The LEAST you need to know about

WordPerfect

About the author

Joel Murach, a former assistant editor of *Strings* and *Acoustic Guitar* magazines, is a new staff writer for Mike Murach and Associates. He brings a working knowledge of *WordPerfect* features from his editing job to his first technical book, *The Least You Need to Know about WordPerfect*.

Joel attended the University of California, Berkeley, and graduated in 1990 with a BA in music. He presently resides in the East Bay area.

About the cover

Kate Solari Baker is the creator of the drawing, *Still Waters #2*, that is featured on the cover of this book. Kate has studied with Wayne Thiebaud at the Santa Fe Institute of Fine Arts and exhibits her work in Marin County and San Francisco. She considers her work to be primarily drawings, but because of her layering technique with chalk pastels, she achieves a "painterly" look.

In addition to our long standing support and concern for the environment, Mike Murach & Associates, Inc., has chosen to show our support for the fine arts by featuring works from California artists on the covers of our technical books. How perfect, then, when Kate Baker wrote to say, "My subject most recently has been Northern Californian scenes with an emphasis on the rivers, lakes, and wetlands so necessary for our survival."

The LEAST you need to know about

WordPerfect

for DOS

Joel Murach

Mike Murach & Associates

4697 West Jacquelyn Avenue, Fresno, California 93722
(209) 275-3335

Production team	**Editor** Cris Allen **Graphics designer** Steve Ehlers
The books in our Least series for DOS users	*The Least You Need to Know About DOS* by Patrick Bultema *The Least You Need to Know About Lotus 1-2-3* by Patrick Bultema
Other books for PC users	*DOS, WordPerfect, and Lotus Essentials* by Joel Murach and Patrick Bultema *The Only DOS Book You'll Ever Need* by Patrick Bultema and Doug Lowe *The Practical Guide to Lotus 1-2-3* by Patrick Bultema *How to Back Up Your PC* by Patrick Bultema *Write Better with a PC* by Mike Murach

10 9 8 7 6 5 4 3 2 1

ISBN: 0-911625-66-6

Library of Congress Cataloging-in-Publication Data

Murach, Joel, 1968-
  The least you need to know about WordPerfect for DOS / Joel
Murach.
    p.   cm.
  Includes index.
  ISBN: 0-911625-66-6 (alk. paper) :
  1. WordPerfect (Computer file) 2. Word processing--Computer
programs. 3. Business writing--Computer programs. 4. IBM
compatible computers--Programming. 5. MS-DOS (Computer file)
I. Title.
Z52.5.W65M86 1992
652.5'536--dc20   92-33846
                                                             CIP

Contents

Preface

During the last several years, dozens of books have been written on *WordPerfect* for DOS users. But *WordPerfect* training and reference is still a problem. Even today, the "easy," "simple," and "quick" *WordPerfect* books are so superficial that they don't teach you what you need to know to be a competent, confident user. And the "fat" *WordPerfect* books are so impractical that they teach you more than you *want* to know, but less than you *need* to know.

So in developing this book, I've kept three goals in mind. The first goal is to teach you *WordPerfect* as quickly as possible...whether you've used other word processing programs before or not.

The second goal is to teach you the skills you need for using *WordPerfect* as efficiently and as productively as possible...whether you're an experienced *WordPerfect* user or whether you're learning to use *WordPerfect* for the first time.

The third goal is to provide you with a *WordPerfect* reference that's quick and easy to use...whether you're looking up a skill that's completely new to you or one that you don't use often enough to have memorized.

What this book does

If you look at the table of contents, you can see that this book is divided into four sections. Sections 2 and 3 are the critical sections of the book, while sections 1 and 4 provide additional perspective that will be useful to many readers.

Section 1 presents the hardware and software concepts and terms that you should be familiar with. Otherwise, you won't understand the interrelationships between *WordPerfect* and your PC that affect your work each day. So if you're new to *WordPerfect* or if you've never quite understood these concepts (they're omitted from most *WordPerfect* books), be sure to read this section. On the other hand, if you're already familiar with these essential hardware and software concepts, you can skip this section.

Section 2 presents a complete tutorial in *WordPerfect* including guided exercises. If you do all of the exercises for each of the three chapters in this section, you should be able to complete the tutorial in six hours or less. If you already know how to use word processing software but you're new to *WordPerfect*, you can probably work your way through this section in just a couple of hours. And if you already know the *WordPerfect* basics, you can skip this section entirely, although you may want to go through it quickly as a refresher course (you're likely to pick up some practical skills that you've never been taught before).

At that point, you'll be able to create and use *WordPerfect* documents. But the title of this book, *The Least You Need to Know about WordPerfect*, implies more than just knowing the basics. So section 3 presents the additional *WordPerfect* skills and shortcuts that will let you work with maximum productivity.

For ease of use, the chapters in section 3 are written as independent modules, so you don't have to read them in sequence. That means you can learn what you want to learn whenever you want to learn it. And it means you can refer back to the chapters whenever you need to quickly refresh your memory about how to use a *WordPerfect* function or feature.

The one chapter in section 4 introduces you to the *WordPerfect* features that aren't covered in section 3 of this book. If you use *WordPerfect* for preparing memos, letters, and reports, you may never need any of the functions and features introduced in this chapter. After you read this chapter, though, you can decide for yourself whether you can benefit from any of the features that it presents. If you decide that you can, you can probably learn how to use them from the *WordPerfect* manual once you've learned the essential *WordPerfect* skills presented in section 3.

How to use the summaries and illustrations

To help you learn more easily, this book is packed with summaries and illustrations. In each chapter, you get summaries of the commands and keystrokes for the functions or features that are presented. You get examples of how the *WordPerfect* commands work. And you get examples of the techniques and procedures that help you work more productively. Summaries and illustrations like these make it easy for you to see how a function or feature works, so you can learn from this book even when you're not at your PC.

But the summaries and illustrations are more than just learning aids. They're also the best reference materials we know of. If, for example, you want to use the Setup command to change the Backup options for your system, figure 6-7 shows you how to do that. If you want to remind yourself what the four ways to delete text are, figure 7-5 summarizes that. If you want to recall how to set the Initial Font for a document without inserting a code into the document, figures 8-5 and 8-6 show you how to do that. And on and on and on. Normally, when you use one of the figures for reference, you don't even have to read the related text because the figure tells you all you need to know.

In appendix C, you'll find quick summaries of the keystroke combinations and commands presented in this book. But no reference appendix is as thorough or as effective as the summaries and illustrations that are used throughout this book. That's why the summaries in appendix C refer you back to the chapter figures.

Who this book is for

I wrote this book with two groups of people in mind. First, I wrote it for anyone who doesn't already know how to use *WordPerfect*. That includes people with no word processing experience as well as people who have experience with other word processing programs but not with *WordPerfect*.

I also wrote this book for the many thousands of *WordPerfect* users who don't work as productively as they ought to because they haven't ever mastered the essential *WordPerfect* skills...people like the editor of this book. When she started reading the manuscript, she was surprised to discover several new commands and features that help her work more productively, even though she's been using *WordPerfect* for several years. She also discovered how useful section 3 can be as a reference to those features and functions that you need only occasionally.

If you're in charge of PC training for your company or if you teach *WordPerfect*, I urge you to try this book in your classes because I'm convinced it will outperform any other instructional materials currently available. Because the book is self-instructional, you can use it for independent study. But you can also use it in a classroom environment. To make it easy for you to develop a course based on our book, we offer an *Instructor's Guide* that provides a full range of instructor's materials.

In terms of hardware and software, this book is for anyone who uses *WordPerfect* 5.0 or 5.1 on a PC with a hard disk. Because subsequent releases of *WordPerfect* probably won't have any effect on the essential skills you need for maximum productivity, this book should continue to be useful for newer *WordPerfect* releases too.

Conclusion

If you glance at the bookstore shelves, you may wonder why anyone would bother to write another *WordPerfect* book. But as I said at the beginning, I wrote this book because there's still a lot of room for improvement when it comes to *WordPerfect* training. I wrote it because the average *WordPerfect* user still hasn't mastered the essential skills needed for maximum productivity. And I wrote it because I have yet to see an efficient reference book for *WordPerfect* users. My hope, of course, is that this book will provide help in all three areas.

If you have any questions, comments, or criticisms, I would enjoy hearing from you. That's why there's a postage-paid comment form at the back of this book. I thank you for reading this book. And I sure hope it will help you become a *WordPerfect* user who is both competent and efficient.

Joel Murach
Berkeley, California
September, 1992

Section 1

PC concepts and terms for every *WordPerfect* user

Before you can use *WordPerfect* effectively, you need to understand some of the concepts and terms that apply to the PC you're using. That's why the two chapters in this section present those concepts and terms. In chapter 1, you'll learn the *hardware* concepts and terms that every *WordPerfect* user should know. In chapter 2, you'll learn the *software* concepts and terms that every *WordPerfect* user should know. In particular, this chapter tells you what you need to know about DOS in order to use *WordPerfect*.

If you're already familiar with PC hardware, you can probably skip chapter 1. But you ought to at least skim the chapter to make sure you know how *WordPerfect* uses internal memory and disk storage. Similarly, if you're already familiar with PC software and DOS, you can probably skip chapter 2.

Chapter 1

Hardware concepts and terms for every *WordPerfect* user

Do you know what kind of processor your PC has? Do you know the difference between internal memory and disk storage? And do you know how *WordPerfect* uses internal memory and disk storage for documents?

If you've answered "yes" to all those questions, you can probably skip this chapter and go on to chapter 2. But if you've answered "no" to any of them, you should read this chapter. To use *WordPerfect* effectively, you need to have a basic understanding of the equipment, or *hardware*, you're using. That's why this chapter presents the hardware concepts and terms that every *WordPerfect* user should know.

An introduction to PCs

As you probably know, *WordPerfect* is used on *personal computers*, or *PCs*. Today, the term *PC* can be used to refer to the original IBM PC, the IBM PC/XT (or just *XT*), the IBM PC/AT (or just *AT*), and the IBM *PS/2*. The term can also be used to refer to PCs that aren't made by IBM like those made by Compaq, Tandy, and Dell. The PCs that aren't made by IBM are often called *clones* or *compatibles* because they work just like the PCs made by IBM.

As I explained in the preface, this book is for people who use *WordPerfect* on PCs. But it doesn't matter whether you have an XT, an AT, a PS/2, or an IBM compatible. Although the type of PC that you have affects how fast *WordPerfect* runs, it works the same on all PCs.

The physical components of a PC

Figure 1-1 shows a typical PC. As you can see, it consists of five physical components: a printer, a monitor, a keyboard, a mouse, and a systems unit. In a laptop PC, the monitor, keyboard, and systems unit are combined into a single carrying case. But on most other systems, these units are separate and can be purchased separately. Because you're probably familiar with these five components already, I'll just describe them briefly.

The systems unit   The *systems unit* is the unit that the other physical components are connected to. As you will soon learn, this unit contains the processor that controls the operations of the PC. In contrast to the systems unit, the four other physical components shown in figure 1-1 are input and output devices.

The monitor   The *monitor* is an output device. Today, most PCs are sold with *color monitors*. Color monitors can display a variety of colors. *Monochrome monitors*, on the other hand, can display only one color, usually green or amber on a dark background.

Like a television set, a monitor uses dot patterns to display characters and images. The more dots a monitor can display, the higher its *resolution* and the sharper its image. Not surprisingly, high-resolution monitors cost more than low-resolution monitors, just as color monitors cost more than monochrome monitors.

When a monitor is in operation, its images are controlled by an electronic circuit card within the systems unit. This circuit card is called a *display adapter*. Today, monitors for PCs are available in five standard forms that are related to their display adapters. The characteristics of these display adapters are summarized in figure 1-2.

The *Monochrome Display Adapter*, or *MDA*, is for the basic monochrome monitor. Because the original IBM version of the MDA could only display text, an MDA monitor couldn't display any graphics. However, a monochrome graphics display adapter called *Hercules* soon became so popular that almost all monochrome monitors and display adapters now support it. The other four display adapters in figure 1-2 are for progressively better color graphics monitors: *CGA* stands for *Color Graphics Adapter*; *EGA* for *Enhanced Graphics Adapter*; *VGA* for *Video Graphics Array;* and *SVGA* for *Super Video Graphics Adapter, or Super VGA..*

The keyboard   The *keyboard* is the main input device of a PC. Although it resembles the keyboard of a typewriter, a PC keyboard has more keys. Figure 1-3 shows the two most common types of PC keyboards: the 84-key and the 101-key keyboards. Although the 84-key keyboard was the original keyboard for the AT, the 101-key keyboard is now a standard component of all PS/2s and most other PCs.

If you study the keyboards in figure 1-3, you can see that they have several types of keys. First, the keyboards include a full set of typewriter keys. Second, they have a numeric pad on the right side of the keyboard in the same arrangement as the ten keys on a calculator. They also have either 10 or 12

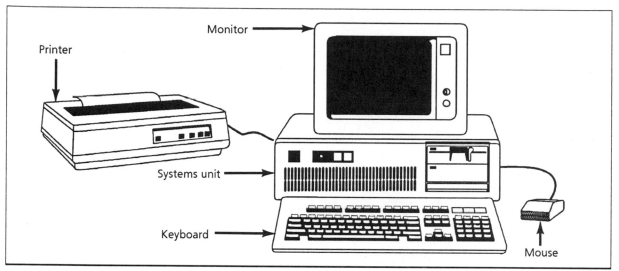

Figure 1-1   The physical components of a PC

function keys (depending on the type of keyboard) numbered F1, F2, F3, and so on. And they have some special control keys such as the Escape key (Esc), the Control key (Ctrl), the Alternate key (Alt), the Page-up and the Page-down keys, and so on.

In chapter 3, you'll learn how to use some of the function and control keys with *WordPerfect*. You'll also learn why it's easier to use the 101-key keyboard with *WordPerfect* than it is to use the 84-key keyboard. Because it's easier to use, we recommend the 101-key keyboard for all *WordPerfect* users.

The mouse   A *mouse* is a small hand-held input device that has two or three buttons on it. If you've ever used a mouse or seen one used, you know that it's just a pointing device. When you move the mouse across a table top (or a *mouse pad* on the table top), a pointer on the monitor moves in the same direction. This pointer on the monitor is called the *mouse cursor*.

With a little practice, you can easily and quickly move the mouse cursor anywhere on the screen. Then, you can *click* or *double-click* the buttons on top of the mouse to perform various actions. If you *click-and-drag* a mouse, you can highlight portions of the screen with the mouse.

Exactly how you use a mouse, or if you can use a mouse at all, depends on the software you're using. For example, the first releases of *WordPerfect* didn't support a mouse. However, release 5.1 of *WordPerfect* does support a mouse.

Even though release 5.1 does support a mouse, using one doesn't make *WordPerfect* any easier to use. In fact, most people can use *WordPerfect* more efficiently using keystrokes than they can using a mouse. That's why we recommend that you don't use a mouse with *WordPerfect*.

Acronym	Adapter name	Standard resolution
MDA	Monochrome Display Adapter	720x348
CGA	Color Graphics Adapter	640x200
EGA	Enhanced Graphics Adapter	640x350
VGA	Video Graphics Array	640x480
SVGA	Super VGA	800x600 or 1024x768

Figure 1-2   A summary of monitor characteristics

The printer   The *printer* of a PC is an output device. Although many different kinds of printers have been developed, the most widely used printers today are dot-matrix printers and laser printers. A *dot-matrix printer* works by striking small pins against an inked ribbon. The resulting dots form characters or graphic images on the paper.

Today, most dot-matrix printers are either 9-pin or 24-pin printers. As you might expect, 24-pin printers print with better quality than 9-pin printers. But both can print text in two different modes: *draft mode* and *letter quality mode*. The draft mode is faster, but the letter quality mode is easier to read. For example, my 24-pin printer prints at 216 cps (characters per second) in draft mode and 72 cps in letter quality mode. As a result, you can use the faster draft mode to print a preliminary version of a document that you're working on. Then, you can use the letter quality mode to print the final version of the document.

In contrast to dot-matrix printers, *laser printers* work on the same principle as photocopiers. These printers are not only faster than dot-matrix printers, but they also print with better quality. Today, most laser printers print with 300 dpi (dots per inch), but 1200-dpi printers are also available. Naturally, the print quality (or resolution) of a laser printer depends on the number of dots per inch, and high-resolution printers are more expensive than low-resolution printers.

The primary components of the systems unit

If you've ever opened up the systems unit of a PC, you know that it is full of electronic components. These components are attached to electronic cards that are inserted into the unit. Although you don't have to understand how any of these components work, you should have a conceptual idea of what the primary components of the systems unit are and how they affect the way you use *WordPerfect*.

The 84-key IBM-AT keyboard

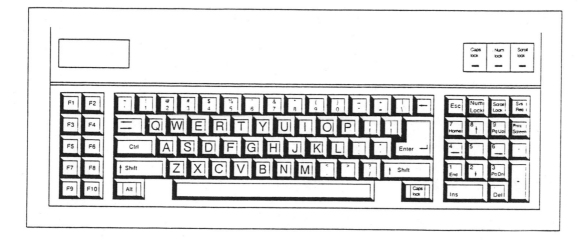

The enhanced 101-key keyboard

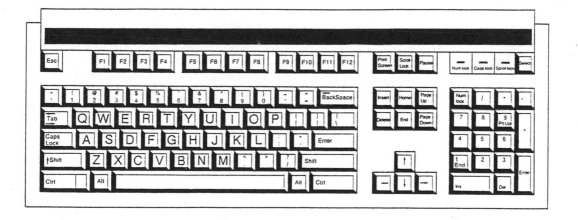

Figure 1-3   The two most common types of PC keyboards

Figure 1-4 is a conceptual drawing of the components of a typical PC. Within the systems unit, you can see four primary components: the diskette drive or drives, the hard disk, internal memory, and the processor.

The diskette drive or drives   A *diskette* is the actual recording medium on which data is stored, and the *diskette drive* is the device that writes data on the diskette and reads data from the diskette. Although diskettes are sometimes called *floppy disks*, I'll refer to them as diskettes throughout this book.

To read data from a diskette or write data on a diskette, you insert the diskette into the slot on the diskette drive and close the drive's latch (if it has a latch). If a PC has two diskette drives, they can be in a left and right arrangement, or they can be in a top and bottom arrangement.

Figure 1-5 illustrates the two sizes of diskettes that can be used with PCs. Originally, all PCs, XTs, and ATs used 5-1/4 inch diskettes, and all PS/2s used the newer 3-1/2 inch diskettes. Today, however, you can install a diskette drive for either type of diskette on an XT, an AT, or a PS/2.

To complicate matters, both types of diskettes come in two storage capacities: *standard capacity* and *high capacity*. These capacities are measured in *bytes* of data. For practical purposes, you can think of one byte of data as one character of data, and you can think of a character as a letter, a digit (0-9), or a special character such as #, %, or &. Thus, ten bytes of diskette storage are required to store the word *impossible*; four bytes are required to store the number *4188*; and two bytes are required to store *$9*.

For 5-1/4 inch diskettes, the standard capacity is 360,000 bytes, or 360KB. Here, KB stands for *kilobyte*. One kilobyte is approximately 1,000 bytes. In contrast, the high capacity is 1,200KB, or 1.2MB. Here, MB stands for *megabyte*. One megabyte is approximately one million bytes. For 3-1/2 inch diskettes, the standard capacity is 720KB, and the high capacity is 1.44MB.

Figure 1-6 summarizes the diskette sizes and capacities. Because the labelling for diskettes is often confusing, this figure also lists the common labelling designations for each type of diskette. Notice, for example, that the standard capacity diskettes are also called *double density* diskettes, and the high capacity diskettes are also called *high density* diskettes.

When you use a diskette to transfer data like a *WordPerfect* document from one PC to another, you must make sure that you're using a diskette that is the right size and capacity for the PC you're transferring the data to. In general, a 5-1/4 inch diskette drive on an XT can only read and write standard capacity diskettes. However, a 5-1/4 inch drive on an AT can read and write diskettes in either standard or high capacity. As a result, you must use standard capacity diskettes to transfer a document between an XT and an AT. Similarly, a standard capacity 3-1/2 inch drive can only read and write standard capacity diskettes, but a high capacity drive can read and write diskettes in either standard or high capacity. Thus, you must use a standard

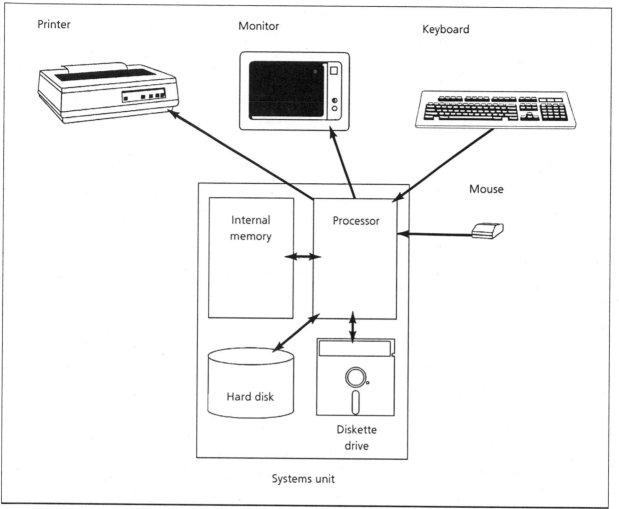

Figure 1-4   The internal components of the systems unit

capacity 3-1/2 inch diskette to transfer a document between a standard and a high capacity drive.

The hard disk   In contrast to diskettes, a *hard disk* is installed inside the systems unit. In this case, the recording medium and the drive are sealed together in a single unit. As a result, a hard disk can't be removed from the PC the way a diskette can. That's why hard disks are sometimes called *fixed disks*. In this book, though, I'll only use the term *hard disk*.

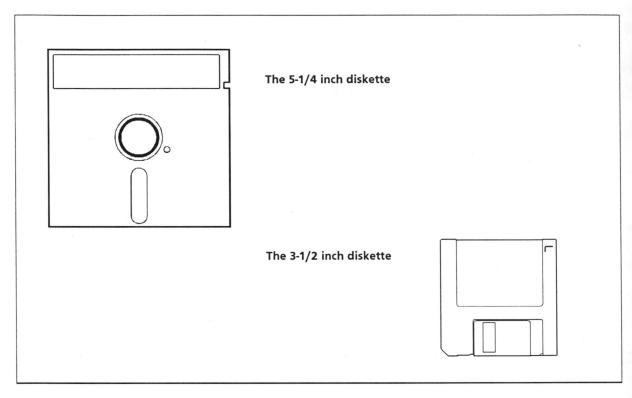

The 5-1/4 inch diskette

The 3-1/2 inch diskette

Figure 1-5   The two diskette sizes

Today, most hard disks have capacities of 20MB or more, and you can buy hard disks with capacities of 320MB or more. To put that into perspective, consider that one megabyte of disk storage can hold about 500 pages of word processing text. So a 30MB hard disk can hold 15,000 pages of text, while a 360KB diskette can hold only about 175 pages. To look at it another way, a 40MB disk can store the equivalent of about 110 diskettes that have a capacity of 360KB.

If your PC has a hard disk, you probably won't use diskettes much because all of your programs will be stored on the hard disk. However, you still need at least one diskette drive on your PC. Then, you can use it to back up the data on your hard disk to diskettes, to install new programs from diskettes to your hard disk, and to transfer data from one PC to another.

When you use *WordPerfect*, a PC with a hard disk is far superior to one that doesn't have a hard disk. That's why I have assumed throughout this book that your PC has a hard disk. Because all of your programs and data can be stored on one hard disk, a hard-disk PC is easier to use than a diskette-based PC. And because a hard disk is much faster than a diskette drive, a hard-disk PC is far more efficient than a diskette-based PC.

Size	Capacity	Common labelling notation
5-1/4"	360KB	5-1/4" Double-Sided Double-Density 5-1/4" DSDD
5-1/4"	1.2MB	5-1/4" Double-Sided High-Density 5-1/4" DSHD
3-1/2"	720KB	3-1/2" Double-Sided Double-Density 3-1/2" 2DD 3-1/2" 1.0M formatted capacity
3-1/2"	1.44MB	3-1/2" Double-Sided High-Density 3-1/2" 2HD 3-1/2" 2.0M formatted capacity

Figure 1-6   A summary of diskette characteristics

Internal memory   Before your PC can operate on the data that is stored on a diskette or a hard disk, the data must be read into the *internal memory* of the systems unit. This memory can also be called *internal storage* or *RAM* (for *Random Access Memory*), but I'll refer to it as internal memory throughout this book.

Like diskette or hard disk storage, the capacity of internal memory is measured in kilobytes or megabytes. Although the original PC was typically sold with either 64KB, 128KB, or 256KB of internal memory, a PC today is usually sold with 512KB or 640KB of internal memory. And the newer, more powerful PCs are sold with 1MB, 2MB, or 4MB of internal memory.

The first 640KB of internal memory can be referred to as *conventional memory*. Since the original PC was designed for a maximum memory of 640K, most programs aren't designed to use more memory than that. But some programs can use either *extended memory* or *expanded memory*. For instance, *WordPerfect* 5.1 can use expanded memory, but not extended memory. However, *WordPerfect* usually works fine on conventional memory alone.

The processor   If you look back to figure 1-4, you can see that all of the components I've described so far are connected to the *processor*. When a program is in operation, the processor controls all of the other components of the PC by executing the instructions of the program. Other terms for a processor are *microprocessor*, *central processing unit*, and *CPU*, but I'll use the term *processor*.

Today, PC processors are identified by the *microprocessor chip* they're based on. In an IBM PC or PC compatible, all of the processors are based on

Processor names	Abbreviated names
8088	None
80286	286
80386SX	386SX
80386DX	386
80486SX	486SX
80486DX	486

Figure 1-7   A summary of PC processors

chips that were originally manufactured by Intel with names like the 8088, the 80286, and the 80386. These are summarized in figure 1-7. As you can see, the shortened versions of the chip names are the 286, the 386SX, the 386, and so on. Because the processor controls all of the operations of a PC, the speed of the processor affects how fast *WordPerfect* runs on your PC.

How *WordPerfect* uses internal memory and disk storage

Now that you know what the basic hardware components of a PC are, you should understand how they relate to *WordPerfect*. In particular, you should understand how *WordPerfect* makes use of internal memory and disk storage.

How *WordPerfect* uses internal memory   Figure 1-8 shows how *WordPerfect* uses conventional memory when it is working on a document. When you start your PC, the operating system (DOS) is loaded into the first portion of internal memory (the first 40KB). Then, when you start *WordPerfect*, it is loaded into the portion of internal memory that follows DOS (from 40KB to 424KB in this example). Next, as you create a document, it is stored in the next portion of internal memory (from 424KB to 560KB in this example). The last portion of memory isn't used so it can be used when you add to the document.

Why you should save a document to disk storage before you exit from *WordPerfect*   Whenever you turn off your PC, the contents of internal memory are lost. Similarly, when you exit improperly from *WordPerfect* and return to the operating system, the document that you've been working on is lost. So if you don't want to lose your work, you must save your document to disk storage on the hard disk or on a diskette before you exit from *WordPerfect* or turn off your PC. Unlike internal memory, the contents of disk storage aren't lost when the PC is turned off.

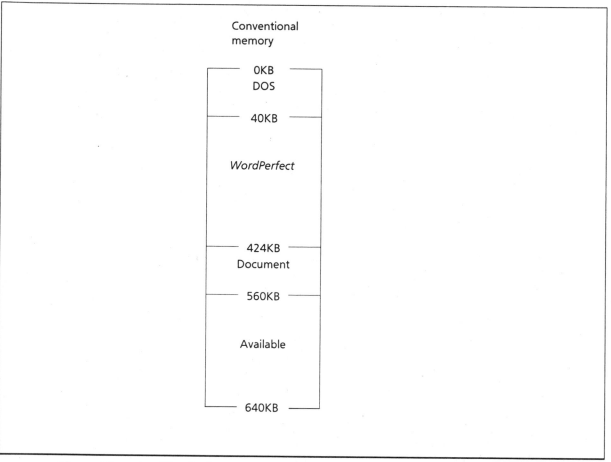

Figure 1-8   How *WordPerfect* uses conventional memory for a document

The process of saving a document to a hard disk is illustrated in figure 1-9. In part 1, you can see that the document in internal memory is saved on the hard disk. After the document has been saved, it is still in internal memory, but it is also on the hard disk. After you exit from *WordPerfect*, you can see that neither the program nor the document is in internal memory in part 2. However, the document is still available on the hard disk for use later on.

When you use *WordPerfect*, you are responsible for saving a document to the disk. To do this, you use one of the *WordPerfect* commands called the Save command. Then, the next time you use *WordPerfect*, you can use the List Files screen or the Retrieve command to retrieve the document from disk storage to internal memory so you continue to work on it. You'll learn how to use these commands in section 2 of this book.

Some perspective on hardware for *WordPerfect* users

Throughout this chapter, I've tried to simplify the concepts and keep the number of new terms to a minimum. In general, I've tried to present only those PC concepts you need to know in order to use *WordPerfect* effectively. And I've tried to present only those terms that you're most likely to encounter in *WordPerfect* manuals and in magazine articles about *WordPerfect*.

Nevertheless, this chapter presents more than you need to know about hardware if all you want to do is use *WordPerfect* effectively. As a result, you shouldn't feel that you need to know all of the terms in this chapter before you continue. That's why I've divided the terms listed at the end of this chapter into two groups. If you're familiar with the terms in the first group, you're ready to go on to the next chapter.

Terms you should be familiar with before you continue

hardware	diskette
personal computer	diskette drive
PC	standard capacity
XT	high capacity
AT	byte
PS/2	kilobyte (KB)
compatible	megabyte (MB)
systems unit	double density
monitor	high density
color monitor	hard disk
monochrome monitor	internal memory
keyboard	conventional memory
mouse	extended memory
mouse cursor	expanded memory
printer	processor
dot-matrix printer	microprocessor chip
laser printer	

Objectives

1. List the four primary physical components of a PC.

2. List the four primary components of a systems unit.

3. Explain how *WordPerfect* uses internal memory.

4. Explain why a document should be saved to disk storage before the PC user exits from *WordPerfect* or turns the PC off.

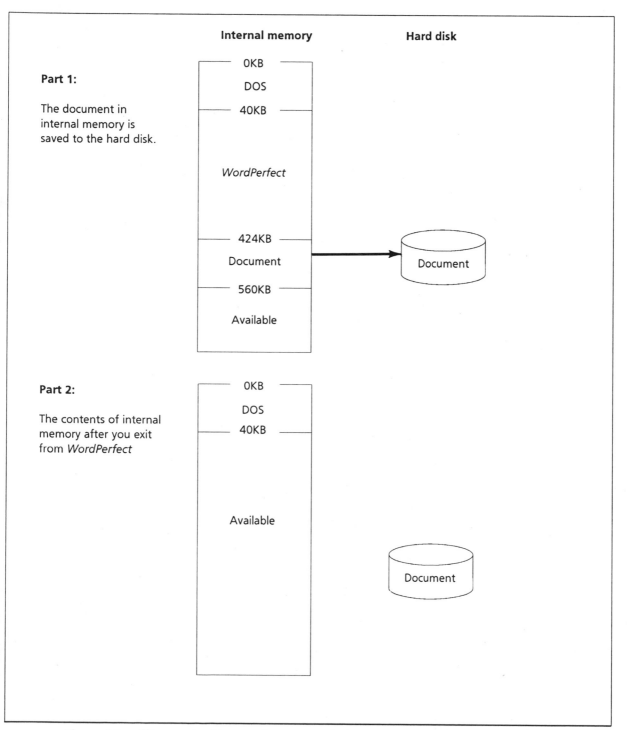

Figure 1-9   Why you should save a document to the hard disk before you exit from *WordPerfect*

Other terms presented in this chapter

clone
resolution
display adapter
Monochrome Display Adapter
MDA
CGA
Color Graphics Adapter
EGA
Enhanced Graphics Adapter
VGA
Video Graphics Array
mouse pad
click the mouse
double-click the mouse
click-and-drag the mouse
draft mode
letter quality mode
floppy disk
fixed disk
internal storage
RAM
Random Access Memory
microprocessor
central processing unit
CPU

Chapter 2

Software concepts and terms for every *WordPerfect* user

Do you know the difference between an application program and an operating system program? Do you know what the primary functions of DOS are? Do you know how to give a complete DOS file specification including drive, directory, and file name? And do you know how to start *WordPerfect* from DOS?

Unless you can answer an unqualified "yes" to those questions, you should read this chapter before you go on to the next one. To use a PC effectively, you must have a basic understanding of PC *software*. The term *software* refers to the *programs* that direct the operations of the PC hardware. When you complete this chapter, you'll have the software background you need for learning how to use *WordPerfect* on your PC.

The two types of programs every PC requires

In broad terms, PC software can be divided into two types: application programs and operating system programs. To do work on your PC, you need both types of programs. In case you're not already familiar with both types, here's some information about each.

Application programs   An *application program* is a program you use to do your work. It lets you *apply* your PC to the jobs that you want to do on a PC. For example, *WordPerfect* is a word processing program that lets you apply your PC to jobs like writing letters, memos, and reports. And *Lotus 1-2-3* is an application program that lets you apply your PC to the job of creating spreadsheets.

Today, word processing and spreadsheet programs are the two most popular types of application programs as summarized in figure 2-1. This figure also lists a couple of the most popular programs of each type. When

Program type	Examples	Operates upon
Word processing	*WordPerfect* *Microsoft Word*	Documents
Spreadsheet	*Lotus 1-2-3* *Quattro Pro*	Spreadsheets

Figure 2-1   The two most popular types of application programs

you use a *word processing program*, you prepare *documents* like letters, memos, and reports. When you use a *spreadsheet program*, you prepare *spreadsheets* like budgets or profit projections.

Operating system programs   An *operating system* is a program that lets your application programs run on your PC. For example, an operating system lets you load an application program into internal memory so you can use it. An operating system also provides functions that let your application programs read a file from a disk drive, print on a printer, and so on.

The concept of an operating system is elusive because much of what the operating system does goes on without you knowing about it. When you save a document on a hard disk, for example, it is the operating system, not *WordPerfect*, that saves the document on the disk. In other words, your application program communicates with the operating system without you knowing about it. Without the operating system, your application program wouldn't work.

DOS (pronounced *doss*) is short for *Disk Operating System*. It is by far the most widely used operating system on PCs, and this book assumes that you're using it on yours. When DOS is sold by Microsoft Corporation, it's called *MS-DOS*; when it's sold by IBM Corporation, it's called *PC-DOS*; and some PC manufacturers provide their own modified versions of DOS. Fortunately, though, all of the DOS versions work essentially the same way, so I'll use the term *DOS* in this book to refer to all versions of DOS.

What DOS provides

When you turn on a hard disk PC, it starts by loading a portion of DOS into internal memory. This portion of DOS occupies a portion of internal memory, usually between 40 and 70KB. Because this portion of DOS remains in internal memory until you turn off your PC, DOS functions are available to you and your application programs whenever your PC is running.

Figure 2-2   A typical DOS command prompt

In general terms, DOS provides three types of functions: command processing, DOS services, and DOS commands. Since you need to have a basic understanding all three of these functions to use *WordPerfect* effectively, I'll introduce you to each of them now.

Command processing   The DOS *command processor* is loaded into internal memory when you start your PC. When the command processor is in control of the system, it displays a *command prompt* like the one shown in figure 2-2. Generally, this command prompt is displayed when your PC finishes its start-up procedure.

When the command prompt is displayed, the command processor is waiting for you to enter a command. For example, you normally enter *wp* to start *WordPerfect*. When you exit from *WordPerfect*, DOS displays the command prompt again. Then, you can enter a command to start another program.

Figure 2-3 illustrates how DOS uses the command processor to load *WordPerfect*. When you enter *wp* at the command prompt as shown in part 1, the command processor loads *WordPerfect* from the hard disk into internal memory, as shown in step 2. Then, the command processor transfers control of the PC to the first instruction of the *WordPerfect* program. When you finish word processing and exit from the *WordPerfect* program, control is passed back to the command processor, as shown in part 3. Then, the command processor waits for your next command.

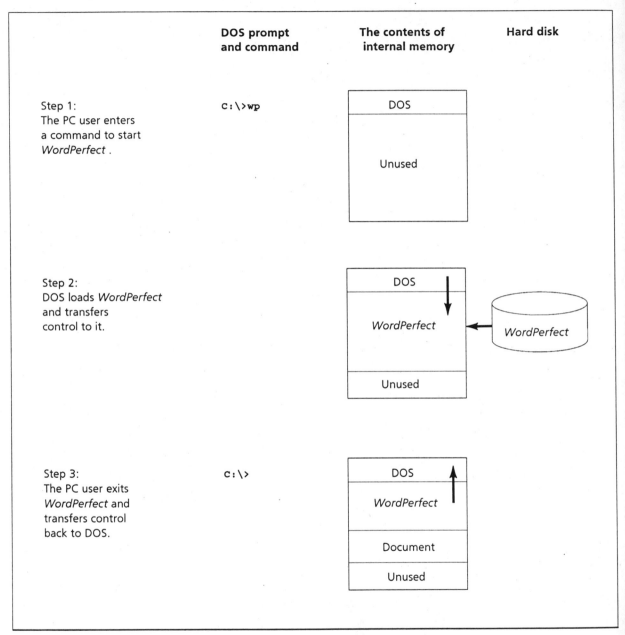

Figure 2-3   How DOS loads an application program into internal memory

DOS services   When an application program is running, DOS provides *DOS services* to the program. Some of the most important of these services are called *input/output services*, or *I/O services*. These services make it possible for the application program to receive input from the input devices of the PC and to give output through the output devices of the PC.

To illustrate, figure 2-4 shows how DOS provides I/O services to *WordPerfect* when you retrieve a document from the hard disk. In step 1, *WordPerfect* requests data from DOS. In step 2, DOS searches the disk for the requested data. In step 3, DOS receives the data from the disk and verifies that the reading operation was successful. In step 4, DOS passes the data on to *WordPerfect*. Then, DOS waits for the next service request.

As part of its services, DOS also manages all of the files that are stored on a hard disk or diskette. In DOS terms, each document, spreadsheet, or program on a hard disk or diskette is called a *file*. To be more specific, you can think of a file as a document file, spreadsheet file, or program file, but DOS makes no distinction between them. It manages all of the files in the same way.

To keep track of the files, DOS requires that they be organized into *directories*. Then, in the directory entry for each file, DOS records the file name, the disk location, the file size in bytes, the date the file was last changed, and the time the file was last changed. As a result, *WordPerfect* doesn't have to know these details when it requests an input or output operation for a disk file. Instead, it has to supply just the name of the file and the name of the directory that contains the file's information. In just a moment, you'll learn how to specify the files and directories that you want to use with *WordPerfect*.

DOS commands   In addition to the DOS services that you use indirectly through an application program, DOS provides *DOS commands* that you can use directly from the command prompt. Most of these commands let you manage the files and directories on a disk. Some commands let you delete, rename, or copy one or more files. Others provide functions for managing directories, backing up the files on a hard disk, and so on.

As you use *WordPerfect*, you are likely to create many documents. Eventually, then, you need to manage the document files by copying, moving, or deleting them from disk storage. And you'll probably want to back up the files on your hard disk to diskette. Since *WordPerfect* provides an easy way to manage document files, you may not need to learn these DOS commands. However, *WordPerfect* doesn't provide a way to back up the files on your hard disk to diskette. In addition, some DOS commands for managing directories are more efficient than *WordPerfect*'s commands for managing directories. So, if you want to use DOS to backup your hard disk, or if you spend a lot of time managing directories, you should know how to use at least a few of the DOS commands.

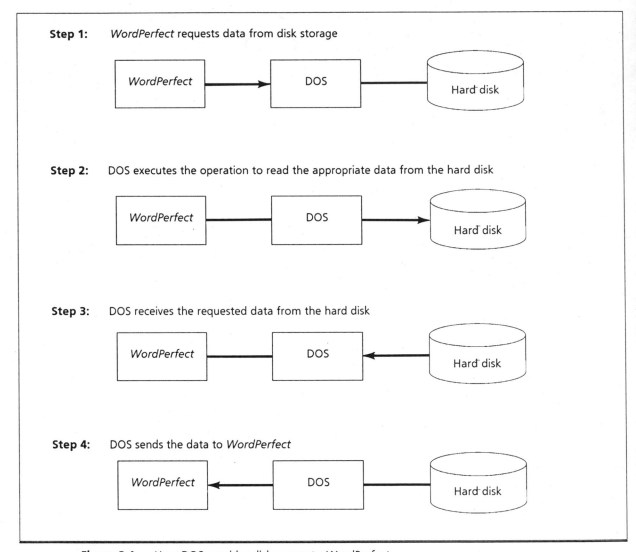

Step 1:   *WordPerfect* requests data from disk storage

Step 2:   DOS executes the operation to read the appropriate data from the hard disk

Step 3:   DOS receives the requested data from the hard disk

Step 4:   DOS sends the data to *WordPerfect*

Figure 2-4   How DOS provides disk access to *WordPerfect*

How to specify the drive, path, and file name for any DOS file

Whenever you use *WordPerfect* to retrieve or save a document, you give a *file specification* for the file. A complete specification consists of a disk drive, a path, and a file name. In figure 2-5, for example, you can see complete specifications for a document file on a diskette and for a document file on a hard disk. Now, I'll explain what each part of a file specification is.

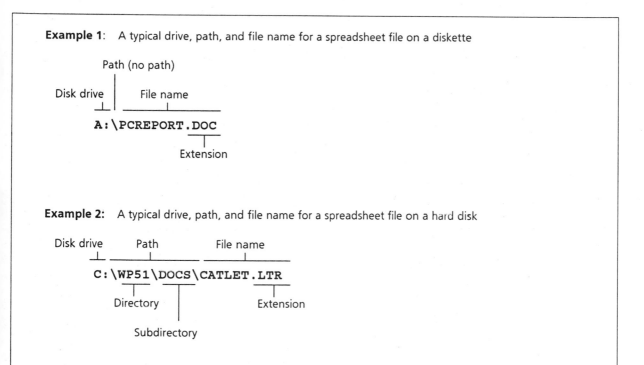

Figure 2-5   Typical drives, paths, and file names for document files

The drive   When you use DOS, the *drives* are identified by letters. For example, the first diskette drive on every system is always drive A, and the second diskette drive is always drive B. Similarly, the hard disk (or at least the first portion of it) is always identified as drive C. When you specify the disk drive in a file specification, you always give the drive letter followed by the colon. In figure 2-5, you can see that example 1 specifies the A drive, and example 2 specifies the C drive.

However, one hard disk can be divided into more than one drive. For example, figure 2-6 shows a hard drive that's divided into two drives. Then, the first portion of the drive is referred to as drive C, the second portion as drive D, and so on. Today, a 40MB drive is likely to be divided into drives C and D, while a 120MB drive is likely to be divided into drives C, D, E, and F.

In PC and DOS literature, the multiple drives that are defined on one hard disk are often referred to as *logical drives* to distinguish them from the *physical drive*. Thus, one physical drive is divided into two or more logical drives. From a practical point of view, however, you can think of each logical drive as a physical drive. As a result, I won't distinguish between the two in the remainder of this book. I'll simply refer to disk drives by letters as in "the C drive" or "drive D."

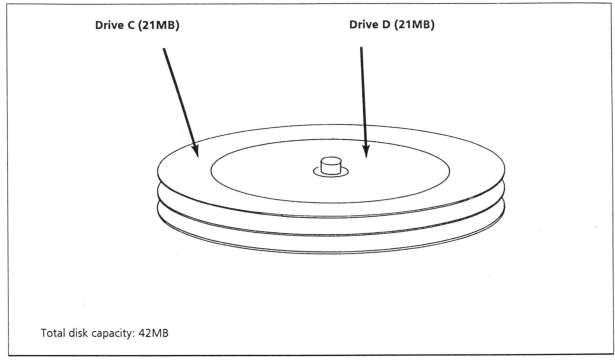

Drive C (21MB)   **Drive D (21MB)**

Total disk capacity: 42MB

Figure 2-6   Two drives on one hard disk

The path   Earlier, I mentioned that DOS lets you organize or group files into directories. The 1,368 files on my system, for example, are organized in 39 different directories. These directories are just a special type of file that DOS uses to keep track of the names and locations of the files that are stored on disk. On a DOS system, every file must be stored in a directory.

Figure 2-7 illustrates a typical directory structure for a hard disk. For each hard disk or diskette, the top-level directory is always called the *root directory*. In this figure, the root directory contains references to five other directories named DOS, UTIL, WP50, 123, and QA. These directories contain the program files for DOS, for some utility programs, for *WordPerfect* 5.0, for *Lotus 1-2-3*, and for *Q&A*. Of course, this figure could just as easily have a WP51 directory containing the program files for *WordPerfect* 5.1 instead of a WP50 directory containing the program files for *WordPerfect* 5.0.

Because one directory can contain entries for other directories, the subordinate directories can be referred to as *subdirectories*. In figure 2-7, for example, the WP50 directory has two subdirectories named SALES and DOCS while the 123 directory has two subdirectories named SALES and WK1. These subdirectories are just like any other directory; they're just subordinate to a higher-level directory. As a result, subdirectories can also be referred to as directories.

The structure for a set of directories

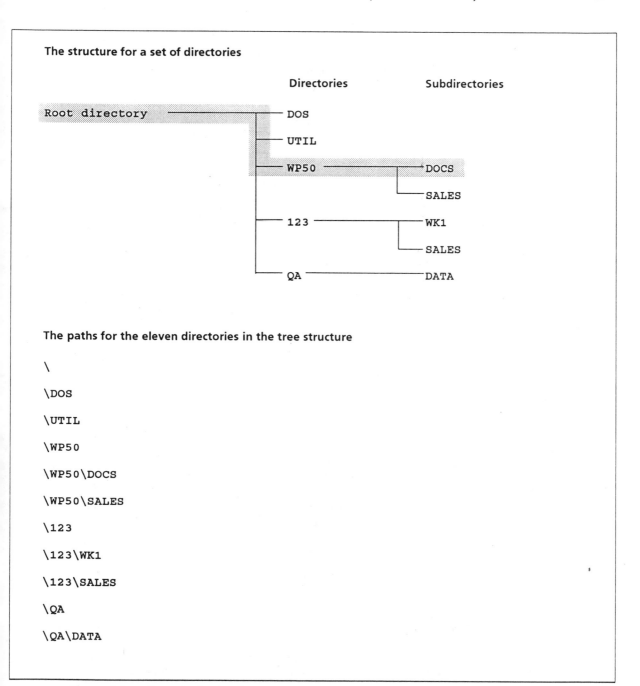

The paths for the eleven directories in the tree structure

\

\DOS

\UTIL

\WP50

\WP50\DOCS

\WP50\SALES

\123

\123\WK1

\123\SALES

\QA

\QA\DATA

Figure 2-7   The paths for the directories on a hard disk

The *path* of a file specification identifies the directory for the file. More specifically, the path tells DOS how to get from the root directory to the directory that contains the entry for the file you want. In the directory structure in figure 2-7, the shaded path goes from the root directory to the WP50 directory to the DOCS directory.

Below the directory structure in figure 2-7, you can see the specifications for the paths of the eleven directories shown in the structure. The root directory is always specified by the backslash (\). The level-1 directories are identified by the backslash followed by the directory name as in \DOS, \UTIL, \WP50, \123, and \QA. And the level-2 directories, or subdirectories, are identified by the backslash for the root directory, the level-1 directory name, another backslash, and the level-2 directory name as in \WP50\SALES and \WP50\DOCS.

Note in figure 2-7 that \DOCS by itself isn't a valid path. To be valid, it must be preceded by its directory as in this path: \WP50\DOCS. Note also that the same subdirectory name can be used within more than one directory. Thus, a SALES directory is subordinate to both the WP50 directory and the 123 directory. To tell them apart, they must be referred to as \WP50\SALES, and \123\SALES.

If you look back to figure 2-5, you can see that the document file on the diskette doesn't have a path. In general, when you specify a file name for document on a diskette, you just use the drive of the diskette and the file name for the document. Since a diskette can't hold as many files as a hard disk, you usually don't need to use directories to organize the files.

The file name   Whenever you use *WordPerfect* to save a new document file on a hard disk or a diskette, you also need to be able to create a valid *file name*. If you refer back to figure 2-5, you can see that a file name is separated into two parts by a period. The part that comes before the period is required. I'll refer to this as the *name* portion of the file name. The part after the period is optional and is called the *extension*.

Figure 2-8 gives the rules for forming valid file names. As you can see, you can use from one to eight characters for the name portion and from one to three characters for the extension. This figure also shows the characters that you can't use in a file name.

Two DOS skills for *WordPerfect* users

Now that you know what DOS does and how to specify a complete DOS file specification, let me present two DOS skills that you'll need for working with *WordPerfect*. First, you need to know how to give a file specification when you're using *WordPerfect*. Second, you need to know how to start *WordPerfect* from DOS.

The rules for forming file names

1.   The name must consist of from one to eight characters.

2.   The extension is optional. If you have one, it must be from one to three characters, and it must be separated from the name by a period as in this example:

     `PCREPORT.DOC`

3.   You can use any character in the name or the extension except for the space and any of these characters:

     `. ,   ? / : ; " ' [ ] | \ + = *`

4.   You can use either lowercase or uppercase letters in the name or the extension of a file name, but they are treated the same. As a result, the two names that follow are the same:

     `PCREPORT.DOC`   and   `pcreport.doc`

Valid file names

`FEB92RPT`

`smith.ltr`

`5-16-92.doc`

`ltr10-21`

`JAN92.WK1`

Invalid file names

`JOHNLETTER.DOC`	(The name is more than 8 characters.)
`JAN:92.WK1`	(The colon is an invalid character.)
`smith.lttr`	(The extension is more than 3 characters.)

Figure 2-8   The rules for forming file names

How to give a file specification when you're using *WordPerfect*

When you use the *WordPerfect* command to list the files in the current directory, it displays a prompt like the one shown in figure 2-9. This means that the current *default directory* is:

   C:\WP50

The *WordPerfect* prompt for the List command

```
DIR C:\WP50\*.*                          (Type = to change default Dir)
```

The *WordPerfect* prompt for the Save command

```
Name of file to save:  _
```

The *WordPerfect* prompt for the Retrieve command

```
Name of file to retrieve:  _
```

Figure 2-9   The types of prompts that are displayed by *WordPerfect* when you save or retrieve a document files

As you can see from the prompt, to change the *WordPerfect* default, you can type = and then type the specification for the directory.

When you use the *WordPerfect* Save command, it displays a prompt like the second one shown in figure 2-9. If you just enter a file name like PCREPORT at this prompt, the file will be saved in the default directory. If that's not what you want, you can override the default by entering a complete file specification that includes the directory that you want the file saved in. For example, you could type:

D:\WPDOCS\PCREPORT

In this case, the file named PCREPORT is saved in the \WPDOCS directory on the D drive.

When you use the *WordPerfect* Retrieve command, it displays a prompt like the third one shown in figure 2-9. If the file you want is in the default directory, you just enter the file name without the extension. Otherwise, you can override the default directory by entering a complete file specification that specifies the drive and directory that you want.

Before you start learning how to use *WordPerfect* in the next section of this book, you should make sure you know what directory you're going to use for your document files. If you're going to put your files in a directory that already exists, you should get the complete specification for that directory. If you're going to put your files in a new directory, you should either make that directory yourself or have someone make it for you before you go on to the next chapter.

How to start *WordPerfect* from the DOS prompt   When you start
your PC, it may finish by displaying a command prompt like the one shown in
figure 2-2. In that case, you need to learn how to start *WordPerfect* from this
prompt. On the other hand, your PC may be set up so that it's easy for you to
start *WordPerfect*. For example, your PC may start with a menu that offers
WordPerfect as one of its selections. Then, all you have to do to start
WordPerfect is to make the right selection.

    If you do have to start *WordPerfect* from the DOS command prompt,
figure 2-10 shows you how to do it on most PCs. First, if the command
prompt doesn't already indicate the C drive, enter

```
c:
```

to change the command prompt to that drive. Second, enter

```
cd \wp50  or
cd \wp51
```

to change the directory to the *WordPerfect* directory. Third, enter *wp* to start
WordPerfect.

    If this doesn't work on your PC, the most likely explanation is that
WordPerfect isn't stored in the \WP50 directory or the \WP51 directory on
the C drive. Then, if you don't know how to use DOS to figure out where
WordPerfect is stored, you probably need to get help. Once you learn the
proper commands for starting *WordPerfect*, you just repeat them each time
you want to start it.

    If you're a competent DOS user and you're using DOS 3.0 or later, you
can use DOS commands to set the default directory before you start
WordPerfect by creating a batch file that contains commands like these:

```
d:
cd\wpdocs
c:\wp50\wp
```

Here, the first two commands set the default drive and directory to the one
that you want for your *WordPerfect* documents. Then, the last command starts
WordPerfect. When you start *WordPerfect* like this, you don't have to use
WordPerfect to set the default directory for your document files.

How *WordPerfect* has evolved

During the last ten years, *WordPerfect* has been improved several times. Using
WordPerfect terminology, each new version is called a *release*, and each release
is identified by a higher *release number*. For example, release 4.1 was an
improvement over 4.0, and release 5.0 was an improvement over 4.2.

Step	Function	Typical command	Examples at the DOS prompt
1	Change the drive to the drive that the *WordPerfect* directory is stored on. Then, press the Enter key to execute the command.	`c:`	`D:\>c:`
2	Change the directory to the one that *WordPerfect* is stored in and press the Enter key.	`cd \wp51`	`C:\>cd \wp51`
3	Enter the command that starts *WordPerfect* (usually, wp) and press the Enter key.	`wp`	`C:\WP51>wp`

Figure 2-10   How to start *WordPerfect* 5.1 from the DOS command prompt

In general, a change in the digit before the decimal point means a major revision of the program so release 5.0 is significantly different than release 4.2. In contrast, a change in the digit to the right of the decimal point means a minor revision so release 5.1 isn't that much different from release 5.0.

Figure 2-11 summarizes the last three releases of *WordPerfect*. You can tell which release you're using by looking at the *WordPerfect* screen that flashes on for a couple seconds when you start *WordPerfect* or by pressing the F3 Key after *WordPerfect* has started.

This book is designed for use with either *WordPerfect* release 5.0 or 5.1. As you can tell by the release numbers, these releases are similar, As a result, both of theses releases provide the same basic functions and a common method for accessing these functions. Although version 5.1 provides a second way to access the functions, this book emphasizes the access method that is common to both releases so you'll be able to use either one of them. Because future releases of *WordPerfect* for DOS will continue to support the access method presented in this book, you should also be able to upgrade to these releases with little difficulty.

Some perspective on DOS for *WordPerfect* users

WordPerfect makes it easy for you to copy files, to move files from one directory to another, or to delete files. And you can use *WordPerfect* to create new directories for files. In fact, many *WordPerfect* users use *WordPerfect* to perform these DOS functions. However, every *WordPerfect* user should know how to use DOS to start *WordPerfect*. In addition, some *WordPerfect* users will

Release number	Release year	Conventional memory requirements	Major improvements
4.2	1987	256KB	Style sheets
5.0	1988	384KB	Improved desktop publishing features
5.1	1989	384KB	New tables feature Context-sensitive help Mouse support and menu access to the commands Improved desktop publishing features

Figure 2-11   The evolution of *WordPerfect*

want to use DOS to back up the files on their hard disk. With that as background, I'd like to recommend two of our other books.

The first book is called *The Least You Need to Know About DOS*. It helps you use DOS to do the functions that can be done most efficiently in DOS. It shows you how to use DOS to back up the files on your hard disk. And it helps you solve the types of PC problems that can only be solved in DOS. As a result, it helps you work smarter, faster, and with less outside help. I especially recommend this book if you've had any trouble with the DOS concepts presented in this chapter because it treats these concepts more thoroughly.

The second book is called *How to back up your PC*. It shows you how to design your backups so they're quick and reliable, no matter what type of software you use. It shows how to use DOS to back up your hard disk. And it shows you how to use the four most popular backup utilities to back up your hard disk. After you read about each of these four backup utilities, you can decide if one is appropriate for your backup needs...all are more efficient and reliable than using the DOS commands.

Terms

software
program
application program
word processing program
document
spreadsheet program
spreadsheet
operating system

DOS
Disk Operating System
MS-DOS
PC-DOS
command processor
command prompt
DOS services
input/output service
I/O service
file
directory
DOS command
file specification
drive
logical drive
physical drive
root directory
subdirectory
path
file name
extension
default directory
release
release number

Objectives

1. Given the drive, directory, subdirectory, and name for a file, type a complete file specification for the file.

2. Explain how the default directory affects your file specifications when you're using *WordPerfect*.

3. Describe the commands that are required for starting *WordPerfect* from the command prompt.

4. Explain the significance of the digits before and after the decimal point in a *WordPerfect* release number.

Section 2

A complete course in *WordPerfect* in six hours or less

If you're new to *WordPerfect*, this section is for you. In just three chapters, you'll learn how to use *WordPerfect* for most business applications. In other words, you will be a competent *WordPerfect* user when you complete this section. Then, you can expand upon what you've learned by reading and referring to the chapters in section 3.

If you do all of the exercises for each of the chapters in this section, you should be able to complete this section in six hours or less. And if you already know how to use word processing software but you're new to *WordPerfect*, you can probably work your way through this section in just an hour or two. That's why we believe this is the most efficient *WordPerfect* tutorial available anywhere. Although some tutorials take less time, they don't teach you what you need to know to be a competent *WordPerfect* user. Worse, many tutorials take more time and still don't teach you enough to be a competent *WordPerfect* user.

When you complete this section, you won't ever have to refer back to it because all of its skills are repeated in a different form in section 3. That means you can review the skills you've learned in this section as you learn the new skills presented in section 3. The chapters in section 3 are designed for efficient learning as well as efficient reference.

Chapter 3

How to create, print, and save a one-page letter

WordPerfect is a complex program that provides hundreds of commands and features. To learn how to use all of them takes many hours. Fortunately, you only need to know how to use a few *WordPerfect* commands and features to create, print, and save a letter. You can learn how to use those commands and features in about an hour, and that's what this chapter is designed to teach you.

As you read this chapter, you can try the skills it teaches on your own PC right after you read about them. If you use the chapter in this way, you'll actually create a simple document like the one in figure 3-1 by the time you complete this chapter. Or if you prefer, you can read the entire chapter first and then try the *WordPerfect* skills it teaches. Because the chapter is heavily illustrated, you shouldn't have any trouble following this chapter even if you don't have *WordPerfect* running on a PC in front of you. Then, you can go through the guided exercises at the end of the chapter.

Whether or not you've used another word processing program, you should be able to go through this chapter rapidly. One of the advantages of *WordPerfect* is that although it is a powerful word processing program, it's also an easy one to learn. However, it does take time to become familiar with the way the program's commands and features work. For that reason, you should make sure that you have a full hour of uninterrupted time to study this chapter. Once you master the material in this chapter, the rest of the book will be easier.

How to start *WordPerfect*

As I explained in chapter 2, how you start *WordPerfect* depends on how your PC is set up. If your PC displays a menu or a shell program when you start it up, you can probably start *WordPerfect* by selecting an option from a menu. If your PC displays the DOS command prompt, you may be able to start *WordPerfect* by entering a batch file command like *wp* at the command prompt:

```
C:\>wp
```

If that doesn't work, you can start *WordPerfect* 5.1 by entering a series of commands like this at the command prompt:

```
D:\>c:
C:\>cd \wp51
C:\WP51>wp
```

To start WordPerfect 5.0, you substitute WP50 for WP51 in the series of commands above. If you don't remember how these commands work, please refer back to chapter 2.

How to interpret the Edit screen

When you start *WordPerfect* 5.0, it displays a blank Edit screen like the top one in figure 3-2. If you're using *WordPerfect* 5.1, however, the program may be set up so it starts with either one of the Edit screens shown in figure 3-2. As you can see, the bottom screen has a bar at the top called the *menu bar*. If your PC displays a screen with the menu bar on it, just ignore the bar for now. It doesn't affect the way *WordPerfect* 5.1 works, and I'll show you how to use it later in this chapter.

Figure 3-3 shows the Edit screen after the document that is printed in figure 3-1 has been entered into *WordPerfect*. The term *document* is used to refer to whatever you're working on when you use *WordPerfect*. For instance, letters, memos, reports, and proposals are all documents. In figure 3-3, the document is a letter. Although the entire document isn't shown because the screen can hold only 24 lines of the document, the entire document is stored in internal memory.

Figure 3-3 also gives the terms that you need to know when you refer to the Edit screen. Here, you can see that the *cursor* is in the middle of the screen right after the colon. The cursor is the blinking underline or the highlight that identifies a specific character or area of a screen.

The *status line* is the bottom line of the screen. If you've saved your document, the left side of the status line shows the file specification for the document. Otherwise, this area is blank. The notation on the right side of the status line gives you the location of the cursor. In figure 3-3, for example, the *document indicator* shows that the cursor is in document 1 (*WordPerfect* lets you work on two different documents at the same time). The *page indicator* shows that the cursor is on page 1 of the document. The *line indicator* shows that the cursor is on the 14th line below the top margin. And the *position indicator* shows that the cursor is 34 characters from the left margin.

August 20, 1992

Tim McCrystle
107 Merring Ct.
Sacramento, CA 95864

Dear Tim:

      Thanks for asking about our PC books. I've enclosed a catalog
that describes them all in detail. As you read through it, I hope
you'll find something you can use right away.

      So there's no risk to you, all our books are backed by our
unconditional guarantee:

      If our PC books aren't the best ones you've ever used for
      both training and reference, you can return them for a
      full refund. <u>No questions asked</u>.

      If you have any questions or if you're ready to place an
order, please call us at our toll-free number: 1-800-221-5528. And
thanks for your interest in our books.

                  Sincerely,

                  Karen DeMartin

Figure 3-1   A letter that was created and printed using *WordPerfect*

**The Edit screen
without the menu bar**

```
                                                              Doc 1 Pg 1 Ln 1 Pos 15
```

**The Edit screen with
the menu bar**

```
File Edit Search Layout Mark Tools Font Graphics Help
_____




                                                              Doc 1 Pg 1 Ln 1 Pos 15
```

Figure 3-2   The starting screen for *WordPerfect* with and without the menu bar

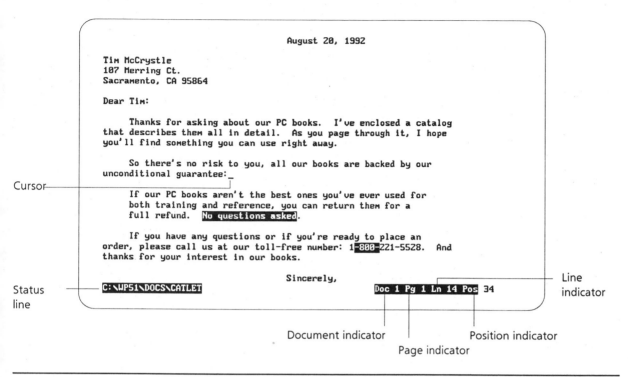

August 20, 1992

Tim McCrystle
107 Merring Ct.
Sacramento, CA 95864

Dear Tim:

Thanks for asking about our PC books. I've enclosed a catalog
that describes them all in detail. As you page through it, I hope
you'll find something you can use right away.

So there's no risk to you, all our books are backed by our
unconditional guarantee:_

If our PC books aren't the best ones you've ever used for
both training and reference, you can return them for a
full refund. No questions asked.

If you have any questions or if you're ready to place an
order, please call us at our toll-free number: 1-800-221-5528. And
thanks for your interest in our books.

Sincerely,

Cursor

Status line

C:\WP51\DOCS\CATLET

Doc 1 Pg 1 Ln 14 Pos 34

Line indicator

Document indicator

Page indicator

Position indicator

Figure 3-3   The terms that apply to the Edit screen

In figure 3-3, the cursor location is given in lines and characters. If you prefer, however, you can set up *WordPerfect* so that it gives the location in inches as in this example:

Doc 1 Pg 1 Ln 1.33" Pos 3.58"

Here, the cursor is 1.33 inches below the top margin and 3.58 inches in from the left margin. You can also set up *WordPerfect* so the file name for the document isn't displayed at the left side of the status line.

In chapter 6, you'll learn how to change the setup for your Edit screen. In particular, you'll learn how to remove the menu bar from the top of your screen and how to change the units of measurement used in the status line. In the meantime, don't be bothered if your Edit screen looks different than the one in figure 3-3 because the differences don't affect the way that *WordPerfect* works.

How to use the keyboard with *WordPerfect*

Figure 3-4 shows the two most common kinds of keyboards in use today: the 84-key keyboard and the 101-key keyboard. If you study these keyboards, you can see that they have several types of keys including a full set of typewriter keys, a set of numeric keys like the ten keys on a calculator, and some control and function keys.

When you use the typewriter keys, most of them work just as they would if you were using a typewriter. You can use these keys to type lower- and uppercase letters, numbers, punctuation marks, and some special symbols. When you hold down the Shift key, you get capital (uppercase) letters when you press the letter keys, and you get the upper symbol of the two symbols on the key when you press one of the other typewriter keys.

Figure 3-5 summarizes the use of the control keys that you will use most often with *WordPerfect*. When you press the Caps-lock key, the keyboard is put in Caps-lock mode. In this mode, the Caps-lock light is on, and the characters *Pos* in the status line are changed to *POS*. Then, all the letter keys that you strike will be entered into *WordPerfect* as capitals. However, the other keys on the keyboard are not affected by this mode. To get the upper symbol on a key, you must still hold down the Shift key while you press the key that you want. To get out of Caps-lock mode, you just press the Caps-lock key again. When a key switches between two or more modes like this, it is called a *toggle key*.

The Tab key is used to indent text like the first line of a paragraph. And the Enter key is used to end a paragraph. As you will see in a moment, you don't need to use the Enter key at the end of each line as you do the Return key when you use a typewriter; you only need to use the Enter key to mark the end of a paragraph. Later, you'll learn that you also use the Enter key to end an entry that's required by *WordPerfect*.

The Backspace and Delete keys are used to delete text. If you press the Backspace key once, *WordPerfect* deletes the character to the left of the cursor. If you press the Delete key once, *WordPerfect* deletes the character at the cursor. If you hold down the Backspace key, *WordPerfect* deletes the character to the left of the cursor and continues deleting in that direction until you release the key or run out of text. If you hold down the Delete key, *WordPerfect* deletes the character at the cursor and continues to delete characters to the right until you release the key or run out of text.

The Arrow keys are sometimes called the *cursor control keys* because they are used to move the cursor through the text in a document. If you press the Right arrow key once, for example, *WordPerfect* moves the cursor one character to the right. If you press the Down arrow key once, *WordPerfect* moves the cursor down one line. And if you hold down any Arrow key, the cursor will continue to move in the direction of the arrow until you release the key. However, the Arrow keys can only be used to move through the existing text. So if you try to move the cursor to an area of the screen that doesn't have any text, *WordPerfect* won't move the cursor.

The 84-key keyboard

Note that the control keys and the numeric keys are combined in a single pad to the right of the typewriter keyboard. To use the numeric keys in the numeric pad, Numeric Lock (Num-lock) must be on. To use the control keys in the numeric pad, Numeric Lock must be off.

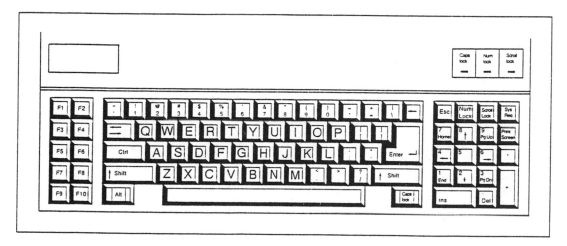

The 101-key keyboard

Note that a separate set of control keys are located between the typewriter keys and the numeric pad. But the numeric pad still includes a second set of control keys. As a result, you still have to turn Numeric Lock (Num-lock) on if you want to enter numbers with the numeric pad. If you keep it on, you can use the control key pad for all control operations and the numeric pad for all data entry.

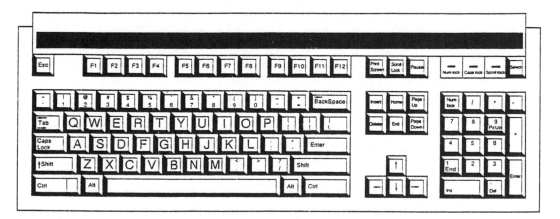

Figure 3-4   The 84-key and 101-key keyboards

Key	Function
Caps-lock	Turns Caps-lock mode on and off. If Caps-lock is on, the Caps-lock light is on, and the position indicator in the status line is displayed in capital letters (POS). Then, all the letter keys you strike appear as capital letters.
Tab	Indents the first line of a paragraph.
Enter	Ends a paragraph or ends an entry that is required by *WordPerfect*.
Backspace	Deletes the character to the left of the cursor.
Delete	Deletes the character at the cursor.
Arrow keys	Moves the cursor one character to the right or left, or moves the cursor one line up or down.
Num-lock	Turns Num-lock mode on and off. If Num-lock is on, the Num-lock light is on, and the position indicator (Pos) in the status line blinks. Then, when you use the numeric key pad, you get the number that's assigned to the key instead of the cursor control function that's assigned to the key.
Insert	Switches between Typeover and Insert modes. If Typeover mode is on, the word *Typeover* appears on the left side of the status line. Then, the characters you type overwrite the characters at the cursor. If Insert mode is on, the characters you type are inserted at the cursor.

Figure 3-5   Control keys that affect *WordPerfect* operations

If you have an 84-key keyboard on your PC like the one shown in figure 3-4, you have to know how the Num-lock key affects the Arrow keys. Within the ten-key numeric pad of that keyboard, every key but the 5-key has a control function. For example, the 6-key is also the Right arrow key, and the 2-key is also the Down arrow key. To access the Arrow keys, you have to turn the Num-lock mode off. To turn this mode off if it's on, you press the Num-lock key. When the mode is off, the Num-lock light is off, and the characters *Pos* in the position indicator of the status line aren't blinking. Since you will use the Arrow keys frequently when you use *WordPerfect*, you will probably want to leave this mode off.

If you are using a 101-key keyboard, on the other hand, you will probably want to leave the Num-lock mode on. On this keyboard, the control keys are duplicated between the typewriter keys and the numeric pad. Then, if you keep the Num-lock mode on, you can use the control pad for control functions and the numeric pad for numeric entries.

The Insert key is used to toggle between *Insert mode* and *Typeover mode*. These two editing modes affect how text is inserted into your document. When you start *WordPerfect*, it is in Insert mode, and this is the mode you'll use most of the time. In Insert mode, the text that you type is inserted into the text by pushing the existing characters to the right.

When you press the Insert key, you switch to *Typeover mode*. In this mode, your Edit screen displays the word *Typeover* on the left side of the status line at the bottom of the screen. Then, the text that you type will overwrite and replace the existing characters.

Once you understand how the Arrow keys and the two text editing modes work, you should be able to correct mistakes anywhere in your document. Just use the Arrow keys to move the cursor to where you want to start editing. Then, use the Delete key or the Backspace key to delete any characters you don't want. Next, use Insert or Typeover mode to type new characters into the document.

In the next chapter, you'll learn how to use other keystrokes to move the cursor around your document more efficiently. And you'll learn how to delete text more efficiently. But for now, the Arrow keys, the Backspace key, and the Delete key are the only keys you need to know how to use.

How to enter the first portion of the letter into *WordPerfect*

If you're creating the letter shown in figure 3-1 as you read this chapter, take the time now to enter the keystrokes as shown in figure 3-6. This figure shows all of the keystrokes required to enter the first portion of the letter. To start, press the Tab key several times so the date is located just past the center of the page. Although figure 3-6 shows that the key should be pressed five times, this depends on how *WordPerfect* has been set up on your PC. Later on, when you enter the signature block for the letter, you should use the same number of tabs that you used before the date.

After you type the date, press the Enter key to move the cursor to the next line. Then, press the Enter key again to skip a line. From this point on, type the keystrokes shown in figure 3-6 to finish the first portion of the letter. When you finish, your screen should look something like the one in figure 3-7. However, it won't look exactly the same unless your margins, tabs, and base font are set the same way they are for this example. I'll show you how to control those settings in chapter 5.

When you type the first paragraph of the letter, you'll notice that you don't have to press the Enter key at the end of each line. Instead, *WordPerfect* automatically moves from the end of one line to the start of the next line. This is called *word wrap*. As a result, you only press the Enter key when you want to end a paragraph.

How to access and cancel *WordPerfect* commands

To enter the second portion of the letter in figure 3-1, you need to know how to use *WordPerfect* commands. Specifically, you need to know how to use the commands for indenting, underlining, and boldfacing. Also, when you complete the letter, you will need to know how to use the commands for printing the letter, saving the letter on the hard disk, and exiting from *WordPerfect*.

[Tab][Tab][Tab][Tab][Tab]**August 20, 1992**[Enter]
[Enter]
Tim McCrystle[Enter]
107 Merring Ct.[Enter]
Sacramento, CA 95864[Enter]
[Enter]
Dear Tim:[Enter]
[Enter]
[Tab]**Thanks for asking about our PC books. I've enclosed a catalog that describes them all in detail. As you read through it, I hope you'll find something you can use right away.**[Enter]
[Enter]
[Tab]**So there's no risk to you, all our books are backed by our unconditional guarantee:**[Enter]
[Enter]

Figure 3-6   The keystrokes for the first portion of the letter in figure 3-1

To access commands when you're using *WordPerfect* 5.0, you use the function keys in combination with the Shift, Alt, and Ctrl keys. To access commands when you're using *WordPerfect* 5.1, you can use the function keys just as you do with release 5.0, or you can use the *WordPerfect* 5.1 menus. I'll show you how to access the commands using both methods, but you can skip the topic on the use of the menus if you're using release 5.0.

How to use the function keys to access the commands   If you look at figure 3-4 again, you'll see that both keyboards include ten function keys numbered from F1 through F10, and the 101-key keyboard includes two additional function keys numbered F11 and F12. Both keyboards include special control keys such as the Ctrl key, the Alt key, and the Shift key. By using the function and control keys in various combinations, you can access any one of the *WordPerfect* commands. To start the Print command, for example, you hold down the Shift key while you press the F7 key (Shift+F7).

A *WordPerfect template* is a piece of cardboard or plastic that summarizes how to access *WordPerfect* commands. The templates for the two types of keyboards are shown in figure 3-8. For the 101-key keyboard, the template lays across the top of the 12 function keys. For the 84-key keyboard, the template fits around the ten function keys. Although there are some minor differences between the templates for *WordPerfect* 5.0 and 5.1, these differences don't affect the commands presented in this book.

Figure 3-9 shows you how to use the Ctrl, Alt, and Shift keys to access the commands on just one of the function keys, the F4 key, but the concept is the same for all of the commands. To access the >Indent command (Single Indent command), you just press the function key. To access the >Indent< command (Double Indent command), you press the function key while holding down

```
                          August 20, 1992

Tim McCrystle
107 Merring Ct.
Sacramento, CA  95864

Dear Tim:

      Thanks for asking about our PC books.  I've enclosed a catalog
that describes them all in detail.  As you read through it, I hope
you'll find something you can use right away.

      So there's no risk to you, all our books are backed by our
unconditional guarantee:


  _




C:\WP51\DOCS\CATLET                              Doc 1 Pg 1 Ln 16 Pos 10
```

Figure 3-7   The Edit screen after the keystrokes in figure 3-6 have been entered into *WordPerfect*

the Shift key. To access the Block command, you press the function key while holding down the Alt key. And to access the Move command, you press the function key while holding down the Ctrl key.

Because the first ten functions keys have four commands each, you can use the command keys to access 40 commands. As you can see in the 101-key template in figure 3-8, the F11 and F12 keys don't provide for additional commands. Instead, they just make it easier to access the Reveal Codes and the Block commands, which can otherwise be accessed using the Alt+F3 and Alt+F4 key combinations.

To enter the second portion of the letter in figure 3-1, you need to access the >Indent< command, the Underline command, and the Bold command. If you look at the templates in figure 3-8, you can see that you access the >Indent< command using the Shift+F4 key combination. To access the Underline command, you press the F8 key by itself. Similarly, to access the Bold command, you press the F6 key by itself. In a moment, I'll explain how these commands work in more detail. But first, I want to show you how to access these commands using the *WordPerfect* 5.1. menu system.

How to use the *WordPerfect* 5.1 menus to access the commands
If you're using *WordPerfect* 5.1, you can use the function keys to access the commands just as you do with *WordPerfect* 5.0. However, you can also access the commands using the 5.1 menus. The menus don't provide new commands; they just provide another way to access the commands.

The 101-key template

F1	F2	F3	F4	F5	F6	F7	F8	F9	F10	F11	F12
Shell	Spell	Screen	Move	Text In/Out	Tab Align	Footnote	Font	Merge/Sort	Macro Define		
Thesaurus	Replace	Reveal Codes	Block	Mark Text	Flush Right	Math/Columns	Style	Graphics	Macro		
Setup	♦Search	Switch	♦Indent♦	Date/Outline	Center	Print	Format	Merge Codes	Retrieve		
Cancel	♦Search	Help	♦Indent	List Files	Bold	Exit	Underline	Merge R	Save	Reveal Codes	Block
F1	F2	F3	F4	F5	F6	F7	F8	F9	F10	F11	F12
			Ctrl				*Ctrl*				
			Alt				*Alt*				
			Shift				*Shift*				

WordPerfect®
for IBM Personal Computers
Delete to End of Ln/Pg   End/Pg Dn
Delete Word   Backspace
Go To   Home
Hard Page   Enter
♦Margin Release   Tab
Screen Up/Down   –/+ (num)
Soft Hyphen
Word Left/Right   –/–
© WordPerfect Corp. 1988   TMXXXWPIV16.0
ISBN 1-55682-200-0

The 84-key template

Ctrl Shift Alt   ©WordPerfect 1988   ISBN 1-55682-200-0   TMXXXWPPII150

F1	F2
Shell	Spell
Setup	♦Search
Thesaurus	Replace
Cancel	♦Search

F3	F4
Screen	Move
Switch	♦Indent♦
Reveal Codes	Block
Help	♦Indent

F5	F6
Text In/Out	Tab Align
Date/Outline	Center
Mark Text	Flush Right
List Files	Bold

F7	F8
Footnote	Font
Print	Format
Math/Columns	Style
Exit	Underline

F9	F10
Merge/Sort	Macro Def
Merge Codes	Retrieve
Graphics	Macro
Merge R	Save

WordPerfect® for IBM Personal Computers
Delete to End of Ln/Pg   End/PgDn   ♦Margin Release   Tab
Delete Word   Backspace   Screen Up/Down   –/+ (num)
Go To   Home   Soft Hyphen   –
Hard Page   Enter   Word Left/Right   –/–

Figure 3-8   The *WordPerfect* command templates for the two styles of keyboards

Keystrokes	Command
Ctrl+F4	Move
Alt+F4	Block
Shift+F4	>Indent<
F4	>Indent

Figure 3-9   How to access the commands on the F4 function key

If you look at figure 3-10, you can see the elements that make up the menu system. At the top of the screen is the *menu bar* with nine menus on it. Since you pull these menus down when you want to use them, they are called *pull-down* menus. In the two examples in figure 3-11, the Layout menu and the Font menu have been pulled down.

If you look closely at the items on the Layout menu, you will see that some of them have a triangle to their right. When you select an item with a triangle, *WordPerfect* gives you another menu with more items. Since this type of menu cascades off to the right of the pull-down menu, it's is called a *cascading menu.* In figure 3-11, for example, the Align menu cascades off to the right of the Align item on the Layout menu, and the Appearance menu cascades off of the Font menu. In contrast, when you select an item that doesn't have a triangle, *WordPerfect* starts the command.

Figure 3-11 summarizes the procedures for using the menus with or without a mouse. First, if the menu bar isn't already displayed on your screen, clicking the mouse will display the menu bar. Second, you move the mouse cursor to the menu you want to pull down, and you click the left mouse button. Third, you move the mouse cursor to the menu item you want and click the left mouse button. If this selection doesn't lead to a cascading menu, the command is started. Otherwise, you move the mouse cursor to the item that you want to select in the cascading menu and press the left mouse button to start that command. If you make a mistake or change your mind, you can cancel the command and return to the Edit screen by clicking the right mouse button.

If you're using the keyboard, you first transfer the cursor from the Edit screen to the menu bar by holding down the Alt key and pressing the Equals key (Alt+=). Or you may have to press just the Alt key, depending on how your PC is set up. This will also display the menu bar if it isn't already displayed. Second, you pull down the menu you want by pressing the highlighted letter of the menu. If, for example, you press the letter *l*, the Layout menu is pulled down. Third, you select an item from the menu by pressing the highlighted letter of the item. If this doesn't lead to a cascading menu, the command is started. Otherwise, you select an item from the cascading menu by pressing

The two menus you use to select the >Indent< command

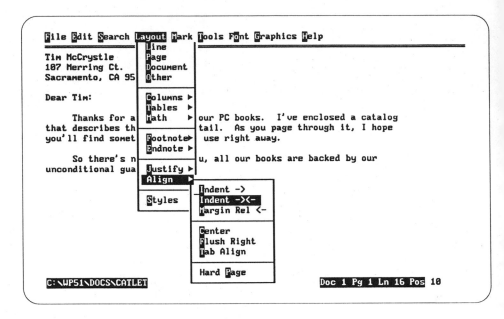

The two menus you use to select the Underline and the Bold commands

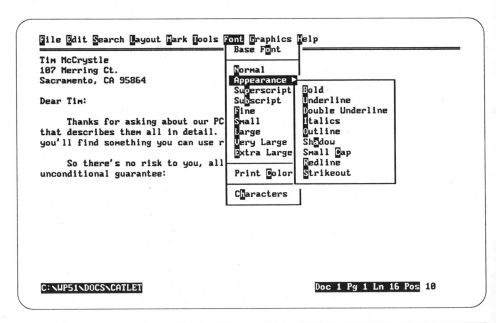

Figure 3-10   Two examples of the pull-down menus and cascading menus that you can use with *WordPerfect* 5.1

How to select commands using a mouse

1. If the menu bar isn't displayed at the top of the Edit screen, click the right mouse button.
2. To pull down a menu, move the mouse cursor to the menu you want and click the left mouse button.
3. To select a command, move the mouse cursor to the command you want and click the left mouse button.
4. If the command that you selected in step 3 leads to a cascading menu, move the mouse cursor to the command on that menu and select it by clicking the left mouse button.

How to select commands using the keyboard

1. If the menu bar isn't displayed at the top of the Edit screen, hold down the Alt key and press the Equals-sign key. On some PCs, all you have to do is press the Alt key to access the menu bar.
2. To pull down a menu, press the highlighted letter of the menu you want.
3. To select a command, press the highlighted letter in that command.
4. If the command that you selected in step 3 leads to a cascading menu, press the highlighted letter of the command on that menu to select it.

Figure 3-11   How to select commands from the *WordPerfect* 5.1 pull-down and cascading menus

the highlighted letter of the item. Incidentally, you can also select a menu or a menu item by moving the cursor to it and pressing the Enter key. But that requires more keystrokes, so I don't recommend it. If you make a mistake or change your mind while you're accessing a command, you can press the Esc key or the Cancel key (F1) to return to the previous screen until you're back at the Edit screen. Or you can press the Exit key (F7) to return immediately to the Edit screen.

In general, I recommend that you avoid using the menu system because you can work more efficiently without it for three reasons. First, when you use the function keys to access commands, you can access any command with just one keystroke combination. In contrast, the menu system requires three or four keystrokes or clicks. Second, when you use the function keys to access commands, you don't have to remove your hands from the keyboard. In contrast, when you use a mouse, you have to switch one of your hands back and forth between the keyboard and mouse. Third, because mouse support and the menu system were added to *WordPerfect* in release 5.1, they aren't an integral part of the product. As a result, the menu interface doesn't work as efficiently or as logically as it ought to. Often, for example, you can't complete a command using the mouse and menu system alone so you end up using the keyboard anyway.

Since I recommend that you use the function keys instead of the menu system to access commands, I won't say any more about the use of menus or a mouse in the rest of this book. Instead, I'll just show you how to use the function keys to access the commands. If you want to use the menu system, though, the summary in appendix B will help you find the commands that you're looking for.

How to use the Cancel command to cancel other commands

When you access commands like the Indent, Bold, and Underline commands, the command is started immediately. But when you access commands like the Move or Print commands, *WordPerfect* displays a screen that gives you options that you must choose from. Then, the command doesn't start until you complete your selections. In the meantime, if you decide that you don't want to perform the command after all, you can cancel it by pressing the Cancel key (F1).

You can also use the Esc key to cancel some commands, but this key won't work for all commands. At some of the screens that are displayed by commands, you can indicate that you don't want any of the options by pressing the Zero (0) key. This too has the effect of canceling a command. In the next chapter, you'll learn more about these alternatives.

How to use the Indent, Underline, and Bold commands as you enter the second portion of the letter

If you're creating the letter shown in figure 3-1 as you read this chapter, take the time now to enter the last portion of it. The commands and keystrokes that are required for this are shown in figure 3-12. In particular, there are three commands that are required to enter this portion of the letter.

To start, you access the Indent command. As you can see in figure 3-9, though, there are two different types of Indent commands. The first one (>Indent) indents only the left side of the paragraph. The second one (>Indent<) indents the left and the right sides of the paragraph, and that's the one you want to use in the letter. To access this command, you hold down the Shift key as you press the F4 key (Shift+F4). This starts the Double Indent command. From that point on, all the characters that you type will be indented from both sides until you press the Enter key.

The second command required in this letter is the Underline command. To access this command, you press the F8 key, which starts underlining immediately. To show that it has started, the number after the Position indicator on the status line is highlighted or changed to a different color. Then, when you type the text that you want to underline, *WordPerfect* colors or highlights it to indicate that it is underlined. Although this text usually isn't underlined on the Edit screen, it is underlined when you print it. To end the Underline command, you can press F8 to access the command again, or you can press the Right arrow key.

[>Indent<]**If our PC books aren't the best ones you've ever used for both training and reference, you can return them for a full refund.** [Underline]**No questions asked**[Underline].[Enter]
[Enter]
[Tab]**If you have any questions or if you're ready to place an order, please call us at our toll-free number: 1**[Bold]**-800-**[Bold]**221-5528. And thanks for your interest in our books.**[Enter]
[Enter]
[Tab][Tab][Tab][Tab][Tab]**Sincerely,**[Enter]
[Enter]
[Enter]
[Enter]
[Tab][Tab][Tab][Tab][Tab]**Karen DeMartin**

Figure 3-12   The commands and keystrokes for the second portion of the letter in figure 3-1

As you enter the last paragraph of the letter, you need the Bold command. This command works like the Underline command. To access it, you press the F6 key. Then, you type the text that you want boldfaced. This text will be colored or highlighted on the screen to indicate that it is boldfaced, and it will be boldfaced when you print the document. To end the command, press F6 to access the command again or press the Right arrow key.

When you enter the signature block of the letter into *WordPerfect*, be sure to use the same number of Tabs that you used before the date. That way, the signature block will be aligned with the date.

As you type the signature block, the top of the letter will disappear, or *scroll off*, the top of the screen. In figure 3-13, for example, you can see that the date and the address have scrolled off the Edit screen. Then, if you want to look at the top of the letter, you can use the Up arrow key to scroll back up the letter.

How to use the Reveal Codes command

When you use *WordPerfect*, it inserts codes into your document. To keep the screen uncluttered, these codes are kept hidden from you. If you want to see these codes, though, you can do so by accessing the Reveal Codes command.

To access the Reveal Codes command, you hold down the Alt key as you press the F3 key (Alt+F3). This works on both the 84-key and the 101-key keyboard. If you have a 101-key keyboard, though, it's easier to access this command by pressing the Reveal Codes key (F11). To return to the Edit screen, just access the Reveal Codes command again.

After you access the Reveal Codes command, your screen will look like the one in figure 3-14. Here, the top half of the screen still looks like a normal Edit screen, but the bottom half of the screen shows both the text and the codes. In other words, the codes are revealed on the bottom half of the

Figure 3-13   The Edit screen after the letter in figure 3-1 has been entered into *WordPerfect*

screen. In this figure, you can see that the status line is just above the line that separates the top and bottom halves of the screen. If you look closely, you can also see that the cursor is on both halves of the screen at the same time and in the same place (between the words *used* and *for*).

Figure 3-15 summarizes all the codes used in the letter in figure 3-14. As you can see, *WordPerfect*'s word wrap function automatically inserts the *soft return* code [SRt] after each line in a paragraph. However, it inserts the *hard return* code [HRt] when you press the Enter key. Similarly, it inserts the Tab code [Tab] when you press the Tab key, and it inserts the Double Indent code [>Indent<] when you access the Double Indent command. Codes like these are referred to as a *single codes*.

In contrast, the Underline [UND][und] and Bold [BOLD][bold] codes are *paired codes*. The first code in the pair activates the command, and the second one turns it off. In figure 3-14, for example, you can see the Underline codes before and after this phrase: "No questions asked." Similarly, you can see the Bold codes before and after the -800- in the phone number.

When the Reveal Codes screen is displayed, it's easy to see why something in your document isn't working the way you want it to. Often, the problem is that the wrong code has been inserted into your document or that the right code is in the wrong place. Then, you can insert or delete the appropriate codes. As soon as you insert or delete a code, the change shows up in the formatting of the document.

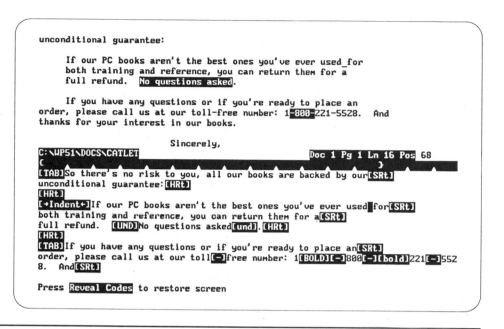

Figure 3-14   The Reveal Codes screen for the letter in figure 3-13

To insert a single code, you move the cursor to the right location and press the key combination that inserts the code. Unfortunately, you can't insert a paired code as easily. To insert a paired code, you need to use an additional command called the Block command. I'll show you how to use that command in the next chapter.

To delete a single code, you move the cursor to the code and press the Delete key. Similarly, to delete a paired code, you move the cursor to one of the codes in the pair and press the Delete key. Once you delete one code in a pair, both of the paired codes are deleted.

How to use the Print command

Figure 3-16 shows you how to use the Print command. To access this command, you hold down the Shift key as you press the F7 key (Shift+F7). When you do this, *WordPerfect* temporarily replaces the Edit screen with the Print screen. To begin printing, you select either the Full Document or Page option from the Print screen. You make your selection by typing either the number of the option (1 or 2) or the highlighted letter in the option (F or P). Since the document in this chapter is less than one page long, either of these options will print the entire document.

After you select Full Document or Page, *WordPerfect* starts the printing operation and returns you to your document. Then, you can continue

Code	Name	Description
[SRt]	Soft Return	A single code that's automatically inserted at the end of each line. This code can't be deleted.
[HRt]	Hard Return	A single code that's inserted when you press the Enter key.
[Tab]	Tab	A single code that's inserted when you press the Tab key.
[>Indent<]	Double Indent	A single code that's inserted when you use the Double Indent command.
[UND][und]	Underline	A paired code that's inserted when you use the Underline command.
[BOLD][bold]	Bold	A paired code that's inserted when you use the Bold command.

Figure 3-15   A summary of the codes used in the completed letter

working on the document while the printer prints. Or you can save your document and start working on another one. However, you can't exit from *WordPerfect* until it has finished the printing operation.

If your printer doesn't start printing after you start the printing operation, you should check to make sure that the printer is on, that the paper is loaded properly in the printer, and that the printer is ready for printing. As soon as the printer is ready, the *WordPerfect* document will start printing.

When your document is printed, you'll see that it doesn't look the same way that it does on the screen. In particular, the text that you underlined and boldfaced will be printed that way, even though they probably don't look that way on your screen. The paragraphs in your printed letter may be aligned at the right margin, even though they aren't aligned that way on the screen. And the text may appear in a typeface (or font) that's different from the typeface that appears on your screen. These differences are controlled by several *WordPerfect* settings. In chapters 5 and 6, I'll show you how to change those settings. Then, you can customize *WordPerfect* so it's appropriate for your work.

How to use the Save command

If you shut off your PC or exit from *WordPerfect* without saving your document, your work is lost. That's why you must understand what the Save command does and how it works. As you will see, this command works slightly differently for a new document than it does for an old one. This is summarized in figure 3-17.

How to access the Print command

Hold down the Shift key and press the F7 key (Shift+F7).

The Print screen

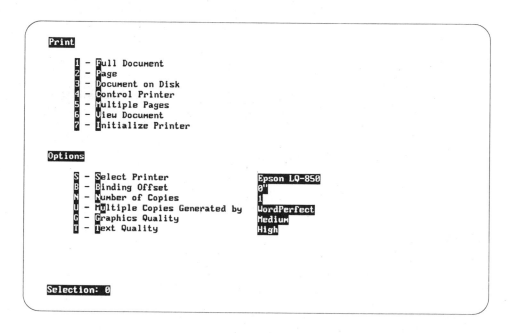

The primary Print options	**Meaning**
1 or F	Print all of the pages in the document.
2 or P	Print only the page of the document that the cursor is on.

Figure 3-16   How to use the Print command to print a document

How to save a document for the first time   The first procedure in figure 3-17 shows you how to use the Save command to save a document for the first time. In step 1, you press the F10 key to start the command. Then, *WordPerfect* displays a message, or *prompt*, that asks for the file specification that you want to use for the document:

Document to be saved:

If you enter just a file name, your document is saved in the *default directory*. If you enter a complete file specification, though, the directory in the specification is used instead of the default directory. After you enter the file specification, press the Enter key to complete the command.

In the next chapter, you'll learn how to set the default directory to the one you want. But for now, just type the complete file specification when you use the Save command. If, for example, you want to save a file named CATLET on the D drive in the \DOCS directory, you enter a file specification like this:

Document to be saved: d:\docs\catlet

When you create a file name for a document, you must follow the DOS rules for file names that I gave you in chapter 2. You should also try to create file names that you'll remember later on. In this example, I used CATLET to indicate that the file is a letter (LET) about a catalog (CAT).

If you try to save a document in a directory that doesn't exist, *WordPerfect* will flash a prompt like this:

ERROR: Invalid drive/path specification

Then, it will give you the save prompt again with your invalid specification. To correct it, you can use the Arrow keys to move the cursor to the right location; you can use the Backspace and Delete keys to delete characters; and you can use the Insert and Typeover modes to insert or typeover characters. When you press the Enter key, *WordPerfect* will try to save the file again.

How to save a document for the second time   Suppose now that you want to change the address of the letter from 107 Merring Ct. to 4112 Redwood Road. Then, after you print the letter, you want to save the document so it will include this address change. The second procedure in figure 3-17 shows you how to do that.

After you access the Save command by pressing the F10 key, *WordPerfect* displays a prompt that gives the complete file specification that you used when you saved the file the first time. Then, since the specification is the way you want it, you don't have to enter it again. Instead, you just press the Enter key.

This time, however, there's already a file on the hard disk with the file name you've just used for the save operation. As a result, *WordPerfect* doesn't store the document on the disk right away. Instead, it displays a prompt that asks you whether you want to replace the old version of the document with the new one. Then, if that's what you want to do, type *y* for Yes. If that isn't what you want to do, type *n* for No so you can change the file specification. And if you decide that you don't want to save the file at all, press the Esc or F1 key to cancel the command.

How to save a revised document with a new name   Suppose now that you decide to make the letter you've been working on a form letter so

How to save a document for the first time

1. Press the F10 key to start the Save command. *WordPerfect* then displays this prompt that asks you to enter a file specification:

   Document to be saved:

2. Type the file specification for the file that you want created like this:

   Document to be saved: c:\wp51\docs\catlet

   Then, press the Enter key. This file specification is for a document to be named CATLET that will be stored in the \DOCS directory that's subordinate to the \WP51 directory on the C drive.

How to replace the document with a revised version of the document

1. Press the F10 key to start the Save command. *WordPerfect* then displays this prompt followed by the complete file specification for the document that you're working on:

   Document to be saved: C:\WP51\DOCS\CATLET

2. Press the Enter key to save the revised version of the document with the same file specification that you used before. Then, *WordPerfect* displays this prompt:

   Replace C:\WP51\DOCS\CATLET? No (Yes)

3. Press *y* for Yes to tell *WordPerfect* that you want to replace the old version of the document with the new version. *WordPerfect* then completes the command.

How to save a revised version of an old document under a new name

1. Press the F10 key to start the Save command. *WordPerfect* then displays this prompt followed by the complete file specification for the document that you're working on:

   Document to be saved: C:\WP51\DOCS\CATLET

2. Change the file specification to the one that you want to use for the revised version of the document like this:

   Document to be saved: C:\WP51\DOCS\CATLET.fm

   Then, press the Enter key. Here, the path remains the same, but the file name has been changed from CATLET to CATLET.FM. To make this change, you can use the Right arrow key to move to the end of the file specification before you type the period and the extension. (CATLET will remain unchanged and the revised version of the document will be saved under the name CATLET.FM.)

Figure 3-17   How to use the Save command to save a document to disk storage

you can use it repeatedly. To do that, delete the date, name and address, and the greeting from the letter, but leave in the tabs and blank lines. When you're done, your document will look like the one in figure 3-18. Then, after you print the letter, you want to save the document with a new name. The last procedure in figure 3-17 shows you how to do that.

After you access the Save command, *WordPerfect* displays a prompt that shows you the file specification that you used to save the file last time. This time, however, you want to change the file name, but not the path. To do that, use the Right arrow key to move to the file name portion of the specification. Then, delete or insert the required characters. In figure 3-17, the name is changed by adding the extension .FM to it (the period followed by the letters *FM*). If you use an extension, remember that it can't be more than three characters.

When you press the Enter key, the command is performed. Then, since the command uses a new file specification, the file is stored on the disk and *WordPerfect* returns to the Edit screen. In this example, that means that the old version of the file is still stored on the disk under the name CATLET, and the new version is stored under the name CATLET.FM.

How to use the Exit command

When you're through with the document you've been working on, you use the Exit command to exit from the document in one of two ways. First, you can use this command to exit from the document, but remain in *WordPerfect*. This will clear your Edit screen so you can start work on another document. Second, you can use this command to exit from *WordPerfect* and return to DOS or the program that you started *WordPerfect* from. Both of these options are summarized in figure 3-19.

The first procedure in figure 3-19 shows how to exit from a document, but not from *WordPerfect*. When you start the Exit command by pressing the F7 key, *WordPerfect* gives you a chance to save your document, but you should have already saved it. To make sure that you've saved your last modifications to the document, though, you can check the right side of the status line to see whether this message is displayed:

(Text was not modified)

If it is displayed, it means that you've already saved your last modifications to the document, so you can answer *n* for No at the first prompt. Then, *WordPerfect* displays a prompt that asks you whether you want to exit from *WordPerfect*. If you enter *n* for No, *WordPerfect* returns you to a blank Edit screen so you can start work on another document.

The second procedure in figure 3-19 shows you how to exit from *WordPerfect*. As in the first procedure, *WordPerfect* gives you another chance to

```
Dear :

      Thanks for asking about our PC books.  I've enclosed a catalog
that describes them all in detail.  As you page through it, I hope
you'll find something you can use right away.

      So there's no risk to you, all our books are backed by our
unconditional guarantee:

      If our PC books aren't the best ones you've ever used for
      both training and reference, you can return them for a
      full refund.  No questions asked.

      If you have any questions or if you're ready to place an
order, please call us at our toll-free number: 1-800-221-5528.  And
thanks for your interest in our books.

                              Sincerely,

C:\WP51\DOCS\CATLET                            Doc 1 Pg 1 Ln 7 Pos 15
```

Figure 3-18   The form letter created by revising the letter in figure 3-1

save your document when you start the Exit command. Assuming that you've already saved your document, you enter *n* for No. Then, *WordPerfect* asks you whether you want to exit from the program and return to DOS. This time, you enter *y* for Yes to return to DOS.

Although you can use the Exit command to save a document before exiting from a document or *WordPerfect*, I recommend that you use the Save command before the Exit command. Then, you can answer No when the first prompt of the Exit command asks you whether you want to save the document you've been working on. Should you answer Yes, the prompts that follow work just like those for the Save command. Then, after you save the document, you can either exit from *WordPerfect* or just from the document.

Discussion   The hardest part about learning *WordPerfect* is getting started. Before you can do anything, you have to learn some basic terminology. You have to learn how to enter text. You have to understand how *WordPerfect* uses codes. And you have to learn how to use the *WordPerfect* commands.

If you've had any difficulty understanding the skills presented in this chapter, I recommend that you do the exercises that follow on your own PC. They force you to use the skills in a more controlled manner than the text

How to exit from a document without saving it and without exiting from *WordPerfect*

1. Press the F7 key to start the Exit command. *WordPerfect* then displays this prompt that asks you if you want to save the document you've been working on:

Save document? **Y**es (**No**)   (Text was not modified)

   If you haven't made any changes to the document since the last time you saved it, you'll see a message on the right side of the prompt that says "Text was not modified."

2. Press *n* for No to indicate that you don't want to save the document you've been working on. *WordPerfect* then displays this prompt that asks you if you want to exit from the program:

Exit WP? **No** (**Y**es)

3. Press *n* for No to indicate that you don't want to exit from *WordPerfect*. This clears the Edit screen so you can start work on another document.

How to exit from *WordPerfect* without saving the document you've been working on

1. Press the F7 key to start the Exit command. *WordPerfect* then displays this prompt that asks you if you want to save the document you've been working on:

Save document? **Y**es (**No**)   (Text was not modified)

   If you haven't made any changes to the document since the last time you saved it, you'll see a message on the right side of the prompt that says "Text was not modified."

2. Press *n* for No to indicate that you don't want to save the document you've been working on. *WordPerfect* then displays this prompt that asks you if you want to exit from the program:

Exit WP? **No** (**Y**es)

3. Press *y* for Yes to indicate that you want to exit from *WordPerfect*.

Figure 3-19   How to use the Exit command to clear the Edit screen or to exit from *WordPerfect*

does. By the time you complete the exercises, you should be able to do all of the tasks presented in this chapter. Then, you'll be ready for the next chapter.

In the next chapter, you'll learn skills that build upon the ones presented in this chapter. For instance, you'll learn how to retrieve an old document from the hard disk; how to put the current date into a document without typing it; and how to use several other *WordPerfect* commands. After that, you'll be on your way to becoming a proficient *WordPerfect* user.

Terms

menu bar
document
cursor
status line
document indicator
page indicator
line indicator
position indicator
toggle key
cursor control key
insert mode
typeover mode

word wrap
template
pull-down menu
cascading menu
scroll off
soft return
hard return
single code
paired code
prompt
default directory

Objectives

1. Enter text into *WordPerfect* using the typewriter keys including the Tab and Enter keys.

2. Make corrections to the text that you've entered by using the Arrow keys, the Backspace key, the Delete key, Insert mode, and Typeover mode.

3. Access any of the *WordPerfect* commands using the template and the function keys.

4. Use the eight commands presented in this chapter to perform any of these functions:

   a) Double indent a portion of text.
   b) Underline a portion of text.
   c) Boldface a portion of text.
   d) Save a document.
   e) Print a document.
   f) Exit from a document and clear the screen.
   g) Exit from *WordPerfect*.
   h) Reveal the codes within a document.
   i) Cancel a command.

5. Use the Reveal Codes screen to locate and delete any of the single or paired codes in a document.

6. Insert single codes in a document after the document has been entered into *WordPerfect*.

Exercises

Part 1: How to enter text into *WordPerfect* and how to use some of the control keys

1. Start *WordPerfect*. Is the menu bar displayed on your Edit screen? Do the line and position indicators in the status line use inches or units? What is the location of the cursor before you enter any characters?

2. Press the Num-lock key to turn the Num-lock light on. When the light is on, the characters *Pos* in the status line blink. Next, use the numeric pad to enter some numbers. Then, press the Num-lock key again to turn the light off and try to use the numeric pad to enter more numbers. Note that *Pos* in the status line stops blinking when the Num-lock light is off. To delete the numbers that you entered, use the Backspace key to return to the first position of the document.

3. Use the typewriter keyboard to type these characters:

   abcdef123456-=[]\;',./<_>!@#$%^&*()_+{}|:"<>?

   Note that you have to use the Shift key to type some of the characters.
   Next, press the Caps-lock key to turn the Caps-lock light on. When you do this, note that the characters *Pos* in the status line are capitalized. Then, type the characters shown above again, but this time with capital instead of lowercase letters. Note that you still have to use the Shift key to type some of the characters.
   To delete the characters that you've entered, use the Arrow keys to move the cursor to the first position in the document. Then, hold down the Delete key to delete all the characters that you entered. Next, press the Caps-lock key again to turn the Caps-lock feature off.

4. Type your name and address. After each line, press the Enter key to return the cursor to the left margin. Next, use the Arrow keys to move the cursor to the start of the second line of the document. Then, type the digits 1 through 9. Note how they are inserted into the line. Press the Insert key to change from Insert to Typeover mode, and enter the digits 1 through 9 again. Note how these digits replace the other characters in the line.
   Hold down the Left arrow key and note the movement of the cursor. When it reaches the left margin, it continues backwards through the lines above it until it reaches the first position of the document and stops. Next, hold down the Right arrow key and note the movement of the cursor. It moves forward through the lines of the document until it reaches the last position in the document and stops.

5. Before you continue with the next set of exercises, you need to: (1) turn off Typeover mode, and (2) return to a blank Edit screen. To turn off

Typeover mode, you press the Insert key; to return to a blank Edit screen, you press the F7 key for the Exit command. Then, when *WordPerfect* asks if you want to save the document, press *n* for No. And when *WordPerfect* asks if you want to exit from WP, press *n* for No. This erases what you've been working on and returns you to a blank screen.

Part 2: How to create, print, and save a letter

6. Type the first portion of the letter shown in figure 3-1 using the keystrokes in figure 3-6. If you prefer, use the current date instead of the date shown and use the name and address of a friend or relative. As you type the first and second paragraphs in the letter, note how the word wrap function works. When you finish, your screen should look similar to the one in figure 3-7. It won't look exactly the same unless your margins, tab settings, and base font happen to be the same as those used for this document.

7. Type the second portion of the letter shown in figure 3-1 using the keystrokes in figure 3-12. To start, look at the template on your keyboard and find the >Indent< command. To access this command, hold down the Shift key while you press the F4 key (Shift+F4) Then, type the first sentence in figure 3-12 followed by two spaces.

   The next sentence in figure 3-12 is supposed to be underlined. To do that, look at the template on your keyboard and find the Underline command. To access this command, just press the F8 key. Then, type "No questions asked," press the F8 key again to end underlining, press the Period key, and press the Enter key to end the double indentation.

   Continue by typing the next paragraph of figure 3-12. When you reach the part of the phone number to be boldfaced, find the Bold command on the template and press the F6 key to access it. Then, type "-800-," press the F6 key again to end the boldfacing, and continue.

   When you type the signature block of the letter, be sure to use the same number of tab characters that you used for indenting the date at the top of the letter. Also, use your own name instead of the name shown.

   When you've finished entering the letter, your Edit screen should look like the one in figure 3-13. Again, your margins and tab settings may not be exactly the same as the ones shown here. Note how your system shows that text has been underlined or boldfaced.

8. Find the Reveal Codes command on your template. If you have a 101-key keyboard you should find this command in two places. Then, start this command to display a Reveal Codes screen like the one in figure 3-14. On the lower half of this screen, find the codes for the Indent, Underline, and Bold commands. Also, find the codes for tabs, soft returns, and hard returns. You can do this by using the Up arrow key to move the cursor up through the document.

Use the Arrow keys to move the cursor to one of the soft return codes [SRt]. Note that each half of the screen has its own cursor and that the cursors are in the same locations on both halves of the screen. Press the Delete key to delete the soft return code, and note that you can't delete it. Instead, the character or space to the left of the code is deleted. Replace this character or space by typing it again.

Use the Arrow keys to move the cursor to the >Indent< code. Press the Delete key to delete it, and note the results. Then, access the command again to insert the code back into the letter. Finally, access the Reveal Codes command again to return to the normal Edit screen.

9. Use the template to find the Print command, and access it by holding down the Shift key while you press the F7 key (Shift+F7). This displays a screen like the one in figure 3-16. Next, press the F1 key to cancel this command.

Start the Print command again. This time, when the Print screen is displayed, press *1* or *f* to print the entire document. Note that you are returned to the Edit screen while the letter is being printed so you can continue your work.

10. Use the template to find the Save command, and access it by pressing the F10 key. This displays a prompt that asks you for the name of the document to be saved, but it doesn't tell you what the default directory is. Enter a complete file specification at this prompt including drive, directory, and file name (CATLET) so you'll know what directory the file is saved in.

11. Use the Arrow keys to move the cursor to the first character in the first line of the address near the top of the letter. Next, press the Insert key to put the keyboard in Typeover mode. Then, type a new address in this line and delete any left over characters at the end of the line. You now have a revised version of the document you saved in the last exercise.

Access the Save command to save this revised version as shown in the second procedure of figure 3-17. This command displays a prompt that gives the complete file specification that you used when you saved the first version of the letter. To save it again with the same name, press the Enter key. *WordPerfect* then displays a prompt that asks you whether you want to replace the old file. Press *y* for Yes to complete the Save command.

Part 3: How to revise an old document and save it with a new name

12. Hold down the Up arrow key to move the cursor to the top of the letter. Next, access the Reveal Codes command to reveal the codes. Then, delete the date, the name and address, and the greeting at the top of the letter, as shown in figure 3-18, but don't delete the Tab [Tab] and Enter [HRt] codes. This revised letter will be used as the basis for a form letter. Last,

access the Reveal Codes command again to return to the normal Edit screen.

13. Use the Print command to print this version of the letter. This time when the Print screen is displayed, press *2* or *p* to print the one-page letter.

14. Use the Save command to save this version of the letter under a new name as shown in the third procedure in figure 3-18. After you start this command, *WordPerfect* will display a prompt that shows the complete file specification that you used the last time you saved the letter. This time, though, change the file name, but not the drive or path. To do that, use the Right arrow key to move to the end of the specification. Then, type a period followed by the letters *fm* to add an extension to the old filename. When you press the Enter key, the revised letter is saved under the new file specification. Now, there are two versions of this letter in your directory: one in the file named CATLET, and another in the file named CATLET.FM.

15. Use the template to find the Exit command. Then, press F7 to access this command. When the prompt asks whether you want to save the document you've been working on, press *n* for No (because you've just saved it). When the next prompt asks whether you want to exit from WP, press *n* for No to return to a blank Edit screen.

    Access the Exit command again. This time press *n* to indicate that you don't want to save the document. Then, press *y* to indicate that you do want to exit from WP. This returns you either to the DOS prompt or to the program that you started *WordPerfect* from.

Chapter 4

How to retrieve and edit the letter

In chapter 3, you learned how to create, print, and save a one-page letter like the one shown in figure 4-1. Now, you'll learn how to retrieve and edit that letter. Along the way, you'll learn how to use seven more commands.

In word processing terms, when you *edit* a document, you make changes to it. That includes changes to words, paragraphs, and sentences like correcting misspellings, improving sentence clarity, adding new ideas, and deleting unnecessary ideas. But it also includes formatting changes like making the left and right margins of a document wider and centering a letter between the top and bottom margins.

As you read this chapter, you can try the *WordPerfect* skills it teaches on your own PC right after you read about them. Or you can read the entire chapter first and then go through the exercises at the end of the chapter. When you do the exercises, you will modify the form letter shown in figure 4-1 so that it looks like the one in figure 4-17.

How to use the List command

The F5 key accesses a command called the List File command in *WordPerfect* 5.0 and the List command in *WordPerfect* 5.1. Since these commands are essentially the same, I'll refer to them both as the List command in this book.

You can use the List command for several different functions that are related to file handling. For instance, you can use it to change the default directory, to retrieve files, to copy files, to delete files, and so on. In this chapter, I'll show you how to use this command for the first two of these functions, and I'll introduce you to some of its other functions too.

How to use the List command to set the default directory   One of the most important uses of the List command is changing the default directory. The *default directory* is the one that *WordPerfect* uses for saving and retrieving files when you don't specify the drive or directory in your file specifications. If, for example, you use the Save command to save a new file

67

with the name CATLET, the file is stored in the default directory. Often, though, the default directory isn't the one that you want your files stored in.

The first procedure in figure 4-2 shows you how to change the default directory. In step 1, you access the List command (F5). Then, *WordPerfect* displays a prompt like this:

    Dir C:\WP51*.*   **(Type = to change default Dir)**

The first part of this prompt tells you the name of the current default directory. In this example, the default directory is C:\WP51. The second part of this prompt tells you to type the equals sign (=) if you want to change the default directory.

In step 2, you tell *WordPerfect* that you want to change the default directory by typing in the equals sign. Then, *WordPerfect* displays a prompt like this:

    New Directory = C:\WP51

In step 3, you replace or modify the directory shown so it's the one that you want for your document files. To do that, you can just type the drive and directory specification that you want. Or if you prefer, you can use the Arrow keys, the Backspace and Delete keys, and the Insert and Typeover modes to modify the specification that's shown. When the drive and directory are correct, you press the Enter key.

At this point, the default directory has been changed, and *WordPerfect* displays a prompt that shows the new default directory. If, for example, you change the directory to the \WPDOCS directory on the D drive, the prompt looks like this:

    Dir D:\WPDOCS*.*

In step 4, you can press the Enter key if you want to see a listing of the files in this directory, or you can press the Esc key or Cancel key (F1) if you want to return to the Edit screen. If you press the Enter key, *WordPerfect* displays a screen like one of the ones in figure 4-3.

How to use the List command to retrieve a file   The second procedure in figure 4-2 shows you how to use the List command to retrieve a file. In step 1, you access the List command. Then, *WordPerfect* displays the prompt that shows the default directory. If this is the one that contains your document files, you press the Enter key to display the List screen.

If the default directory isn't the one that you want to list, you have two options. First, you can change the default directory by typing an equals sign and continuing as in the first procedure in figure 4-2. Then, when you press the Enter key, the new default directory is displayed. Second, you can modify the directory that is displayed in the prompt and press the Enter key. This displays the List screen for the directory that you specify, but it doesn't change the default directory. When you exit from the List screen, the old default directory is still in effect.

```
Dear :

     Thanks for asking about our PC books.  I've enclosed a catalog
that describes them all in detail.  As you read through it, I hope
you'll find something you can use right away.

     So there's no risk to you, all our books are backed by our
unconditional guarantee:

     If our PC books aren't the best ones you've ever used for
     both training and reference, you can return them for a
     full refund.  No questions asked.

     If you have any questions or if you're ready to place an
order, please call us at our toll-free number: 1-800-221-5528.  And
thanks for your interest in our books.

                    Sincerely,


                    Karen DeMartin
```

Figure 4-1   The CATLET.FM form letter from chapter 3

Once a List screen like the one in figure 4-3 is displayed, it's easy to retrieve a file. Just use the Arrow keys to move the highlight to the file you want to retrieve. Then, press either *1* or *r* as indicated by the options at the bottom of the screen. If, for example, you want to retrieve the file named CATLET.FM, you move the highlight to the second file listed in figure 4-3 and press *r*. *WordPerfect* then retrieves the file and returns you to the Edit screen.

Before you retrieve a file, you usually want to be sure that the Edit screen is empty. That means that you haven't entered any codes or characters into it and that you haven't retrieved another document into it. If you try to retrieve a document into an Edit screen that isn't empty (even one that contains just one space), *WordPerfect* displays a prompt like this one:

Retrieve into current document? No (Yes)

Although there are times when you want to retrieve one document into another document, you probably won't want to do that this early in your training. So you can press *n* for No. Then, after you use the Exit command to clear the screen, you can retrieve the file without getting this prompt.

How to use the List command for other functions   If you look at the options at the bottom of the screens in figure 4-3, you can see that you can use this screen to perform several functions. The second and third options, for example, let you Delete and Move (or rename) files. And the eighth option lets you Copy files. These options make it easy for you to manage files without using DOS.

The fourth option lets you Print a file on disk without retrieving it first. And the seventh option gives you another way to change the default directory. Normally, though, you just type the equals sign to change the directory when you first access the List command. So you won't use this option often.

The sixth option is the Look option. This option lets you display the document that's highlighted before you retrieve it. This option comes in handy when you're not sure that the document you highlighted is the one that you want to retrieve. To access the Look option, you press the Enter key because this option is the default option for the List command. You can tell that 6 is the default by looking at the number that appears at the end of the option selections. After you press the Enter key to look at a file and confirm that it's the right one, you press Enter or Exit to return to the List screen and *1* or *r* to retrieve the file.

If you compare the options in figure 4-3 for *WordPerfect* 5.0 and 5.1, you can see that there are some minor differences. In particular, the fifth options have different functions, and the ninth options have different words (but similar functions). In chapter 9, I'll present all of the options of the List command for both releases of *WordPerfect*.

How to use the List command to change the default directory

1. Access the List command (F5) to display the prompt for the default directory:

   `Dir C:\WP51\*.*`   (Type = to change default Dir)

2. When you type the equals sign (=), *WordPerfect* displays this prompt:

   `New Directory = C:\WP51`

3. Type the drive and directory that you want as the default directory as in this example:

   `New Directory = d:\wpdocs`

   Then, press the Enter key to change the directory and complete the command.

   `Dir D:\WPDOCS\*.*`

4. If you want to see the List screen for the default directory, press the Enter key. If you want to return to the Edit screen, press the Esc or Cancel key. Either way, the new default directory is in effect for the current work session.

How to use the List command to retrieve a file

1. Access the List command (F5) to display the prompt for the default directory:

   `Dir D:\WPDOCS\*.*`   (Type = to change default Dir)

2. If the file you want is in this directory, press the Enter key to display the List screen.

   If the file you want isn't in the default directory, you can continue in one of two ways. First, you can change the default directory as described above. Second, you can specify the directory you want by typing it in at the prompt. If you don't type the equals sign before you type in the directory specification, the default directory won't be affected. Then, when you have the directory you want, press the Enter key to display the List screen.

3. Use the Arrow keys to move the cursor on the List screen to the file you want to retrieve.

4. Use the Retrieve option to retrieve the file by pressing *1* or *r*.

Figure 4-2   How to use the List command to set the default directory and retrieve a file

In the meantime, though, you should be able to use most of the options for the List command just by experimenting with them. All you have to do is highlight the file you want to perform a function on, press the number or letter of the function that you want to perform, and do whatever the prompts ask for after that. To return to the Edit screen from the List screen without performing a function, you can press the Esc or Cancel key (F1); you can press the Exit key (F7); or you can press the Zero key to indicate that you don't want to perform any of the numbered options.

How to use the Retrieve command to retrieve a file

Another way to retrieve a file is to use the Retrieve command. If you look at the command template, you'll find it right above the Save command. To access it, you use the Shift+F10 keystroke combination.

Like the Save command, this command works best when the default directory is set to the one that you want to use for your files. Then, the file specification that you give doesn't have to include the drive and directory. Instead, you just supply the file name.

Figure 4-4 shows you how to use this command to Retrieve a file when the default directory is set the way you want it. In step 1, you access the command. In step 2, you enter the name of the file that you want to retrieve and press the Enter key. Of course, this assumes that you know the name of the file. If you do, you can usually retrieve a file more quickly with this command than you can with the List command. If you don't know the file name, you can use the List command to both find and retrieve the file.

Unlike the Retrieve function for the List command, the Retrieve command doesn't display a warning message when you're about to retrieve a file into a document that isn't empty. It just retrieves the file into the current document at the cursor location.

How to move the cursor more efficiently

In the last chapter, you learned how to use the Arrow keys to move the cursor through existing text. Often, though, you can move the cursor more efficiently by using the keystroke combinations shown in figure 4-5. As a result, it's worth taking the time to memorize these combinations.

If you hold down the Ctrl key as you use the Right and Left arrow keys, the cursor jumps one word at a time. If you're using *WordPerfect* 5.1, you can also use the Up and Down arrow keys while you hold down the Ctrl key. These keys jump the cursor up and down one complete paragraph.

If you press the Home key one or more times followed by an Arrow key, you get the movement shown in the second group in figure 4-5. If, for example, you press the Home key once followed by the Left or Right arrow key, the cursor moves to the left or right of a line. If you press the Home key once followed by the Up or Down arrow keys, the cursor moves to the top or bottom of the Edit screen.

If you press the Home key twice followed by the Up arrow key, the cursor moves to the top of the document before any text, but after any control codes. If you press the Home key three times, though, followed by the Up arrow key, the cursor moves to the top of the document before both codes and text. Similarly, pressing the Home key twice followed by the Down arrow moves the cursor to the end of the document after both text and codes. And pressing the Home key three times followed by the Left arrow moves the cursor to the left of a line before any codes. As you use more codes, you'll realize that there are times when you want to move the cursor before the

The List screen for
WordPerfect **5.1**

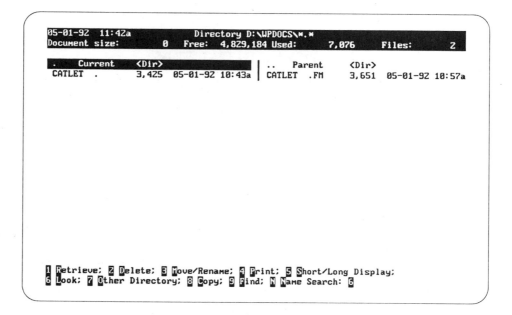

The List Files screen
for *WordPerfect* **5.0**

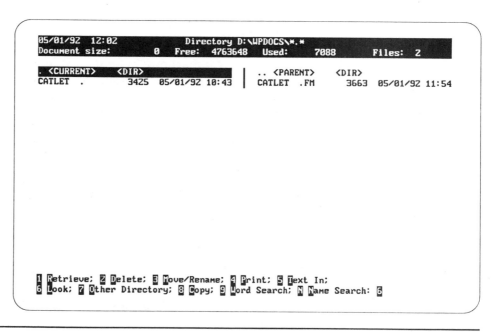

Figure 4-3   The List screens for releases 5.0 and 5.1

1. Access the Retrieve command (Shift+F10) to display this prompt:

   Document to be retrieved:

2. If the default directory is set to the one that contains the file you want, type the name of the file as in this example:

   Document to be retrieved: catlet

   Then, press the Enter key to complete the command.

Figure 4-4   How to use the Retrieve command to retrieve a file

codes at the top or left of a document, and there are times when you want to move it after the codes but before the text.

The last key in figure 4-5 is the End key. When you press this key, it moves the cursor to the right of a line after all codes. This is the same as pressing the Home key once followed by the Right arrow key, but you'll usually use the End key for this purpose because it takes only one keystroke.

How to delete more efficiently

In the last chapter, you learned how to delete by using the Backspace key and the Delete key. However, you can usually delete text more quickly by using the keystroke combinations shown in figure 4-6. As a result, you should take the time to memorize these combinations so you can work more efficiently.

To delete an entire word at a time, you can press either the Backspace or Delete key while you hold down the Ctrl key. This deletes the word at the cursor. For this purpose, a *word* is any group of characters that is preceded and followed by one or more spaces. When you use this keystroke combination, the cursor doesn't have to be at the first character of the word; it can be anywhere in the word. If you use the Ctrl key with the Arrow keys to find the words that you want to delete, you just continue to hold down the Ctrl key while you press the Delete or Backspace key to delete one or more of the words.

If you press the End key while you hold down the Ctrl key, *WordPerfect* deletes all the characters from the location of the cursor to the end of the line. Similarly, if you press the Page-down key while you hold down the Ctrl key, *WordPerfect* deletes all the characters and codes from the location of the cursor to the end of the page. In this case, though, *WordPerfect* displays a prompt like this:

Delete Remainder of Page? No (Yes)

This warns you that the remainder of the page is about to be deleted. Then, if you don't want to delete the remainder of the page, press *n* for No. If you do, press *y* for Yes.

Keystrokes	Function
The Control key and the Arrow keys	
Ctrl+Right	Moves the cursor right one word at a time
Ctrl+Left	Moves the cursor left one word at a time
Ctrl+Up (5.1)	Moves the cursor up one paragraph at a time
Ctrl+Down (5.1)	Moves the cursor down one paragraph at a time
The Home key and the Arrow keys	
Home Left	Moves the cursor to the left of the line after all codes
Home Right	Moves the cursor to the right of the line after all codes
Home Up	Moves the cursor to the top of the Edit screen
Home Down	Moves the cursor to the bottom of the Edit screen
Home Home Up	Moves the cursor to the top of the document after all codes
Home Home Home Up	Moves the cursor to the top of the document before all codes
Home Home Down	Moves the cursor to the bottom of the document after all codes
Home Home Home Left	Moves the cursor to the left of the line before all codes
The End Key	
End	Moves the cursor to the right of the line after all codes

Figure 4-5   How to move the cursor efficiently

How to use the Cancel command to restore codes and text that have been deleted

As you develop your *WordPerfect* skills, you start to work more quickly and less cautiously. As a result, you occasionally delete a portion of a document by accident. Fortunately, though, *WordPerfect* provides a feature that lets you *restore* the text and codes that you have deleted in any one of your last three deletions. This puts the text and codes back into the document at the location of the cursor.

Figure 4-7 gives the procedure for restoring text. In step 1, you move the cursor to the point at which you want to restore a deletion. Then, you access the Cancel command (F1). *WordPerfect* then displays the last deletion that you made at the cursor location, and it displays the prompt shown in figure 4-7.

If the deletion shown is the one that you want to restore, just press *1* or *r* to restore it as shown in step 2. If it isn't, you press *2* or *p* to see the previous

Keystrokes	Function
Ctrl+Backspace	Deletes the word the cursor is on
Ctrl+Delete	Deletes the word the cursor is on
Ctrl+End	Deletes all text and codes from the cursor to the end of the line
Ctrl+Page-down	Deletes all text and codes from the cursor to the end of the page

Figure 4-6   How to use the control keys to delete text

deletion. When you do this, *WordPerfect* displays the previous deletion at the cursor location and continues to display the prompt shown in figure 4-7. Then, if it still isn't the right deletion, you can press 2 or *p* to see the third most recent deletion. If you continue to press 2 or *p*, *WordPerfect* will cycle through the three most recent deletions again. When you press 1 or *r*, the deletion that is shown is restored. To cancel the command without restoring text, you can press the Esc, Cancel (F1), or Zero key.

How to use the Date command to insert the current date into a document

Most PCs today automatically keep track of the current date and time. On the older PCs, you are asked to enter the correct date and time as part of the DOS start-up procedure. But either way, the current date is available to *WordPerfect*, and you can insert it in your documents without typing it.

Figure 4-8 shows how to insert the current date into a document. In step 1, you move the cursor to where you want the date inserted. Then, you access both the Date and Outline commands by finding the Date/Outline key (Shift+F5) on the template and pressing it. This displays a prompt with three date options:

1 Date Text; 2 Date Code; 3 Date Format

The other options in the prompt are for the Outline command, not the Date command.

In step 2, if you select the Date Text option, the current date is inserted in your document just as if you typed it. This way, you don't have to manually enter the date. If you select the Date Code option, though, a date code is inserted in your document. This code is automatically updated each time you retrieve the document. This is useful when you work on a document over several days, and you always want the document printed with the current date.

The third date option in the prompt is Date Format. You can use this option to set the format of the date before you use options 1 or 2. You can use the Date Format option to display the date in several formats including this one: mm/dd/yy. You can also include the time of day in the format.

1. Move the cursor to where you want to restore text that was deleted. Then, access the Cancel command (F1). This displays the last deletion at the cursor and this prompt:

   Undelete: 1 Restore; **2** Previous Deletion: **0**

2. To restore the deleted text that's shown at the cursor, press *1* or *r*.

3. To restore a previous deletion, press *2* or *p* to display it at the cursor. Remember, you can restore up to two previous deletions. When the text you want to restore is shown above the prompt, press *1* or *r* to restore it.

Figure 4-7   How to use the Cancel command to restore text

Usually, though, the format for the date is set the way you want it so you probably won't have to use this third option.

How to use the Move command to move, copy, or delete a sentence or a paragraph

You can use the Move command to move a sentence or a paragraph from one part of a document to another. However, you can also use this command to Copy or Delete a sentence or a paragraph. In fact, the most efficient way to move, copy, or delete a sentence or paragraph is to use the Move command.

Figure 4-9 shows you how to use the Move command for any of these three functions. In step one, you move the cursor to the sentence or paragraph that you want to move, copy, or delete. To operate on a sentence, the cursor can be anywhere from the first character in the sentence to the period. To operate on a paragraph, the cursor can be anywhere from the first character of the paragraph to the hard return code at the end of the paragraph.

In step 2, you access the Move command (Ctrl+F4). This displays the prompt shown in figure 4-9. Then, in step 3, you select either Sentence or Paragraph. When you do this, the entire sentence or paragraph at the cursor is highlighted, and the second prompt in figure 4-9 is displayed.

In step 4, you select either Move, Copy, or Delete. If you select Move, the highlighted sentence or paragraph disappears from the Edit screen and is copied into *WordPerfect*'s memory. If you select Copy, the highlighting disappears, but the text remains. If you select Delete, the highlighted sentence or paragraph disappears and you are returned to the Edit screen.

In step 5, you continue with the function if you selected Move or Copy in step 4. Then, you move the cursor to the point where you want the sentence or paragraph moved or copied to. To complete the function, you press the Enter key.

1. Position the cursor where you want to insert the date. Then, access the Date/Outline command (Shift+F5) to display this prompt:

   `1 Date Text; 2 Date Code; 3 Date Format; 4 Outline; 5 Para Num; 6 Define: 0`

2. As you can see, the first three options are for the Date command and the last three are for the Outline command. To insert the date, select Date Text by pressing *1* or *t*, or select Date Code by pressing *2* or *c*. If you want to change the date format, select Date Format (*3* or *f*) before you select Date Text or Date Code.

Figure 4-8   How to use the Date command to insert the current date into a document

It may take a bit of practice using the Move or Copy functions before you are able to move the cursor to exactly the right spot before pressing the Enter key. When you move a sentence, for example, you should note that the sentence includes the spaces after it. As a result, you need to move the cursor to the first character of the sentence you want to insert the new sentence in front of before you press the Enter key. If you don't get the Move or Copy function quite right, though, you can make whatever corrections are needed.

How to use the Block command

The Block command is used to identify a block of text that you want to perform a function on. After you identify the *block*, you can perform various *WordPerfect* functions on it. For instance, you can delete, move, or copy it. In addition, you can insert paired codes around the block.

How to use the Block command to block text   The first procedure in figure 4-10 shows you how to block text. In step 1, you move the cursor to the start of the text that you want to block. In step 2, you access the Block command by pressing F12 if you have the 101-key keyboard or Alt+F4 if you don't. This displays a flashing prompt that says "Block On." In step 3, you move the cursor to the end of the text that you want to block. At this point, you haven't performed a function yet, but the block has been identified and the prompt is still flashing.

To move the cursor as efficiently as possible when you're blocking text, you just press the character that you want the cursor to jump to. If, for example, you press the Period key, the cursor jumps to the next period in the text. As a result, this is an efficient way to block to the end of the next sentence. Similarly, if you press the Enter key, the cursor jumps to the next hard return code [HRt] in the text. As a result, this is an efficient way to block to the end of the next paragraph. With a little practice, you can highlight

1. Move the cursor to the sentence or paragraph that you want to move, copy, or delete. For a sentence, the cursor can be anywhere from the first letter of a the sentence to the period. For a paragraph, the cursor can be anywhere from the first letter of the paragraph to the hard return code [HRt] at the end of the paragraph.

2. Access the Move command (Ctrl+F4) to display this prompt:

   Move: 1 Sentence; **2** P**a**ragraph; **3** P**a**ge; **4** Retrieve: **0**

3. Select Sentence or Paragraph by pressing the related highlighted number or letter. Then, the sentence or paragraph that the cursor is in is highlighted, and *WordPerfect* displays this prompt:

   1 Move; **2 C**opy; **3** Delete; **4 A**ppend: **0**

4. Select Move, Copy, or Delete by pressing the related number or letter. If you select Move, the highlighted sentence or paragraph is removed from the screen, and this prompt is displayed:

   Move cursor; press **Enter** to retrieve.

   If you select Copy, the highlighting is removed from the sentence or paragraph, and the prompt shown above is displayed. If you select Delete, the highlighted sentence or paragraph is removed from the screen, and the command is finished.

5. If you selected Move or Copy, position the cursor where you want to insert the text and press the Enter key.

Figure 4-9   How to use the Move command to move, copy, or delete a sentence or paragraph

blocks more quickly this way than you can using the normal keystroke combinations for cursor movement.

How to perform functions on a block   The second, third, and fourth procedures in figure 4-10 show you how to perform functions on a block. To delete a block, for example, you just press the Delete key as summarized in the second procedure. Then, when the prompt asks for confirmation, you press *y* for Yes. This deletes the block and returns you to the Edit screen.

To move or copy a block, you use the Move command as summarized in the third procedure in figure 4-10. After you access the Move command, you press *1* or *b* to indicate that you want to operate on the block. Then, you select either the Move or Copy function. To complete the command, you position the cursor where you want the block inserted and press the Enter key.

To insert paired codes around a block, just access the related command. If, for example, you want to boldface a block, press F6 for the Bold command. If you want to underline a block, press F8 for the Underline command.

These examples are designed to show you how you can perform functions on blocks of text. But they aren't the only functions you can perform. For instance, you can use the Print command to print a block and the Save command to save a block. To use one of these commands after you've blocked the text, just access the command and do whatever the prompts require. If you try to perform a command that isn't appropriate for a block, your attempt to access the command will be ignored.

Because the Move command is designed for moving, copying, or deleting sentences, paragraphs, and pages, you don't need the Block command for these operations. Instead, you should use the Block command when you want to move, copy, or delete odd portions of text like part of one paragraph plus the two full paragraphs that follow it.

How to use the Format command

When you create a new document with *WordPerfect*, it automatically formats the document according to its *default settings*, or just *defaults*. As much as possible, these defaults should be the way you want them to be for most of your documents. So in chapter 6, you'll learn how to change these settings to make them appropriate for your purposes. In the meantime, though, you can use the Format command to override these settings for any document that you work on.

If you look at the command template, you can see that you access the Format command by using the Shift+F8 keystroke combination. This displays the Format screen shown in figure 4-11. Although this screen has many words on it, there are only four options: Line, Page, Document, and Other. To access one of them, you type the number or letter of the option. In this chapter, though, I'm going to show you how to use only the Line and Page formats.

When you access the Line or Page option, you get the Line or Page screen shown in figure 4-12. The settings shown on these screens are the default settings for your system. As you can see in this figure, the Line screen has nine options; the Page screen has eight. If you're using *WordPerfect* 5.0, your Page screen has nine options, but this doesn't affect the skills presented in this chapter, so you can ignore the difference for now.

When you change one of the Line or Page options, *WordPerfect* inserts a code that controls the formatting of the document. As a result, you should be sure to put the cursor where you want the code to be inserted before you access the Format command. Since some of these codes only affect text below them and others only work right if they're at the start of a document, you insert most formatting codes at the start of a document.

If the codes you insert don't work the way you want them to, you can use the Reveal Codes command that you learned about in the last chapter. Then, you can insert, delete, and correct the placement of the codes so they work correctly.

How to set Line options   Figure 4-13 summarizes the procedures for changing three of the Line options. These are the options that you're most

How to use the Block command to block text

1. Position the cursor where you want to begin the block.
2. Access the Block command (F12 or Alt+F4); then, this flashing prompt is displayed:
   Block On
3. Move the cursor to the last character of the block. The characters within the block are highlighted as you move the cursor.

How to use the Delete key to delete a block

1. Block the text you want to delete.
2. Press the Delete key; then, this prompt is displayed:
   Delete block? No (Yes)
3. Press *y* for yes and the blocked text is deleted.

How to use the Move command to move or copy a block

1. Block the text you want to move or copy.
2. Access the Move command (Ctrl+F4) to display this prompt:
   Move: 1 Block; **2** Tabular Column; **3** Rectangle: **0**
3. Select Block by pressing *1* or *b*; then, this prompt is displayed:
   1 Move; **2** Copy; **3** Delete; **4** Append: **0**
4. Select Move or Copy by pressing the related number or letter; then, this prompt is displayed:
   Move cursor; press **Enter** to retrieve.
5. Position the cursor where you want to insert the text and press the Enter key.

How to insert paired codes on each side of a block

1. Block the text you want to code.
2. Access the paired code you want to insert. For example, press F8 for underline or F6 for boldface. This inserts the paired codes on each side of the block. As a result, the blocked text is boldfaced or underlined when the document is printed.

Figure 4-10   How to use the Block command

likely to change. Then, in chapter 8, I'll show you how to use and change the other Line options.

The first procedure in figure 4-13 shows you how to change the *justification* for a document. This term refers to the alignment of the text when it's printed, although this alignment doesn't appear on the Edit screen. In figure 4-1, for example, the letter is printed with *justified text*. This means that the text is flush with both the left and right margins. You can see this most clearly in the first and last paragraphs of the letter. In contrast, the same letter is printed without justification in figure 4-17. This type of printing can be referred to as *ragged-right text*.

For simple business documents like letters, ragged-right text is preferable to justified text for a couple of reasons. First, studies have shown that ragged-right text is easier to read than justified text. Second, studies have shown that letters are more effective when they don't have the formal appearance that is associated with justified text. So if your default setting is for justified text, that's the first Line option that you should change.

To change this option, just follow the first procedure in figure 4-13. When you reach the Line format screen, select the Justification option by pressing *3* or *j*. Unfortunately, though, the *WordPerfect* 5.1 terminology for justification differs from the traditional typesetting terminology. So to set the justification for ragged right when using release 5.1, select the Left option from the four given in the prompt. This means that the text should be aligned on the left margin only. For *WordPerfect* 5.0, type *n* for No. This means that the justification should be turned off.

If you use the Reveal Codes screen when you return to the Edit screen, you can see the justification codes that *WordPerfect* has inserted. Depending on which release of *WordPerfect* you're using, your code will look like one of these:

[Just Off] or [Just:Left].

The second procedure in figure 4-13 shows you how to set the left and the right margins for a document. You'll probably change the Margins option more often than any of the other Line options because the margins help determine how much can be printed on a page. To get more on a page, you just decrease the size of the margins.

When you reach the Line screen, you select the Margins option by pressing *7* or *m*. The cursor then moves to the entry for the Left margin. If you want to leave it the way it is, press the Enter key to move to the entry for the Right margin. Otherwise, type the value that you want for the Left margin and press Enter. Next, type the value for the Right margin, or leave it as is if it's the way you want it. Then, when you press the Enter key, the margin code is inserted into the document, and the cursor moves to the selection prompt at the bottom of the Line screen.

If the measurements on your system are set for inches, you enter decimal numbers for the left and right margins. For instance, 1.25 means 1-1/4 inches, and 1.75 means 1-3/4 inches. If the measurements are set for units, you enter numbers that represent the number of characters that should be skipped on the left and right margins. For instance, 15 means that 15 characters should be skipped. Then, if your system is set for printing at 10 characters per inch, 15 units leads to a 1-1/2 inch margin; if your system is set for printing at 12 characters per inch, 15 units leads to a 1-1/4 inch margin.

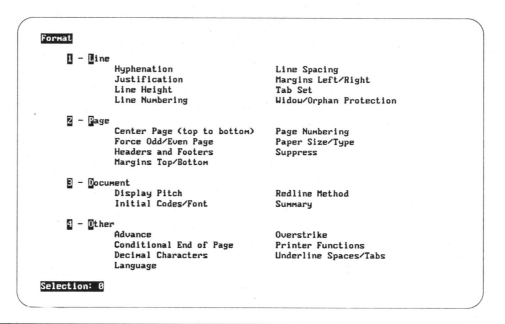

```
Format

  1 - Line
          Hyphenation                     Line Spacing
          Justification                   Margins Left/Right
          Line Height                     Tab Set
          Line Numbering                  Widow/Orphan Protection

  2 - Page
          Center Page (top to bottom)     Page Numbering
          Force Odd/Even Page             Paper Size/Type
          Headers and Footers             Suppress
          Margins Top/Bottom

  3 - Document
          Display Pitch                   Redline Method
          Initial Codes/Font              Summary

  4 - Other
          Advance                         Overstrike
          Conditional End of Page         Printer Functions
          Decimal Characters              Underline Spaces/Tabs
          Language

Selection: 0
```

Figure 4-11   The main Format screen

In general, you should set the margins to print fewer than 66 characters in each line. This makes your document easier to read. If your system is set for printing at 10 characters per inch, margins of about 1 inches (10 units) are appropriate. If your system is set for printing at 12 characters per inch, margins of about 1.5 inches (18 units) are appropriate. If you're using a printer that doesn't print a set number of characters per inch, you may have to count the characters in a line or two to see how many characters a typical line contains. Then, you can adjust your margins accordingly.

Although inches and units are the most commonly used measurements, *WordPerfect* also provides for measurements in centimeters, picas, or points. The last two of these measurements are used only in desktop publishing applications, though, so I doubt that the default setting on your system is for one of them. In chapter 6, I'll show you how to set up *WordPerfect* so it uses the measurements that you prefer. For now, just use whatever your system is set up for.

If you reveal codes when you return to the Edit screen, you can see that *WordPerfect* inserts a code like one of these into the document:

[L/R Mar:1.5i,1.5i] or [L/R Mar:18,18]

Here, the first code is in inches, and the second one is in units.

The third procedure in figure 4-13 shows you how to change the line spacing for a document from single to double spacing. This is useful if you're preparing a report (like a college paper) that has to be double spaced or if

The Line screen

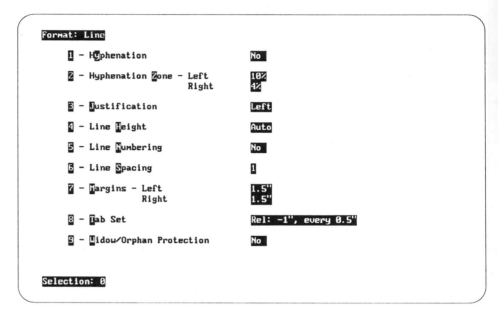

```
Format: Line
        1 - Hyphenation                    No
        2 - Hyphenation Zone - Left        10%
                              Right        4%
        3 - Justification                  Left
        4 - Line Height                    Auto
        5 - Line Numbering                 No
        6 - Line Spacing                   1
        7 - Margins - Left                 1.5"
                     Right                 1.5"
        8 - Tab Set                        Rel: -1", every 0.5"
        9 - Widow/Orphan Protection        No


Selection: 0
```

The Page screen

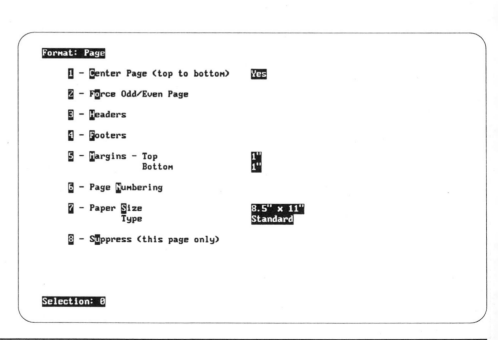

```
Format: Page
        1 - Center Page (top to bottom)    Yes
        2 - Force Odd/Even Page
        3 - Headers
        4 - Footers
        5 - Margins - Top                  1"
                     Bottom                1"
        6 - Page Numbering
        7 - Paper Size                     8.5" x 11"
                 Type                      Standard
        8 - Suppress (this page only)


Selection: 0
```

Figure 4-12   The Line and Page screens of the Format command

How to set the justification to ragged-right

1. Move the cursor to the top of the document by pressing Home Home Up.
2. Access the Format command (Shift+F8). This displays the screen shown in figure 4-11.
3. Select the Line option. This displays the Line screen shown in figure 4-12.
4. Select the Justification option. If you're using release 5.1, select the Left option from the prompt that's displayed:

    Justification: 1 Left; 2 Center; 3 Right; 4 Full: 0

    If you're using release 5.0, just type *n* for No.
5. Press the Exit key (F7) to return to the Edit screen.

How to set the left and right margins

1. Move the cursor to the top of the document by pressing Home Home Up.
2. Access the Format command (Shift+F8). This displays the screen shown in figure 4-11.
3. Select the Line option. This displays the Line screen shown in figure 4-12.
4. Select the Margins option.
5. If your system is set for inches, type the decimal number for the number of inches you want for the Left margin and press the Enter key. Then, repeat this procedure for the Right margin. If you type 1.25, for example, the margin will be 1-1/4 inches.

    If your system is set for units, type the number of units you want for the Left margin and press the Enter key. Then, repeat the procedure for the Right margin. If you type the number 15, for example, the margin is set to 15 characters. Then, if your system is set to print at 10 characters per inch, this sets the margin at 1-1/2 inches. If your system is set to print at 12 characters per inch, this sets the margin at 1-1/4 inches.
6. Press the Exit key (F7) to return to the Edit screen.

How to set the line spacing for double spacing

1. Move the cursor to the top of the document by pressing Home Home Up.
2. Access the Format command (Shift+F8).
3. Select the Line option from the Format screen.
4. Select the Line Spacing option from the Line screen.
5. Type *2* for double spacing and press the Enter key.
6. Press the Exit key (F7) to return to the Edit screen.

Figure 4-13   How to set three Line options of the Format command

you want to have extra room for editorial marks on a preliminary draft of a document. In steps 1 through 4, you move the cursor to the top of the document; you access the Format command; you select the Line option; and you select the Line Spacing option. In step 5, you type *2* for double spacing and press the Enter key. In step 6, you exit from the command.

When you specify double spacing, the lines on the screen are double spaced. As a result, the Edit screen can only display half as much text when this option is on as it can otherwise. For this reason, you probably won't want to set the code for double spacing until you're ready to print the document. While you work on the document, you'll want to keep the code set for single spacing.

How to set Page options   Figure 4-14 summarizes the procedures for changing two of the Page options. These are the two options that you're most likely to change. Then, in chapter 8, I'll show you how to use and change the other Page options.

The first procedure in figure 4-14 shows you how to center a page from top to bottom. When you reach the Page screen, you select the Center Page option by pressing *1* or *c*. Then, if you're using *WordPerfect* 5.0, the option is turned on right away. But if you're using *WordPerfect* 5.1, you have to press *y* for Yes before the option is turned on. In either case, the cursor returns to the selection prompt at the bottom of the Page screen.

If you reveal codes, you will see that the code for page centering looks like this: [Center Pg]. Later, when the document is printed, it will be centered on the page with equal amounts of space above and below the printed text. This option is especially useful for letters because it helps make them look more appealing.

The second procedure in figure 4-14 shows how to set the Top and Bottom margins for each page of a document. If you reveal codes after you set the margins, you will see a code like one of these for the Top and Bottom margins: [T/B:1i,1i] or [T/B:6,6].

In terms of inches, a one-inch margin is appropriate for most business documents. In terms of units, which represent lines when they're applied to Top and Bottom margins, 6 is the equivalent of a one-inch margin because most printers print six lines to the inch.

How to move from one screen to another within a command

With the Format command, you've seen how one screen can lead to another after you access a command. To move between these command screens efficiently, you should use the keystrokes that are summarized in figure 4-15.

To move from one screen to the next, you select an option by pressing the highlighted letter or number for the option. Then, to go back one screen, you can press the Esc key or the Cancel key (F1). On most screens, you can also press the Zero key (0) to indicate that you're not making any selection.

How to center the printed page from top to bottom

1. Move the cursor to the top of the document by pressing Home Home Up.
2. Access the Format command (Shift+F8). This displays the screen shown in figure 4-11.
3. Select the Page option. This displays the Format Page screen shown in figure 4-12.
4. Select the Center Page option. If you're using release 5.1, press *y* for Yes at this prompt to turn on the option:

   ### No (Yes)

   If you're using release 5.0, the option is turned on automatically when you select the Center Page option .
5. Press the Exit key (F7) to return to the Edit screen.

How to set the top and bottom margins for the printed page

1. Move the cursor to the top of the document by pressing Home Home Up.
2. Access the Format command (Shift+F8). This displays the Format screen shown in figure 4-11.
3. Select the Page option. This displays the Format Page screen shown in figure 4-12.
4. Select the Margins option.
5. If your system is set for inches, type the decimal number for the number of inches you want for the Top margin and press the Enter key. Then, repeat this procedure for the Bottom margin. If you type 1, for example, the margin will be 1 inch. If you type 1.5, the margin will be 1-1/2 inches.

   If your system is set for units, type the number of units you want for the Top margin and press the Enter key. Then, repeat this procedure for the Bottom margin. If you type the number 6, for example, the margin will be set at 6 lines. Since a standard printer prints 6 lines per inch, this sets the Top and Bottom margins at 1 inch.
6. Press the Exit key (F7) to return to the Edit screen.

Figure 4-14   How to set two Page options of the Format command

And if you want to return immediately to the Edit screen without going back through the screens one at a time, you can press the Exit key (F7).

If you press the Esc key when you're not trying to escape from a command or a screen, you may be surprised to see a message on the left side of the status line. Although the number may be different, the message looks like this:

Repeat Value = 8

Keystroke	Function
Highlighted letter or number	Selects an option
Esc	Returns to the previous screen
Cancel (F1)	Returns to the previous screen
Zero (0)	Returns to the previous screen
Exit (F7)	Returns to the Edit screen

Figure 4-15   Keystrokes you can use to move between command screens

This means you've accessed a function that is designed to repeat whatever you enter next. If, for example, you press the letter *w* while the message is displayed, eight *w*'s will be entered into your document. Since this repeat function has limited use, I'm not going to present it in detail until chapter 7. In the meantime, cancel the repeat function by pressing the Esc key again.

Discussion

You have now been introduced to seven new commands as well as several keystroke combinations that will help you move the cursor and delete text more efficiently. If you combine these commands and skills with those in chapter 3, you should be able to retrieve and modify the letter that you created in the last chapter. You should be able to add a sentence and a paragraph to it so it looks like the letter in figure 4-16. You should be able to use the Move command to edit the letter in figure 4-16 so it looks like the one in figure 4-17. And when you've got the letter the way you want it, you should be able to print it and save it under its old name.

If you feel confident about your *WordPerfect* skills already, you should be able to make the changes shown in figures 4-16 and 4-17 without any help. But if you don't feel confident, do the exercises at the end of this chapter. The first ten exercises guide you through some experimentation with commands and keystrokes that you probably won't do on your own. Then, the last three exercises guide you through the steps of the revision process.

Once you master all of the skills presented in chapters 3 and 4, you will have a respectable set of *WordPerfect* skills. However, since this section is designed as a tutorial, the skills presented in this section aren't covered as completely as they will be in the next section. For instance, editing skills like using the Move and Block commands will be covered in more detail in chapter 7. Using the Format command to format your documents will be covered more completely in chapter 8. And using the List command to manage your files will be covered more completely in chapter 9.

August 20, 1992

Dear :

    Thanks for asking about our PC books. I've enclosed a catalog that describes them all in detail. As you read through it, I hope you'll find something you can use right away.

    So there's no risk to you, all our books are backed by our unconditional guarantee:

    You must be satisfied. If our PC books aren't the best ones you've ever used for both training and reference, you can return them for a full refund. <u>No questions asked</u>.

    Our best-selling PC title, <u>The Least You Need to Know about DOS</u>, is described on page 7. Our newest book, <u>The Least You Need to Know about Lotus</u>, is described on page 8. The descriptions in the catalog will help you decide if one of these books is right for you or your company.

    If you have any questions or if you're ready to place an order, please call us at our toll-free number: 1-800-221-5528. And thanks for your interest in our books.

    Sincerely,

    Karen DeMartin

Figure 4-16   The letter in figure 4-1 after it has been retrieved, edited, and printed

```
                                      August 20, 1992




        Dear :

              Thanks for asking about our PC books.  I've
        enclosed a catalog that describes them all in detail.
        As you read through it, I hope you'll find something
        you can use right away.

              Our newest book, The Least You Need to Know about
        Lotus, is described on page 8.  Our best-selling PC
        title, The Least You Need to Know about DOS, is
        described on page 7.  The descriptions in the catalog
        will help you decide if one of these books is right for
        you or your company.

              So there's no risk to you, all our books are
        backed by our unconditional guarantee:

              You must be satisfied.  If our PC books
              aren't the best ones you've ever used for
              both training and reference, you can return
              them for a full refund.  No questions asked.

              If you have any questions or if you're ready to
        place an order, please call us at our toll-free number:
        1-800-221-5528.  And thanks for your interest in our
        books.

                                    Sincerely,



                                    Karen DeMartin
```

Figure 4-17   The letter in figure 4-16 after it has been edited and printed

At this point, though, you have already learned how to use 15 of the most useful *WordPerfect* commands. Since there are only 40 keystroke combinations on the template, this means that you're well on the way to *WordPerfect* proficiency. In the next chapter, you'll learn how to use seven more commands and a few more keystroke combinations. After that, you'll be on your way to *WordPerfect* mastery.

Terms

default directory
restore
block
default setting
default
justification
justified text
ragged-right text

Objectives

1. Use the new commands presented in this chapter to perform any of the following functions:

   a) Change the default directory.
   b) Retrieve a file.
   c) Restore text that has recently been deleted.
   d) Insert the current date into a document in either text or code form.
   e) Move, copy, or delete a sentence or paragraph.
   f) Move, copy, or delete a block of text.
   g) Insert paired codes on the sides of a block of text.
   h) Set the line or page margins for a printed document.
   i) Vertically center a document on a printed page.
   j) Set the justification code so the document is printed with ragged right text.

2. Use any of the skills or commands presented in this chapter or the previous chapter to modify a document in ways that are similar to those indicated by figures 4-16 and 4-17.

Exercises

Part 1: How to use the new commands and keystrokes

1. Start *WordPerfect* and access the List command by pressing F5. *WordPerfect* then displays a prompt at the bottom of the screen in this form:

   Dir C:\WP50*.*

   The directory shown is the *default directory*. If this is the directory that you want to store your document files in, press the Cancel key (F1) to cancel the command and return to the Edit screen. But if it isn't, press equals (=) to change the directory. *WordPerfect* then displays a prompt in this form:

New Directory = C:\WP50

To change the directory, just type the drive and path for the directory that you want; it will replace the directory shown. Or if you prefer, modify the directory shown by using the Arrow keys, Typeover or Insert mode, and so on. When the drive and directory are correct, press the Enter key to complete the change of directory. Then, press the Esc or Cancel key (F1) to return to the Edit screen.

2. Access the List command again. This time, when *WordPerfect* displays the default directory at the bottom of the screen, it should be the one you want for your files. Then, press the Enter key to tell *WordPerfect* that you want it to display the List screen for that directory. If you saved your files correctly at the end of the last chapter, your list screen should display the two files in figure 4-3.

3. Use the Arrow keys to move the highlight from one file to another. When the highlight is on the file named CATLET (not CATLET.FM), press the Enter key. This starts the Look function, which lets you review the contents of the file. Press Enter again to return to the List screen. Then, press *l* or *r* to retrieve the file. This returns you to the Edit screen with the CATLET document displayed on the screen.

4. Use the keystroke combinations shown in figure 4-5 to move the cursor through the letter. To start, use the Ctrl+Right arrow key combination to move the cursor forward one word at a time. Then, use the Ctrl+Left arrow key combination to move the cursor backwards one word at a time. If you're using *WordPerfect* 5.1, continue to hold the Ctrl key down as you experiment with the Up and Down arrow keys. Do they jump the cursor up and down one paragraph at a time?

   Now, use the Home key combinations shown in figure 4-5 to move the cursor to the left of a line, to the right of a line, to the top of the screen, to the bottom of the screen, and to the end of the document. Next, try two Homes and an Up to move the cursor to the top of the document. Last, move the cursor to the start of the second paragraph in the body of the letter. Then, press the End key to move the cursor to the end of the line.

5. Use the keystroke combinations in figure 4-6 to delete text. To start, hold the Ctrl key down and press the Right arrow key to move to the word *or* in the first sentence of the last paragraph of the letter. When you reach it, continue to hold down the Ctrl key. Then, press the Backspace key to delete the word; press the Backspace key three more times to delete the next three words; and press the Delete key four more times to delete the words through *an order*. Note that the comma is deleted along with the

word *order*, so release the Ctrl key and re-enter the comma in the appropriate place.

Move the cursor to the start of the second paragraph in the letter. Next, hold down the Ctrl key and press the End key. This deletes the entire line. Press the Delete key by itself to move the cursor to the next line, and use the Ctrl+End key combination again to delete that line.

Now, hold down the Ctrl key and press the Page-down key. When the prompt asks whether you want to delete the remainder of the page, press *y* for Yes. Is the rest of the document gone?

To restore it, press the Cancel key. This shows the last deletion starting at the cursor location. But press the letter *p* to show the previous deletion, and press it two more times to return to the first deletion. Then, press the letter *r* to restore the highlighted text.

6. With the restored document on the Edit screen, access the List command. Then, move the highlight to CATLET and press *r* for the Retrieve function. Since a document is already on the screen, *WordPerfect* displays this prompt:

   Retrieve into current document? No (Yes)

   Type *n* for No, and you are returned to the Edit screen.

   Next, use the Retrieve command to retrieve CATLET. If you're using release 5.0, you get the warning prompt that's shown above. For this exercise, press *y* for Yes to retrieve the document. If you're using release 5.1, however, you don't get the warning prompt and the document is instantly retrieved into the current document. When you return to the Edit screen, you'll see that you have a mess.

   No problem, though. Clear the screen by accessing the Exit command (F7), pressing *n* to indicate that you don't want to save the file, and pressing *n* again to indicate that you don't want to exit from the program. This returns you to a blank Edit screen. Then, use the Retrieve command again to retrieve CATLET. Since the changes (deletions) that you made in exercise 5 were never saved, the document is just as you left it at the end of the last chapter.

7. Move the cursor to the first character in the date of CATLET. Press Reveal Codes to look at the characters in the date, and press Reveal Codes again to return to the normal Edit screen. With the cursor still at the first character in the date, use Ctrl+End to delete the date. Then, start the Date command (Shift+F5), and press *2* or *c* to insert the date code into the document. Press Reveal codes to look at the date code, and press the Backspace key one time to delete the code and the entire date with it. Last, start the Date command again, and press *1* or *t* to insert the date text into the document. This time, characters are inserted just as if you had typed the date. Press Reveal Codes to return to the normal Edit screen.

8. Move the cursor to the middle of the first sentence in the first paragraph in the letter. Use the Move command to delete the sentence. To do that, start the command (Ctrl+F4); press the highlighted number or letter for Sentence; and press the highlighted number or letter for Delete. The sentence is gone.

    Next, use the Move command to copy the paragraph that the cursor is in. Start the command; press 2 for Paragraph; press 2 for Copy; press Home Home Down to move the cursor to the end of the document; and press Enter to complete the copy function.

    To clear the screen, use the Exit command. Then, use the Retrieve command to retrieve CATLET one more time in its original form.

9. Move the cursor to the start of the underlined phrase, "No questions asked." Then, press Reveal Codes, move the cursor to the Underline code at the start of the phrase, press the Delete key to delete the underlining, and press Reveal Codes again to return to the normal Edit screen.

    Next, move the cursor to the first letter of the phrase. Then, start the Block command (Alt+F4 or F12). To jump the cursor to the end of the sentence, press the Period key. To jump the cursor to the ends of the next paragraphs, press the Enter key a few times. This shows that *WordPerfect* will move the cursor to the first occurrence of whatever character you press. This helps you move the cursor more quickly. Now, press the Cancel key to cancel the blocking operation.

    Next, start the Block command again and highlight the entire phrase except the period. Then, press the Underline key (F8) to put the paired Underline codes around the phrase. This returns the letter to the way it was when you retrieved it.

10. Start the Format command (Shift+F8) to display the main Format screen. Then, press *p* to display the Page screen. The values shown are the default formatting options for your system. Are inches or units used for the top and bottom margins? What are the settings for these margins?

    Press the Esc, Cancel, or Zero key to return to the main Format screen. Then, press *l* to display the Line screen. Here again, the values shown are the default formatting options for your system. Are inches or units used for the left and right margins? What are the settings for the Justification option and the left and right margins?

    Press *m* to change the Margin settings. Enter new values that increase both the Left and Right margins by an inch or more. Then, press Exit to return to the Edit screen. Move the cursor up and down the screen to see how the margins change at the point where the margin code has been inserted into the document. Press Reveal Codes to see what the margin code looks like.

    Move the cursor to the top of the document; start the Format command; and press *l* for Line options. Then, select the Line Spacing option; type 2; press Enter; and press Exit to return to the Edit screen. Note how the lines on the screen are double spaced as you move the cursor through the document. Last, press the Reveal Codes and Exit keys. Then, press *n* twice to clear the Edit screen.

Part 2: How to retrieve and edit a letter

11. Use the List command to retrieve the file named CATLET.FM that you saved for the last chapter. If necessary, change the default directory to the one for your files before you display the List screen and retrieve the document. To modify the document so it looks like the letter in figure 4-16, do the following.

    At the top of the letter, use the Date command to insert the date code, not the date text. That way, the form letter will always have the current date.

    Move the cursor to the start of the last paragraph in the body of the original letter. Then, use Insert mode to insert the new paragraph that starts, "Our best-selling PC title..." into the letter. Next, move the cursor to the start of the indented guarantee, and type the new sentence shown in figure 4-16: "You must be satisfied." Last, use the Print command to print the revised letter.

12. Now, suppose that you decide to modify the revised the letter so it looks like the one in figure 4-17. To do that, use the Move command to move the new paragraph to the location shown in the figure. Then, use the Move command to switch the sequence of the second and third sentences in the new paragraph. Last, use the Block command to underline the new sentence in the guarantee.

13. Move the cursor to the top of the document. Then, start the Format command and move to the Line screen. If the Justification option isn't set to Left (release 5.1) or Off (release 5.0), change it. Then, change the left and right margins so they're a half-inch larger. Press the Exit key twice to return to the Edit screen, and press Reveal Codes so you can see the codes that have been inserted at the top of the document.

    Next, start the Format command again and move to the Page screen. Select the Center Page option and turn it on. Then, press the Zero key twice to return to the Edit screen. Note the code that has been inserted at the top of the document.

    Last, print the letter again. Then, compare it to the letter you printed in exercise 11. Note the differences in the margins. And if you changed the Justification option too, note the differences in the way the paragraphs in the body of the letter are printed. To complete the exercises, save the revised document under its original name (CATLET.FM).

Chapter 5

How to create and edit a two-page report

In chapters 3 and 4, you learned how to create and edit a one-page letter. Now, you'll learn how to work with multi-page documents. Along the way, you'll learn how to use seven more commands and some new keystroke combinations.

As you read this chapter, you can try the *WordPerfect* skills it teaches on your own PC right after you read about them. Or you can read the entire chapter first and then go through the exercises at the end of the chapter. When you do the exercises, you will create a two-page report like the one in figure 5-1.

Five keystroke combinations for working with a multi-page document

Figure 5-2 presents some keystroke combinations that are useful when you're working on documents that are two or more pages long. You can press the Page-up or Page-down key to move the cursor to the top of the previous page or to the next page. If you press the Page-down key when you're on the last page of the document, the cursor moves to the end of the document after all codes.

When you hold down the Ctrl key and press the Home key, you access the Go-to function, which displays this prompt:

Go to

Then, when you type the number of the page that you want and press the Enter key, the cursor moves to that page.

The fourth keystroke combination in figure 5-2 is for the *hard page break*. When you type this key combination (Ctrl+Enter), *WordPerfect* inserts a hard page break code [HPg] into the document and a new page is started whether or not the previous page has been filled. In contrast, *WordPerfect* automatically inserts a *soft page break* [SPg] when it reaches the bottom of a page. As you can see in figure 5-3, a single dashed line on the Edit screen represents a soft page break, and a double dashed line represents a hard page break.

August 19, 1992   51REPORT   Page 1

Why we should upgrade from <u>WordPerfect</u> 5.0 to 5.1

Unlike <u>WordPerfect</u> 4.2 and 5.0, <u>WordPerfect</u> 5.0 and 5.1 share the
same structure. Although some of the existing features have been
enhanced, none of them have been drastically changed. <u>WordPerfect</u>
5.1 does, however, offer some new features including a Tables
feature, Mouse support, and Pull-down menus.

     At the end of this report, I'm going to recommend that our
editors upgrade from <u>WordPerfect</u> 5.0 to 5.1. But first, I'm going
to briefly describe the **Tables** feature. I think that this feature
alone makes it worthwhile to upgrade. I'm also going to present a
brief analysis of the benefits and costs of converting to
<u>WordPerfect</u> 5.1. When you finish this report, you can decide
whether you would like more information on any of these subjects.
If so, I'll be happy to get it for you.

The Tables feature The Tables feature can be used for several
purposes, even as a simple spreadsheet. If you combine the Tables
feature with the Math feature, for example, you can use formulas
to calculate each cell within the table. However, the Tables
feature is no substitute for a spreadsheet. It doesn't provide as
many features as a spreadsheet, it's not as efficient, and it's
not as easy to use.

     However, the Tables feature is an efficient way to present
tabular data. For example, we often use tables to present
information in our reports. Right now, we use the Columns feature
or Tabs to present this information, and we waste a lot of time.
We set and reset our Tab stops until the table looks right. Or,
we adjust and readjust the widths of the Columns feature. This
can be tricky and time consuming. Since the Tables feature
provides an easier way to adjust the width of each column in a
table, it could save us a lot of time. The other day, for
example, I used the Tables feature to create a table that I would
have created with Tabs if I had been using 5.0. Although I'm
still learning how to use the Tables feature, I finished this
table in about five minutes.

     Since a table like this used to take me about 20 minutes to
create, I saved about 15 minutes on this table alone. If I'm
right, converting to release 5.1 should save our editors about
five to 20 minutes per table, depending on whether they are
creating or editing the table. Since we need to create and edit
many tables, I think converting to release 5.1 will save our
editors time that is measurable in hours, not minutes.

The cost of converting to 5.1 The cost of upgrading to 5.1 will
be about $85 per editor. In addition, the cost of converting from
5.0 to 5.1 includes the time it will take our editors to learn how
to use the Tables feature. However, I think our editors can
quickly learn how to use the Tables feature. In my opinion, the

Figure 5-1   A two-page report (part 1 of 2)

August 19, 1992   51REPORT   Page 2

hard part of learning the Tables feature is learning how to use
the math functions to calculate data for each cell. Since our
editors don't need to calculate any data, it shouldn't take an
editor more than an hour to learn how to use Tables. The other
day, for example, I showed Monica how to use Tables. After about
45 minutes of learning how to use the feature, she created her
first table in five minutes.

Analysis If you calculate each editor's time to be worth $15 per
hour, I think you'll see that all of our editors should upgrade to
5.1 as soon as possible. If you estimate that it will take each
editor an hour to learn how to use the Tables feature, the costs
of converting to 5.1, including training time, will be $100 per
editor. If you assume that the Tables feature will save each
editor two hours a month, the savings for each editor will be $30
a month. Therefore, the upgrade to 5.1 should pay for itself
within four or five months. And since I'm confident these
estimates are conservative, the actual payback time should be even
shorter.

Figure 5-1   A two-page report (part 2 of 2)

You can use the fifth keystroke combination in figure 5-2 to insert an
automatic page number into a document. To enter this code, you hold down
the Ctrl key while you press the letter *b* (Ctrl+B). Then, the entry in the
document looks like this:

^B

When you print your document, the correct page number is substituted for
this code. As a result, this code prints as 1 on page 1, 2 on page 2, and so on.

How to set the Document options of the Format command

When you start a new document, it is given the default settings for your
system. If, for example, the default settings for the left and right margins are
one inch, a new document is given those settings. Then, if you want to change
those defaults, you can use the Document options of the Format command.
In contrast to the Line and Page options of the Format command, the
Document options let you change the defaults for the entire document
without inserting codes into the document.

Keystrokes	Function
Page-up	Moves the cursor to the top of the previous page
Page-down	Moves the cursor to the top of the next page
Ctrl+Home	Goes to the page number indicated by the entry that follows
Ctrl+Enter	Inserts a hard page break [HPg] into the document
Ctrl+B	Inserts an automatic page number (^B) into the document

Figure 5-2   Keystroke combinations for multi-page documents

Figure 5-4 displays the Document screen of the Format command. You reach this screen by accessing the Format command (Shift+F8) and selecting the Document option. Then, you can use the Initial Base Font option to select the font that you want to use for your document. And you can use the Initial Codes option to change the default settings for the entire document without inserting codes into the document. I'll show you how to use both of these options now.

How to set the Initial Base Font for a document   The third option on the Document screen is Initial Font for *WordPerfect* 5.0 and Initial Base Font for *WordPerfect* 5.1, but I'll refer to both as the Initial Base Font option from now on. In *WordPerfect* terms, the *font* is the type that is going to be used when the document is printed; the *base font* is the font that's in force as you work on a portion of a document; and the *initial base font* is the base font that is in force when you start work on a document.

To change the initial base font for a document when you're using a typical dot-matrix printer, you use the procedure that's summarized in figure 5-5. In step 1, you access the Initial Base Font option of the Format command. This displays a listing of all the fonts that are available for the current printer. In step 2, you select one of the fonts by moving the the highlight to it and pressing the Enter key. This returns you to the Document screen where you can see the change in the initial font.

When you use a dot-matrix printer, the size of the font is usually expressed in the number of characters per inch, or *cpi*. In figure 5-5, for example, you can see that most of the font selections have a size ranging from 5 cpi to 20 cpi. The ones that don't have a specific size have an implied size, and they are likely to have a varying number of characters per inch. For business documents, a font at either 10 or 12 characters per inch is appropriate. However, because a font at 12 cpi is usually easier to read than a font at 10 cpi, I recommend a 12 cpi font.

The soft page break
[SPg]

```
have created with Tabs if I had been using 5.0.  Although I'm
still learning how to use the Tables feature, I finished this
table in about five minutes.

        Since a table like this used to take me about 20 minutes to
create, I saved about 15 minutes on this table alone.  If I'm
right, converting to release 5.1 should save our editors about
five to 20 minutes per table, depending on whether they are
creating or editing the table.  Since we need to create and edit
many tables, I think converting to release 5.1 will save our
editors time that is measurable in hours, not minutes.

The cost of converting to 5.1  The cost of upgrading to 5.1 will
be about $85 per editor.  In addition, the cost of converting from
5.0 to 5.1 includes the time it will take our editors to learn how
to use the Tables feature.  However, I think our editors can
quickly learn how to use the Tables feature.  In my opinion, the
--------------------------------------------------------------------
hard part of learning the Tables feature is learning how to use
the math functions to calculate data for each cell.  Since our
editors don't need to calculate any data, it shouldn't take an
editor more than an hour to learn how to use Tables.  The other
day, for example, I showed Monica how to use Tables.  After about
45 minutes of learning how to use the feature, she created her
D:\LWPDOCS\51REPORT                       Doc 1 Pg 1 Ln 50 Pos 18
```

The hard page break
[HPg]

```
have created with Tabs if I had been using 5.0.  Although I'm
still learning how to use the Tables feature, I finished this
table in about five minutes.

        Since a table like this used to take me about 20 minutes to
create, I saved about 15 minutes on this table alone.  If I'm
right, converting to release 5.1 should save our editors about
five to 20 minutes per table, depending on whether they are
creating or editing the table.  Since we need to create and edit
many tables, I think converting to release 5.1 will save our
editors time that is measurable in hours, not minutes.

====================================================================
The cost of converting to 5.1  The cost of upgrading to 5.1 will
be about $85 per editor.  In addition, the cost of converting from
5.0 to 5.1 includes the time it will take our editors to learn how
to use the Tables feature.  However, I think our editors can
quickly learn how to use the Tables feature.  In my opinion, the
hard part of learning the Tables feature is learning how to use
the math functions to calculate data for each cell.  Since our
editors don't need to calculate any data, it shouldn't take an
editor more than an hour to learn how to use Tables.  The other
day, for example, I showed Monica how to use Tables.  After about
D:\LWPDOCS\51REPORT                       Doc 1 Pg 2 Ln 3 Pos 18
```

Figure 5-3   How soft and hard page breaks are shown on the Edit screen

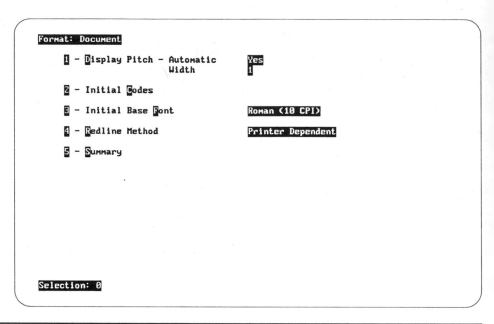

Figure 5-4   The Document screen of the Format command

To change the initial base font for a document when you're using a laser printer or a dot-matrix printer with *scalable fonts*, the procedure can be a bit more complicated as summarized in figure 5-6. In step 1, you access the Initial Base Font option of the Format command. This displays a listing of all the fonts that are available for the current printer. In step 2, you select one of the fonts by moving the highlight to it and pressing the Enter key.

When the current printer is a laser printer or a dot-matrix printer with scalable fonts, the size of the font is usually expressed in *points* with 72 points to the vertical inch. For most business documents, a size from 10 through 12 points is appropriate. If a font isn't scalable, the size of the type is given right after it in points as in this example:

Times Roman 12pt

Then, when you select the font and press the Enter key in step 2 of the procedure in figure 5-6, *WordPerfect* returns you to the Document screen where you can see the change in the initial font. That ends the procedure.

If the font is scalable, though, no size is given after it as illustrated by the fonts in the screen in figure 5-6. Then, when you select a font in step 2, *WordPerfect* displays this message:

Point size:

Here, you type the size that you want for the initial font and press the Enter key as described in step 3. That ends the procedure.

The Initial Font screen

```
Document: Initial Font
 Roman ( 5 CPI)
 Roman ( 6 CPI)
 Roman ( 7 CPI)
 Roman (10 CPI)
* Roman (12 CPI)
 Roman (15 CPI)
 Roman (17 CPI)
 Roman (20 CPI)
 Roman 12pt (PS)
 Roman 12pt (PS) Condensed
 Roman 12pt (PS) Dbl-Wide
 Roman 12pt (PS) Italic
 Roman Italic ( 5 CPI)
 Roman Italic ( 6 CPI)
 Roman Italic ( 7 CPI)
 Roman Italic (10 CPI)
 Roman Italic (12 CPI)
 Roman Italic (15 CPI)
 Roman Italic (17 CPI)
 Roman Italic (20 CPI)
 San Serif ( 5 CPI)

 1 Select; N Name search: 1
```

How to change the Initial Font

1. Access the Initial Font screen through the Format command (Shift+F8) like this:

   WordPerfect 5.0: Format > Document > Initial Font
   WordPerfect 5.1: Format > Document > Initial Base Font

   This displays a screen like the one above.

2. Move the cursor to the font you want to use. When you press the Enter key, *WordPerfect* returns you to the Document screen where you can see the change in the initial font.

Note: If you're using *WordPerfect* 5.1, you can also use Initial Codes to set the initial font. If you do, the font specified by Initial Codes overrides the font specified by Initial Font.

Figure 5-5   How to change the Initial Font for a document when you use a printer without scalable fonts

In chapter 8, you can learn more about the selection of fonts for the documents that you prepare. In particular, you can learn the difference between serif and sans serif fonts and why you should use a serif font as the initial font for most business documents. For now, though, you can just concentrate on selecting a font that has an appropriate size for your documents.

How to set the Initial Codes for a document   To change the default settings for a new document, you can use the Initial Codes option of the Document options as summarized in figure 5-7. When you access this option, a screen like the one in this figure is displayed. If nothing is shown below the separating line in the middle of the screen, all of *WordPerfect*'s defaults for the initial codes remain in effect. However, if there are codes below the line, someone has changed *WordPerfect*'s defaults by using the Setup command as explained in chapter 6. As a result, the codes below the line override the original default settings that came with *WordPerfect*. In this example, the second and third codes override the justification setting and the left and right margin settings.

To add a code to those shown below the line when you're at the Initial Codes screen, you access the Format command again as indicated by step 2 in the procedure in figure 5-7. I know that isn't logical since you've just accessed the Format command to get to the Initial Codes screen option, but that's the way this works. To change the left and right margins, for example, you access the Format command while you're at the Initial Codes screen. Then, you select Line from the Format screen and Margins from the Line screen. After you change the margin settings, you press the Exit key to return to the Initial Codes screen (which means you're still using the original Format command). You will then see the code for the margin settings below the line in the center of the screen. To change any of the other Format options for the document, you proceed in the same way.

If the Initial Codes screen doesn't have a code for justification, you should add one. As I said in the last chapter, ragged-right documents are easier to read than justified documents. As a result, the Justification option of the Line screen should be set to Off for *WordPerfect* 5.0 and to Left for *WordPerfect* 5.1.

If the Initial Codes screen doesn't have a code for the Left and Right margins, you should probably add one also. As I said in the last chapter, you should try to keep the number of characters in each line of a report to 66 or fewer because that makes the document easier to read. As a result, if you're using a font of 12 cpi or more or a font of 12 points or fewer, you should set larger margins than the one-inch defaults that *WordPerfect* provides. For fonts that are measured in points, you may have to count the number of characters in a line or two of a document to figure out how many characters the average line contains. Then, you can figure out how wide the margins should be.

If you decide that you want to delete one of the codes below the line of the Initial Codes screen, you move the cursor to the code and press the Delete key as described in step 3 of the procedure in figure 5-7. This returns that setting to the original *WordPerfect* default setting. If, for example, you don't want left and right margins of 1.5 inches as shown in the Initial Codes screen in figure 5-7, you move the cursor to this code and press the Delete

The Initial Font screen

```
Document: Initial Font
* ITC Avant Garde Gothic Book Oblique
  ITC Avant Garde Gothic Demi
  ITC Avant Garde Gothic Demi Oblique
  ITC Bookman Demi
  ITC Bookman Demi Italic
  ITC Bookman Light
  ITC Bookman Light Italic
  ITC Zapf Chancery Medium Italic
  New Century Schoolbook
  New Century Schoolbook Bold
  New Century Schoolbook Bold Italic
  New Century Schoolbook Italic
  Palatino
  Palatino Bold
  Palatino Bold Italic
  Palatino Italic
  Symbol
  Times Roman
  Times Roman Bold
  Times Roman Bold Italic
  Times Roman Italic

Point size: 12
```

How to change the Initial Font

1. Access the Initial Font screen through the Format command (Shift+F8) like this:

   WordPerfect 5.0: Format > Document > Initial Font
   WordPerfect 5.1: Format > Document > Initial Base Font

   This displays a screen like the one above.

2. Move the cursor to the font you want to use and press the Enter key. If the font isn't scalable, *WordPerfect* returns you to the Document screen where you can see the change in the initial font.

3. If you select a scalable font, a prompt like this appears:

   `Point size:`

   Type the point size that you want to use. When you press the Enter key, *WordPerfect* returns you to the Document screen where you can see the change in the initial font.

Note: If you're using *WordPerfect* 5.1, you can also use Initial Codes to set the initial font. If you do, the font specified by Initial Codes overrides the font specified by Initial Font.

Figure 5-6 How to change the Initial Font for a document when you use a printer with scalable fonts

key. This returns the margins to the *WordPerfect* defaults of one inch. Then, if necessary, you can add another code to replace the one you've deleted. If you see two codes for the same option on the Initial Codes screen, the last one on the screen is the one that's in force.

In figure 5-7, you should delete the first code on the Initial Codes screen. This code sets the initial font for the document, and it takes precedence over the Initial Base Font code. As a result, you should delete the font code on the Initial Codes screen if you want the Initial Base Font code to be in force. (If you're using *WordPerfect* 5.0, you can't use the Initial Codes screen to set the initial font so you don't have to worry about this.)

When you've got the Initial Codes the way you want them, you press the Exit key to return to the Document options menu. And you press the Exit key again to return to the Edit screen. Then, you can start preparing the document with the knowledge that the initial base font and the formatting codes are set the way you want them.

Later, if you want to change one of the codes for the entire document, you can access the Format command again, select the Document options, and change the codes just as though you hadn't started work on the document. This applies the codes to the entire document without inserting them into the document.

If this seems like a cumbersome way to set the formatting options for a document, it is. Why then should you bother to use Initial Codes and Initial Base Font instead of inserting the formatting codes into the document? First, if you use the Document options, you don't have to worry about putting the codes in the wrong place in the document or about deleting them accidentally. Second, it's sometimes easier to change the default formats by using Initial Codes than it is to insert overriding codes. For example, if you want to return to *WordPerfect*'s default setting, you just delete the code that you don't want. Third, if you combine two or more documents with inserted codes that conflict, you have to find and delete the codes that you don't want. In contrast, if you combine two or more documents that have used the Document options, the second document just assumes the codes of the first one.

In chapter 6, you can learn how to use the Setup command to change the default options for the Initial Codes. If you get these set so they're appropriate for most of the documents that you work on, you won't have to change the defaults for individual documents as often. This, of course, helps you increase your productivity.

How to use the Format command to create a header for a document

If you look at the report in figure 5-1, you'll see the date, file name, and page number at top of each page. This information comes from the *header* for the document. Although you enter a header only once, it prints automatically on each page of the document.

The Initial Codes screen

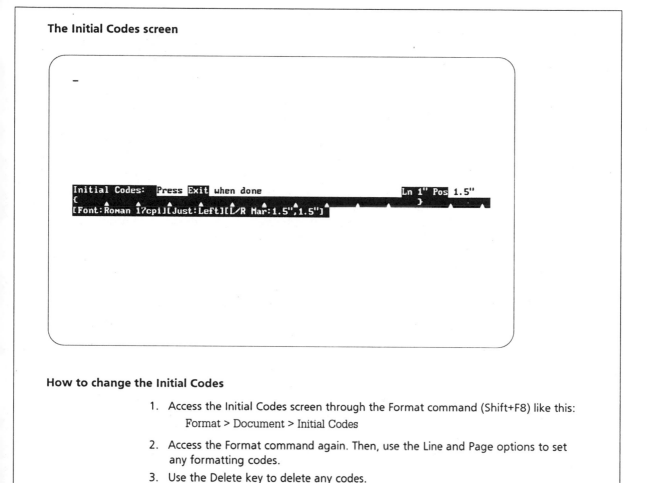

How to change the Initial Codes

1. Access the Initial Codes screen through the Format command (Shift+F8) like this:
   Format > Document > Initial Codes
2. Access the Format command again. Then, use the Line and Page options to set any formatting codes.
3. Use the Delete key to delete any codes.
4. Press the Exit key to return to the Document screen.
5. Press the Exit key again to return to the Edit screen.

Figure 5-7   How to change the Initial Codes for a document without inserting codes into the document

The first procedure in figure 5-8 shows you how to create a simple header that prints on every page of a document. In step 1, you move the cursor to the top of the first page of the document that you want the header to be printed on. If you want the header to start on the first page, the cursor must be at the top of the document before any text. However, the cursor should be after any formatting codes that apply to the header as well as to the rest of the document.

In step 2, you access the Format command and select the Page option. Then, the Page screen is displayed. In steps 3 through 5, you select the appropriate options from the prompts that are displayed: Headers from the Page screen; Header A from the next prompt; and Every Page from the next prompt. At that point, a Header screen like the first one in figure 5-9 is displayed, and the Edit screen disappears. Then, in step 6, you type the header. In step 7, you press the Exit key (F7) twice: once to exit from the Header screen; once to exit from the Format command.

The Header shown in figure 5-9 is for the report in figure 5-1. When you reach the Header screen, you type the text that you want to be printed at the top of every page of the document. This header can be one or more lines, but one line is often all that you need. *WordPerfect* automatically skips one line between the header and the first line of text as shown in figure 5-1. If you want more than one line skipped, type your header and then press the Enter key once for each extra line that you want skipped between the header and the text.

When you complete the procedure for creating a header, *WordPerfect* inserts a header code into the document at the cursor location. Depending on which release of *WordPerfect* you're using, the code will look like one of these:

[Header A; Every page; ...] or [Header A;2; ...]

If you find a mistake in the header or you want to modify it for some other reason, you can delete the header code and create a new header. Or you can correct the header by using the editing procedure in figure 5-8. As you can see, the procedure for editing a header is similar to the procedure for creating one. When you edit a header, however, the cursor doesn't have to be in any specific location. And you select the Edit option from the second prompt instead of the Every Page option.

The second screen in figure 5-9 shows the Header screen with the codes revealed. The first code inserts the current date. You should remember this code from the last chapter. The second code centers the file name, and the third code aligns the page number flush with the right margin. Now, I'll show you how to use the Center and Flush Right commands for your headers.

How to use the Center command

If you look at the command template, you'll see that you access the Center command using the Shift+F6 key combination. To center text as you enter it, you first access the command. This jumps the cursor to the center of the line. Then, you type the text that you want centered. As you type, the characters are centered automatically. Normally, you end the centering function by pressing the Enter key to move to the next line of the document. To center an existing line of text, you move the cursor to the start of the line and access the Center command. *WordPerfect* then automatically centers the line.

How to create a header

1. Move the cursor to the top of the document before any text but after any formatting codes that affect the header.
2. Access the Format command (Shift+F8) and select the Page option.
3. Select the Headers option from the Page screen to display this prompt:

   1 Header **A**; **2** Header **B**: **0**

4. Select Header A.
5. Select the Every Page option from the next prompt:

   1 Discontinue; **2** Every Page; **3 O**dd Pages; **4 E**ven Pages; **5** Edit: **0**

6. At the Header screen, type a header like the one in figure 5-9; it's the header for the report in figure 5-1.
7. After you enter the header, press the Exit key twice to return to the Edit screen.

How to edit a header

1. From anywhere in your document, access the Format command (Shift+F8) and select the Page option.
2. At the Page screen, select the Headers option to display this prompt:

   1 Header **A**; **2** Header **B**: **0**

3. Select Header A.
4. Then, select the Edit option at the next prompt:

   1 Discontinue; **2** Every Page; **3 O**dd Pages; **4 E**ven Pages; **5** Edit: **0**

5. Edit the header. Then, when you're done, press the Exit key twice to return to the Edit screen.

Figure 5-8   How to create and edit a header that prints on each page of the document

If you look at the Header screen in figure 5-9, you can see that the file name, 51REPORT, is centered. If you look at the Reveal Codes portion of this screen, you can see that a Center code

[Center]

precedes the file name. Note in this example that the centered text isn't the only text on the line. In fact, it is preceded by the date and followed by the page number.

If you're using release 5.0, your Center code will be different. In this release, the Center command uses two codes if the centered text is followed by any other keystroke. If you typed the header in figure 5-9 using release 5.0, this is what the codes look like:

[Cntr] [C/A/Flrt]

The first code is placed at the beginning of the centered text, and the second code is placed at the end of the text. Although there are these slight differences between the 5.0 and 5.1 codes, the Center command works the same for both releases.

How to use the Flush Right command

If you look at the command template, you'll see that you access the Flush Right command using the Alt+F6 key combination. To right align text as you enter it, you access this command. This jumps the cursor to the right side of the line. Then, you type the text that you want aligned. To end this function, you press the Enter key to move to the next line of the document.

To right align text after you have entered it, you move the cursor to the start of the text that you want right aligned. Then, you access the Flush Right command. When you move the cursor to the next line of the document, the text is aligned on the right margin.

In figure 5-9, you can see that the page number is right aligned. If you look at the Reveal Codes portion of this screen, you can see that the page number is preceded by the Flush Right code:

[Flsh Rgt]

Like the Center code, *WordPerfect* 5.0 uses two Flush Right codes if the text that is right aligned is followed by any other keystrokes. But again, the differences between the release 5.0 and 5.1 codes are trivial; they don't affect the way the Flush Right command works.

How to use the Search command

If you look at the command template, you can see that it includes two Search commands: >Search and <Search. You can use these commands to search for a string of letters, numbers, characters, or codes in your document. A *forward search* (F2) searches from the cursor to the end of a document. A *backward search* (Shift+F2) searches from the cursor to the start of the document.

Figure 5-10 shows you how to use the Search command. In step 1, you move the cursor to where you want the search to begin. In step 2, you access the appropriate Search command. *WordPerfect* then displays a prompt that asks you to enter a *search string* that contains the characters and codes that you want to search for. In step 3, you enter that search string. In step 4, you press the F2 key again, not the Enter key, to start the search. If you press the Enter key, you enter a hard return [HRt] into the search string.

In figure 5-10, you can also see some typical search strings. If, for example, you want to search for the word *analysis*, you just type it in. If you want to search for words that are boldfaced, you press the F6 key to enter the Bold code as the search string. If you want to search for the ends of paragraphs, you press the Enter key twice to enter the hard return codes.

The Header screen

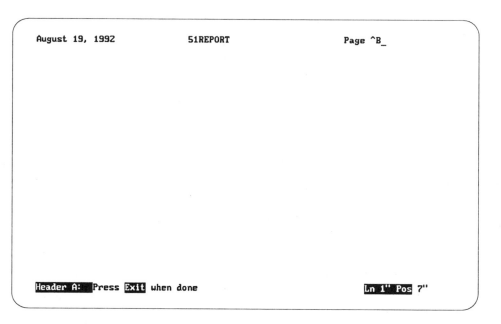

```
August 19, 1992              51REPORT                    Page ^B_
```

```
Header A:  Press Exit when done                          Ln 1" Pos 7"
```

The same screen with the codes revealed

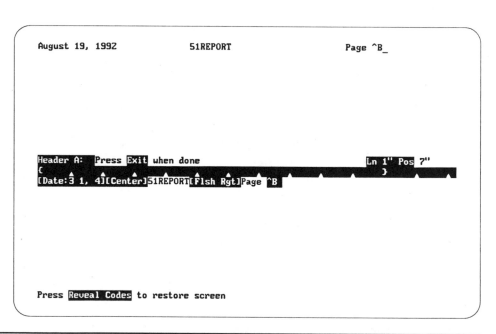

```
August 19, 1992              51REPORT                    Page ^B_
```

```
Header A:  Press Exit when done                          Ln 1" Pos 7"
{                                                                }
[Date:3 1, 4][Center]51REPORT[Flsh Rgt]Page ^B
```

```
Press Reveal Codes to restore screen
```

Figure 5-9   The Header screen for release 5.1 after a header has been entered into it

To find all occurrences of a word like *analysis*, you type it in lowercase letters as shown in figure 5-10. Then, *WordPerfect* finds the word whether or not any of its letters are capitalized. In contrast, if you type the word in the search string with any capital letters, *WordPerfect* will find the word only if it's capitalized exactly the same way as it is in the search string.

When the search starts, *WordPerfect* searches for the first occurrence of the search string. If it finds one, it moves the cursor to the end of that occurrence. Then, if you want to search for the next occurrence of the search string, you start the forward or backward search again by pressing F2 or Shift+F2 twice. The first time you press it, the search string is displayed again; the second time you press it, the search begins. You can continue in this way until *WordPerfect* has found all of the occurrences of the search string. When *WordPerfect* can't find another occurrence, it flashes this message

* Not Found *

and leaves the cursor where it was when the search began.

When you use the Search command, you'll find that you often need to limit your search by making the search string more specific. For instance, if your search string is *one*, *WordPerfect* will also find the words *bone*, *none*, and *alone*. So if you want to limit your search to the word *one*, you can put one space before the word when you enter it in the search string.

Often, you can use spaces to limit a search as shown in the last two examples in figure 5-10. Even though you can't see the spaces when you type them in the search string, *WordPerfect* recognizes them. You can also use codes, punctuation marks, and capitalization in a search string to limit a search.

If you decide to change a search string, you press the F2 key once to display the previous search string. Then, if you want to replace the old search string, you just enter the new string. However, if you want to modify the old search string, you can use the Arrow keys, the Backspace and Delete keys, and Insert and Typeover modes to edit the old string.

There are several ways that you can use the Search command to improve your efficiency as you edit a document. For instance, you can use the Search command to move the cursor to where you want to begin editing. You can use the command to search for a frequently misused word like *it's* to make sure that you used the word correctly. You can use the command to search for terms to make sure that you used them consistently. And you can use the command to search for codes within the document to make sure that your formatting was consistent.

How to use the Replace command

Once you know how to use the Search command, you won't have any trouble using the Replace command. This command searches for a search string just like the Search command, but when it finds an occurrence of the search

How to search for a search string

1. Move the cursor to where you want to begin the search.
2. Access the appropriate Search command. If you want to search forward, press F2. If you want to search backward, press Shift+F2.
3. Enter the search string at the prompt:

   `>Srch:`   (prompt for a forward search)

   `<Srch:`   (prompt for a backward search)

Note: An arrow appears before the prompt to tell you which direction the search will proceed.

4. After you enter the string, press the F2 key (not the Enter key) to start the search. If *WordPerfect* finds a sequence of characters that matches the search string, it stops the cursor at the end of the matching string. If *WordPerfect* doesn't find a match, it briefly displays this message

   `* Not Found *`

   and ends the search.

Some typical search strings

>Srch: analysis
<Srch: [Bold]
<Srch: [HRt][HRt]
>Srch: one
>Srch: [sp]one   (where [sp] equals one space)
>Srch: .[sp][sp]   (where [sp] equals one space)

Figure 5-10   How to use the Search command

string, it replaces that string with the *replace string* that you've entered. Because the Replace command is closely related to the Search command, it's sometimes referred to as the Search and Replace command.

If you look at the command template, you'll see that you access the Replace command using the Alt+F2 key combination. Figure 5-11 shows you how to use this command. In step 1, you move the cursor to where you want the replace function to start. Usually, this is at the beginning of a document. When you start the Replace command in step 2, *WordPerfect* displays this prompt:

w/Confirm? No (Yes)

Then, you select No if you're sure that you to want to replace every occurrence of the search string with the replace string. If you're not sure, you select Yes. Then, *WordPerfect* gives you a chance to either skip each occurrence or to replace it with the replace string. In steps 3, and 4, you enter the search string for the function followed by the replace string.

When the Replace function starts, it searches for the first occurrence of the search string. If you selected Yes in step 2 to confirm each replacement, *WordPerfect* displays a prompt like this:

Confirm? No (Yes)

If you select Yes, the first occurrence of the search string is replaced by the replace string, and *WordPerfect* looks for the next occurrence of the search string. If you select No, that occurrence of the search string will be left as it is and *WordPerfect* will continue to search for the next occurrence.

If you selected No in step 2 to indicate that you don't want to confirm each replacement, the Replace command automatically replaces every occurrence of the search string with the replace string without any prompting. In this case, the function can be called a *global replace*.

Because a global replace function can drastically change a document in just a few seconds, here are two precautions you can take when you use it. First, you can save your document before you execute the global replace. Then, if the global replace function doesn't work quite the way you want it to, you can clear the screen, retrieve the old document, and try it again. Second, you can try the search string that you're going to use in a Search command before you try it in the Replace command. That way, you can be sure that the search string is only going to find what you want it to.

Like the Search command, the Replace command can help you edit more efficiently. For instance, you can search for the numbers 1 through 10 and replace them with their spelled-out form (a common editorial standard) as shown in the first example in figure 5-11. You can search for the word *which* and replace it with the word *that* (whenever *that* is appropriate) to make your writing less formal as shown in the second example. If you've been writing about *WordPerfect* and have been spelling it without capitalizing the letter *p*, you can search for *wordperfect* and replace it with *WordPerfect* as shown in the third example. If you decide that you want to underline all occurrences of *WordPerfect* because it is a product name, you can do that as shown in the fourth example. If you decide that you want to indent all paragraphs, you can do that as shown in the fifth example. And if you decide that you don't want to use boldfacing to emphasize words, you can remove the boldfacing by replacing the boldface codes with nothing as shown in the sixth example.

How to use the Spell command

You can use *WordPerfect*'s Spell command to check a document for spelling and for certain types of typographical errors. To check for spelling,

How to replace text with other text

1. Move the cursor above any text that you want to replace. (Unlike the Search command, the Replace command only searches forward.)
2. Access the Replace command (Alt+F2) and select a confirm option at this prompt:

   `w/Confirm? No (Yes)`

   If you want to confirm each replacement, select Yes. If you don't, select No.
3. Enter the search string at this prompt:

   `>Srch:`

   Then, press the F2 key.
4. Enter the replace string at this prompt:

   `Replace with:`

   Then, press the F2 key to start the search and replace function.

Some typical search and replace strings

w/Confirm?	Search string	Replace string
Yes	[sp]5	five
Yes	which	that
No	wordperfect	WordPerfect
No	wordperfect	[UND]WordPerfect[und]
Yes	[HRt][HRt]	[HRt][HRt][Tab]
Yes	[Bold]	

Figure 5-11 How to use the Replace command

WordPerfect looks up each word in an electronic dictionary of about 115,000 words. If the word is in the dictionary, *WordPerfect* assumes it's correct. If it isn't, *WordPerfect* displays a screen that lets you correct the word. This feature of *WordPerfect* is often referred to as the *spell check feature* or as the *spelling checker*. *WordPerfect*'s spelling checker runs so fast on most PCs that you'll be able to check most documents in less than 30 seconds.

Although the spelling checker usually finds most of the errors in a document, it won't catch all spelling and typographical errors. If, for example, you spell *there* as *their*, the checker won't catch the error because both words are in its dictionary. Similarly, if you type *though* when you mean to type *through*, the checker won't catch the error. Nevertheless, the spelling checker is a useful feature that you should use on just about every document that you create.

---

1. Access the Spell command (Ctrl+F2). Then, *WordPerfect* displays this prompt:

   Check: 1 Word; **2 P**age; **3 D**ocument; **4 N**ew Sup. Dictionary; **5 L**ook up; **6 C**ount: **0**

2. Select the Document option.
3. Respond to the Not Found, Double Word, and Irregular Case screens that *WordPerfect* then displays.

Figure 5-12   How to use the Spell command

Figure 5-12 shows you how to use the Spell command. First, you access the command by pressing the Ctrl+F2 key combination. This displays a prompt with six options, but the first three are the ones you'll use most of the time:

Check: 1 Word; 2 Page; 3 Document

These options let you check the spelling of a single word, a single page, or the entire document.

When you select an option, *WordPerfect* starts the search for errors. Whenever it finds one, it displays a screen with options you can select to correct the error. To correct the errors, you respond to the screens that are displayed.

Both release 5.0 and 5.1 display these two screens: Not Found and Double Word. The Not Found screen indicates a spelling error. The Double Word screen indicates the use of the same word two times in a row (a common typing error). If you're using release 5.1, it also displays a third screen: Irregular Case. This screen indicates that a word is entered in a way that usually isn't correct, like *firSt* instead of *first*.

You can see a typical Not Found screen in figure 5-13. Here, the highlighted word *analisis* is the one that *WordPerfect* couldn't find in its dictionary. Then, just below the horizontal line that divides the screen, *WordPerfect* lists some possible corrections for the word. At the bottom of the screen, *WordPerfect* displays a selection line.

If one of the listed words is correct, type its letter. Then, *WordPerfect* replaces the incorrect word with the word you selected, and it continues the spelling check. If, for example, you press *a* for *analysis*, *WordPerfect* replaces the word *analisis* in the document with the word *analysis*. Since you use letters to select from the list of possible corrections, you must use numbers to select the options from the selection line at the bottom of the screen.

If the word that's highlighted is correct, you can press *1* to skip it for this time only or *2* to skip it for the rest of the spelling check. If you want to add the word to the spelling dictionary, you press *3*. If you want to edit the word, you press *4*. This moves the cursor to the word so you can correct it. Then,

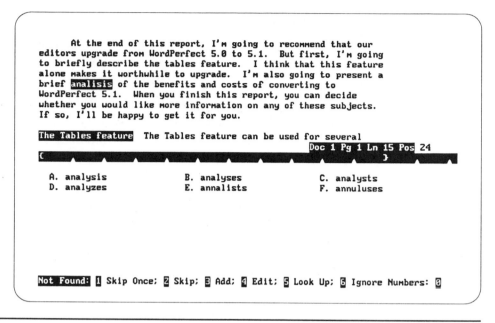

Figure 5-13   The Not Found screen of the Spell command

after you correct it, you press the Enter or Exit key to continue with the spelling check. If the highlighted word consists of a combination of letters and numbers like F3, you can press *6* if you want to ignore words with embedded numbers for the rest of the spelling check.

The Double Word and Irregular Case screens work much like those for the Not Found screen. For a double word, you can press *2* to skip it, *3* to delete the second word, *4* to edit it, or *5* to stop checking for this type of error for the rest of the spelling check.

For an irregular case, you can press *2* to skip it, *3* to replace it, *4* to edit it, or *5* to stop this type of checking. You should be careful how you correct an irregular case, though, because the Replace option doesn't always work the way you would expect. That's why I suggest that you choose the Edit option instead of the Replace option to correct an irregular case. This way, you can make sure that the word is corrected properly.

If you want to cancel the spelling checker at any time during its operation, you can press the Cancel key (F1). When you do, *WordPerfect* displays a message that gives you a count of the number of words that were checked. *WordPerfect* also gives you a word count when the spelling checker is allowed to run to its normal completion. As a result, you can use the spelling checker to count the number of words on a page or the number of words in your whole document. This is useful when you have to keep your document within a certain word count.

How to use the Help command

WordPerfect provides a Help feature that you can use to access much of the information that's in the *WordPerfect* manuals. Since you can access the help information while you're working on a document, this feature is often referred to as *on-line help*.

Figure 5-14 summarizes the main keystroke combinations you need for using the Help feature. To access this feature, you use the Help command (F3). To exit from this feature and return to the Edit screen, you press the Enter key or the Spacebar. This is important to remember because the keys that you usually use to exit from a command (like the Esc, Cancel, or Exit keys) don't work with the Help feature.

When you access Help, a screen is displayed that gives you most of the same information that's in figure 5-14. Then, to display the command template, you can press F3 again. Or to display the help information for a command, you press the keystroke combination that accesses that command. If, for example, you want information on the Spell command, you press Ctrl+F2. Then, *WordPerfect* displays a Help screen like one of the ones shown in figure 5-15. Similarly, if you want to display the information for one of the control keys, you just press that key.

When you get the first Help screen for a command, it is likely to offer options for more information. For instance, the Help screens for the Spell command in figure 5-15 offer six additional options. Then, if you want more information on the Document option, you press *3* or *d*. *WordPerfect* 5.1 then displays the screen shown in figure 5-16. *WordPerfect* 5.0 displays a similar screen.

If you don't know how to access a command or function but you know its name, you can look it up in the Help index. You access the Help index from the main Help screen. To use this index, you press the first letter of the command or function that you want. *WordPerfect* then displays an alphabetic list of the features that begin with that letter. For instance, figure 5-17 shows you the screen that you get if you press the letter *p*. As you can see, if you want to get the information for *Page Break, Hard*, you press the Ctrl+Enter key combination. To see the next screen for the index list, you press the number *1* if you're using *WordPerfect* 5.0 or the letter that you used to access the index if you're using *WordPerfect* 5.1.

As you can see from looking at the screens in figures 5-15 and 5-17, the differences between the Help screens for *WordPerfect* 5.0 and 5.1 are mostly cosmetic. For instance, the 5.1 Spell screen is somewhat easier to read than the 5.0 screen. And the columns for the index screens are in a different order.

Although most of the differences between the 5.1 and 5.0 Help features are minor, the 5.1 Help feature does offer one major improvement. It is called *context sensitive help*. This means that you can press the Help key (F3) at any time to get information about the command you're using. If, for example,

Keystrokes	Function
How to access and exit from the Help feature	
F3	Accesses the Help feature
Enter or Spacebar	Exits from the Help feature
How to access the Help information that you want	
F3	Displays the *WordPerfect* command template so you can find the keystroke combination for the command that you want to get information about. You shouldn't need to do this unless you don't have a template of your own.
Function or control key	Accesses the screen that explains the related command or function. Often, these screens lead to other screens that present more detailed information.
Any letter	Displays the Help Index, an alphabetic list of the Help topics, for the letter entered. If the list doesn't fit on one screen, you go to the next screen by pressing the letter again (5.1) or the number *1* (5.0).

Figure 5-14   How to access and use the Help feature

you are at a Not Found screen for the Spell command, you can press the F3 key to get information about the options for that screen. If you're using *WordPerfect* 5.0, you have to exit from the command before you can access the Help feature and the appropriate Help screen. Unfortunately, the 5.1 Help feature doesn't provide context-sensitive help for all functions. When it does, though, this is a significant improvement over the 5.0 Help feature.

Discussion

You have now been introduced to seven more commands that can be accessed from the command template, and 22 commands in all. If you feel confident about your ability to use those commands, you should be able to create and edit a report like the one in figure 5-1 without any help. But if you have any confusion or doubts, please do the exercises at the end of this chapter. They should clear up any doubts that you still have.

As you read this chapter, you may have noticed that I didn't present the new commands with as much detail as the commands in the last two chapters. I did this deliberately to get you to try the commands on your own. If you try them, you'll find that they just aren't that difficult to use. Once you know how to access the commands and how to select options from *WordPerfect* prompts, you can learn a lot just by experimenting.

In fact, you can think of your PC with *WordPerfect* running on it as a teaching machine. This machine does whatever you tell it to do. If you use the

WordPerfect commands correctly, the machine does what you want it to do and positively reinforces your learning. If you use the *WordPerfect* commands incorrectly, the machine doesn't do what you want it to do, and you learn from your mistakes. As a result, all you have to do to keep learning is to keep trying. With this book as a guide, your learning will proceed efficiently because you will be directed to the most essential commands and the most efficient techniques.

As you experiment with *WordPerfect*, you should remember that you can usually recover from a serious error without much trouble. Once you save a document, for example, you can always retrieve it in that earlier form. For that reason, you may want to save your work frequently when you're experimenting with something you haven't used before. Also, remember that you can use the Cancel command to restore (undelete) any one of the last three deletions that you made to a document.

Now that you've completed the tutorial section of this book, you should be able to prepare letters, memos, and reports easily. In fact, you're probably as competent as most *WordPerfect* users in industry. And yet, I hope you aren't satisfied with that. To get the maximum benefit from *WordPerfect*, you should take the time to master the essential skills that are presented in the next section of this book.

To make it easier for you to master those skills, the chapters in the next section of this book present the skills in a form that is designed both for efficient learning and for efficient reference. That means you can read these chapters in whatever sequence you prefer. Although these chapters present plenty of new information that will help you use *WordPerfect* more productively, they also summarize all of the skills presented in chapters 3, 4, and 5 so you won't have to refer back to those chapters. In short, the more you use the chapters in the next section, the more productive you'll become.

Terms

hard page break
soft page break
font
base font
initial base font
cpi
scalable font
non-scalable font
point

header
forward search
backward search
search string
replace string
spell check feature
spelling checker
on-line help
context sensitive help

The 5.1 Help Screen for the Spell command

```
Speller

    Helps you check the spelling in your document.  The Speller also checks
    capitalization errors and double words.  You can spell-check a word,
    page, document, or block of text.

    If you are running WordPerfect from two disk drives, retrieve the
    document you want to check, insert the Speller diskette into drive B,
    then press Spell.

    1 - Word

    2 - Page

    3 - Document

    4 - New Supplementary Dictionary

    5 - Look up

    6 - Count


 Selection: 0                                    (Press ENTER to exit Help)
```

The 5.0 Help Screen for the Spell command

```
Speller

    Helps you check the spelling in your document as well as look for double
    words. You can check a word, page, document, or block of text.

    Disk Drives: If you are running WordPerfect from disk drives, retrieve
          the document you want to check, insert the Speller diskette in drive
          B, then press Spell.

    Check the spelling of the current:
    1 Word; 2 Page; 3 Document

    You can also choose:
    4 New Supplementary Dictionary; 5 Look up; 6 Count

                        Type a menu option for more help: 0
```

Figure 5-15   The 5.1 and 5.0 Help screens for the Spell command (Ctrl+F2)

```
 Speller

    When the Speller encounters a word that is not in its dictionary(s), the
    word is highlighted, and the Speller suggests a list of replacement
    words.  To automatically replace the misspelled word, press the letter
    corresponding to the correct word in the list.  For information on Double
    Word occurrences, press D.  For information on Case Checking, press C.

    Skip Once - Accept the word as correct for this occurrence only.

    Skip - Accept the word as correct throughout this spell-check.

    Add Word - Add the word to the supplementary dictionary.  The Speller
           uses the supplementary dictionary as a secondary dictionary, meaning
           that the Speller will always accept the added word as correct.

    Edit - Position the cursor on the word so that you can edit it.  (You can
           also press Left or Right Arrow to begin editing).  When you are
           finished editing, press Exit to continue spell checking.

    Look Up - Look up words that match a pattern.

    Ignore Numbers - Do not check the spelling of words with numbers.

 Selection: 0                                         (Press ENTER to exit Help)
```

Figure 5-16   The 5.1 Help screen for the Spell command after you select Document from the Help screen in figure 5-15

Objectives

1. Use the new commands presented in this chapter to perform any of the following functions:

    a) Use the Format command to set the Initial Base Font for a document.
    b) Use the Format command to set the Initial Codes for a document.
    c) Create or edit a header.
    d) Center the text on one line of a document.
    e) Right align the text on one line of a document.
    f) Search any portion of a document, forward or backward, for a given search string.
    g) Replace any occurrences of a search string with a given replace string.
    h) Check the spelling within a document.
    i) Check for double words and irregular cases (5.1) within a document.
    j) Use the help feature of *WordPerfect* 5.0 or 5.1.
    k) Get context sensitive help from *WordPerfect* 5.1.

2. Use any of the skills or commands presented in this chapter to create or edit a multi-page document.

Exercises

Part 1: How to use the new commands and keystrokes

1. Start *WordPerfect*. Then, press the F3 key to access the Help feature, and press Ctrl+Enter to get information about hard page breaks. Next, press

The 5.1 Help Index

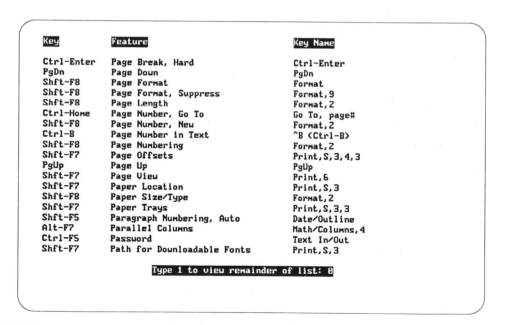

```
Features [P]                        WordPerfect Key   Keystrokes

Page Break, Hard                    Hard Page         Ctrl-Enter
Page Down                           Page Down         PgDn
Page Format                         Format            Shft-F8,2
Page Format, Suppress               Format            Shft-F8,2,8
Page Length                         Format            Shft-F8,2,7
Page Number, Go To                  Go To             Ctrl-Home, page#
Page Number in Text                 ^B (Ctrl-B)       Ctrl-B
Page Number in Text                 Format            Shft-F8,2,6,3
Page Number, New                    Format            Shft-F8,2,6,1
Page Number Style                   Format            Shft-F8,2,6,2
Page Numbering                      Format            Shft-F8,2,6,4
Page Offsets                        Format            Shft-F8,2,7,5,9
Page Up                             Page Up           PgUp
Page View                           Print             Shft-F7,6
Paper Location                      Format            Shft-F8,2,7
Paper Size/Type                     Format            Shft-F8,2,7
Paper Trays                         Print             Shft-F7,s,3,3
Paragraph Down                      Paragraph Down    Ctrl-Down
Paragraph Numbering                 Date/Outline      Shft-F5,5
Paragraph Numbering, Auto           Date/Outline      Shft-F5,5
More... Press p to continue.

Selection: 0                                    (Press ENTER to exit Help)
```

The 5.0 Help Index

```
Key          Feature                         Key Name

Ctrl-Enter   Page Break, Hard                Ctrl-Enter
PgDn         Page Down                       PgDn
Shft-F8      Page Format                     Format
Shft-F8      Page Format, Suppress           Format,9
Shft-F8      Page Length                     Format,2
Ctrl-Home    Page Number, Go To              Go To, page#
Shft-F8      Page Number, New                Format,2
Ctrl-B       Page Number in Text             ^B (Ctrl-B)
Shft-F8      Page Numbering                  Format,2
Shft-F7      Page Offsets                    Print,S,3,4,3
PgUp         Page Up                         PgUp
Shft-F7      Page View                       Print,6
Shft-F7      Paper Location                  Print,S,3
Shft-F8      Paper Size/Type                 Format,2
Shft-F7      Paper Trays                     Print,S,3,3
Shft-F5      Paragraph Numbering, Auto       Date/Outline
Alt-F7       Parallel Columns                Math/Columns,4
Ctrl-F5      Password                        Text In/Out
Shft-F7      Path for Downloadable Fonts     Print,S,3

              Type 1 to view remainder of list: 0
```

Figure 5-17   The 5.1 and 5.0 Help Index screens for the letter *p*

Ctrl+F2 to get information about the Spell command. Select the Look Up option on the Spell screen to get information about that option. Is it self explanatory, or would you need information about it before you could use it effectively? To exit from the Help feature, try pressing the Cancel or Esc key. What happens? Now, press the Enter key or the Spacebar to return to the Edit screen.

Access the Help feature again. This time press the letter *s* to get the index for items starting with that letter. Then, find the entry for the Spell command. Note that the index tells you only what keystrokes you need to use (Ctrl+F2) to access the command, and this information is already on the template. Now, press the Enter key to exit from the Help feature.

If you're using *WordPerfect* 5.1, try using the context sensitive help. To do that, access the Format command, select the Page option, and select the Margin option. Then, press the F3 key. Note that the help information for that option is displayed. Next, press the Enter key to exit from the Help feature and then exit from the Format command. Now, see how many keystrokes it takes to access the information on the Page Margins option of the Format command without using context sensitive help. Finally, return to the Edit screen.

2. Your Edit screen should still be blank. Now, access the Print command. Here, in the Select Printer line, you can see the name of the current printer. What is it?

    Then, return to the Edit screen. Next, access the Format command and select Document. Here, in the Initial Base Font line (Initial Font line on *WordPerfect* 5.0), you can see the initial base font for the current printer. What is its name and what is its size?

    Now, select Initial Base Font. This displays a list of the fonts that are available for the current printer. Are sizes given for these fonts? If sizes are given, are they measured in characters per inch or in points?

    Move the highlight to one of the fonts and press the Enter key. If the font isn't scalable, this returns you to the Document screen. But if the font is scalable, *WordPerfect* asks you to enter a type size in points. So type 12 and press the Enter key to return to the Document screen. Here, you can see the initial base font that you've selected for the current document.

3. Assuming that you're still at the Document screen, select Initial Codes. This displays the Initial Codes screen. Are any codes listed below the line in the center of the screen? If so, someone has modified the original *WordPerfect* default settings. Can you tell what each of the codes does? If not, you'll learn about most of the formatting codes in chapter 8.

    Does one of the codes change the Justication default to ragged right? Whether or not it does, access the Format command, select Line, select Justification, and change the code to Left or Off, depending on which release of *WordPerfect* you're using. Next, while you're still at the Line screen, select Margins and change the left and right margins to 1.5 inches (or 18 units). Then, press the Exit key to return to the Initial Codes screen from the Format command. Here, you can see that Justification and Margin codes have been added to the codes on this screen.

Now, move the cursor to one of the codes on the Initial Codes screen and press the Delete key. This deletes the code. If for example, there are two codes for the same setting, delete the first of the two codes. Then, make a mental note of the the codes that are shown, and press the Exit key to return to the Edit screen.

At this point, you've changed the default settings for the current document, but not for the system. To prove that, use the Exit command to clear the screen and start a new document. Next, access the Format command, and select Document. On this screen, you can see that the Initial Base Font isn't the font that you selected in exercise 2. Instead, it has been returned to its original default setting. Similarly, if you select Initial Codes from the Document screen, you can see that these codes have been returned to their original settings. To end this exercise, press the Exit key twice to return to a blank Edit screen.

4. Your Edit screen should still be blank, and the cursor should be at the top of it. Now, access the Center command, type your name, and press the Enter key. Your name should be centered on the first line of the screen.

    Press Home Home Up to move the cursor to the top of the screen. Then, press the Delete key. This deletes the Center code so your name is no longer centered. Next, access the Flush Right command, and press the Down arrow key. Your name should now be right aligned on the first line of the screen.

5. Use the Exit command to clear the Edit screen. Then, use the List command to set the default directory to the one you use for your document files. Next, retrieve the CATLET.FM file that you edited in the last chapter. It should look like the one in figure 4-17 except that the date should be the current date.

    Use the appropriate Search command to find the word *catalog*. How many times is it used in the letter? Next, use the appropriate Search command to find all occurrences of the Underline code. How many times does the command find this code? Last, use the Search command to search first for the word *I* and then for the word *you*. What search string or strings do you have to use to find each of these words without finding other words?

6. Use the Replace command without the Confirm option to replace all occurrences of the term *PC* with the words *Personal Computer*. Next, use the Replace command with the Confirm option to remove all the Tab codes so the paragraphs in the letter aren't indented. To do that, just press the F2 key when it's time to enter the replace string. This way, the Tab characters will be removed but not replaced. Last, use the Replace command to replace all occurrences of the letters *sk* with the letters *ks* (this will create some spelling errors for the next exercise).

7. Move the cursor to the start of the word *for* in the first paragraph. Then, insert another word *for* so the spelling checker will find a double word. Next, move the cursor to the first sentence in the second paragraph, and change the word *Least* to *LeaST*.

   Access the Spell command to check the spelling in the letter. When the double word is highlighted, press *3* to delete the extra word. When the first misspelling with *ks* is highlighted, press the letter of the proper replacement word. When the next one is highlighted, press *4* to edit the word. After you correct it, press the Exit or Enter key to continue with the spelling check. If you're using *WordPerfect* 5.1, edit the irregular case when it is highlighted. When all the words have been checked, note the word count of your letter.

   If you're using *WordPerfect 5.0*, the spelling checker didn't recognize *LeaST* as an error. So use the Search command to find it; then, correct it.

8. Move the cursor to the start of the second paragraph. Press Ctrl+Enter to insert a hard page break into the letter. Note that the cursor is below the double line, and note that the page indicator shows page 2. Press the Page-up key to move to page 1 and note the page indicator. Press Ctrl+Home to start the Go-to function. Then, type *2* at the prompt and press the Enter key. This moves the cursor to page 2 again. Although this function isn't useful in a short document like this, you can see that it comes in handy when you work with long documents. Now, with the cursor at the top of page 2, press the Backspace key to delete the hard page break code. If that doesn't work, use the Reveal Codes command so you can be sure to delete the right code. Once it's deleted, note that the entire letter is on one page again.

9. Move the cursor to the start of the second paragraph and press Ctrl+Enter to insert a hard page break into the letter. Next, move the cursor to the start of the second paragraph on the second page and press Ctrl+Enter to create a third page.

   Move the cursor to the top of the first page. Then, use the Format command to create a header for the document. To do that, access the Format command; press *p* for Page; press *h* for Header; press *a* for Header A; and press *p* for Every Page. This should bring you to the Header screen. At that screen, type your name and press the Enter key; type the word *Page* followed by one space; and press Ctrl+B. The left corner of the Header screen should now look like this:

   Your Name
   Page ^B

   Then, press the Exit key twice to exit from the Header screen and from the Format command. When you return to the Edit screen, note that the header doesn't show. Press Reveal Codes, though, so you can see the Header code at the start of the document. Next, return to the normal Edit screen.

Press the Page-down key to move to the second page of the document. Then, edit the header. To do that access the Format command; press *p* for Page; press *h* for Header; press *a* for Header A; and press *e* for Edit. Then, at the Header screen, edit the header so your name and the page number are on the same line with the page number aligned on the right margin of the document.

Now, use the Print command to print all three pages of the document. After the pages are printed, use the Exit command to clear the screen without saving this version of the letter.

Part 2: How to create and edit a report

10. Start with a blank Edit screen. Then, use the Format command to change the Initial Base Font and the Initial Codes for a report like the one in figure 5-1. If, for example, the size of the initial base font isn't 12 cpi or 10 points, select a base font that does have that size. If the justification isn't set for ragged right, change that code so it is. And if the left and right margin settings aren't appropriate for the initial base font you just selected, set them for 1-1/2 inches or the equivalent.

11. Use the Format command to insert a header like the one in figure 5-1. At the Header screen, access the Date/Outline command, and insert a date code at the left margin. Next, access the Center command and type the file name that you're going to use for the report in capital letters. Then, access the Flush Right command and type *Page* followed by one space and Ctrl+B. To finish the header, press the Exit key twice. This should return you to the Edit screen.

12. At this point, type a report. If you're working on a multi-page report of your own, type that report into *WordPerfect*. Otherwise, you can type the report in figure 5-1. Or if you want to save time, just type the first two paragraphs of that report. Then, copy the paragraphs four times each so the paragraphs go beyond the first page of the document.

    Whether you type an entire report or just a few paragraphs, type quickly and don't worry about mistakes. Later on, the spelling checker will catch most of them.

    As the document goes from the first page to the second page, note the dashed line that indicates a soft page break. Press Reveal Codes so you can see that this line is just a single code [SPg]. Then, press Reveal Codes again to return to the normal Edit screen.

    Now, move the cursor to the top of the last paragraph on the first page and press Ctrl+Enter. This inserts a hard page break [HPg] into the document. As you move the cursor down the second page, note that the soft page break is removed.

    Press the Page-up key to move to the top of the first page, and press the Page-down key to move to the top of the second page. Now, press the Backspace key to delete the hard page break. This removes the hard page break and returns the soft page break farther down in the document.

13. Use the Spell command to check the report for spelling errors. Even if you haven't made any mistakes, *WordPerfect* will probably stop at some of the words in the report because they aren't in its dictionary. If these words are okay the way they are, use one of the Skip options to skip them.

14. Use the Print command to print the entire report. Then, use the Page option of the Print command to print just the second page of the report. Next, use the List command to make sure the default directory is the one you're using. And use the Save command to save the report with the file name you used in the heading. Last, use the Exit command to exit from *WordPerfect*.

Section 3

The essential *WordPerfect* skills for maximum productivity

Most *WordPerfect* users don't work as efficiently or as productively as they ought to. That's why this section presents the skills that all *WordPerfect* users should have if they want to work with maximum productivity. For ease of use, the chapters in this section are written as independent modules, so you don't have to read them in sequence. That means you can learn what you want to learn whenever you want to learn it.

In contrast to the tutorial presentations in section 2, the chapters in this section are designed for efficient learning as well as efficient reference. That means you can learn the essential *WordPerfect* skills as efficiently as possible. Also, the chapters in this section repeat all of the skills presented in section 2 in a new form. This repetition reinforces your learning as you read through the chapters in this section.

What I recommend, then, is that you first read through the chapters in this section to learn what the essential skills are. Then, you can master the ones you need for the types of documents that you usually work on. Later, when you require one of the skills that you haven't yet mastered, you can refer back to the chapters in this section for an efficient review of the required skill.

Chapter 6

How to set up *WordPerfect* so it works the way you want it to

When you install *WordPerfect*, the installation program sets up several values and codes that affect the way that *WordPerfect* works. These are called the *default settings*, or just *defaults*. When you start a new document, for example, it uses the default settings for the top, bottom, left, and right margins. Similarly, when you use the Date command to insert the current date into a document, the command uses the default date format.

If you don't want to use the default settings for a document that you're working on, you can override them. If, for example, you want to override the default settings for the left and right margins, you can use the Format command to do that. And if you want to change the date format, you can use the Format command to do that too. However, if you find that you repeatedly change the default settings for the documents you work on, you should take the time to change the default settings themselves. Once you get them set up right, you won't have to change the settings for individual documents as often.

To change most of the *WordPerfect* default settings, you use the Setup command. This command not only lets you change the formatting settings for the new documents that you create, but it also lets you set defaults that affect the way *WordPerfect* works. For instance, you can use this command to control the way the *WordPerfect* backup feature works, to change the units of measure that you use, to change the speed at which the cursor moves on your screen, and so on. As a result, it's worth taking the time to learn how to use this command.

To change the default setting for the size or appearance of the type that's used for printing a document, you use the Print command instead of the Setup command. Since the default setting for the type size or appearance can affect some of the other default settings, you need to get it set up right. And because this is the only default setting that you don't use the Setup command for, I'll start by showing you how to do that.

In the rest of the chapter, I'll show you how to use the Setup command. First, I'll introduce you to the Setup command and identify those options that you should consider resetting. Then, you'll learn how to set the formatting defaults for new documents, how to set the options for *WordPerfect*'s automatic backup feature, and how to tell *WordPerfect* where some critical files are located. All *WordPerfect* users should know how to use the Setup command for these purposes. Next, you'll learn how to set ten more Setup options that affect the way both *WordPerfect* 5.0 and 5.1 work. Last, you'll learn how to set four more options that affect the way just *WordPerfect* 5.1 works.

How to use the Print command to set the initial base font for a printer

One of the most important default settings is the *initial base font*. In *WordPerfect* terms, the *font* is the type that's used when the document is printed; the *base font* is the font that's in force as you work on a document; and the *initial base font* is the default font that's in force when you start work on a document. If you have more than one printer attached to your PC, each of the printers has an initial base font. Often, though, the initial base font is not the best one for business documents.

To change the initial base font, you use the procedure that's summarized in figure 6-1. In step 1, you access the Print command to display the Print and Options menus. In step 2, you select the Select Printer option from the Options menu. In step 3, you move the highlight to the printer that you want to set the initial base font for. If you have only one printer on your PC, only one printer will be listed. Then, you select the Edit option. After you select this option, another menu with several other printer options is displayed. One of these options is Initial Base Font, and that's the one you select in step 4. This selection displays a listing of fonts like the one shown in this figure.

To select a font in step 5, you move the highlight to it and press the Enter key. Then, if the font is scalable, *WordPerfect* prompts you for the size of the type that you want to use. When you complete this step, the initial base font for the printer is changed to the one you've selected. To return to the Edit screen, you press the Exit, Esc, or Cancel key three times.

If you're not familiar with fonts, you should read the portion of chapter 8 that explains the characteristics of fonts. It also explains the differences between scalable and non-scalable fonts. After you read this material, you'll be able to select an appropriate initial base font for your documents.

An introduction to the Setup command

If you look at the command template, you can see that you access the Setup command by pressing the Shift+F1 key combination. This displays one of the two screens shown in figure 6-2. As you can see, the Setup menu for

The Initial Font screen

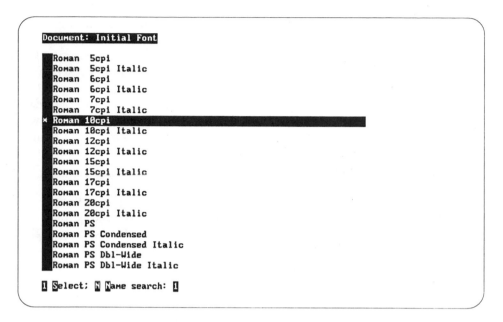

Document: Initial Font

Roman 5cpi
Roman 5cpi Italic
Roman 6cpi
Roman 6cpi Italic
Roman 7cpi
Roman 7cpi Italic
* Roman 10cpi
Roman 10cpi Italic
Roman 12cpi
Roman 12cpi Italic
Roman 15cpi
Roman 15cpi Italic
Roman 17cpi
Roman 17cpi Italic
Roman 20cpi
Roman 20cpi Italic
Roman PS
Roman PS Condensed
Roman PS Condensed Italic
Roman PS Dbl-Wide
Roman PS Dbl-Wide Italic

1 Select; N Name search: 1

How to change the initial base font for a printer

1. Access the Print command (Shift+F7) to display the Print and Options menus.
2. Select the Select Printer option from the Options menu to display a listing of the printers that are available for your PC.
3. Move the highlight to the printer you're using and select the Edit option. Then, a menu with six options that you can edit is displayed.
4. From this menu, select Initial Base Font. Then, an Initial Font screen like the one above is displayed.
5. Move the highlight to the font you want to use as the initial base font and press the Enter key. If the font is scalable, *WordPerfect* prompts you for the type size that you want to use. In that case, type the size and press the Enter key.
6. Press the Exit key three times to return to the Edit screen.

Figure 6-1   How to use the Print command to set the initial base font for a printer

WordPerfect 5.0 has eight options, and the menu for *WordPerfect* 5.1 has only six. However, *WordPerfect* 5.1 actually has many more Setup options than *WordPerfect* 5.0 because four of the selections in the main Setup menu lead to other menus.

If you know how to use the Format command, you shouldn't have any trouble using the Setup command because it works the same way. In general, to move from one Setup menu to another, you just press the number or letter of the option that you want to select. Then, when you reach an option that asks for a value or code, you type in the value or code and press the Enter key. If, at any time, you want to go back one screen, you can press the Esc key or Cancel key. And if you want to go all the way back to the Edit screen, you can press the Exit key.

With that in mind, the most difficult part of using the Setup command is figuring out what options to change and where to find them if you do want to change them. To simplify this problem, I'll present two summaries of all the options that you should be aware of. The first summary is for *WordPerfect* 5.0 users; the second one is for *WordPerfect* 5.1 users.

A Setup summary for *WordPerfect* 5.0 users Figure 6-3 presents a summary of the Setup options for *WordPerfect* 5.0. Although this summary doesn't include all of the Setup options, it includes all of those that apply to the functions and features presented in this book. It also includes most of the other options that you're likely to want to change.

If you look at the first column in this table, you can see that it presents the eight options of the main Setup menu. Then, if you look at the second column, you can see that only two of these options lead to other menus: the Display and the Initial Settings options. In contrast, the Backup, Cursor Speed, Fast Save, Keyboard Layout, Location of Files, and Units of Measure options lead directly to screens that let you change these settings.

At this point, you can probably use the Setup command to change many of the defaults in figure 6-3 without reading any further. As a result, the rest of this chapter presents each of the options as briefly as possible. If the purpose of an option isn't obvious, that's explained. If the procedure for setting the option isn't obvious, that's explained. As you will soon learn, however, the purposes and procedures for a few of the options aren't at all obvious.

A Setup summary for *WordPerfect* 5.1 users Figure 6-4 presents a summary of the Setup options for *WordPerfect* 5.1. Although this summary doesn't include all of the Setup options, it includes all those that apply to the functions and features presented in this book. It also includes most of the other options that you're likely to want to change.

If you look at the first column in this table, you can see that it presents the six options of the main Setup menu. Of these, the Display, Environment, and Initial Settings options lead to menus that offer most of the options that you're likely to want to change. In contrast, the Keyboard Layout and Location of Files options lead directly to screens that let you change these settings.

The main Setup screen for *WordPerfect* **5.0**

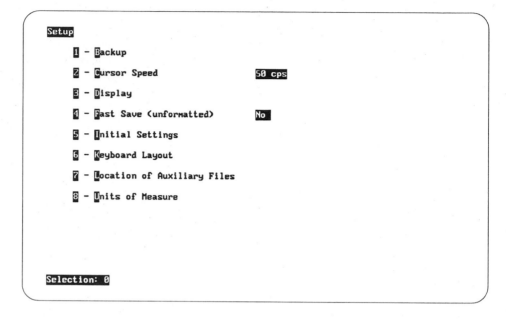

```
Setup

    1 - Backup
    2 - Cursor Speed                    50 cps
    3 - Display
    4 - Fast Save (unformatted)     No
    5 - Initial Settings
    6 - Keyboard Layout
    7 - Location of Auxiliary Files
    8 - Units of Measure




Selection: 0
```

The main Setup screen for *WordPerfect* **5.1**

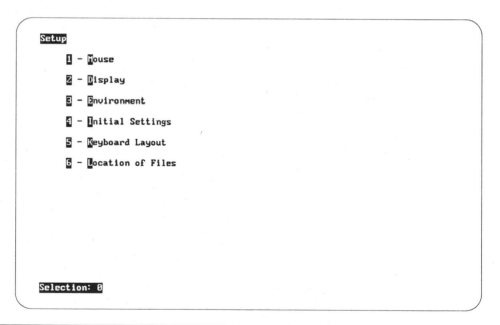

```
Setup

    1 - Mouse
    2 - Display
    3 - Environment
    4 - Initial Settings
    5 - Keyboard Layout
    6 - Location of Files






Selection: 0
```

Figure 6-2   The main Setup screens for *WordPerfect* 5.0 and 5.1

Setup menu option	Next menu option	Recommendation
Backup		Set for timed document backups.
Cursor Speed		Set for 50 cps once you've worked up to that speed; set for a slower speed if 50 cps is too fast for you.
Display	Automatically Format and Rewrite	Set to Yes so documents are reformatted before you move the cursor through them.
	Colors/Fonts/Attributes	Set these so they are appropriate for your documents and your working style.
Fast Save		Set to No so you can use the Print option of the List Files screen.
Initial Settings	Beep Options	Set the three beep options the way you want them.
	Date Format	Set the date format to the one you're going to use in most documents.
	Document Summary	Set the Create on Save/Exit option to No so you don't have to take the extra time to create document summaries.
	Initial Codes	Set these codes so they are appropriate for most of the documents you work on.
	Repeat Value	This is the repeat value that's used by the Esc key as explained in chapter 7. This option is probably OK as it is.
Keyboard Layout		Can be used to change the functions of the Esc, F1, and F3 keys, if you think that will improve your efficiency.
Location of Auxiliary Files		Set the locations of the backup and macro directories.
Units of Measure		Set the units to the ones you want to use.

Figure 6-3   A setup summary for *WordPerfect* 5.0 users

At this point, you can probably use the Setup command to change many of the defaults in figure 6-4 without reading any further. As a result, the rest of this chapter presents each of the options as briefly as possible. If the purpose of an option isn't obvious, that's explained. If the procedure for setting the option isn't obvious, that's explained. As you will soon learn, however, the purposes and procedures for a few of the options aren't at all obvious.

Setup menu option	Next menu option	Next menu option	Recommendation
Mouse	Left-Handed Mouse		If you're left handed, set the mouse for left-handed use. Otherwise, the Mouse options are probably OK as they are.
Display	Colors/Fonts/Attributes	Screen Colors	Set the Colors/Fonts/Attributes and the Screen Colors so they are appropriate for your documents and your working style.
	Menu Options	Menu Bar Remains Visible	This removes the menu bar from the top of the Edit screen until you access the menus. Set to No.
	Edit-Screen Options	Automatically Format and Rewrite	Set to Yes so documents are reformatted before you move the cursor through them.
		Reveal Codes Window Size	This sets the size of the Reveal Codes window. Probably OK as it is.
Environment	Backup Options		Set for timed document backups.
	Beep Options		Set the three beep options the way you want them.
	Cursor Speed		Set for 50 cps once you've worked up to that speed; set for a slower speed if 50 cps is too fast for you.
	Document Management/Summary	Create Summary on Save/Exit	Set to No so you don't have to take the extra time to create document summaries.
		Long Document Names	Set to No so you don't have to take the extra time for creating long document names and using them on the List screen.
	Fast Save		Set to Yes if you want to improve the speed of save and retrieve operations.
	Units of Measure		Set the units to the ones that you want to use.

Figure 6-4   A setup summary for *WordPerfect* 5.1 users (part 1 of 2)

Setup menu option	Next menu option	Next menu option	Recommendation
Initial Settings	Date Format		Set the date format to the one you're going to use for most documents.
	Format Retrieved Documents for Default Printer		Set to Yes if your system has only one printer. Set to No if it has two or more printers.
	Initial Codes		Set these codes so they are appropriate for most of the documents that you work on.
	Repeat Value		This is the repeat value that's used by the Escape key as explained in chapter 7. This option is probably OK as it .
Keyboard Layout			Can be used to change the functions of the Esc, F1, and F3 keys, if you think that will improve your efficiency.
Location of Files			Set the locations of the backup, macro, and default directories.

Figure 6-4   A setup summary for *WordPerfect* 5.1 users (part 2 of 2)

Three Setup options that every *WordPerfect* user should set up right

This chapter presents 13 Setup options for *WordPerfect* 5.0 users and four more for *WordPerfect* 5.1 users. Most of these options, however, have only a minor effect on the way *WordPerfect* works. As a result, learning how to set them will have only a minor effect on your efficiency. In contrast, every *WordPerfect* user should know how to set the three options that follow.

Initial Codes   When you install *WordPerfect* on your PC, it sets the defaults for the *initial codes* that apply to each new document. Some of these defaults are summarized in figure 6-5. As you can see, the initial codes provide for left, right, top, and bottom margins of one inch on an 8-1/2 by 11 inch page. They provide for single spacing and tabs that are set every half inch. They provide for justified text, and they don't provide for widow/orphan protection.

Because these settings aren't the best ones for many types of documents, figure 6-5 also makes some recommendations for changes. Although the *WordPerfect* default is for justification, studies have shown that ragged-right text is easier to read. As a result, the first recommendation in figure 6-5 is to change the Justification option to Off for *WordPerfect* 5.0 or Left for *WordPerfect* 5.1.

The *WordPerfect* default settings

Option	Default setting
Justification	Justified text (On for *WordPerfect* 5.0; Full for *WordPerfect* 5.1)
Line spacing	1
Left margin	1"
Right margin	1"
Tab settings	Every 0.5"
Top margin	1"
Bottom margin	1"
Paper Size	8.5" x 11"
Widow/Orphan Protection	No (Off)

Recommended changes in the settings

Option	Recommended setting
Justification	Ragged-right text (Off for *WordPerfect* 5.0; Left for *WordPerfect* 5.1).
Left margin Right margin	This depends on the base font. The left and right margins should be set so the width of the line is 66 characters or fewer.
Widow/Orphan Protection	Yes (On).

Figure 6-5   The *WordPerfect* default settings and the recommended settings for Initial Codes

The left margin and right margin settings should be based on the size of the initial base font that you use. In general, these margins should be set so the length of the line doesn't exceed 66 characters. Studies have shown that lines longer than that are difficult to read. If, for example, you're using a font that prints at 10 characters per inch, one inch margins are okay because the length of the line is 65 characters. But if you're using a font that prints at 12 characters per inch, the margins should be larger than that, perhaps one and one-half inches. Otherwise, the line will be too long to be read easily.

The last recommendation in figure 6-5 is that the Widow/Orphan Protection option be turned on. If this option is on, *WordPerfect* won't print the first line of a paragraph as the last line on a page, and it won't print the last line of a paragraph as the first line on a page. Because that improves the appearance of a report or proposal, it makes sense to keep this option on for all documents.

If you often work on documents with special requirements, you may want to change some of the other initial codes. For instance, you may want to change the defaults for tab settings or for the top and bottom margins. At the least, though, you should consider making the changes that are recommended in figure 6-5.

If you want to change the default settings for your system, you use the Initial Codes screen as summarized in figure 6-6. If nothing is shown below the separating line in the middle of the screen, all of defaults that were set by the installation program are in effect. However, if you add codes below the line, they change the initial default settings. In this figure, for example, the justification default has been changed to Left. The Left and Right margins have been changed to 1.5 inches. And the Widow/Orphan option (W/O) has been turned on.

To access the Initial Codes screen, you select the Initial Settings option from the main Setup screen and the Initial Codes option from the Initial Settings screen. Then, to change any of the formatting options, you use the Format command. To change the left and right margins, for example, you access the Format command while you're at the Initial Codes screen. Then, you select Line from the Format screen and Margins from the Line screen. After you change the margin settings, you press Exit to return to the Initial Codes screen. You will then see the code for the margin settings below the line in the center of the screen. To change any of the other Format defaults, you proceed in the same way.

In chapter 8, you can learn more about the Format command and the options that you can set with it. So if you have any trouble setting the Initial Codes the way you want them, you can refer to that chapter.

If you want to delete one of the changed default settings on the Initial Codes screen, move the cursor to the code and press the Delete key. Then, if necessary, you can add another code to replace the one you've deleted. If you see two codes for the same option on the Initial Codes screen, the last one on the screen is the one that's in force.

When you change the Initial Codes, you should keep in mind that the changes don't affect any existing documents. Instead, the changes apply only to the new documents that you create. In chapter 9, though, you will learn how to apply the new default settings to an old document by retrieving it into a document that contains one space.

Backup Options   To set the Backup options the way you want them, you access the Backup screen as summarized in figure 6-7. If you're using *WordPerfect* 5.0, you just select the Backup option from the main Setup screen. If you're using *WordPerfect* 5.1, you select Environment from the main Setup menu, and Backup Options from the next menu. When you reach the Backup screen, you can see that *WordPerfect* provides two kinds of backup options. One of the options automatically saves your document at timed intervals, and the other option creates a duplicate copy of your document.

The Initial Codes screen

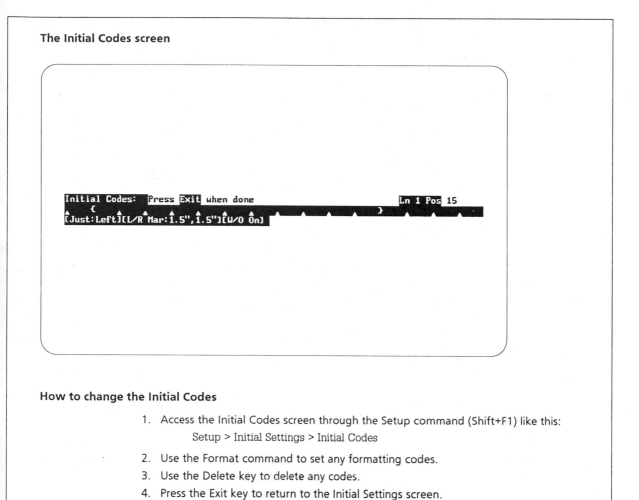

```
Initial Codes:  Press Exit when done                        Ln 1 Pos 15
      {                                                   }
[Just:Left][L/R Mar:1.5",1.5"][W/O On]
```

How to change the Initial Codes

1. Access the Initial Codes screen through the Setup command (Shift+F1) like this:
   Setup > Initial Settings > Initial Codes
2. Use the Format command to set any formatting codes.
3. Use the Delete key to delete any codes.
4. Press the Exit key to return to the Initial Settings screen.
5. Press the Exit key to return to the Edit screen.

Figure 6-6   How to change the Initial Codes

When you select the Original Document Backup option, a backup copy of a document is made each time that you save it. The backup copy is stored in the same directory with the same name as the other document file, but the backup copy has BK! as the extension. This option is meant to protect you from losing a file by making two copies of it. Then, if you accidentally damage one copy, you have a second copy. Once you get used to working with *WordPerfect*, though, you shouldn't have any trouble saving and replacing files. As a result, this option will rarely be of value. In the meantime, it clutters your directories by putting twice as many files in them as are necessary. That's why

I recommend that you turn this option off and use the other backup option instead.

When you select the Timed Backup option, *WordPerfect* asks you to specify the number of minutes between backups. If you're working on two documents at the same time as described in chapter 7, *WordPerfect* backs up both documents at the specified interval. In general, you should specify the fewest number of minutes of work that you think you can afford to lose. For most people, that's probably between 5 and 15 minutes. However, if you work in an area that has frequent power outages or you suspect that your PC is about to fail, you may want to set the backup interval to just a few minutes.

In the second or two that it takes *WordPerfect* to save the document or documents, *WordPerfect* displays a prompt like this:

* Please Wait *

In fact, if this feature has been on while you've been using *WordPerfect*, you may have already noticed this message, but you didn't know what it meant.

If you exit from *WordPerfect* properly, *WordPerfect* deletes the timed backup files. As a result, you still have to save your files properly before you exit from *WordPerfect*. However, if you aren't able to exit from *WordPerfect* properly because of an equipment or power failure, the timed backup files remain on the hard disk. In figure 6-7, you can see that the name of the backup file for Document 1 is WP{WP}.BK1; the name of the backup file for Document 2 is WP{WP}.BK2. These backup files are stored in the backup directory shown on the Backup screen. Or if no backup directory is specified on the Backup screen, these files are stored in the *WordPerfect* directory.

When you restart *WordPerfect* after a power failure or a PC failure, *WordPerfect* displays a prompt like this:

Are other copies of WordPerfect currently running? (Y/N)

If you aren't running *WordPerfect* on a network, you should select No. Then, you can recover the documents that you weren't able to save properly by retrieving the backup files.

Later, when it's time for *WordPerfect* to do its timed document backups, it displays this prompt:

Old backup file exists. 1 Rename; 2 Delete:

This shows that the backup files (WP{WP}.BK1 and WP{BK}2) weren't deleted the last time you used *WordPerfect* because you didn't exit properly. If you've already recovered the documents that you were working on from these backup files, you select Delete so *WordPerfect* can continue with its timed backups. Otherwise, you select Rename so you can rename the old backup files and recover your documents from them later on.

If you understand how the Timed Document Backup feature works, you already realize that it is no substitute for backing up your hard disk. In fact, it only protects you from losing the documents you're working on when some

The Backup screen

```
Setup: Backup

     Timed backup files are deleted when you exit WP normally.  If you
     have a power or machine failure, you will find the backup file in the
     backup directory indicated in Setup: Location of Files.

          Backup Directory                    D:\WPBACK

     1 - Timed Document Backup                Yes
         Minutes Between Backups              10


     Original backup will save the original document with a .BK! extension
     whenever you replace it during a Save or Exit.

     2 - Original Document Backup             No













Selection: 0
```

How to access the Backup screen

WordPerfect 5.0:	Setup > Backup
WordPerfect 5.1:	Setup > Environment > Backup Options

Recommendation

Timed Backups at 5 to 15 minute intervals.

The file names for timed backups

Document 1 = WP{WP}.BK1
Document 2 = WP{WP}.BK2

Figure 6-7   How to set the Backup options

sort of PC failure, power failure, or user error prevents you from exiting properly from *WordPerfect*. So if your hard disk fails or you accidentally delete all the files in a directory, the Timed Document Backup option won't help at all. That's why you should regularly back up your hard disk when you use a PC. If you don't already know how to do that by using DOS or a backup utility, you should find out how to do efficient backups on your PC as soon as you can.

Location of Files   Figure 6-8 shows the Location of Files screens for
WordPerfect 5.0 and 5.1. As you can see, the screen for release 5.0 is called the
Location of Auxiliary Files screen, while the screen for release 5.1 is called the
Location of Files screen. To keep things simple, I'll refer to both screens as
the Location of Files screen. Whether you're using release 5.0 or 5.1, I
recommend that you use this screen to specify the directories for your backup
files and your macro files. If you're using *WordPerfect* 5.1, you may also want
to use this screen to specify the directory for your document files.

By default, the timed backup files are stored in the same directory as the
program files. That usually means your timed backup files are stored in either
C:\WP50 or C:\WP51. To simplify the recovery of the backup files, though, I
recommend that you create a directory that's just for timed backup files. If
you're comfortable with DOS, you can use DOS to create this directory.
Otherwise, you can use *WordPerfect* to create this directory as explained in
chapter 9.

Once you've created a directory for the timed backup files, you need to
tell *WordPerfect* that you want to store your timed backup files in that
directory. To do that, access the Location of Files screen, select the Backup
option, and enter the drive and path of the directory. When you change this
directory on the Location of Files screen, this directory will also be shown on
the Backup screen in figure 6-7. From then on, *WordPerfect* will store your
timed backup files in that directory, and that will make it easier for you to
find the backup files when you need them.

The macro files are also stored in the same directory as the program files
by default. As you can learn in chapter 12, though, you can manage your
macro files more easily if they are stored in a separate directory. That's why
chapter 12 explains how to create a new directory for the macro files and how
to copy the old macros from the *WordPerfect* directory to the macro directory.
Once that's done, you must use the Setup command to change the
Keyboard/Macro Files directory on the Location of Files screen. But don't
make that change until you've read chapter 12.

A little later in this chapter, you'll learn how you can use a special
keyboard known as the ALTRNAT keyboard. If you decide to use that
keyboard and you decide to use a separate directory for your macros, you also
need to copy the ALTRNAT keyboard file to the new macro directory. Since
all keyboard files have a WPK extension, the complete filename for that
keyboard is ALTRNAT.WPK.

If you're using *WordPerfect* 5.1, you can also use the Location of Files
screen to set the default directory for your document files. To do that, just
select the Documents option from the Location of Files screen and type the
drive and directory that contains the document files you want to work on. In
figure 6-8, for example, the directory for documents is set to D:\WPRPTS.
When you set the default directory in this way, you don't have to use the List
command to set it each time that you start a *WordPerfect* session.
Unfortunately, you can't use *WordPerfect* 5.0 to set the default directory in this
way, but chapter 9 shows you how to set it in two other ways.

The Location of Auxiliary Files screen for *WordPerfect* 5.0

The Location of Files screen for *WordPerfect* 5.1

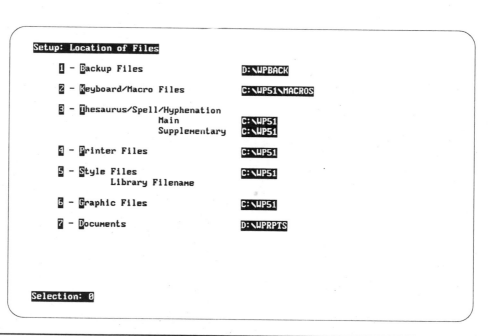

Figure 6-8   The Location of Files screens for *WordPerfect* 5.0 and 5.1

Ten more Setup options that affect the way *WordPerfect* works

Once you get the Initial Codes, Backup Options, and Location of Files set up properly, you've set the defaults that will affect your work the most. However, many of the other Setup options have a minor effect on the way *WordPerfect* works. If you're interested in these, here are ten more options that apply to both *WordPerfect* 5.0 and 5.1.

Units of measure   Figure 6-9 presents the Units of Measure screen. To access this screen, you use the selections shown at the bottom of this figure. Then, when you reach the Units of Measure screen, you can use the first option to set the units of measure for displaying and entering numbers like those for margins and tabs. And you can use the second option for displaying the location of the cursor in the status line of the Edit screen.

Today, most people prefer to use inches as the units of measure. That way, it's easy to enter measurements for margins, tab stops, and so on. If, for example, you want one inch left and right margins, you enter 1 when you set these margins. If you want one and one-half inch margins, you enter 1.5. If you're going to use more than one type size in the same document, you should definitely use inches as the units of measure because that makes it easier for you to format the document. You should also use inches if you're using a laser printer because the number of characters that are printed per horizonal inch usually vary.

If you use units (*WordPerfect* 4.2 Units) as the units of measure, the numbers represent characters when you're moving from left to right across the screen, and they represent lines when you're going from top to bottom. This is consistent with typewriter notation from years past. If, for example, you're using a dot-matrix printer that is going to print at 10 characters per inch, you set the left margin to 10 if you want one-inch margins, and you set it to 15 if you want one and one-half inch margins. This works well as long as you use only one type size in each document.

Date Format   Figure 6-10 shows the Date Format screen. You can use this screen to change the way the date appears when you use the Date command to insert the date in your document. When you use this command, the date probably appears in this format: July 4, 1992. If you want it to appear in a different format like this: 07/04/92, you need to use the Date Format screen to change the format.

If you read the text on the Date Format screen shown in figure 6-10, you should be able to figure out how to set the date format. This screen gives a list of the characters that you can use in a date format, the meanings of each of the characters, and some examples of how they can be used. Then, after you type the new date format, you press the Enter key to complete the format change.

Keyboard Layout   Figure 6-11 shows the Keyboard Layout screen. You can access this screen by selecting the Keyboard Layout option from the main

The Units of Measure screen

```
Setup: Units of Measure

      1 - Display and Entry of Numbers          i
            for Margins, Tabs, etc.

      2 - Status Line Display                   i

  Legend:

      i = inches
      i = inches
      c = centimeters
      p = points
      w = 1200ths of an inch
      u = WordPerfect 4.2 Units (Lines/Columns)




  Selection: 0
```

How to access the Units of Measure screen

WordPerfect 5.0:	Setup > Units of Measure
WordPerfect 5.1:	Setup > Environment > Units of Measure

Recommendation

Use either inches or units.

Figure 6-9 How to change the units of measure

Setup screen for either *WordPerfect* 5.0 or 5.1. Then, you can use this screen to select or create a customized keyboard. In this book, though, I'll only show you how to select one of the customized keyboards, the ALTRNAT keyboard.

If the ALTRNAT keyboard is available on your system, ALTRNAT will be one of the options on the Keyboard Layout screen shown in figure 6-11. To select this keyboard, you just move the highlight to ALTRNAT and press the Enter key. Once you've done that, the meanings of three of the keys on the keyboard are changed. The Esc key becomes the Cancel key; the Cancel key (F1) becomes the Help key; and the Help key (F3) takes on the repeat functions of the Esc key that are presented in chapter 7. Because many programs use the Esc key for canceling commands and the F1 key for accessing the help facility, these changes make the use of these keys more consistent with their use in other programs. When you complete the keyboard change, *WordPerfect* returns you to the main Setup screen. At that screen, you can see that ALTRNAT.WPK is displayed to the right of the Keyboard Layout option.

If someone else has set up your system, the default keyboard may be a customized keyboard like ALTRNAT instead of the normal keyboard. To find out, you can check the main Setup screen to see whether a file name is displayed to the right of the Keyboard Layout option. If a name is present, the keyboard has been customized. Then, if you want to switch back to the original *WordPerfect* keyboard, you can access the Keyboard Layout screen and select the Original option from the selection line at the bottom of the screen. When you do that, *WordPerfect* returns you to the main Setup screen and the customized keyboard name is no longer displayed to the right of the Keyboard Layout option. Throughout this book, I have assumed that you're using the original *WordPerfect* keyboard layout on your PC.

Create Summary on Save/Exit   This feature lets you prepare and print a summary for each document that you create each time you save the document. For most *WordPerfect* users, though, this is a time consuming step that reduces productivity. As a result, I recommend that you turn off the Create Summary on Save/Exit option. To turn this option off in release 5.0, select the Document Summary option from the Initial Settings menu. If you're using *WordPerfect* 5.1, select the Document Management/Summary option from the Environment menu. Even with this option off, you can still use the Format command to create a summary for an individual document. You just won't be prompted to create a summary every time you save a document. Throughout this book, I have assumed that this option has been turned off on your PC.

Fast Save (*WordPerfect* 5.0)   If the Fast Save option is on when you're using release 5.0, *WordPerfect* saves all documents to disk without formatting them. Although this allows *WordPerfect* to save documents more quickly, you can't print fast-saved documents from disk. Instead, you have to retrieve them before you can print them. Because printing a document from disk is a useful feature that is presented in chapter 10, I recommend that you keep the Fast Save option turned off.

Fast Save (*WordPerfect* 5.1)   If you're using release 5.1, I recommend that you turn the Fast Save option on. Although the difference in speed between a regular save and a fast save usually isn't noticeable, this option can save some time when you're working with large files. And unlike the Fast Save option for *WordPerfect* 5.0, there's no disadvantage to using the Fast Save option with *WordPerfect* 5.1 because you can print fast-saved documents from disk.

Cursor Speed   Does the cursor on your screen move too fast or too slow for your level of proficiency? If it does, you can use the Cursor Speed option to change the speed. When you access this option, you are given choices that

The Date Format screen

```
Date Format
    Character   Meaning
    1           Day of the Month
    2           Month (number)
    3           Month (word)
    4           Year (all four digits)
    5           Year (last two digits)
    6           Day of the Week (word)
    7           Hour (24-hour clock)
    8           Hour (12-hour clock)
    9           Minute
    0           am / pm
    %,$         Used before a number, will:
                  Pad numbers less than 10 with a leading zero or space
                  Abbreviate the month or day of the week

    Examples:  3 1, 4        = December 25, 1984
               %6 %3 1, 4    = Tue Dec 25, 1984
               %2/%1/5 (6)   = 01/01/85 (Tuesday)
               $2/$1/5 ($6)  =  1/ 1/85 (Tue)
               8:90          = 10:55am

Date format: 3 1, 4
```

How to access the Date Format screen

Setup > Initial Settings > Date Format

Recommendation

The default is probably the way you want it. If it isn't, set this to the format that you're going to use in most of your documents.

Figure 6-10   How to change the default date format

range from 15 to 50 characters per second. If the speed is already set to 50 characters per second, you can't increase it any more. But you can reduce the speed if the cursor movement is too fast for your level of proficiency.

Automatically Format and Rewrite   When this option is turned off, formatting changes aren't shown on the Edit screen until you move the cursor through the reformatted text. In contrast, when this option is turned on, you don't have to move the cursor through the reformatted text to see the changes. As a result, you probably will want to keep this option turned on.

Repeat Value   In chapter 7, you can learn how to use the Esc key to repeat functions. You use the Repeat Value to set the number of times that the Esc key repeats a function. To change default setting for the Repeat

Value, you use the Repeat Value option of the Initial Settings menu. Normally, though, you don't need to change this setting because the default setting works fine.

Beep Options   Does your PC beep at you more than you want it to when you use *WordPerfect*? If so, you can access Beep Options. Then, you can change one or more of the three beep options. My preference is to turn all three options off because the prompts at the Edit screen let you know what's happening with or without accompanying beeps.

Colors/Fonts/Attributes   When you select Colors/Fonts/Attributes from the Display menu, the menu in figure 6-12 is displayed. You can use these options to change the way your screen displays text. If you have a color monitor, you can use the first option to change the background color of the screen and the color of the text. If your monitor can display graphics, you can also use one of the other options to change the way that text with special attributes like italics or underlining is displayed or what kinds of characters you want displayed. If you don't have a color monitor, the first option isn't available to you, but you might still be able to use one of the other options.

When you select option 1, Screen Colors, a screen like the one in figure 6-13 is displayed that shows the available colors. Then, you can select a foreground color and a background color for each font attribute. And you can use the Move and Switch commands to copy the settings from document 1 to document 2. (If you don't already know how to work on two documents at the same time, you can find out how to do that in chapter 7.) Many people, however, like to use one set of colors for document 1 and another set for document 2 so they can tell which document they're working on without looking at the status line.

Options 2, 3, 4, and 6 in figure 6-12, let you change the way some types of text are displayed or are not displayed on your screen. If, for example, you select the second option, italic characters are displayed in italic form. Similarly, if you select the third option, underlined characters are displayed with a line under them. If you select the sixth option, though, all text is displayed as normal text, but more colors for option 1 are available to you.

Option 5 reduces the total number of colors that *WordPerfect* can display, but it increases the number of special characters that can be displayed. I doubt that you'll select this option unless your work requires Greek symbols, advanced mathematical symbols, or other special characters.

As you would expect, the type of monitor (Monochrome, CGA, EGA, VGA) you have not only affects which options in the Colors/Fonts/Attributes menu are available, it also affect how they work on your screen. So experiment with the options to see what they do. You don't have to worry about getting stuck with a setting that doesn't work for you because they're easy to change.

The Keyboard Layout screen

```
Setup: Keyboard Layout

  ALTRNAT
  ENHANCED
  EQUATION
  MACROS
  SHORTCUT














1 Select; 2 Delete; 3 Rename; 4 Create; 5 Copy; 6 Original;
7 Edit; 8 Map; N Name search: 1
```

How to select the ALTRNAT keyboard

1. Move the highlight to ALTRNAT.
2. Press *1* or *s* to Select that keyboard.

How to return to the regular keyboard

Press *6* or *o*.

The changes in the ALTRNAT keyboard

Key	Normal function	Alternative keyboard function
Esc	Repeat	Cancel
F1	Cancel	Help
F3	Help	Repeat

Figure 6-11   How to change the keyboard layout to the ALTRNAT keyboard

---

The Colors/Fonts/Attributes screen

```
Setup: Colors/Fonts

     1 - Screen Colors

    *2 - Italics Font, 8 Foreground Colors

     3 - Underline Font, 8 Foreground Colors

     4 - Small Caps Font, 8 Foreground Colors

     5 - 512 Characters, 8 Foreground Colors

     6 - Normal Font Only, 16 Foreground Colors




Selection: 0
```

How to access the Colors/Fonts/Attributes screen for *WordPerfect* 5.0 and 5.1

Setup > Display > Colors/Fonts/Attributes

Figure 6-12   The Colors/Fonts/Attributes screen

Four more Setup options that affect the way *WordPerfect* 5.1 works

WordPerfect 5.1 provides many more Setup options than *WordPerfect* 5.0. Some of these are trivial; some aren't. Here are four more options worth mentioning because they can affect how efficiently you use *WordPerfect* 5.1.

Left-Handed Mouse   If you select Mouse from the main Setup menu, you can set the characteristics for the mouse on your PC. If you're left handed, you may want to change the Left-Handed Mouse option from No to Yes. Then, you can use the mouse naturally without having to think about it.

Menu Bar Remains Visible   In chapter 3, I presented the menu interface that comes with *WordPerfect* 5.1, and I recommended that you avoid using it. Now, if your system is set up so the menu bar is displayed across the top of the Edit screen, you can use the Setup command to remove the menu bar. To do that, you select Menu Options from the Display menu. Then, you turn off the Menu Bar Remains Visible option.

The Screen Colors screen

```
Setup: Colors/Fonts              A B C D E F G H
                                 A B C D E F G
Attribute          Font  Foreground  Background  Sample
Normal              N        H           A       Sample
Blocked             N        A           H       Sample
Underline           N        A           H       Sample
Strikeout           N        A           H       Sample
Bold                N        A           H       Sample
Double Underline    N        A           H       Sample
Redline             N        A           H       Sample
Shadow              N        A           H       Sample
Italics             Y        H           A       Sample
Small Caps          N        A           H       Sample
Outline             N        A           H       Sample
Subscript           N        A           H       Sample
Superscript         N        A           H       Sample
Fine Print          N        A           H       Sample
Small Print         N        A           H       Sample
Large Print         N        A           H       Sample
Very Large Print    N        A           H       Sample
Extra Large Print   N        A           H       Sample
Bold & Underline    N        A           H       Sample
Other Combinations  N        A           H       Sample

Switch documents; Move to copy settings      Doc 1
```

How to access the Screen Colors screen for *WordPerfect* 5.0 and 5.1

Setup > Display > Colors/Fonts/Attributes > Screen Colors

Figure 6-13   The Screen Colors screen

Long Document Names   When you use *WordPerfect* 5.1, you can create
long names of up to 68 characters for the documents you save in addition to
the short, 8-character names required by DOS. In theory, this lets you create
names that are more descriptive so you can find your documents more easily.
In practice, though, this also means that you have to take the extra time to
create the long names; that the List screen is only able to display half as many
names on the screen at one time; and that file-handling operations work more
slowly than they do when you use only the short names. As a result, using
long document names tends to reduce your productivity. That's why I
recommend that you avoid using long names.

If you agree, be sure to turn off the Long Document Names option. You
get to this option by selecting Document Management/Summary from the
Environment menu. Throughout this book, I've assumed that this option has
been turned off on your PC.

Format Retrieved Documents for Default Printer   If you often switch files from one PC to another and the PCs have different types of printers, you probably want this option turned on. Then, when you use your PC to retrieve a document that has been prepared on another PC, *WordPerfect* automatically converts the document to the form required by the default printer on your PC. Otherwise, you have to use the Print command to select the correct printer for the document before you print it.

On the other hand, if your PC has access to two or more printers, you probably want this option turned off. Otherwise, when you retrieve a document that is intended to be printed on one type of printer, *WordPerfect* will automatically convert it to the form required by whatever the current default printer is. And that may not be what you want.

Discussion

As you read the other chapters in this section, you'll find that many of the Setup options presented in this chapter will make more sense to you. For instance, chapter 7 shows you how to use the Esc key to repeat functions. After that, you'll have a better understanding of what the F3 key does when you use the ALTRNAT keyboard. Similarly, chapter 8 presents more of the options of the Format command that you may want to set as defaults for the Initial Codes; and chapter 12 explains why it makes sense to set up a separate directory for macros and keyboards.

Similarly, setting the initial base font for a printer will make more sense to you after you read about fonts in chapter 8. This will help you select a font that's appropriate for most of your documents. And if the font is scalable, it will show you how to specify an appropriate type size.

So for now, you should be satisfied to get the Initial Codes, Backup Options, and Location of Files set up right. Later, as you learn more about the other options or as you realize that some of the options aren't working the way you want them to, you can reset those defaults.

Terms

default setting	base font
default	initial base font
font	initial codes

Objectives

1. Use the Print command to change the initial base font for a printer.

2. Use the Setup command to change the defaults for Initial Codes, Backup Options, and Location of Files so that these options are appropriate for your PC and your working style.

3. If you use *WordPerfect* 5.0, use the Setup command to change any of the other ten options that are presented in this chapter. If you use *WordPerfect* 5.1, use the Setup command to change any of the other 14 options that are presented in this chapter. Of course, you should change these options only if *WordPerfect* isn't working the way you want it to.

Chapter 7

The most useful editing skills

If you took the tutorial in section 2 of this book, you have already learned many of the most useful editing skills. As a result, you should already know how to move and copy portions of text, how to delete and restore portions of text, how to search and replace, and how to put a header on the pages of a multi-page document. With that as background, you shouldn't have much difficulty learning other editing skills.

When I speak of "editing skills," I'm referring to those skills that help you enter and modify the words, paragraphs, and pages within a document. That distinguishes editing skills from formatting, file-handling, and printing skills. These skills are presented in the chapters that follow. Because you spend most of your time editing a document, not printing, saving, or formatting it, editing skills are likely to have a major effect on your productivity.

With that in mind, this chapter presents a complete summary of the most useful editing skills. That includes the skills that you were introduced to in section 2, and it includes some new skills. If you experiment with all of these skills as you use *WordPerfect*, you'll soon have most of them mastered. But whenever you need to refresh your memory, you can use the summaries in this chapter for quick and efficient reference.

How to move the cursor efficiently

Figure 7-1 summarizes the keystroke combinations that you use for moving the cursor as efficiently as possible. Here, the plus sign (+) means that you press the second key while you hold down the first key. To move the cursor one word to the right, for example, you hold down the Ctrl key and press the Right arrow key. On the other hand, a space between two key names means that you press each key in succession. To move the cursor to the left of a line, for example, you press the Home key followed by the Left arrow key.

If you use *WordPerfect* much, you should probably memorize all of the keystrokes in this summary because speeding up cursor movement is a quick way to improve your efficiency. At the least, you should memorize the combinations in the first four groups. In addition, you may want to experiment with the Plus and Minus keys on the numeric pad when Num-lock is off; these keys provide another way of moving to the top and bottom of a screen. And if you work with multi-page documents much, you may want to experiment with the Go to command to see whether it helps you move from one page to another faster than you can by using the Page-up and Page-down keys.

When you use the Home key and the Arrow keys, notice how the number of times that you press the Home key affects where the cursor is placed in relation to codes. If you press the Home key three times and then press the Up arrow key, *WordPerfect* moves the cursor to the beginning of the document before any codes. If you press the Home key three times and then press the Left arrow key, *WordPerfect* moves the cursor to the left of the current line before any codes. Otherwise, *WordPerfect* moves the cursor after the codes. When you work with formatting codes, cursor movement can be critical because some codes need to be placed before other codes.

How to use the Block command to block text

The Block command is used to identify a block of text as illustrated by the highlighted text in figure 7-2. After you have identified a block, you can perform functions on it. For instance, you can move, copy, or delete it; you can put paired formatting codes around it; you can print or save it; and you can check the spelling in it.

Figure 7-2 summarizes the procedure for blocking text. In step 1, you move the cursor to the first character or code that you want in the block. In step 2, you access the Block command. A blinking "Block on" message then appears in the status line. Then, in step 3, you move the cursor to the right of the last character or code that you want included in the block. At that point, you're ready to perform a function on the block. If you change your mind, you can cancel the command by accessing the Block command again or by accessing the Cancel command.

Once you access the Block command, you can move the cursor by pressing the key of the character that you want to move the cursor to. If, for example, you press the letter *k*, the cursor will jump to the next *k* in the text. If you press the Period key, the cursor will jump to the next period (usually, the end of a sentence). And if you press the Enter key, the cursor will jump to the next hard return code (usually, the end of a paragraph). In most cases, this is the most efficient way to move the cursor. At times, however, it's more efficient to use the keystroke combinations for cursor movement that are summarized in figure 7-1.

	Keystrokes	Function

Ctrl key and the Arrow keys

	Keystrokes	Function
	Ctrl+Right	Moves the cursor right one word at a time
	Ctrl+Left	Moves the cursor left one word at a time
	Ctrl+Up (5.1)	Moves the cursor up one paragraph at a time
	Ctrl+Down (5.1)	Moves the cursor down one paragraph at a time

The Home key and the Arrow keys

Home Left	Moves the cursor to the left of the line after all codes
Home Right	Moves the cursor to the right of the line after all codes
Home Up	Moves the cursor to the top of the Edit screen
Home Down	Moves the cursor to the bottom of the Edit screen
Home Home Up	Moves the cursor to the top of the document after all codes
Home Home Home Up	Moves the cursor to the top of the document before all codes
Home Home Down	Moves the cursor to the bottom of the document after all codes
Home Home Home Left	Moves the cursor to the left of the line before all codes

The End key

End	Moves the cursor to the right of the line after all codes

The Page keys

Page-up	Moves the cursor to the top of the previous page
Page-down	Moves the cursor to the top of the next page

The Plus (+) and Minus (-) keys on the numeric pad with Num-lock off

+	Moves the cursor to the bottom of the Edit screen
-	Moves the cursor to the top of the Edit screen

How to use the Go to command to go to a specific page

1. Access the Go to command (Ctrl+Home) to display this prompt:

   `Go to`

2. Type the page number you want to move the cursor to and press the Enter key. This moves the cursor to the top of that page.

Figure 7-1   How to move the cursor efficiently

How to use the Move command to move or copy text

The Move command lets you move or copy text from one part of your document to another. This command works on sentences, paragraphs, pages, and blocks of text. Since it is one of *WordPerfect*'s most useful commands, you should take the time to master it.

How to move or copy a sentence, paragraph, page, or block

Figure 7-3 summarizes the use of the Move command for moving or copying. If you're going to move or copy a complete sentence, paragraph, or page, you should use this command without blocking as shown in the first procedure. In step 1, you move the cursor to any point in the sentence, paragraph, or page that you want to move or copy. Note that you don't have to put the cursor on the first character of the sentence, paragraph, or page. In step 2, you access the Move command. And in step 3, you select Sentence, Paragraph, or Page. When you do that, *WordPerfect* highlights the entire sentence, paragraph, or page automatically. As you can see, this is more efficient than using the Block command to highlight a sentence, paragraph, or page because you use fewer keystrokes.

In step 4, you select Move or Copy. If you select Move, the text is deleted from the Edit screen and copied into *WordPerfect*'s memory. If you select Copy, the text remains on the Edit screen, but it is also copied into *WordPerfect*'s memory. Then, in step 5, when you move the cursor and press the Enter key, the text in *WordPerfect*'s memory is copied into the document at the cursor location. This completes the move or copy function.

If you're not going to move or copy a complete sentence, paragraph, or page, you use the second procedure in figure 7-3. In this procedure, you start by using the Block command to identify the text that you want to move or copy. This block can be as short as a single code or a single character, or it can extend over many pages. Then, in step 2, you access the Move command. In step 3, you select Block. And in steps 4 and 5, you continue just as you would if you were moving a sentence, paragraph, or page.

If you're using *WordPerfect* 5.1, you can move or copy a block of text more efficiently by using the third procedure in figure 7-3. In step 2, you use Ctrl+Insert to tell *WordPerfect* that you want to copy the block or Ctrl+Delete to tell it that you want to move the block. Then, in step 3, you move the cursor to where you want the block inserted into the document and press the Enter key.

When you use the Move command, it's often difficult to put the cursor in exactly the right place before you complete the move or copy function. After you move a sentence, for example, you're likely to end up with four spaces after the sentence you moved and none before it. To deal with this problem, you just have to pay attention to what's being moved or copied. When you use the Move command to select a sentence, for example, notice how *WordPerfect* highlights the period and the space or spaces after the period, but not the spaces before the sentence. Then, if you want to move this sentence to the

An Edit screen with blocked text

```
         Why we should upgrade from WordPerfect 5.0 to 5.1

Unlike WordPerfect 4.2 and 5.0, WordPerfect 5.0 and 5.1 share the
same structure.  Although some of the existing features have been
enhanced, none of them have been drastically changed.  WordPerfect
5.1 does, however, offer some new features including a Tables
feature, Mouse support, and Pull-down menus.

        At the end of this report, I'm going to recommend that our
editors upgrade from WordPerfect 5.0 to 5.1.  But first, I'm going
to briefly describe the tables feature.  I think that this feature
alone makes it worthwhile to upgrade.  I'm also going to present a
brief analysis of the benefits and costs of converting to
WordPerfect 5.1.  When you finish this report, you can decide
whether you would like more information on any of these subjects.
If so, I'll be happy to get it for you.

The Tables feature  The Tables feature can be used for several
purposes, even as a simple spreadsheet.  If you combine the Tables
feature with the Math feature, for example, you can use formulas
to calculate each cell within the table.  However, the Tables
feature is no substitute for a spreadsheet.  It doesn't provide as
many features as a spreadsheet, it's not as efficient, and it's
not as easy to use.
Block on                               Doc 1 Pg 1 Ln 2.84" Pos 5.33"
```

How to block text

1. Position the cursor at the first character that you want in the block.
2. Access the Block command (Alt+F4 or F12).
3. Highlight the block by moving the cursor past the last character in the block. If you change your mind and want to cancel the block, access the Block command again or access the Cancel command (F1).

Tips for efficient blocking

1. If you're using a 101-key keyboard, use F12 to access the Block command, not Alt+F4.
2. To move the cursor after you access the Block command, press the key for any character to move the cursor to that character. To move to the end of a sentence, for example, press the Period key. To move to the end of a paragraph, press the Enter key. Usually, this method of blocking is faster than using the cursor control keys.

Figure 7-2   How to use the Block command to block text

beginning of a paragraph, you must move the cursor to the first letter in the first word of the paragraph and press the Enter key. This will put the sentence at the start of the paragraph with two spaces after it so the spacing should be correct.

Similarly, when you use the Move command to select a paragraph, *WordPerfect* selects the paragraph plus all of the hard returns after the paragraph. Although you can't see these hard returns highlighted on your Edit screen, they're still going to be moved with the rest of the paragraph. Then, if you want to move the paragraph ahead of another paragraph, you must move the cursor to the start of that paragraph before you complete the command.

How to use the Retrieve function of the Move command   When you use the Move command to move or copy a sentence, paragraph, page, or block, you press the Enter key to retrieve the text the first time. However, the text remains in *WordPerfect*'s memory. Then, if you want to retrieve that text again, you can use the Retrieve function of the Move command as summarized in figure 7-4.

In step 1, you move the cursor to where you want to retrieve the last sentence, paragraph, page, or block that has been copied or moved. That's what has been stored in *WordPerfect*'s memory. Then, in steps 2 and 3, you access the Move command and select Retrieve from the four options shown in the prompt. In step 4, you select Block from the three options shown in the prompt. This retrieves the text into the document.

You can repeat this function as many times as you want to duplicate text within a document because *WordPerfect* continues to save the last sentence, paragraph, page, or block that has been operated upon by the Move command. You can also use this function to retrieve text that has been deleted by the Move command. However, it's usually easier to use the Cancel command to restore text that has been deleted. I'll show you how to do that in a moment.

How to delete and undelete text and codes

WordPerfect provides several methods for deleting text and codes. At the simplest level, you can use the Backspace key to delete the character or code to the left of the cursor. And you can use the Delete key to delete the character at the cursor. To delete as efficiently as possible, though, you should learn all of the methods that are summarized in figure 7-5.

How to use keystroke combinations for deleting   Figure 7-5 shows you the keystroke combinations for deleting a word, for deleting text from the cursor to the end of the line, and for deleting text from the cursor to the end of the page. When you delete a word, the cursor doesn't have to be on the first character of the word. (In *WordPerfect* terms, a *word* is any group of

How to move or copy a sentence, paragraph, or page

1. Position the cursor somewhere within the sentence, paragraph, or page that you want to move or copy.
2. Access the Move command (Ctrl+F4).

   `Move: 1 Sentence; 2 Paragraph; 3 Page; 4 Retrieve: 0`

3. Select Sentence, Paragraph, or Page.

   `1 Move; 2 Copy; 3 Delete; 4 Append: 0`

4. Select Move or Copy.

   `Move cursor; press Enter to Retrieve.`

5. Position the cursor where you want the text to be inserted and press the Enter key.

How to move or copy a block of text

1. Use the Block command (Alt+F4 or F12) to block the text you want to move or copy.
2. Access the Move command (Ctrl+F4).

   `Move: 1 Block; 2 Tabular Column; 3 Rectangle: 0`

3. Select Block.

   `1 Move; 2 Copy; 3 Delete; 4 Append: 0`

4. Select Move or Copy.

   `Move cursor; press Enter to Retrieve.`

5. Position the cursor where you want the text to be inserted and press the Enter key.

How to use Ctrl+Insert and Ctrl+Delete to move or copy a block of text (*WordPerfect* 5.1)

1. Use the Block command to block the text you want to move or copy.
2. To copy the block, press Ctrl+Insert. To move the block, press Ctrl+Delete.

   `Move cursor; press Enter to retrieve.`

3. Position the cursor where you want the text to be inserted and press the Enter key.

Tips for efficient moving and copying

1. To move or copy sentences, paragraphs, and pages, use the Move command without blocking any text.
2. To move or copy text that isn't a sentence, paragraph, or page, block the text and then move or copy it.

Figure 7-3   How to use the Move command to move or copy text

1. Move the cursor to where you want the text to be retrieved.
2. Access the Move command (Ctrl+F4).

   Move: 1 Sentence; **2** Paragraph; **3** Page; **4** Retrieve: **0**

3. Select Retrieve.

   Move: 1 Block; **2** Tabular Column; **3** Rectangle: **0**

4. Select Block and the text will be retrieved into the document just to the left of the cursor.

Figure 7-4   How to use the Retrieve option of the Move command

characters that has one or more spaces before and after it.) When you delete to the end of the line, *WordPerfect* deletes to the end of the line that the cursor is on, not to the end of the sentence. And when you delete to the end of the page, *WordPerfect* displays this prompt:

Delete Remainder of page? No (Yes)

This prevents you from accidentally deleting a large portion of text.

How to use the Move command to delete a sentence, paragraph, or page   When you want to delete a sentence, paragraph, or page, the Move command provides an efficient way for doing that as summarized in figure 7-5. In steps 1 through 3, you use the Move command just as though you were going to perform a move or copy function. In step 4, you select the Delete function to complete the command. If a sentence is short, you can often delete it just as fast by using the keystroke combinations for deleting single words and for deleting text to the end of the line. But otherwise, this method is more efficient for deleting sentences, paragraphs, and pages than any of the other methods.

How to delete a block of text   When you want to delete a portion of text that isn't a complete sentence, paragraph, or page, you can use the Block command to highlight the block that you want to delete as summarized in figure 7-5. Then, you can press the Delete key to delete the block. This displays a prompt like the one shown in the figure. When you select Yes, the deletion is completed. If you're deleting a block of text that's shorter than a sentence, you can probably delete more efficiently by using the keystroke combinations for deleting words and deleting text to the end of the line. But otherwise, this is the most efficient method for deleting a portion of text that isn't a complete sentence, paragraph, or page.

How to delete codes   When you delete a sentence, paragraph, page, or block of text, the codes within that unit are also deleted. When you delete one

Keystrokes	Function

How to use keystroke combinations for deleting

Ctrl+Delete	Deletes the word the cursor is at
Ctrl+Backspace	Deletes the word the cursor is at
Ctrl+End	Deletes from the cursor to the end of the line
Ctrl+Page-down	Deletes from the cursor to the end of the page

How to use the Move command to delete a sentence, paragraph, or page

1. Position the cursor anywhere within the sentence, paragraph, or page that you want to delete.
2. Access the Move command (Ctrl+F4).

   `Move: 1 Sentence; 2 Paragraph; 3 Page; 4 Retrieve: 0`

3. Select Sentence, Paragraph, or Page.

   `1 Move; 2 Copy; 3 Delete; 4 Append: 0`

4. Select Delete.

How to delete a block

1. Use the Block command (Alt+F4 or F12) to block the text that you want to delete.
2. Press the Delete key.

   `Delete Block? No (Yes)`

3. Select Yes.

Tips for efficient deleting

1. Use the keystroke combinations to delete words, to delete to the end of line, and to delete to the end of the page.
2. Use the Move command to delete a sentence, paragraph, or page.
3. Use the Block command to delete blocks of text that you can't delete efficiently with either of the first two methods.

Figure 7-5   How to delete text

word at a time, though, the codes before or after the words aren't deleted. In some cases, this can lead to formatting results that you don't want. Then, you have to find the codes that are causing the problems and delete them. If necessary, you can access the Reveal Codes command to display the codes. Then, you can delete the codes by pressing the Delete or Backspace key.

---

1. Position the cursor where you want to restore text.
2. Access the Cancel command (F1).

   Undelete: 1 Restore; **2** Previous Deletion: **0**

3. To cycle through the previous three deletions, select Previous Deletion. When you find the text you want to restore, select Restore. If you want to exit from this feature, press the Cancel or Esc key.

Figure 7-6   How to use the Cancel command to restore text

If you use the Delete or Backspace keys to delete characters when the Reveal Codes screen isn't displayed, *WordPerfect* displays a message like this when it reaches certain types of formatting codes:

Delete [BOLD]? No (Yes)

In this case, the message asks whether you want to delete a code for boldfacing. Then, if you want to delete the code, you can select Yes. Otherwise, you can press the Delete or Backspace key again to skip over the code. In chapter 8, you'll get complete information about finding and deleting different types of formatting codes.

How to use the Cancel command to restore text that you've deleted   If you delete text accidentally or decide that you shouldn't have deleted it after all, you can use the Cancel command to *restore* the text that you have deleted. Since this function can bring back text that has been deleted, it is sometimes referred to as the *undelete* function. This function is summarized in figure 7-6.

In step 1, you move the cursor to the point where you want to restore a deletion. In step 2, you access the Cancel command. This displays the last text that was deleted at the cursor. Then, in step 3, if you want to restore the text that is displayed, you select Restore. Otherwise, you can select Previous Deletion to see the previous deletion. If you continue to select Previous Deletion, you will cycle through the last three deletions that were made by any of the methods shown in figure 7-5. If you want to restore one of the previous deletions, you select Restore. Otherwise, you can access the Cancel command again to cancel the restore function.

In some cases, it's more efficient to use the delete and restore functions to move text than it is to use the Move command. If, for example, you want to move three words from one part of a sentence to another, you can delete the three words using the Ctrl+Delete key combination. Then, you can move the cursor to the place in the sentence where you want to retrieve the words and use the restore function to retrieve them. You can also use the restore function when you want to insert a deletion into a document more than once.

How to use the Search command

You can use the Search command to quickly move the cursor to any string of letters, numbers, characters, or codes in your document. Although the Search command may seem complicated at first, it's easy to use. And once you master it, you'll find that it makes editing documents, especially long ones, much easier.

There are several ways that you can use the Search command to improve your efficiency as you edit a document. For instance, you can use the command to move the cursor to where you want to begin editing. You can use the command to search for frequently misused words like *it's* to make sure that you used them correctly. You can use the command to search for terms to make sure that you used them consistently. And you can use the command to search for formatting codes within the document to make sure that your document was formatted consistently.

How to search for a search string   If you look at the command template, you can see that it includes two Search commands. The *forward search* (F2) searches from the cursor to the end of a document. The *backward search* (Shift+F2) searches from the cursor to the start of the document.

Figure 7-7 shows how to use the Search command. In step 1, you move the cursor to where you want the search to begin. In step 2, you access the command for either a forward or backward search. *WordPerfect* then displays a prompt that asks you to enter a *search string*. This string contains the combination of characters and codes that you want to search for. In step 3, you enter the search string. And in step 4, you press the F2 key to start either a forward or backward search. Be sure to press the F2 key, though, not the Enter key. If you press the Enter key, a hard return code [HRt] is inserted into the search string.

When you start the Search command in step 2 of the procedure in figure 7-7, the prompt that follows indicates the direction of the search. For a forward search, the prompt starts with an arrow to the right. For a backward search, the arrow goes to the left. At this prompt, you can enter a search string of up to 59 letters, numbers, characters, and codes. You can also change the direction of the search at the prompt by using the Arrow keys. To change to a backward search, press the Up arrow key. To change to a forward search, press the Down arrow key.

When the search begins, *WordPerfect* searches for the first occurrence of the search string. If it finds one, it moves the cursor to the first character to the right of that occurrence. If it can't find an occurrence of the search string, *WordPerfect* flashes a Not Found prompt on the left side of the status line.

If one occurrence of the search string is found, you can search for the next occurrence by performing the forward or backward search again. When you access the Search command, the old search string is displayed again. Then, you just have to press the F2 key to search for the next occurrence of that string.

How to search forward and backward for text

1. Move the cursor to where you want the search to begin.
2. If you want to search forward, press the F2 key. If you want to search backward, press Shift+F2.

   | >Srch: | (prompt for a forward search) |
   | <Srch: | (prompt for a backward search) |

3. Enter the search string.
4. Press the F2 key, not the Enter key to start the search. If *WordPerfect* finds a sequence of characters that matches the search string, it stops with the cursor to the right of the match. If *WordPerfect* can't find a match, it briefly displays this message:

   | * Not Found * |

Some typical search strings

>Srch: analysis
>Srch: [BOLD]
<Srch: [HRt][HRt]
>Srch: [HRt][BOLD]

Figure 7-7   How to use the Search command

In figure 7-7, you can see some typical search strings. If, for example, you want to search for the word *analysis*, you just type it in. If you want to search for words that are boldfaced, you press the F6 key to enter the Bold code as the search string. If you want to search for the ends of paragraphs in single-spaced documents, you press the Enter key twice to enter two hard return codes. If you want to search for boldfaced headings, you press the Enter key followed by the Bold key to find Bold codes that are on the left margin of the document.

How to edit or replace the search string   Each time you start a forward or backward search, *WordPerfect* recalls the previous search string if there was one. Then, if you want to search for something that is slightly different from your previous search string, use the Right arrow key, the Left arrow key, or the End key to move the cursor to the part of the string that you want to change. This tells *WordPerfect* that you want to edit the existing search string. At that point, you can use Insert mode to insert characters or codes into the search string. Or you can use Typeover mode to replace characters or codes in the existing string.

On the other hand, if you want to erase the previous search string completely and enter a new one, just start typing when the old search string is displayed. In this case, *WordPerfect* erases the old string as soon as you type the first character of the new string. You can then enter a new search string from scratch.

The effects of case and spaces in the search string   Figure 7-8 presents examples that will help you understand the effects of case (uppercase and lowercase) and spaces in the search string. As you can see, uppercase (capital) letters in a search string will only find other uppercase letters. Lowercase letters, on the other hand, will find both uppercase and lowercase letters. So if you want to find all occurrences of a word, you use all lowercase letters in the search string. But if you want to find a word only when it's at the beginning of a sentence or only when it's capitalized, you must use uppercase letters in the search string.

To limit the words that a search will find, you can use spaces as illustrated in figure 7-8. If, for example, you want to find the word *table* but not the word *tables*, you can end the search string with a space. However, this search string will still find the word *stable*. Although you can't see the spaces when you type them in the search string, they can help make your search strings more specific.

How to use the Replace command

If you know how to use the Search command, you shouldn't have any trouble with the Replace command. This command searches for a search string just like the Search command. But when it finds an occurrence of the search string, it replaces that string with the *replace string* that you entered. Because the Replace command is closely related to the Search command, it's often referred to as the Search and Replace command.

How to use the Confirm option   Figure 7-9 shows you how to use the Replace command. In step 1, you move the cursor to where you want the replace function to start. Often, this is at the top of a document. Then, when you start the Replace command in step 2, *WordPerfect* displays this prompt:

w/Confirm? No (Yes)

In step 3, if you're not sure that you want to replace every occurrence of your search string with the replace string, select Yes. In step 4, if you want to search backwards, press the Up arrow key. Then, in steps 5 and 6, you enter the search string for the function, and you end it by pressing the F2 key. In step 7, you enter the replace string. And in step 8, you start the Replace function by pressing the F2 key.

When the function starts, it searches for the first occurrence of the search string. When it finds one, *WordPerfect* displays a prompt like this:

Confirm? No (Yes)

If you select Yes, the first occurrence of the search string is replaced by the replace string, and *WordPerfect* looks for the next occurrence of the search

The effect of case in the search string

Search string	Finds	Doesn't Find
tables	TABLES Tables tables	
Tables	TABLES Tables	tables
TABLES	TABLES	Tables tables

The effect of spaces [sp] in the search string

Search string	Finds	Doesn't Find
table	table tables stable table.	
table[sp]	table stable	table. tables
[sp]table[sp]	table	tables stables table.

The combined effects of case and spaces [sp] in the search string

Search string	Finds	Doesn't find
[sp]TABLE[sp]	TABLE	TABLES STABLE Table table
table	every occurrence	

Figure 7-8   The effects of case and spaces in the search string

string. If you select No, that occurrence of the search string is left as it is, and *WordPerfect* looks for the next occurrence. This process continues until you've had a chance to confirm or deny the replacement of all occurrences of the search string. If you decide that you want to cancel the command at any point along the way, you can press the Cancel key.

How to replace a search string with a replace string

1. Move the cursor to the starting point for the Replace Function.
2. Access the Replace command (Alt+F2).

   `w/Confirm? No (Yes)`

3. If you want to confirm each replacement, select Yes. If you don't, select No.

   `>Srch:`

4. If you want to search backward, press the Up arrow key.
5. Enter the search string.
6. Press the F2 key.

   `Replace with:`

7. Enter the replace string.
8. Press the F2 key.

Some typical search and replace strings

w/Confirm?	Search string	Replace string
Yes	[sp]5	five
Yes	which	that
No	wordperfect	WordPerfect
No	wordperfect	[UND]WordPerfect[und]
Yes	[HRt][HRt]	[HRt][HRt][Tab]
Yes	[BOLD]	

Figure 7-9   How to use the Replace command

Like the Search command, the Replace command can help you edit more efficiently. For instance, you can search for the numbers 1 through 10 and replace them in their spelled-out form (a common editorial standard) as shown in the first example in figure 7-9. You can search for the word *which* and replace it with the word *that* (whenever *that* is appropriate) to make your writing less formal as shown in the second example. If you've been writing about *WordPerfect* and have been spelling it without capitalizing the letter *p*, you can search for *wordperfect* and replace it with *WordPerfect* as shown in the third example. If you decide that you want to underline all occurrences of *WordPerfect* because it is a product name, you can do that as shown in the fourth example. If you decide that you want to indent all paragraphs, you can do that as shown in the fifth example. And if you decide that you don't want to use boldfacing to emphasize words, you can remove the boldfacing as shown in the sixth example. Here, since there is no replace string, the boldface codes are replaced with nothing. In other words, the codes are deleted. Because it takes only a second or two for each replacement, this command works much more quickly than you can.

How to globally replace   If you selected No in step 3 to indicate that you didn't want to confirm each replacement, the Replace command replaces every occurrence of the search string with the replace string without any prompting. In this case, the function can be called a *global replace*.

Because a global replace function can drastically change a document in just a few seconds, here are two precautions you can take when you use it. First, you can save your document before you execute the global replace. Then, if the global replace function doesn't work quite the way you want it to, you can clear the screen, retrieve the old document, and try it again. Second, you can try the search string that you're going to use in a Search command before you try it in the Replace command. That way, you can be sure that the search string will find just what you want it to find.

Global replaces are often used to clean up documents that have been imported into *WordPerfect* from another program. To delete unnecessary codes, for example, you can use a global replace with an empty replace string. Global replaces can also be used to prepare documents for desktop publishing. For this purpose, the search string usually contains one or more formatting codes, and the replace string usually contains one or more desktop publishing codes.

How to work on two documents at the same time

When you use *WordPerfect*, you usually work on just one document at a time. When you finish your work on one document, you save your work, clear the screen, and start work on the next document. Sometimes, though, it makes sense to work on two documents at the same time. Then, you can copy or move text from one of the documents to the other.

How to use the Switch command to work on two documents at the same time   To work on two documents at the same time, you use the Switch command to switch from one document to the other. The use of this command is summarized in figure 7-10.

To start, you can retrieve two documents into *WordPerfect* as summarized by the first procedure in figure 7-10. In step 1, you retrieve the first document. In step 2, you access the Switch command. This clears the Edit screen and switches you to Document 2. This is indicated by the designation *Doc 2* in the status line. Then, in step 3, you retrieve the second document.

At this point, you can access the Switch command whenever you want to switch from one document to the other. When you leave one document, *WordPerfect* remembers the cursor location. Then, when you switch back to that document, the cursor is in the same place.

How to retrieve two documents

1. Retrieve the first document.
2. Access the Switch command (Shift+F3). If your screen isn't divided into windows, document 1 will disappear and you will get a blank Edit screen. However, the status line on this Edit screen will show you're on document 2. If your screen is divided into windows, the Switch command moves the cursor from one window to the other one.
3. Retrieve the second document. Now, the Switch command will switch back and forth between these two documents.

How to move or copy text from one document to the other

1. Start the move or copy function for a sentence, paragraph, page, or block in one of the two documents.

   `Move cursor; press **Enter** to Retrieve.`

2. Access the Switch command (Shift+F3) to move to the other document.
3. Move the cursor to where you want to move or copy the text. Then, press the Enter key.

How to exit from document 2

1. Use the Save command (F10) to save the document.
2. Access the Exit (F7) command.

   `Save document? Yes (No)                    (Text was not modified)`

3. Select No.

   `Exit Doc 2? Yes (No)`

4. Select Yes. This returns you to document 1.

Tips for working on two documents at the same time

1. The Switch command switches between document 1 and document 2.
2. The status line always shows what document you're working on.
3. If you use the Screen command (see figure 7-11) to divide your Edit screen into windows, the top window is always document 1 and the bottom window is always document 2.

Figure 7-10   How to use the Switch command to work on two documents at the same time

One of the primary uses of the Switch command is to copy or move text from one document to another. To do that, you use a procedure like the second one in figure 7-10. When the Move command prompts you to move the cursor, you use the Switch command to switch to the other document. Then, you can move the cursor to the appropriate location in that document and press the Enter key to complete the command.

When you're through working on one of the documents, you can save the document and exit to the other document. To do that, you use the third procedure shown in figure 7-10. Although this example is for exiting from Document 2, it works the same way in reverse if you're exiting from Document 1. After you save the document and access the Exit command, the final prompt asks if you want to exit from the document:

Exit Doc 2? Yes (No)

If you do, select Yes, to return to the other document. If you don't, select No, to clear the screen. Then, you can start work on another Document 2.

How to use the Screen command to divide the screen into windows   In some cases, you can work more efficiently if Document 1 and Document 2 are both on the same screen. To make that possible, you use the Screen command to divide the screen into two *windows*. Then, you can switch your eyes from one document to the other without using any keystrokes.

To divide a screen into windows, you use the first procedure in figure 7-11. In steps 1 and 2, you access the Screen command and select Window. In step 3, you type the number of lines that you want in the first window and press the Enter key. For a standard 24 line screen, a value of 12 divides the screen into two windows as shown in this figure. Here, the top window has 12 lines plus a status line; the bottom window has 10 lines plus a status line; and one line is used to separate the two windows.

If you look at the status line in the top window in figure 7-11, you can see that it is for Document 1. Similarly, the bottom window is for Document 2. To switch from one window (or document) to the other, you use the Switch command just as though the screen weren't divided into windows.

When you want to return to the full Edit screen, you use the second procedure in figure 7-11. Then, when you get the prompt in step 2, you enter a number that's equal to or larger than the number of lines in a full screen. Usually, 24 is large enough, but you can use a number like 99 if you're not sure how many lines the screen can hold.

How to use the Switch command to switch case

If you block a portion of text before you access the Switch command, you can use the command to switch the text in the block from uppercase to lowercase, or vice versa. This procedure is summarized in figure 7-12. This is useful, for instance, when you want to capitalize a block of text for use in a heading. When you use the Switch command this way, you don't have to re-enter the text you want capitalized.

The Edit screen with two windows

```
Outline for WordPerfect 5.1 report

Introduction
        Evolutionary upgrade
        The Tables feature

The Tables feature
        Spreadsheet functions
        Presentation of tabular data

The cost of converting to 5.1


                                        Doc 1 Pg 1 Ln 2.67" Pos 4.4"
```

Window 1
Doc 1

```
{                                        }

The Tables feature  The Tables feature can be used for several
purposes, even as a simple spreadsheet.  If you combine the Tables
feature with the Math feature, for example, you can use formulas
to calculate each cell within the table.  However, the Tables
feature is no substitute for a spreadsheet.  It doesn't provide as
many features as a spreadsheet, it's not as efficient, and it's
not as easy to use.

        However, the Tables feature is an efficient way to present
D:\WPRPTS\51REPORT                      Doc 2 Pg 1 Ln 4.01" Pos 1.5"
```

Window 2
Doc 2

How to divide the Edit screen into two windows

1. Access the Screen command (Ctrl+F3).

    0 Rewrite; **1** Window; **2** Line Draw: **0**

2. Select Window.

    Number of lines in this window: 24

3. Type the number of lines for the first window (usually, 12, which is half the number of lines shown), and press the Enter key.

How to restore the Edit screen to a single window

1. Access the Screen command (Ctrl+F3).

    0 Rewrite; **1** Window; **2** Line Draw: **0**

2. Select Window

    Number of lines in this window: 12

3. Type the number of lines for a full screen (usually, 24), and press the Enter key.

Figure 7-11   How to use the Screen command to divide the Edit screen into two windows

1. Use the Block command (Alt+F4 or F12) to mark the text.
2. Access the Switch command (Shift+F3).
   1 Uppercase; 2 Lowercase: 0
3. Select Uppercase or Lowercase.

Figure 7-12   How to use the Switch command to change the case of a block of text

How to insert the current date into a document

Most PCs today automatically keep track of the current date and time. On the older PCs, you are asked to enter the correct date and time as part of the DOS start-up procedure. But either way, the current date is available to *WordPerfect*, and you can insert it in your documents without typing it.

The first procedure in figure 7-13 shows how to insert the current date into a document. In step 1, you move the cursor to where you want the date inserted, and you access the Date/Outline command. In step 2, you select the Date Text or the Date Code option. If you select the Text option, the current date is inserted into the document as if you typed it. If you select the Code option, *WordPerfect* inserts a code into your document that is automatically updated each time you retrieve the document. As a result, the date in the document is always the current date.

When the date is inserted into your document, it is in the default date format for your system. If you want to use a different format, you must change the date format before you insert the date into your document. To do that, you use the second procedure in figure 7-13. When you select the Date Format option in step 2, the screen shows you the characters that you can use in a format specification along with their meanings and examples. Although this screen may seem formidable at first, you should be able to figure out what the format codes should be for the date format that you want. Then, in step 3, you type the codes and press the Enter key. This changes the date format until you change the format again or end the *WordPerfect* session. If you want to change the date format for future sessions too, you use the Setup command as described in chapter 6.

How to use headers and footers with multi-page documents

When you prepare a document of two or more pages, it often makes sense to put a *header* on each page of the document. A header usually contains identifying information like the date, file name, and page number. Although you enter a header only once, you can set it so it's printed automatically on

How to insert the date into a document

1. Position the cursor where you want the date to be inserted. Then, access the Date/Outline command (Shift+F5).

    `■ 1 Date Text; 2 Date Code; 3 Date Format`

2. Select Date Text by pressing *1* or *t*, or select Date Code by pressing *2* or *c*. If you want to change the date format, select Date Format before you select Date Text or Date Code.

How to change the date format

1. Access the Date/Outline command (Shift+F5).

    `■ 1 Date Text; 2 Date Code; 3 Date Format`

2. Select Date Format by pressing *3* or *f* to get this screen:

```
Date Format

        Character   Meaning
        1           Day of the Month
        2           Month (number)
        3           Month (word)
        4           Year (all four digits)
        5           Year (last two digits)
        6           Day of the Week (word)
        7           Hour (24-hour clock)
        8           Hour (12-hour clock)
        9           Minute
        0           am / pm
        %,$         Used before a number, will:
                      Pad numbers less than 10 with a leading zero or space
                      Abbreviate the month or day of the week

        Examples:   3 1, 4        = December 25, 1984
                    %6 %3 1, 4    = Tue Dec 25, 1984
                    %2/%1/5 (6)   = 01/01/85 (Tuesday)
                    $2/$1/5 ($6)  =  1/ 1/85 (Tue)
                    8:90          = 10:55am

Date format: 3 1, 4
```

3. Type a format string like one of the examples, and press the Enter key. This format will stay in effect until you end the *WordPerfect* session.

Figure 7-13   How to use the Date command to insert the current date into a document

each page of the document. A *footer* works the same way a header does, but a footer is printed at the bottom of each page.

When you use *WordPerfect*, you can use two different headers (A and B) and two different footers (A and B) for a single document. From a practical point of view, though, you can usually get by with just a single header or a single footer. With that in mind, this book only shows you how to use a single header (Header A) with a document. But if you understand how to use a single header, you shouldn't have any trouble using a second header or a footer if that need develops. To work with footers instead of headers, you just select Footers from the Format Page screen.

How to create a header   Figure 7-14 gives the steps for creating a header. In step 1, you move the cursor to the top of the first page that you want the header to be printed on. If you want the header to start on the first page, the cursor must be at the top of the document before any text. However, the cursor should be after any formatting codes that are supposed to apply to the header as well as to the rest of the document.

In step 2, you access the Format command and select the Page option so the Page screen is displayed. In steps 3 and 4, you select the appropriate options from the prompts that are displayed: Headers from the Page screen, and Header A from the next prompt. Then, in step 5, you decide whether you want the header printed on Every Page, Odd Pages only, or Even Pages only. If you're using both a header A and a header B, you can set one up for odd pages and one for even pages. Usually, though, you'll select Every Page so the one header that you use prints on every page.

At that point, a Header screen like the one in figure 7-14 is displayed and the Edit screen disappears. Then, in step 6, you enter the header into this screen. And in step 7, you press the Exit key twice: once to exit from the Header screen; once to exit from the Format command.

The Header shown in figure 7-14 is only one line long. It contains the date, a centered file name, and a right aligned page number (I'll explain the ^B code in a moment). If necessary, though, a header can be more than one line. If you want just one line skipped between the header and the rest of the document, don't press the Enter key at the end of the last line in the header because one line is skipped automatically. If you want more than one line skipped, press the Enter key once for each extra line that you want skipped.

When you complete the procedure for creating a header, *WordPerfect* inserts a header code into the document at the cursor location. If you want to delete the header, you can delete the header code with a single keystroke.

How to edit a header   If you discover a mistake in the header or you want to modify it for some other reason, you can delete the header code and create a new header. Or you can correct the header by using the first procedure in figure 7-15. This is like the procedure for creating a header with

A Header screen

August 19, 1992   51REPORT   Page ^B

`Header A:` Press `Exit` when done   `Ln 1" Pos` 7"

The procedure for creating a header

1. Move the cursor to the top of the first page that you want the header to print on.
2. Access the Format command (Shift+F8) and select Page to get to the Page screen.
3. Select Headers from the Format Page screen.

   1 Header **A**; **2** Header **B**: **0**

4. Select Header A.

   1 Discontinue; **2** Every **P**age; **3 O**dd Pages; **4 E**ven Pages; **5 E**dit: **0**

5. Select Every Page to display the Header screen.
6. Enter a header. *WordPerfect* will automatically skip one line between the header and the document, so don't type a hard return at the end of the header unless you want more than one line skipped.
7. Press the Exit key twice to return to Edit screen

Figure 7-14   How to use the Format command to create a header for a document

two exceptions. First, the cursor doesn't have to be in any specific location when you edit a header. Second, you select the Edit function in step 4 of the procedure.

How to stop the printing of a header   If you want to stop the header from printing after a certain page, you can use the second procedure in figure 7-15. This is like the procedure for creating a header with two exceptions. First, the cursor should be at the point in the document where you want to discontinue the printing of headers. Second, you select the Discontinue function in step 5 of the procedure. This inserts a Discontinue code in the document that prevents the header from printing after the code.

Three more skills for working with multi-page documents

When you work with documents of more than one page, moving the cursor from page to page as summarized in figure 7-1 is one important skill. Using headers and footers as summarized in figures 7-14 and 7-15 is another. Now, here are three more skills that are important for working with multi-page documents.

How to start a new page   As you enter a document into your PC, *WordPerfect* keeps track of the page and line number that you're on. Then, when you reach the bottom of one page, *WordPerfect* automatically inserts a *soft page break* code [SPg] into the document and starts a new page. This kind of *page break* is indicated by a single dashed line on the screen.

Sometimes, though, you want to start a new page before you reach the bottom of a page. Then, you use the first keystroke combination (Ctrl+Enter) in figure 7-16. This inserts a *hard page break* code [HPg] into the document. This kind of page break is indicated by a double dashed line on the screen. If you decide later that you don't want to start the new page at that point, you can delete the hard page break code with the Backspace or Delete key.

How to insert the page number on a page or in a header   If you want to print the page number on a page, you use the second keystroke combination (Ctrl+B) in figure 7-16. This keystroke combination inserts a code into the document that looks like this:

^B

Although this looks like two characters, it is actually a single code that represents the current page number. As a result, this code prints as 1 on page 1 of a document, and it prints as 7 on page 7 of a document.

Usually, you use this code in the header or footer of a document as illustrated by the Header screen in figure 7-14. Here, you can see the code on the right side of the header. However, you can use this code outside of a header or footer whenever you want to print the current page number on a page.

How to edit a header

1. Access the Format command (Shift+F8) and select Page to get to the Format Page screen. (Cursor location doesn't affect this step.)
2. Select Headers from the Format Page screen.

   1 Header **A**; **2** Header **B**: **0**

3. Select Header A or Header B to identify the header that you want to edit.

   1 Discontinue; **2** Every Page; **3** Odd Pages; **4** Even Pages; **5** Edit: **0**

4. Select Edit.
5. Edit the header on the Header screen.
6. Press the Exit key twice to return to Edit screen.

How to stop the printing of a header

1. Move the cursor to where you want to discontinue printing the header. Usually, this is at the top of a new page.
2. Access the Format command (Shift+F8) and select Page to get to the Page screen.
3. Select Headers from the Format Page screen.

   1 Header **A**; **2** Header **B**: **0**

4. Select Header A or Header B to identify the header that you want to stop printing.

   1 Discontinue; **2** Every Page; **3** Odd Pages; **4** Even Pages; **5** Edit: **0**

5. Select Discontinue to insert the Discontinue code into the document.
6. Press the Exit key to return to the Edit screen.

Figure 7-15   How to edit a header or stop the printing of a header

How to number pages without using headers or footers   When you prepare a multi-page document, you may want to number the pages of a document without using a header or a footer. To do that, you can use the Format command as summarized in figure 7-17.

In step 1, you move the cursor to the top of the page that you want to start the numbering on. In steps 2 and 3, you start the Format command, select Page, and select Page Numbering. If you're using *WordPerfect* 5.1, this leads you to the menu shown in step 3. From this menu, you select Page Number Position in step 4. Then, the screen at the top of figure 7-17 is displayed. But if you're using *WordPerfect* 5.0, you can skip this step because the selection in step 3 goes directly to the screen at the top of the figure.

In step 5, you type the number of the page number position that you want for page numbering. You get this number from the screen that is displayed. If, for example, you want the page number printed in the upper left corner on every page, type *1*. If you want the number printed in the upper left corner of even numbered pages and the upper right corner of odd

Keystrokes	Function
Ctrl+Enter	Inserts a hard page break [HPg] into the document
Ctrl+B	Inserts an automatic page number into the document

Figure 7-16   Keystroke combinations for working with multi-page documents

numbered pages, type *4*. When you type the number, the page numbering code is inserted into your document and you are returned to the Format Page screen. Then, in step 6, press the Exit key to return to the Edit screen.

How to use the Esc key to repeat functions

When you're in the middle of a command, you can often press the Esc key to back out of the command. But when you're not using a command, the Esc key has another use. Then, it can be used to repeat functions as summarized in figure 7-18.

When you press the Esc key while you're at the Edit screen, it displays a prompt like this one:

Repeat Value = 8

This shows how many times the next keystroke combination that you enter is going to be repeated. If you want to change this Repeat Value, you type a new number at the prompt and press the Enter key. This returns you to the Edit screen.

To repeat a function, you use the second procedure in figure 7-18. In step 1, you press the Esc key to display the current Repeat Value. If this value is the one you want, you can skip to step 3. But otherwise, you can type the number of times you want the function repeated in step 2. This time, though, you shouldn't press the Enter key to change the Repeat Value; just leave the new value displayed on the screen.

Then, in step 3, you press the keystroke combination that starts the function that you want to repeat. If, for example, the Repeat Value is 8 and you press the Esc key followed by the letter *x*, 8 *x*'s are entered into the document. If you press the Esc key followed by the Up arrow key, the cursor moves up 8 lines. If you press the Esc key followed by the Ctrl+Right arrow key combination, the cursor moves eight words to the right. If you press the Esc key followed by the Page-down key, the cursor moves down eight pages. And if you execute a macro (you can learn how to do that in chapter 12) after you press the Esc key, the macro is executed 8 times. If you decide that you want to cancel a repeat function before you press the keystroke combination, you press the Esc key again.

The Page Number Position screen

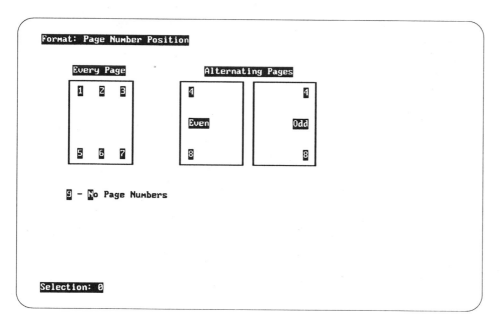

The procedure for numbering the pages without using a header or footer

1. Move the cursor to the top of the page that you want to start page numbering on. Usually, this is the first page.
2. Access the Format command (Shift+F8) and select Page to get to the Format Page screen.
3. Select Page Numbering from the Format Page screen. For *WordPerfect* 5.0 users, the screen above is displayed. For *WordPerfect* 5.1 users, this menu is displayed:

   ```
   1 - New Page Number      1
   2 - Page Number Style    ^B
   3 - Insert Page Number
   4 - Page Number Position No Page Numbering
   ```

4. For *WordPerfect* 5.1 users only: Select Page Number Position to display the screen above. *WordPerfect* 5.0 users skip this step.
5. Type the number of the position that you select from the Page Number Position screen shown above. For instance, the number *3* means that the page numbers will be printed in the upper right corner within the margins of every page.
6. Press the Exit key to return to the Edit screen.

Figure 7-17   How to use the Format command to number pages without using a header or footer

I'm presenting this use of the Esc key last because it isn't an important editing skill. However, it is useful occasionally. If, for example, you want to enter a series of ruled lines in a document, you can set the repeat value to the length of your line. Then, you can press the Esc key followed by the Underline key (not the Underline command) for each line that you want to enter into the document.

Discussion

As you master the skills presented in this chapter, your productivity should increase. In a matter of seconds, you should be able to move your cursor to the spot in your document that you want to edit. In a few keystrokes, you should be able to move, copy, or delete sentences, paragraphs, pages, or blocks of text. You should be able to use the Search and Replace commands whenever they can help you find and correct editorial problems. You should be able to work on two documents at the same time when you need to copy or move text from one document to another. And you should be able to use headers and footers on multi-page documents, and to number the pages without headers or footers whenever that's appropriate.

Although each chapter in this section of the book is designed to be as independent as possible, you may have noticed that editing skills are closely related to formatting skills. In particular, you can use many of the editing skills in this chapter as you work with formatting codes. For instance, you can block, delete, move, copy, search for, and replace codes. After you read the next chapter that presents the most practical formatting skills, you'll better understand how editing and formatting skills are related. Then, you'll be able to use both types of skills with maximum efficiency.

Terms

restore
undelete
forward search
backward search
search string
replace string
global replace
window
header
footer
soft page break
page break
hard page break

Objectives

1.   Move the cursor efficiently through a document by using the keystroke combinations presented in this chapter.

How to set the repeat value

1. Press the Esc key.

   ▌**Repeat Value = 8**

2. Type the new value and press the Enter key.

How to repeat functions

1. Press the Esc key to display the Repeat Value (n).
2. If you want to change the Repeat Value, type the new value, but don't press the Enter key.
3. Use any of the following keystrokes or keystroke combinations to repeat a function n times:

Keystrokes	Function
Any character	Inserts the character into the document n times
Up arrow	Moves the cursor up n lines
Down arrow	Moves the cursor down n lines
Left arrow	Moves the cursor left n lines
Right arrow	Moves the cursor right n lines
Page-down	Moves the cursor n pages forward
Page-up	Moves the cursor n pages backward
Ctrl+Right arrow	Moves the cursor n words forward
Ctrl+Left arrow	Moves the cursor n words backward
Delete	Deletes n characters to the right starting at the cursor
Ctrl+Delete	Deletes n words to the right starting at the cursor
Ctrl+End	Deletes n lines down starting at the cursor
Execute a macro	Performs the macro n times (Chapter 12 shows you how to define and execute macros.)

How to cancel a repeat function after you press the Esc key

Press the Esc key again or press the Cancel key.

Figure 7-18   How to use the Esc key to repeat functions

2. Move, copy, or duplicate a sentence, paragraph, page, or block within a document as efficiently as possible.

3. Delete any of the following as efficiently as possible:

   Words
   Text to the end of the line
   Text to the end of the page
   Sentences, paragraphs, or pages
   Blocks

4. Restore any of the last three deletions.

5. Use the Search command to find any valid search string consisting of text or codes.

6. Use the Replace command to replace any valid search string with any replace string.

7. Use the Switch command to work on two documents at the same time.

8. Use the Screen command to divide the Edit screen into two windows and the Switch command to switch between the windows.

9. Use the Switch command to switch the case of a block of text.

10. Insert a date into a document in either text or code form.

11. Create, edit, or stop the printing of a header or footer for a document.

12. Number the pages of a document without using a header or footer.

13. Use the Esc key to repeat functions.

Chapter 8

The most practical formatting skills

If you read the tutorial in section 2 of this book, you have already learned some of the most practical formatting skills. As a result, you should already know how to indent paragraphs, how to boldface or underline text, how to center and right align lines of text, and how to change some of the formatting options like the left, right, top, and bottom margins. With that as background, you shouldn't have much trouble learning other formatting skills.

Because *WordPerfect* offers so many formatting options, you can waste a lot of time if you experiment with all of them. As a result, this chapter presents only the most practical formatting skills. That includes the skills that you were introduced to in section 2, and it includes many new skills. If you master these skills, you'll be able to present your documents in an attractive form that's easy to read. And you'll be able to concentrate on the content of your writing instead of the formatting details.

When I speak of "formatting skills," I mean those skills that change the way a document looks when it is printed. That distinguishes formatting skills from editing, file-handling, and printing skills. These skills are presented in other chapters in this section of the book. Because the font that you use for a document has a major effect on the way the document looks, I'll start by introducing you to fonts.

An introduction to fonts

The term *font* refers to the kind of type, or typeface, that is used when a document is printed. When you prepare documents like letters and memos, you're likely to use only one font in an entire document. For documents like proposals or newsletters, though, you may decide to use more than one font in a single document. To identify a font, you give its type family and its type size.

The name of the *type family* determines the general characteristics of the font. In figures 8-1 and 8-2, for example, you can see a couple of typical type families for dot-matrix and laser printers. In figure 8-1, the name of the first type family is Roman; the name of the second one is Sans Serif. In figure 8-2, the name of the first family is Times Roman; the name of the second one is Helvetica.

A *serif* is a horizontal line on the bottom or top of a vertical line in a character such as an *l* or an *m*. Some type families have serifs, and some don't. The ones that don't are referred to as *sans serif* type families. In figure 8-1, the Roman font has serifs; the Sans Serif font doesn't. In figure 8-2, the Times Roman font has serifs; the Helvetica font doesn't. Since sans serif typefaces are more difficult to read than typefaces with serifs, the primary font that you use for a document should be from a type family with serifs. Then, if necessary, you can use a sans serif font for special purposes within a document.

After you select a type family, you should select a *type size*. If you're using a dot-matrix printer, this size is usually expressed in characters per inch, or *cpi*, and the two most common sizes are 10 cpi and 12 cpi. Besides these two sizes, most dot-matrix printers also provide for larger and smaller type sizes, but you should only need these for special purposes such as report titles or footnotes. In figure 8-1, you can see some of the type sizes that are available on my dot-matrix printer.

If you're using a laser printer, the type size is expressed in *points* with 72 points to the vertical inch. When you use points, the larger the number, the larger the type size. For most documents, 10- or 12-point type is appropriate for the primary font. In figure 8-2, you can see a range of type sizes for a laser printer.

A dot-matrix printer usually prints at six lines per inch, no matter what type size you use. As a result, the *line height* is 1/6 of an inch. That means that there's more white space between the lines when you use a 12 cpi font than there is when you use a 10 cpi font. Since this makes the 12 cpi font easier to read, I recommend this size for most business documents, although the 10 cpi size is also acceptable.

In contrast, a laser printer varies the line height based on the type size. If you let *WordPerfect* adjust the line height automatically, two points are added to the type size to get the line height. If, for example, you use a 10 point font, the line height is 12 points. If you use a 12 point font, the line height is 14 points. This two point space between the lines is called *leading* (pronounced ledding). Although two points of leading is appropriate when you're working with 10 or 12 point type, it often isn't appropriate when you're using larger or smaller type.

Generally, most of the fonts on a dot-matrix printer are *mono-spaced fonts*. That means that the same amount of space is used for each character in the font. For example, an *i* in a mono-spaced font takes up the same amount of space as a *w*. In contrast, when you use a *proportionally-spaced font*, the amount of space used for each letter depends on the width of the letter. For instance, an *i* in a proportionally-spaced font takes up less space than a *w*. In figure 8-1, you can see these differences in mono-spaced and proportionally-spaced fonts. When you select a proportionally-spaced font for a dot-matrix printer,

Type families

Roman (a font with serifs)

This font is from a type family called Roman. It has serifs, so it is easier to read than a sans serif font.

Sans Serif (a sans serif font)

This font is from a type family called Sans Serif. Since this is a sans serif font, you'll probably want to use it sparingly.

Type sizes

5   characters   per   inch
10 characters per inch
12 characters per inch
15 characters per inch
17 characters per inch

Line height

Most printing on a dot-matrix printer is done at six lines per vertical inch, no matter how many characters per inch are printed horizontally. As a result, the line height is 1/6 of an inch, or 12 points.

Mono-spaced and proportional fonts

A mono-spaced font

Most fonts on a dot-matrix printer are mono-spaced. This one is Roman 12 cpi so it prints at 12 characters per inch. Note that each character, including the space before and after the character, takes up the same amount of space.

A proportional font

This is Roman PS, a proportionally-spaced font. Note that the letter *i*, including the space before and after it, takes up less space than the letter *m* or *o.*

Figure 8-1   Typical type families and type sizes for dot-matrix printers

the letters *PS* usually appear after the type family name, and the number of characters per inch isn't specified.

When you use a laser printer, all of the fonts are likely to be proportionally spaced. In addition, some fonts are relatively wide and some are relatively narrow as illustrated in figure 8-2. As a result, you often have to count the number of characters in a line or two of a document to see how many characters there are in an average line. If you want your documents to be easy to read, you should set your margins so the average line contains no more than 66 characters.

If you're a graphics designer, you shouldn't have any trouble selecting fonts and formatting your documents so they are attractive and easy to read. But if you don't have any graphics training, this can be a problem. In that case, the best advice is to keep your fonts and formatting simple. For most documents, select a font with serifs in the 10 to 12 cpi or 10 to 12 point size. Then, make sure that your margins are set so the average line contains 66 characters or fewer.

How to prepare for efficient formatting

Before you start a entering text for a document, you should prepare it for efficient formatting. To do that, you should make sure that the units of measure are set up right and that the appropriate printer has been selected for the document.

How to use the Setup command to set the units of measure   In chapter 6, you can learn how to use the Setup command to set the units of measure that *WordPerfect* uses. This procedure is summarized in figure 6-9. Because measurements in inches are easier to understand, most people prefer to use inches as the units of measure. Also, inches work best when you use more than one font in a single document or when you use proportionally-spaced fonts.

Some people, however, still prefer to use *WordPerfect* 4.2 units as the units of measure. These units represent characters when you see them in left to right measurements, and they represent lines when you see them in top to bottom measurements. When you use units, the numbers of characters per inch depends on the type size. As a result, an 8-1/2 by 11 inch form is 85 characters wide and 66 lines long when it's printed at 10 cpi, and it's 102 characters wide and 66 lines long when it's printed at 12 cpi. Because of these complexities, I recommend that you use units only when you use a dot-matrix printer and a single font for a document.

How to select the printer for a document   If your PC has only one printer attached to it, you don't have to worry about selecting a printer for the document. But if your PC has more than one printer or if you're on a network that provides more than one printer, you should select the printer that you're going to use for a document before you start it.

Type families

Times Roman (a font with serifs)

This font is from a type family called Times Roman. It has serifs, so it is easier to read than a sans serif font.

Helvetica (a sans serif font)

This font is from a type family called Helvetica. Since this is a sans serif font, you'll probably want to use it sparingly.

Type sizes

7 points
10 points
12 points

20 points

Line height

This is Times Roman in 9 point size with two points leading so the line height is 11 points.

This is Helvetica in 12 point size with two points leading so the line height is 14 points.

Number of characters per horizontal inch

Most laser fonts are proportionally spaced so you may have to count the number of characters in a line or two of printing to make sure that the lines are 66 characters or less. This is Times Roman, which is a relatively wide font.

Most laser fonts are proportionally spaced so you may have to count the number of characters in a line or two of printing to make sure that the lines are 66 characters or less. This is Helvetica, which is a relatively narrow font.

Figure 8-2   Typical type families and type sizes for laser printers

The Select Printer screen

```
Print: Select Printer
 Apple LaserWriter Plus
* Epson LQ-850
```

```
1 Select; 2 Additional Printers; 3 Edit; 4 Copy; 5 Delete; 6 Help; 7 Update: 1
```

How to select the printer

1. Access the Print command (Shift+F7).
2. Select the Select Printer option. This displays a screen like the one above.
3. Move the highlight to the printer that you're going to use for the document. Then, press the Enter key.
4. Press Exit to return to the Edit screen. This printer selection stays in force for new documents until you change it.

Figure 8-3 How to select the printer for a document

To select a printer, you use the procedure in figure 8-3. In step 1, you access the Print command. On the Print screen next to the Select Printer option, you can see the name of the *current printer*. If this is the printer that you want to use for the document, you can return to the Edit screen. Otherwise, you select the Select Printer option in step 2. This displays a Select Printer screen like the one in figure 8-3. Then, in steps 3 and 4, you move the highlight to the printer that you want to use, press the Enter key to select it, and press the Exit key to return to the Edit screen.

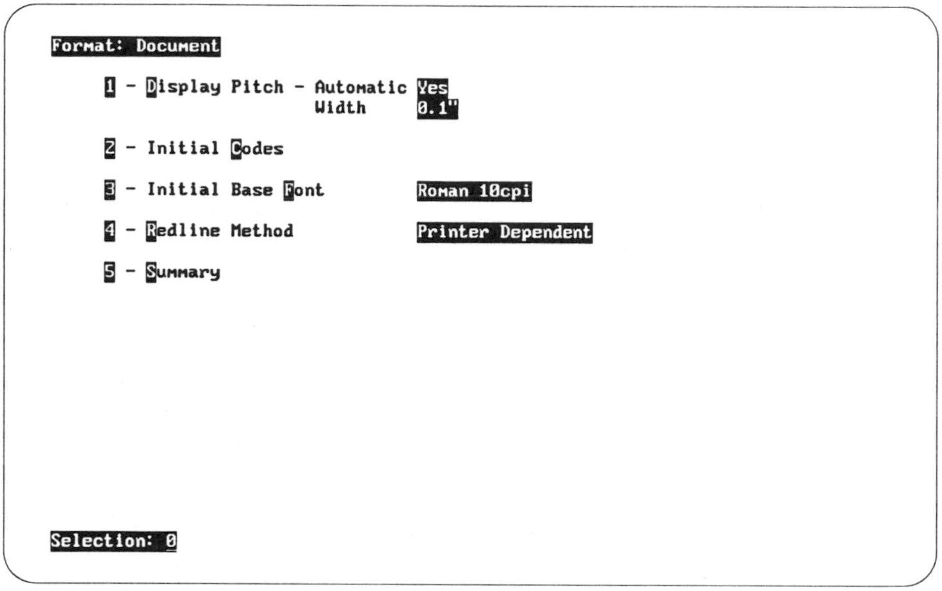

```
Format: Document
        1 - Display Pitch - Automatic  Yes
                            Width       0.1"

        2 - Initial Codes

        3 - Initial Base Font           Roman 10cpi

        4 - Redline Method              Printer Dependent

        5 - Summary




Selection: 0
```

Figure 8-4   The Document screen of the Format command

When and how to set the Document options of the Format command

When you start a new document, it's given the default settings for your system. If, for example, the default settings for the left and right margins are one inch, a new document is given those settings. Then, if you want to change those defaults, you can use the Document options of the Format command. In contrast to the Line and Page options of the Format command, the Document options let you change the defaults for the entire document without inserting codes into the document.

Figure 8-4 displays the Document screen of the Format command. You reach this screen by accessing the Format command and selecting the Document option. Then, you can use the Initial Base Font option to select the font that you want to use for your document. And you can use the Initial Codes option to change the default settings for the entire document. I'll show you how to use both of these options now.

How to set the Initial Base Font for a document   The third option on the Document screen is Initial Font for *WordPerfect* 5.0 and Initial Base Font for *WordPerfect* 5.1, but I'll refer to both as the Initial Base Font option from now on. In *WordPerfect* terms, the *base font* is the font that's in force as you work on a document; and the *initial base font* is the base font that is in force when you start work on a document.

In figure 8-5, you can see some of the font choices for the current printer. In this example, the current printer is a dot-matrix printer. If the font selection isn't followed by a size in characters per inch, its size is implied by words like *condensed* and *dbl-wide*. And PS means that the font is proportionally spaced.

To change from the initial base font for a document when you're using a typical dot-matrix printer, you use the procedure that's summarized in figure 8-5. In step 1, you access the Initial Base Font option of the Format command. This displays a listing of all the fonts that are available for the current printer. In step 2, you move the highlight to font you want and press the Enter key to select it. This returns you to the Document screen where you can see the change in the initial font.

To change from the initial base font for a document when you're using a laser printer, you follow the procedure in figure 8-6. In step 1, you access the Initial Base Font option of the Format command. This displays a listing of all the fonts that are available for the current printer. In step 2, you move the highlight to the font you want and press the Enter key to select it. What you do next depends upon whether you selected a *scalable font* or a *non-scalable font*.

If a font is non-scalable, its type size is given in points as in this example:

Times Roman 12pt

Then, when you select the font and press the Enter key in step 2 of the procedure in figure 8-6, *WordPerfect* returns you to the Document screen where you can see the change in the initial font.

If the font is scalable, though, no size is given after it as illustrated by the fonts in the screen in figure 8-6. Then, when you select a font in step 2, *WordPerfect* displays this message:

Point size:

So in step 3, you type the point size that you want for the initial base font and press the Enter key. This returns you to the Document screen. There, you can see the change in the initial font.

In the past, only laser printers supported scalable fonts. Today, however, you can buy dot-matrix printers that support scalable fonts. If your dot-matrix printer is one of these, follow the procedure in figure 8-6 when you want to change the initial base font for your document to a scalable font.

How to set the Initial Codes for a document   To change the default settings for a new document, you can use the Initial Codes option of the Document menu as summarized in figure 8-7. When you access this option, a screen like the one in this figure is displayed. If nothing is shown below the separating line in the middle of the screen, all of *WordPerfect*'s original defaults for the initial codes remain in effect. If there are codes below the line, however, someone has made changes to *WordPerfect*'s defaults by using the Setup command as explained in chapter 6. As a result, the codes below the line override the original default settings that came with *WordPerfect*. In

The Initial Font screen for a dot-matrix printer

```
Document: Initial Font
  Roman  5cpi
  Roman  5cpi  Italic
  Roman  6cpi
  Roman  6cpi  Italic
  Roman  7cpi
  Roman  7cpi  Italic
* Roman 10cpi
  Roman 10cpi  Italic
  Roman 12cpi
  Roman 12cpi  Italic
  Roman 15cpi
  Roman 15cpi  Italic
  Roman 17cpi
  Roman 17cpi  Italic
  Roman 20cpi
  Roman 20cpi  Italic
  Roman PS
  Roman PS Condensed
  Roman PS Condensed Italic
  Roman PS Dbl-Wide
  Roman PS Dbl-Wide Italic

1 Select; N Name search: 1
```

How to change the Initial Font

1. Access the Initial Font screen through the Format command (Shift+F8) like this:

   WordPerfect 5.0:   Format > Document > Initial Font
   WordPerfect 5.1:   Format > Document > Initial Base Font

   This displays a screen like the one above.

2. Move the cursor to the font you want to use. For most business documents, a font with serifs that prints at 12 characters per inch is appropriate. When you press the Enter key, *WordPerfect* returns you to the Document screen where you can see the change in the initial font.

Note: If you're using *WordPerfect* 5.1, you can also use Initial Codes to set the initial font. If you do, the font specified by Initial Codes overrides the font specified by Initial Font.

Figure 8-5   How to change the Initial Font for a document without inserting codes into the document when the current printer is a typical dot-matrix printer

this example, the second and third codes override the original justification setting and the original left and right margin settings.

To add a code to those shown below the line of the Initial Codes screen, you access the Format command again as indicated by step 2 in the procedure in figure 8-7. I know that this is confusing because you just accessed the Format command to get to the Initial Codes option, but that's the way this formatting option works. To change the left and right margins, for example, you access the Format command while you're at the Initial Codes screen. Then, you select Line from the Format screen and Margins from the Line screen. After you change the margin settings, you press Exit to return to the Initial Codes screen. You will then see the code for the margin settings below the line in the center of the screen. To change any of the other Format options for the document, you proceed in the same way.

If you want to delete one of the codes below the line of the Initial Codes screen, move the cursor to the code and press the Delete key as described in step 3 of the procedure in figure 8-7. This returns that setting to the original *WordPerfect* default setting. If, for example, you don't want left and right margins of 1.5 inches as shown in the Initial Codes screen in figure 8-7, you move the cursor to this code and press the Delete key. This returns the margins to the *WordPerfect* default setting of 1 inch.

In figure 8-7, you should delete the first code on the Initial Codes screen. If you leave it there, this code takes precedence over the Initial Base Font code. Since that can be confusing, it's better to delete the code on the Initial Codes screen and to use the Initial Base Font option of the Document screen to set the initial base font.

You should know that if you see two codes for the same option on the Initial Codes screen, the last one on the screen is the one that's in force. Also, if you're using *WordPerfect* 5.0, you can't use the Font command at the Initial Codes screen to set the initial base font for a document. Instead, you have to set it using the Initial Base Font option of the Document screen shown in figure 8-4.

When you've got the Initial Codes the way you want them, you press the Exit key once to return to the Document screen or twice to return to the Edit screen. Then, you can start preparing the document with the knowledge that the initial base font and the formatting codes are set the way you want them.

Later, if you want to change one of the codes for the entire document, you can access the Format command again, select the Document option, and change the codes just as though you hadn't started work on the document. This applies the codes to the entire document without inserting them into the document.

If this seems like a cumbersome way to set the formatting options for a document, it is. Why then should you use the Document options of the Format command to code your document instead of inserting the formatting codes into the document using the Line and Page options of the Format command? First, if you use the Document options, you don't have to worry about putting the codes in the wrong place in the document or about deleting

The Initial Font screen for a laser printer

```
Document: Initial Font
× Courier
 Courier Bold
 Courier Bold Oblique
 Courier Oblique
 Helvetica
 Helvetica Bold
 Helvetica Bold Oblique
 Helvetica Narrow
 Helvetica Narrow Bold
 Helvetica Narrow Bold Oblique
 Helvetica Narrow Oblique
 Helvetica Oblique
 ITC Avant Garde Gothic Book
 ITC Avant Garde Gothic Book Oblique
 ITC Avant Garde Gothic Demi
 ITC Avant Garde Gothic Demi Oblique
 ITC Bookman Demi
 ITC Bookman Demi Italic
 ITC Bookman Light
 ITC Bookman Light Italic
 ITC Zapf Chancery Medium Italic

1 Select; N Name search: 1
```

How to change the Initial Font

1. Access the Initial Font screen through the Format command (Shift+F8) like this:

    WordPerfect 5.0:   Format > Document > Initial Font
    WordPerfect 5.1:   Format > Document > Initial Base Font

    This displays a screen like the one above.

2. Move the cursor to the font you want to use. If you select a font that isn't scalable, a point size of 10 or 12 is appropriate for most business documents. When you press the Enter key, *WordPerfect* returns you to Document screen where you can see the change in the initial font.

3. If you select a scalable font, a prompt like this appears:

    Point size: 10

    Type the point size that you want to use. Here again, a point size of 10 or 12 is appropriate for most business documents. When you press the Enter key, *WordPerfect* returns you to the Document screen where you can see the change in the initial font.

Note: If you're using *WordPerfect* 5.1, you can also use Initial Codes to set the initial font. If you do, the font specified by Initial Codes overrides the font specified by Initial Font.

Figure 8-6   How to change the Initial Font for a document without inserting codes into the document when the current printer is a laser printer

The Initial Codes screen

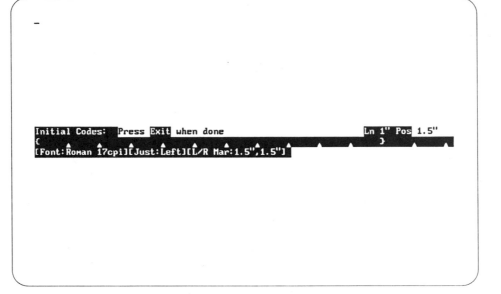

```
Initial Codes:  Press Exit when done                          Ln 1" Pos 1.5"
{                                                                  }
[Font:Roman 17cpi][Just:Left][L/R Mar:1.5",1.5"]
```

How to change the Initial Codes

1. Access the Initial Codes screen through the Format command (Shift+F8) like this:
    Format > Document > Initial Codes

2. Access the Format command again. Then, use the Line and Page options to set any formatting codes.

3. Use the Delete key to delete any codes.

4. Press the Exit key to return to the Document screen of the Format command.

5. Press the Exit key to return to the Edit screen.

Figure 8-7   How to change the Initial Codes for a document without inserting codes into the document

them accidentally. Second, it's sometimes easier to change the default formats by using the Initial Codes screen than it is to insert overriding codes. If, for example, you want to return to your systems's default settings, you just delete the codes on the Initial Codes screen that you don't want. Third, if you combine two or more documents with inserted codes that conflict, you have to find and delete the codes that you don't want. In contrast, if you combine two or more documents that have used the Document options, the codes of the first document are applied to other ones.

How to set the primary Line, Page, and Other options of the Format command

By the time you read this chapter, you should know how to use a command like the Format command. To access it, you use the keystroke combination shown on the template (Shift+F8). Then, to move from one of its menus to another, you press the number or letter of the option that you want to select. When you reach an option that asks for a response, you type the response and press the Enter key. If, at any time, you want to go back one screen, you can press the Escape or Cancel key. And if you want to go all the way back to the Edit screen, you can press the Exit key. In general terms, that's the way all *WordPerfect* commands work.

When you access the Format command, a screen like the one in figure 8-8 is displayed. This screen is simply a menu with four options: Line, Page, Document, and Other. Then, if you select Line, a screen like the first one in figure 8-9 is displayed. If you select Page, a screen like the second one in figure 8-9 is displayed. These are the screens that you'll use most of the time when you want to insert a formatting code into a document. As I've already explained, though, you should use the Document options to change the defaults that apply to the entire document.

Figure 8-10 summarizes the primary options of the Format command. These are the ones that are presented in this book, and these are the ones you should know how to use. To make sure that you know what each of the options does, I'll describe each one briefly. These descriptions will be in the same sequence as the options in figure 8-10. Although that sequence isn't completely logical, that's the sequence that you have to work with when you use *WordPerfect*.

Justification   This term *justification* refers to the alignment of the text when it's printed, although this alignment doesn't appear on the Edit screen. If a document is printed with *justified text*, the text is flush with both the left and right margins of the document. If a document is printed with *ragged-right text*, the text is flush on the left but not on the right.

For most business documents like letters, memos, and internal reports, ragged-right text is preferable to justified text for a couple of reasons. First, studies have shown that ragged-right text is easier to read than justified text. Second, you rarely have to worry about hyphenating words when you use ragged-right text. That's why I recommend that you use ragged right text for most of the documents that you prepare.

For *WordPerfect* 5.0, that means the Justification option should be set to No. For *WordPerfect* 5.1, this option should be set to Left. Because the *WordPerfect* default setting is for justified text, you should use either the Setup command to change this default for your system or the Document options of the Format command to change this default for the document.

Line Spacing   This option specifies the line spacing for a document. For instance, a value of 1 represents single spacing, and a value of 2 represents

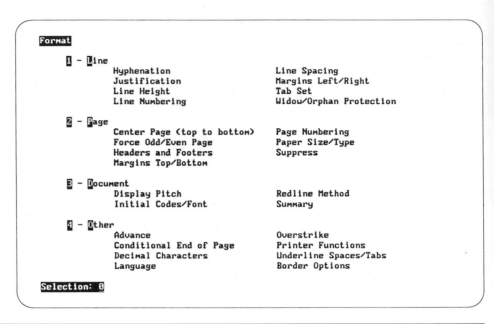

Figure 8-8   The main Format screen

double spacing. Since this spacing shows on the Edit screen as well as in the printed document, the default setting for this option should be 1. This setting allows you to see as many lines on the screen as possible when you work on a document. Then, when you want to print a document that is doubled spaced, you can change this value to 2, print the document, and delete the code so the Edit screen returns to single spacing. Although you normally use a value of 1 or 2 for single or double spacing, you can also use decimal values like 1.5 or 2.25.

Margins Left/Right   The left margin and right margin settings should be based on the number of characters that are printed in a line. In general, these margins should be set so the width of the line doesn't exceed 66 characters. If, for example, you're going to print a document at 10 characters per inch, one inch margins are fine because the length of the line is 65 characters. But if you're going to print the document at 12 characters per inch, the margins should be larger than that (perhaps one and one-half inches). Otherwise, the line will be too long to be read easily.

Usually, the margin settings apply to the entire document, so you should use the Document options of the Format command to set margins that are different from your system defaults. Then, you only have to insert margin codes into the document when you want to change the margins for a portion of the document.

**The Format Line
screen**

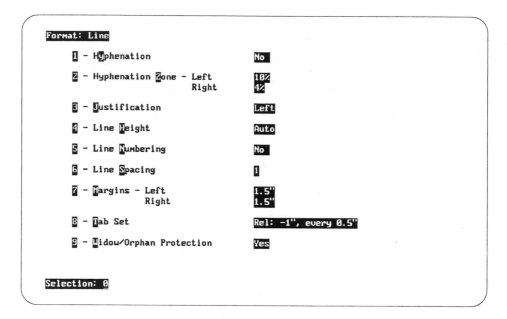

```
Format: Line

    1 - Hyphenation                      No

    2 - Hyphenation Zone - Left          10%
                          Right          4%

    3 - Justification                    Left

    4 - Line Height                      Auto

    5 - Line Numbering                   No

    6 - Line Spacing                     1

    7 - Margins - Left                   1.5"
                  Right                  1.5"

    8 - Tab Set                          Rel: -1", every 0.5"

    9 - Widow/Orphan Protection          Yes


Selection: 0
```

**The Format Page
screen**

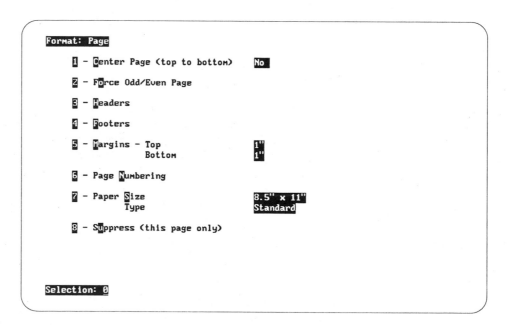

```
Format: Page

    1 - Center Page (top to bottom)      No

    2 - Force Odd/Even Page

    3 - Headers

    4 - Footers

    5 - Margins - Top                    1"
                  Bottom                 1"

    6 - Page Numbering

    7 - Paper Size                       8.5" x 11"
        Type                             Standard

    8 - Suppress (this page only)


Selection: 0
```

Figure 8-9   The Line and Page screens of the Format command

Tab Set   This option is used to set the tab stops for a document. Because the *WordPerfect* default setting for tab stops is for one every half inch across the page, this is acceptable for many documents. If it isn't, though, you can use the Document options of the Format command to set the tab stops for a document. Later, if you want to enter tabular information into the document, you can adjust the tab stops to suit the table. Because you don't make a simple entry on the Line screen to set the tab stops, I'll explain how to set them in detail later in this chapter.

Widow/Orphan Protection   When this option is on, *WordPerfect* won't print the first line of a paragraph at the bottom of a page or the last line of a paragraph at the top of a page. In other words, *WordPerfect* tries to keep a minimum of two lines together at the top or bottom of a page. Because this feature improves the appearance and readability of a report or proposal, I recommend that you keep this option on for all documents. However, the *WordPerfect* default setting for this option is off. As a result, you should use the Setup command to change this default setting for your system.

Center Page   If you use this option to insert a code into a document, the page that follows the code will be centered from top to bottom. As a result, this is a useful option for letters. It is also useful when you prepare title pages for reports, proposals, or term papers. This option applies only to one page at a time, and to work properly, the code for this option must be at the top of the page.

Margins Top/Bottom   For most documents, the *WordPerfect* default settings of one inch for the top and bottom margins are acceptable. However, you may want to adjust them so they coordinate properly with your printer. On my printer, for example, a one inch top margin setting leads to an actual margin of 1-1/3 inches, and a one inch bottom margin setting leads to an actual margin of 2/3 inch. As a result, I used the Setup command to adjust the defaults for the top and bottom margins accordingly.

Paper Size/Type   Most documents in America are printed on standard 8-1/2 by 11 inch paper. If you work in a legal office, though, the standard size may be 8-1/2 by 14. As a result, the default setting in most businesses should be for one of these two sizes. Then, when you're preparing a form like an envelope, you can use this option to set the paper size for the form you're going to use. Because you can't make a simple entry on the Page screen to set this option, I'll explain how to set it in detail in a moment.

Underline Spaces/Tabs   This option is on the Other screen, and you use it to specify whether the underlines for spaces and Tab characters should be printed when they have been marked for underlining. The *WordPerfect* default setting underlines for spaces but not for tabs, and this is usually what you

Format menu option	Next menu option	Recommendation
Line	Justification	Set for ragged right (Off for *WordPerfect* 5.0; Left for *WordPerfect* 5.1).
	Line Spacing	Set for single spacing while you're editing. Set to other spacing (if needed) just before you print a document.
	Margins Left/Right	This depends on the base font. In general, these margins should be set so the width of the line is 66 characters or fewer.
	Tab Set	If you use units as the units of measure, set tabs every five units (characters) relative to the margin. If you use inches, set tabs every half inch relative to the margin.
	Widow/Orphan Protection	Set to Yes. This keeps at least two lines together at the bottom and top of a page.
Page	Center Page (top to bottom)	Use this for a letter or title page when you want to center the text between the top and bottom margins.
	Margins Top/Bottom	Default margins of 6 lines or one inch are appropriate for most documents.
	Paper Size/Type	The default is usually standard 8-1/2 by 11 inch paper, but if you work in a legal office the default may be standard 8-1/2 by 14 inch paper. Use this option when you want to work on non-standard sizes.
Other	Underline Spaces/Tabs	Use this to specify whether you want spaces or tabs underlined in a block of text that has been marked for underlining.

Figure 8-10   A summary of the primary formatting options of the Format command

want. But if the default setting isn't appropriate for most of your work, you can change it by using the Setup command.

How to use the Format command to set the paper size and type

When you access the Paper Size option of the Page screen, you don't just type the new page size and press Enter. Instead, another screen is displayed. Since the procedure for setting this option is different for each release of *WordPerfect*, I'll present the procedures separately. With either procedure, though, you should set this option through the Document options of the Format command if this option applies to the entire document. Otherwise, the cursor should be at the top of the page that marks the start of a new paper size or type.

Paper Size/Type (*WordPerfect* 5.0)

If you're using *WordPerfect* 5.0, the Paper Size screen in figure 8-11 is displayed when you select the Paper Size option from the Page menu. From this screen, you select the size of the paper that you're going to use for the document. If, for example, you're preparing a report on legal size paper, you select Legal. If you're preparing an envelope, you select Envelope. And if you're not going to use any one of the standard paper sizes, you select Other. Then, *WordPerfect* will prompt you for the width and length of the paper that you're going to be using.

When you complete this selection, *WordPerfect* displays the Paper Type screen in figure 8-11. From this screen, you select the type of the paper you're going to use for the document. If you're using continuous form paper, select Standard so *WordPerfect* will print your document without requiring any responses before it starts printing. If you're using individual letterhead pages or envelopes, you can select Letterhead or Envelope. Although this varies from one printer to another, selecting one of these types usually means that *WordPerfect* will require a response from you before it starts printing. It may even require a response before it prints each page of a document. As a result, you may find that Standard works best for both continuous forms and individual forms. After you make a selection, *WordPerfect* returns you to the Page screen. Then, when you Exit from the Format command, you can use Reveal Codes to see that the appropriate code has been inserted into the document.

Paper Size/Type (*WordPerfect* 5.1)

If you're using *WordPerfect* 5.1, the Paper Size/Type screen in figure 8-12 is displayed when you select the Paper Size option from the Page menu. In this example, you can see that four options are listed: one for standard 8-1/2 by 11 inch paper, one for standard 8-1/2 by 14 inch paper (legal size), one for an envelope that's 9-1/2 by 4 inches, and one for ALL OTHERS. In the third and fourth columns of this listing, you can see that the first two forms are continuous and that no prompting from *WordPerfect* is required. In contrast, the third form is manual, and *WordPerfect* prompts you for a response before it starts to print.

If you're going to use one of the forms that's listed on the Paper/Size Type screen, you move the highlight to it and press the Enter key. That's the first procedure in figure 8-12. But if the form you're going to use isn't listed, you need to use the second procedure. In step 1, you move the highlight to ALL OTHERS and press the Enter key; that displays a Paper Size screen like the one in figure 8-11. In step 2, you select one of the paper sizes. If you're not going to use any one of the standard paper sizes, you select Other. Then, *WordPerfect* prompts you for the width and length of the paper that you're going to use. When you complete that selection, *WordPerfect* displays a Paper Type screen like the one in figure 8-11. So in step 3, you select the type of

**The Paper Size
screen**

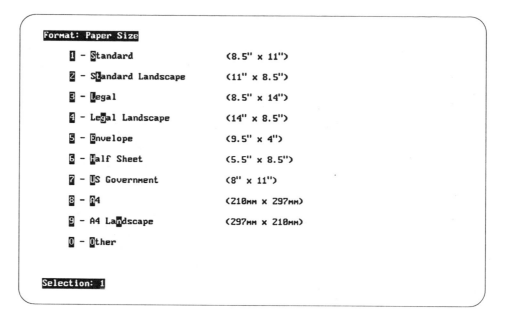

**The Paper Type
screen**

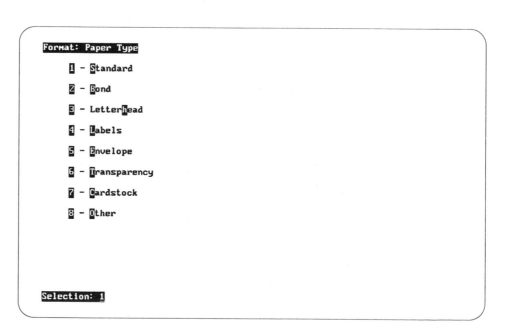

Figure 8-11   The two screens for setting the paper size and type when you're using *WordPerfect* 5.0

The Paper Size/Type screen

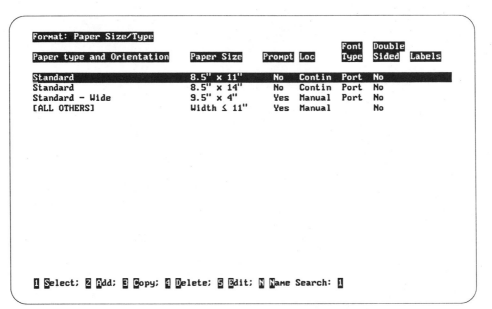

```
Format: Paper Size/Type

                                                      Font Double
Paper type and Orientation    Paper Size    Prompt Loc  Type Sided  Labels

Standard                      8.5" x 11"    No    Contin Port  No
Standard                      8.5" x 14"    No    Contin Port  No
Standard - Wide               9.5" x 4"     Yes   Manual Port  No
[ALL OTHERS]                  Width ≤ 11"   Yes   Manual       No
```

```
1 Select; 2 Add; 3 Copy; 4 Delete; 5 Edit; N Name Search: 1
```

How to select one of the listed forms

Move the highlight to the paper definition that you want to use. Then, press the Enter key. This returns you to the Format Page screen.

How to select a form that isn't listed

1. Move the highlight to [ALL OTHERS]. Then, press the Enter key.
2. Select a paper size from the Paper Size screen in figure 8-11.
3. Select a paper type from the Paper Type screen in figure 8-11. This returns you to the Format Page screen.

Figure 8-12   How to set the paper size and type when you're using *WordPerfect* 5.1

paper that you're going to use. That completes the selection and returns you to the Page screen.

If you repeatedly use a form size that isn't listed on the Paper Size/Type screen like the one in figure 8-12, it makes sense to add that form to the listing. To do that, you use the procedure in figure 8-13. In step 1, you select the Add option listed at the bottom of the Paper Size/Type screen. In step 2, you select the paper type from a Paper Type screen like the one in figure 8-11. *WordPerfect* then displays a screen like the one in figure 8-13. At that screen,

The Edit Paper Definition screen

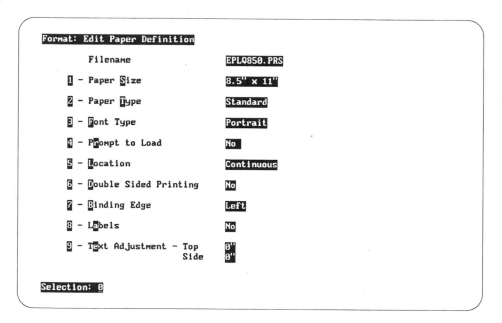

```
Format: Edit Paper Definition

         Filename                    EPLQ850.PRS

     1 - Paper Size                  8.5" x 11"

     2 - Paper Type                  Standard

     3 - Font Type                   Portrait

     4 - Prompt to Load              No

     5 - Location                    Continuous

     6 - Double Sided Printing       No

     7 - Binding Edge                Left

     8 - Labels                      No

     9 - Text Adjustment - Top       0"
                           Side      0"


Selection: 0
```

How to add a paper definition to the Paper/Size Type listing

1. Select Add from the Paper Size/Type listing in figure 8-12. This displays a Paper Size screen like the one in figure 8-11.

2. Select a paper type from the Paper Type screen in figure 8-11. This displays an Edit Paper Definition screen like the one above.

3. Change any values in the Edit Paper Definition screen so the paper definition is the way you want it. If you select Paper Size, you can select the paper size from a screen like the one in figure 8-11. If you select Paper Type, you can re-select a paper type from a Paper Type screen. If you select Prompt to Load, you can specify whether you want *WordPerfect* to require a response before it starts printing (Yes) or whether you want *WordPerfect* to start printing as soon as it gets the Print command (No). If you select Location, you can specify whether the form is Continuous, Manual, or coming from a specific Bin of your printer.

4. Press the Zero (0) or Enter key to add the new paper definition to the list.

Figure 8-13   How to add a paper definition to the Paper/Size Type listing when you're using *WordPerfect* 5.1

you can change any one of the nine characteristics shown, but you usually only need to work with three of them. If the paper size or type isn't set the way you want it, you can select either of these options to change it. If the Prompt to Load option isn't set the way you want it, you can change it to either Yes or No. If it's set to Yes, *WordPerfect* will ask you for a response before it starts to print a document; otherwise, it won't. When you have all the options set the way you want them, press the Enter key to complete the operation. That adds the new form to the Paper/Size Type listing. Then, you can select it from the listing to insert its code into your document.

In chapter 10, you can learn more about setting the Paper Size/Type option so the codes work properly with your printer. If you have a laser printer, for example, you can use the Font Type option to print your document horizontally instead of vertically. Or if your PC has a printer with two form feeding bins, you can use the Location option to specify the bin that contains the form you want to use. This, however, goes way beyond formatting considerations. So for now, just concentrate on getting the paper size right.

How to use the Format command to set the tab stops for a document

For most documents, you should have some general-purpose tab stops set across the page. Then, if you want to indent a paragraph or align some data, you can use these tab stops. Later on in this chapter, I'll show you how to set specific tab stops for tabular data, but general tab stops are all that you need for most documents.

How to set evenly spaced tab stops   The first procedure in figure 8-14 shows you how to set evenly spaced tab stops across a page. In the first four steps, you access the Tab Set option of the Format command, select the type of tab stops to be used, move the cursor to the left of the Tab ruler that is displayed, and delete all of the old tab stops. Then, in step 5, you type an entry that identifies the placement of the first tab stop and the distance between the tab stops that should follow. If, for example, you're using inches as the units of measure, this entry

   0,.5

means that the first tab stop should be at location zero and tabs should be set every half inch to the right. The appropriate entry in step 5, though, varies depending on which type of tab stops you're using. To complete the command, you press the Exit key twice in step 6 to return to the Edit screen.

If you're using release 5.0, all tab entries represent *absolute tab stops*. That means that the tab settings are measured from the left edge of the page, and they aren't automatically adjusted if the left and right margins are changed. As a result, you must make sure that your tab settings are coordinated with the margin settings. If, for example, the left margin is set at 1.25 inches and

---

The Tab Ruler

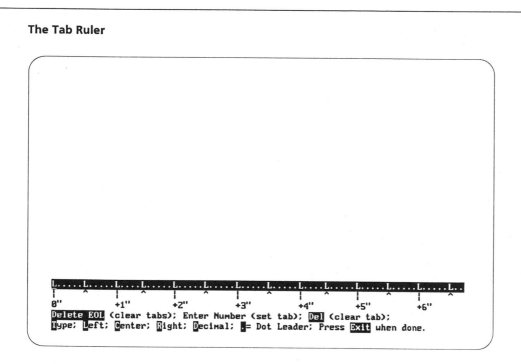

How to set general-purpose tab stops for a document (part 1 of 2)

How to set a series of evenly spaced tab stops

1. Access the Format Line screen and select the Tab Set option. This displays the Tab Set ruler shown above.
2. If you want to switch the type of the tab stops in *WordPerfect* 5.1, press T for Type. Then, select either Absolute or Relative tab stops.
3. If necessary, press Home Home Left arrow to move the cursor to the far left side of the tab ruler.
4. Press Ctrl+End to delete all tab stops to the right of the cursor.
5. Type a measurement for the location of the first tab stop; this moves the cursor to the lower right hand corner of the tab ruler. For absolute tab stops, an entry of zero (0) represents the left edge of the page. For relative tab stops, an entry of zero (0) represents the left margin. Then, type a comma, and type a measurement for the distance that you want between tab stops. When you press the Enter key, the cursor returns to the tab ruler and the new tab settings are displayed.
6. Press the Exit key twice to return to the Edit screen.

Figure 8-14   How to set general-purpose tab stops for a document (part 1 of 2)

How to set one tab at a time

1. Access the Format Line screen and select the Tab Set option. This displays the Tab Set ruler shown above.
2. If you want to switch the type of the tab stops in *WordPerfect* 5.1, press T for Type. Then, select either Absolute or Relative tab stops.
3. Press Home Home Left arrow to move the cursor to the far left side of the tab ruler.
4. Press Ctrl+End to delete all tab stops to the right of the cursor.
5. Type the location of the first tab stop. This moves the cursor to the lower right side of the tab ruler. Then, press the Enter key. This returns the cursor to the tab ruler with the new tab stop shown. If, for example, you're using inches as the unit of measure and you enter *2*, a tab stop is shown at the 2 inch mark. If you're using units as the units of measure and you enter *24*, a tab is shown at the 24 unit mark.
6. Enter the locations of the other tab stops that you want.
7. Press the Exit key twice to return to the Edit screen.

Figure 8-14   How to set general-purpose tab stops for a document (part 2 of 2)

you want half-inch indents for paragraphs, one of the tab stops has to be at 1.75 inches.

If you're using *WordPerfect* 5.1, you can use absolute tab stops, but you can also use *relative tab stops*. With relative stops, the tab settings are measured from the left margin, and they are automatically adjusted if the left and right margins are changed. As a result, you should start the entry in step 5 with a negative number if you want to be able to release the margin (Shift+Tab) and tab to the first tab stop to the left of the margin. For instance, if you're using inches as the units of measure, this entry

> **-1,.5**

means that the first tab stop should be one inch to the left of the margin and the tab stops that follow should be set every half inch to the right.

When you enter the first measurement for absolute tab stops, you must start with a number, not a decimal point. Similarly, when you enter the first measurement for relative tab stops, you must start with a number or a minus sign, not a decimal point. This tells *WordPerfect* that you're setting a series of evenly spaced tabs. If, for example, you want the first tab stop setting at one-half inch, you must enter 0.5, not .5. For absolute tab stops, you often start with a zero (the left edge of the page) and set your left margin so it coordinates with the tab settings.

How to set one tab stop at a time   If you know exactly where you want the tab stops for a document, you can use the second procedure in figure 8-14 to set them. In steps 1 through 4, you clear the old tab stops. Then, in step 5, you type the location of the first tab stop that you want to enter. If, for example, you're using inches as the units of measure and you want the first tab stop at 2 inches, you type *2* and press the Enter key. In step 5, if you want the next tab stop at 4.75 inches, you type that number and press the Enter key. And you continue like that until all the tab stops have been entered. To complete the command, you press the Exit key twice in step 7.

A summary of the primary formatting commands and keystrokes and the type of codes they use

Figure 8-15 summarizes the formatting commands and keystroke combinations presented in this chapter. When you use any one of them, a single code or a pair of codes is inserted into your document. In contrast, when you use the Document options of the Format command, no codes are inserted into your document.

Single code commands   For all but a few of the commands and for both keystroke combinations, the code that is inserted is a *single code*. That type of code changes the formatting of the text that follows the code. It also overrides a corresponding default code, and it overrides a corresponding code that precedes it in the document. For instance, you can use the Font command to change the base font in a document from the initial base font to another font.

Paired code commands   When you use commands like the Bold or Underline commands, *paired codes* are inserted into the document. Then, the first code in the pair starts the formatting change, and the second code in the pair stops it. When you use the Font command to change the size or appearance of the base font, but not the base font itself, it also inserts paired codes into a document. As a result, the Font command is the only command that can insert both single and paired codes into a document.

How to use the Font command

The Font command lets you change the base font that's being used for a document. It also lets you change the size and appearance of the base font without changing the base font. As I said earlier, you should use the Document option of the Format command to set the Initial Base Font for a document. But when you want to change the font within a document, you use the Font command.

Command name	Access	Function	Code type
Format	Shift+F8	Sets many formatting codes and options	Single
Font	Ctrl+F8	Inserts a code that changes the font	Single
		Inserts a code that changes the type size or the type appearance	Paired
>Indent	F4	Indents a paragraph one tab stop from the left margin	Single
>Indent<	Shift+F4	Indents a paragraph one tab stop from the left margin and an equal amount from the right margin	Single
Center	Shift+F6	Centers text between the left and right margins	Single
Flush Right	Alt+F6	Aligns text with the right margin	Single
Bold	F6	Boldfaces text	Paired
Underline	F8	Underlines text	Paired
Tab Align	Ctrl+F6	Aligns the decimal point in a number on a tab stop	Single

Keystrokes	Name	Function	Code type
Tab	Tab	Indents a line one tab stop	Single
Shift+Tab	Margin release	Moves a line one tab stop to the left past an indent code or a left margin	Single

Figure 8-15   A summary of the formatting commands and keystrokes and the type of codes they use

How to change the base font   The first procedure in figure 8-16 shows you how to change the base font within a document when you're using a non-scalable font. In step 1, you access the Font command. In step 2, you select Base Font. In step 3, you select the font that you want to use from the list of fonts displayed on the Base Font screen. This is the same list of fonts that you get when you use the Document option of the Format command to set the Initial Base Font (see figure 8-5). To complete the font change, you press the Enter key.

The second procedure in figure 8-16 shows you how to change the base font when you're using a scalable font. In step 2, when you select Base Font, *WordPerfect* displays the same list of fonts that you get when you use the Document option of the Format command to set the Initial Base font (see figure 8-6). If you select a scalable font from this list in step 3, a prompt is displayed that asks you for the type size. Then, in step 4, you have to enter the size of the font and press the Enter key. This completes the font change.

How to change the Base Font for a non-scalable font

1. Access the Font command (Ctrl+F8) to get this prompt:

   `1 Size; 2 Appearance; 3 Normal; 4 Base Font; 5 Print Color: 0`

2. Select Base Font. This displays a Base Font screen.

3. Move the cursor to the font you want to use and press the Enter key. This inserts a single code in your document that changes the base font. This stays in effect until you change the base font again.

How to change the Base Font for a scalable font

1. Access the Font command (Ctrl+F8) to get this prompt:

   `1 Size; 2 Appearance; 3 Normal; 4 Base Font; 5 Print Color: 0`

2. Select Base Font. This displays a Base Font screen.

3. Move the cursor to the font you want to use and press the Enter key. Then, this prompt is displayed:

   `Point size: 10`

4. Type the point size you want to use and press the Enter key. This inserts a single code in your document that changes the base font. This stays in effect until you change the base font again.

Figure 8-16   How to use the Font command to change the Base Font for a non-scalable or a scalable font

When you change the base font, a single code is inserted into the document at the cursor. This code changes the initial base font to the new font, and the new font stays in effect until you change it again. In other words, the new base font replaces the initial base font.

How to change the type size or appearance of the base font   The first procedure in figure 8-17 shows you how to change the appearance of the base font. After you access the Font command, you select Appearance. This gives you the list of options shown in step 2. Examples of these options are given in figure 8-18. In step 3, you select the option that you want, and the paired codes are inserted into your document. If you use the Block command to block text before you use the Font command to change the appearance, the paired codes are inserted on both sides of the block. Otherwise, the cursor is between the paired codes so the characters that you enter next get the changed appearance. To end this change, press the Right arrow key to move past the right code in the pair.

Of the several appearance options in figure 8-18, the one you're most likely to use is italics. However, it takes three keystroke combinations to insert

How to change the type appearance

1. Access the Font command (Ctrl+F8).

   `1 Size; 2 Appearance; 3 Normal; 4 Base Font; 5 Print Color: 0`

2. Select Appearance.

   `1 Bold 2 Undln 3 Dbl Und 4 Italc 5 Outln 6 Shadw 7 Sm Cap 8 Redln 9 Stkout: 0`

3. Select one of the Appearance options. This inserts paired codes in the document just like the Boldface or Underline commands do. If a block is active when you insert the codes, the codes go on either side of the block. Otherwise, because the cursor is between the codes, the text that you type next is inserted between them. To end this appearance change, press the Right arrow key.

Note: Chapter 12 shows how to make a macro that makes it easy for you to insert the paired codes for an appearance change.

How to change the type size

1. Access the Font command.

   `1 Size; 2 Appearance; 3 Normal; 4 Base Font; 5 Print Color: 0`

2. Select Size.

   `1 Suprscpt; 2 Subscpt; 3 Fine; 4 Small; 5 Large; 6 Vry Large; 7 Ext Large: 0`

3. Select one of the Size options. This inserts paired codes in the document. If a block is active when you insert the codes, the codes go on either side of the block. Otherwise, the text that you type next is inserted between the codes. To end this size change, press the Right arrow key.

How to return to the normal base font

1. Access the Font command.

   `1 Size; 2 Appearance; 3 Normal; 4 Base Font; 5 Print Color: 0`

2. Select Normal. This moves the cursor past the second code in a pair of appearance or size codes.

Figure 8-17   How to use the Font command to change the appearance or size of the base font or to return to the normal base font

the paired codes for italics into a document. So if you use italics much, be sure to read chapter 12. It shows you how to create a simple macro for inserting the italic codes into a document. Using this macro, you can insert italic codes with a single keystroke combination.

As you can see in the second procedure in figure 8-17, you can use a similar procedure to change the type size without changing the base font. For instance, figure 8-18 illustrates the way the size options are applied to the base

Type appearances	Type sizes
Bold	WordPerfect ᴿSuperscript
Underline	WordPerfect ᴿSubscript
Italic	WordPerfect Fine
Double Underline	WordPerfect Small
Outline	WordPerfect Large
Shadow	WordPerfect Very large
Sᴍᴀʟʟ Cᴀᴘs	WordPerfect Extra large

Figure 8-18   Type appearances and type sizes when the current printer is a matrix printer and the base font is 12 cpi

font for a dot-matrix printer. If you intend to transfer a document from one printer to another, this way of setting the size for the base font makes the conversion more likely to work the way you want it to. If that's not your intent, though, you're better off using the Font command to change the base font so you know exactly what size you've selected.

How to return to the base font   The third procedure in figure 8-17 shows you how to return to the base font after you've changed its appearance or size. To do that, you just select Normal from the list of options. Since this simply moves the cursor past the second code in a pair, though, you shouldn't ever need this option. Instead, just press the Right arrow key.

Three formatting skills for most documents

For most documents, you'll use some type of indenting for paragraphs, quotations, and numbered lists. You'll occasionally use centering or right alignment. And you'll use boldfacing, underlining, or italics for headings, book titles, and the like. In case you don't already have these skills, I'll present them in detail now.

How to indent and outdent text   Figure 8-19 gives the keystroke combinations that you need for all types of indenting. To *indent* the first line of a paragraph, for example, you use the Tab key. To indent all the lines of a paragraph, you use the >Indent command (Single Indent command). And to

indent all the lines of a paragraph from both sides, you use the >Indent<
command (Double Indent command). Both of the Indent commands end
when you press the Enter key.

In the first example in figure 8-19, the Tab key has been used to indent
the first line of a paragraph. In the second example, the >Indent command
has been used after the period in each of the numbered items. In the third
example, the >Indent< command has been used to indent a quotation from
both sides of the margins. If you experiment with these keystroke
combinations, you'll find that they're easy to use. However, you must set the
tab stops the way you want them to get the right amount of indentation from
the left margin.

The fourth keystroke combination in figure 8-19 is referred to as the
margin release, or *outdent*. When you use this keystroke combination, the
cursor is moved to the first tab stop to the left. If this tab stop is to the left of
the left margin, the cursor goes beyond the left margin. In either case,
though, the lines that follow are indented or aligned on the left margin as if
the Margin release combination hadn't been used. The result is an effect
called a *hanging indent*. This can be useful when you enter the items in a
bibliography or for special effects. Here again, you must set the tab stops
properly to get this keystroke combination to work the way you want it to.

How to center or right align one or more lines of text

Figure 8-20
summarizes the commands you need for centering and right aligning a line of
text. It also gives a procedure for centering or right aligning one line at a time
and a procedure for working on more than one line at a time.

To center or right align one line, you access the appropriate command
while the cursor is at the start of the line. If you've already entered the line
with a hard return at its end, this will center or right align it. Otherwise, you
type the line. Then, when you press the Enter key, the cursor jumps to the
next line and the line above it is centered or right aligned.

To center or right align more than one line at a time, use the Block
command to block them. Then, access the Center or Flush Right command.
This inserts the appropriate code at the start of each of the lines in the block
so those lines are centered or right aligned.

How to boldface or underline

Figure 8-21 gives two ways to boldface
or underline text. The first way is to access the Bold or Underline command;
type the text that you want boldfaced or underlined; and press the Right
arrow key to end the command. The second way is to block the text that you
want boldfaced or underlined; then, access the Bold or Underline command.
Either way, paired codes are inserted the document.

You can also use the Font command in either of these ways to change the
appearance of text. In fact, you can use the Font command to insert the Bold
and Underline codes into a document. However, since the Bold and
Underline commands require only a single keystroke, it's easier to use these
commands for boldfacing and underlining than it is to use the Font command.

The commands and keystrokes for indenting and outdenting

Keystrokes	Name	Function
Tab	Tab	Indents the current line one tab stop
F4	>Indent	Indents all the lines of a paragraph one tab stop
Shift+F4	>Indent<	Indents all the lines of a paragraph one tab stop on both the right and left sides
Shift+Tab	Margin release	Outdents the current line one tab stop; if necessary, it goes beyond the left margin

Examples

The Tab key used at the start of a paragraph

Sooner or later, you're going to lose some or all of the files on your hard disk. It's as simple as that. Eventually, for example, the hard disk on your PC will fail, and all of the data on it will be lost.

The >Indent command used after the numbers in a numbered list

1. You can use the DOS Backup and Restore commands to back up and restore your hard disk data to diskettes. However, these commands are slow, hard to use, and unreliable.
2. You can use a commercial backup utility to back up your hard disk to diskettes. This is faster and more reliable than using the DOS command, but you still have to swap diskettes during the process.

The >Indent< command used to set off a quotation

Pat Bultema, the author of *How to back up your PC*, starts the book this way:

Sooner or later, you're going to lose some or all of the files on your hard disk. It's as simple as that. Eventually, for example, the hard disk on your PC will fail, and all of the data on it will be lost.

The >Indent command followed by the Margin-release key combination to create an effect called a hanging indent

Sooner or later, you're going to lose some or all of the files on your hard disk. It's as simple as that. Eventually, for example, the hard disk on your PC will fail, and all of the data on it will be lost.

Figure 8-19   The keystrokes and commands for indenting and outdenting

The commands and keystrokes for centering and right aligning

Keystrokes	Name	Function
Shift+F6	Center	Centers the current line or the lines in the current block
Alt+F6	Flush Right	Right aligns the current line or the lines in the current block

How to center or right align the current line

1. Access the Center or Flush Right command.
2. Type the text that you want centered or right aligned.
3. Finish the operation by pressing the Enter key.

How to center or right align the current block

1. Use the Block command to block the lines that you want centered or right aligned.
2. Access the Center or Flush Right command. This inserts the Center or Flush Right code at the start of each of the lines in the block.

Figure 8-20   The commands for centering and right aligning

How to use tab stops to align tabular data within a document

As I said earlier, the default settings for a document should provide the tab stops that you use most often. So you should at least include a tab stop for indenting paragraphs. And you may also need tab stops for dates and signature blocks on letters. Often, you need evenly spaced tab stops across a page so the stops can be used for any requirements that develop.

In some documents, though, you will want to modify the tab settings so you can use them to align tabular data within a document. Then, you can use the Tab key to align text or numbers on the tabs. Or you can use the Tab Align command to align the decimal points in a column of numbers on the tab.

How to set the tab stops for tabular data   Figure 8-22 summarizes the keystrokes you need for setting or resetting tab stops after you access the Tab Set option from the Line screen of the Format command. Often, you want to delete some or all of the existing tab stops. You can do this by using the Ctrl+End key combination to delete all tab stops to the right of the cursor on the tab ruler. Then, if you want to enter a series of evenly spaced tab stops or you want to enter tab stops one at a time, you can use the procedures that

How to insert paired codes as you enter text

1. Access the command for the type of paired code that you want. To access the Boldface command, for example, press the F6 key. To access the Underline command, press the F8 key. This inserts the paired codes into the document with the cursor between them.
2. Type the text.
3. Press the Right arrow key to move the cursor past the second code in the pair.

How to insert paired codes around existing text

1. Block the text.
2. Access the command for the type of paired code that you want.

Figure 8-21   How to insert paired codes like the Boldface or Underline codes into a document

I summarized earlier in figure 8-15. However, these procedures only set tab stops for left alignment (L).

When you set the tab stops for tabular data, though, you often want to set tab stops for right (R) or decimal alignment (D). And you may occasionally want to set tab stops for centered (C) alignment. Then, you move the cursor to the location on the tab ruler where you want to set a tab stop and press the letter for the type of tab stop that you want.

In the first example in figure 8-23, you can see how I set the tab stops for a table with six columns. To keep the table simple, I used only Left and Right tabs. Then, I aligned the columns that contained dollar amounts on the Right tabs, and I aligned the other columns on Left tabs.

If you want to have a *dot leader* precede the aligned data, you type a decimal point (or dot) on the tab ruler in the same location as a Left, Right, Center, or Decimal tab stop. Then, when you tab to that stop, a series of dots precedes it as shown in the second example in figure 8-23. If you type a decimal point on the tab ruler without an L, R, C, or D, a Left tab stop with a dot leader is assumed.

How to align text or numbers on the tab stops   Once you've got the tab stops set the way you want them, it's easy to align text or numbers on the tabs. You just use the Tab key before each column entry. Then, if the next tab stop is for right alignment, *WordPerfect* inserts a code for that purpose into the document. If the next tab is for center alignment, *WordPerfect* inserts a code for that purpose into the document. And so on.

How to use the Tab Align command to align decimal data without resetting the tab stops   Occasionally, it makes sense to align decimal data without using a Decimal tab stop. To do that, you can use the Tab Align

The Tab Ruler

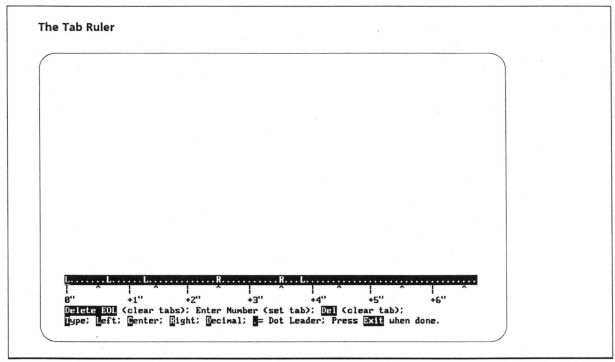

Figure 8-22 How to set the tab stops for tabular data (part 1 of 2)

command. To access this command, you press the Ctrl+F6 keystroke combination. *WordPerfect* then inserts an alignment code into your document, moves the cursor one tab stop to the right, and displays a prompt like this at the bottom of the screen:

    Align char = .

This means that *WordPerfect* will align the next characters that you type with the decimal point at the tab stop. If the characters don't include a decimal point, they will be right aligned on the tab stop.

If you want to change the character that is used for alignment with the Tab Align command, you can use the Decimal/Align Character option. This option is on the Other screen that you access from the Format command. When you change this option, a code is inserted into the document. So if you want to change the decimal alignment character for the entire document, you should move the cursor to the top of the document before inserting the code.

Some practical advice for aligning tabular data   Because *WordPerfect* offers so many options for aligning tabular data, you'll work more efficiently if you try to keep your tables simple. Often, for example, you can get by with

The keystroke combinations for deleting and setting tab stops

Keystrokes	Function
Arrow key	Moves the cursor one space in the direction of the arrow.
Ctrl+End	Deletes all tabs to the right of the cursor.
Any number	Starts an entry for setting one tab stop or a series of evenly spaced tab stops as summarized in figure 8-15.
Delete	Deletes the tab stop at the cursor.
L	Inserts a left tab stop at the cursor. If you tab to this type of tab stop, a code is inserted into the document so the characters that follow will be left aligned on the tab stop.
R	Inserts a right tab stop at the cursor. If you tab to this type of tab stop, a code is inserted into the document so the characters that follow will be right aligned on the tab stop.
C	Inserts a center tab stop at the cursor. If you tab to this type of tab stop, a code is inserted into the document so the characters that follow will be centered on the tab stop.
D	Inserts a decimal tab stop at the cursor. If you tab to this type of tab stop, a code is inserted into the document so the characters that follow will be decimally aligned on the tab stop.
Decimal point	Inserts a code that calls for dot leaders. This can be used in combination with L, R, C, or D. If you tab to a tab stop with this code, the characters that follow will be preceded by dots as shown in figure 8-23.
Minus sign (5.1 only)	Starts an entry for setting one tab stop or a series of evenly spaced tab stops as summarized in figure 8-15.
Alt+Arrow (5.1 only)	Moves the cursor one tab stop in the direction of the arrow.
Ctrl+Arrow (5.1 only)	Moves the tab stop at the cursor one space in the direction of the arrow.

Figure 8-22   How to set the tab stops for tabular data (part 2 of 2)

Left and Right tab stops alone even if you're aligning decimal data. That's illustrated by the first example in figure 8-23. In this case, if I had used Decimal tab stops for the third, fourth and fifth columns, I couldn't have used the same tab stops for both the headings of the columns and for the data in the columns. Similarly, you can usually get the alignment you want by using the Tab key and the appropriate tab stops, so you shouldn't have to use the Tab Align command.

A table that uses just Left and Right tab stops

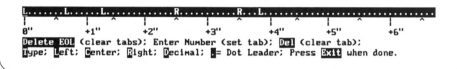

```
                        Rev/      Avg.
     Date   Qty.  Resp. Cost      Order   Comments

     2/92   2443  6.9%  $3.84     $33.82  $10 off, no letter
            2443  8.9    4.31      34.83  $10 off, letter

     6/92   2403  4.7    4.08      56.85  10% off, letter
            2554  5.5    4.93      58.72  20% off, letter
            2558  2.0    1.30      43.45  No discount, letter
```

```
L......L.....L..................R.........R..L....................................
^        ^       ^              ^         ^       ^         ^         ^         ^
0"       +1"     +2"            +3"       +4"     +5"       +6"
Delete EOL (clear tabs); Enter Number (set tab); Del (clear tab);
Type; Left; Center; Right; Decimal; .= Dot Leader; Press Exit when done.
```

A table that uses a Right tab with dot leaders

```
Lee Chae . . . . . . . . . . . . . . . . (415) 922-2531
Penny Mapa  . . . . . . . . . . . . . .  (916) 991-0743
Braden McKeighan . . . . . . . . . . .   (209) 431-4922
Jenny Evert . . . . . . . . . . . . . .  (510) 548-3641
Mike Farino . . . . . . . . . . . . . .  (415) 224-9497
```

Figure 8-23   Two examples of tables that are easy to create and edit

If you want to adjust the alignment of a table after you get it set up, you start by moving the cursor to the right of the tab setting code for the table. You can do this by using the Reveal Codes key to locate the first code. Then, you can access the Tab Set option of the Line screen of the Format command. When you do that, the tab ruler displays the tab stops of the previous tab setting code. That makes it easy for you to adjust the tab stops. If you're using *WordPerfect* 5.1, for example, and you just want to move one code, you can use the last keystroke combination in figure 8-22. After you move the cursor to the tab stop that you want to move, you hold down the Ctrl key and press an Arrow key. Each time you press it, it moves the tab stop one space in the

Keystrokes	Hyphen name 5.1	5.0	Function
Ctrl+Hyphen	Soft	Soft	Inserts an invisible hyphen. Then, *WordPerfect* hyphenates the word at the end of a line only if that is appropriate. When hyphenation is appropriate, the word is split. Otherwise, it's not.
Hyphen	Normal	Hard	Inserts a visible hyphen. Then, *WordPerfect* splits the word at the hyphen if the hyphen is the last character in the line. Otherwise, the whole word including the visible hyphen is rolled over onto the next line.
Home Hyphen	Hard	Hyphen	Inserts a visible hyphen that tells *WordPerfect* not to break the word at the hyphen at the end of a line but to always keep the hyphenated word on one line.

Figure 8-24   The three types of hyphens and their functions

direction of the arrow. After you've got the tab stops the way you want them, you press the Exit key twice to return to the Edit screen. Then, to clean up the document, you delete the code for the previous tab settings.

When and how to use hyphenation

If you set your *WordPerfect* defaults for ragged right printing, you shouldn't have to hyphenate words at the end of a line. That's one reason why ragged right text is easier to read than justified text. However, if you use justified text, you may want to hyphenate some words so the gaps between the words in some lines aren't so large. This becomes even more important when you set your margins for short lines of text.

Figure 8-24 summarizes the keystrokes you can use for hyphenation. As you can see, releases 5.0 and 5.1 don't use the same names for all three kinds of hyphens. For the sake of simplicity, I'll use the 5.1 names in this chapter.

The easiest way to provide for hyphenation at the end of a line is to use the *soft hyphen*. To insert a soft hyphen into a word, press the hyphen key while you hold down the Ctrl key. Then, if *WordPerfect* can get more characters on a line by hyphenating the word at that point, it will do so. Later, if you add a word that changes the need for hyphenation, *WordPerfect* will pull the word back together. In that case, the soft hyphen disappears from the screen and isn't printed, but it is still there if you display the Reveal Codes screen.

The hyphen you're already familiar with is the *normal hyphen*. This is the character you get when you press the hyphen key on the keyboard. In this case, *WordPerfect* will hyphenate the word at the hyphen if the word has to be divided to fit properly at the end of a line.

WordPerfect also provides for a *hard hyphen*, but you should rarely need it. When this hyphen is used, *WordPerfect* won't divide the word at the hyphen at the end of a line. Instead, it will always move the entire word to the next line. To insert a hard hyphen into a word, you press the Home key followed by the hyphen.

You should know that in addition to these three types of hyphens, *WordPerfect* provides an advanced feature for automatic hyphenation. This feature hyphenates words based on the hyphenation in the *WordPerfect* dictionary or based on a set of programmed rules. Unless you're using *WordPerfect* for advanced desktop publishing applications, though, you shouldn't need the automatic hyphenation feature.

How to work with formatting codes

To keep the normal Edit screen uncluttered, *WordPerfect* doesn't show the formatting codes. If some formatting option isn't working the way you want it to, though, you can use the Reveal Codes command to reveal the codes. Then, you can delete, insert, or edit the codes to correct the problem.

How to use the Reveal Codes screen　You can access the Reveal codes command using the Alt+F3 key combination or the F11 key. When you access this command, a Reveal Codes screen like the one in figure 8-25 is displayed. When you're done with the Reveal Codes screen, you use one of the keystroke combinations again to return to the normal Edit screen.

As you can see in figure 8-25, the Reveal Codes screen is actually a combination of two screens. The top half of the screen is an Edit screen, and the bottom half shows the text as well as the formatting codes. The status line separates the two screens. And the two cursors, one on the top half of the screen and one on the bottom half, represent the same location in the document.

When you study the Reveal Codes screen, you can usually figure out why a formatting option isn't working the way you want it to. The screen in figure 8-25 illustrates two common formatting problems. The first problem is sometimes referred to as *competing codes*. In this example, you can see that there are two single codes in succession for setting the left and right margins. In the case of single codes, the second code overrides the first code. Then, if you want the first code to be in effect, you delete the second code.

A Reveal Codes screen that illustrates a couple of formatting problems

```
          _          Why we should upgrade from WordPerfect 5.0 to 5.1

Unlike WordPerfect 4.2 and 5.0, WordPerfect 5.0 and 5.1 share the same
structure.  Although some of the existing features have been enhanced, none of
them have been drastically changed.  WordPerfect 5.1 does, however, offer some
new features including a Tables feature, Mouse support, and Pull-down menus.

        At the end of this report, I'm going to recommend that our editors
upgrade from WordPerfect 5.0 to 5.1.  But first, I'm going to briefly describe
the tables feature.  I think that this feature alone makes it worthwhile to
upgrade.  I'm also going to present a brief analysis of the benefits and costs
D:\WPRPTS\51REPORT                              Doc 1 Pg 1 Ln 1 Pos 18
        {
[L/R Mar:1.5",1.5"][L/R Mar:1",1"][Center][BOLD]Why we should upgrade from [UND]
WordPerfect[und] 5.0 to 5.1[bold][HRt]
[Header A:Every page;August 19, 1992[Center]51REPORT[Flsh Rgt]Page ^B][HRt]
Unlike [UND]WordPerfect[und] 4.2 and 5.0, [UND]WordPerfect[und] 5.0 and 5.1 shar
e the same[SRt]
structure.  Although some of the existing features have been enhanced, none of[S
Rt]
them have been drastically changed.  [UND]WordPerfect[und] 5.1 does, however, of
fer some[SRt]
new features including a Tables feature, Mouse support, and Pull[-]down menus.[H

Press Reveal Codes to restore screen
```

How to access the Reveal Codes screen

84-key keyboard:	Alt+F3
101-key keyboard:	Alt+F3 or F11

How to return to the normal Edit screen

Access Reveal Codes again

Figure 8-25   How to use the Reveal Codes screen

The second problem illustrated by the screen in figure 8-25 is that some single codes don't work properly unless they're at the top of the page. In this example, the header code comes after text in a document. As a result, the header won't print on the current page, but it will print on the next page. Then, if you want the header to print on the first page, you have to move the code to the top of the page before any text. You can do this by using the Block command to move the code or by deleting the header code and using the Format command to enter a new header.

How to delete, insert, move, or copy single codes   If you want to delete a single code while the Reveal Codes screen is displayed, you move the cursor to the code and press the Delete key. When the Reveal Codes screen is displayed, you can delete any single code, and no warning message is displayed before the code is deleted.

Often, though, you can tell where a single code is without displaying the Reveal Codes screen. Then, you can use the Delete or Backspace key to delete it. For simple formatting codes like >Indent or Tab, no message is displayed when you delete the code. However, you can tell that the code has been deleted because the formatting on the Edit screen gets changed. For some formatting codes, though, a message is displayed when you try to delete a single code. If, for example, you try to delete a base font code, a message like this is displayed:

> **Delete [Font:Roman 10cpi]? No (Yes)**

Then, you must select Yes to delete the code.

If you want to insert a single code into a document, you first move the cursor to where you want the code inserted. Then, you use the keystroke combination or command that inserts the code. For many formatting codes, the formatting on the screen also gets changed when you move the cursor down through the text.

If you want to move or copy formatting codes, you almost always begin by revealing them. Once you reveal the codes, the procedure for moving or copying a code is the same as the procedure for moving or copying a block of text. First, block the code. Next, start the move or copy function. Last, move the cursor to the spot where you want the codes moved or copied to and press the Enter key. Because this is a relatively cumbersome process, though, it's often more efficient to delete old codes and to insert new ones than it is to move or copy codes.

How to delete and insert paired codes   If you want to delete paired codes while the Reveal Codes screen is displayed, you move the cursor to either the first or second code in the pair and press the Delete key. When the Reveal Codes screen is displayed, you can delete any pair of codes, and no warning message is displayed before the pair is deleted.

Often, though, you can tell where paired codes are without displaying the Reveal Codes screen. Then, you can use the Delete or Backspace key to delete one code in the pair. In this case, a message is displayed when you try to delete the code. If, for example, you try to delete a pair of underline codes, a message like this is displayed:

> **Delete [UND]? No (Yes)**

Then, to delete the pair of codes, select Yes.

If you want to insert paired codes into a document after you've entered the text, you must use the second procedure in figure 8-21. First, you use the Block command to block the text that you want to put the paired codes around. Then, you access the command that inserts the paired codes into the document.

How to view a document before printing it

WordPerfect for DOS is not a *WYSIWYG* (what-you-see-is-what-you-get) program. As a result, the Edit screen doesn't show you how a document will look when it's printed. If, for example, a document has a header or a footer or if it's going to be printed with right justification, that's not shown on the Edit screen. Similarly, the fonts that are used in a document are not shown on the screen, and font appearances like boldface, underline, and italics are usually not displayed on the Edit screen in the same way that they will look when they're printed. Font sizes aren't shown either, although they will affect the number of characters that *WordPerfect* allows on each line of the Edit screen.

If you want to see how the document will look when it's printed, you can use the View Document option of the Print command. This displays a screen like the one in figure 8-26. Although the text on this screen may be more difficult to read than the Edit screen, it shows you the formatting of the document so you can make sure that it's going to come out the way you want it.

When you're at the View Document screen, you can use the normal keystroke combinations to move the cursor from one page to another and from one area of a page to another. You can also select any one of the four options shown at the bottom of the screen. If, for example, you want to see what an entire page is going to look like, select the full page option. You probably won't be able to read any of the text when you use this option, but you'll able to see the format of the entire page. Then, if you want to display the text in a larger size, you can select the 100% or 200% option.

If you discover a formatting problem when you use the View Document screen, you have to return to the Edit screen to make any formatting changes. So if you find several problems, you may have to go back and forth between the Edit screen and the View Document screen several times before you fix all of them. Since this can be time consuming, it is often more efficient to print a short document or the first page or two of a long document. Then, you can use the printed copy as a guide to the changes that you need to make. This is particularly true if your PC takes a long time to prepare the View Document screen.

How to format your documents with maximum efficiency

When you're formatting a document, it's tempting to insert single codes into the document to get whatever you want done and not worry about the system defaults or the document defaults. For maximum efficiency, though, you should take the time to set up your system defaults properly. And you should know when to use the Document options of the Format command.

Set the system defaults so they're right for most of your documents   In chapter 6, you can learn how to use the Setup command to set the system defaults for the Format command. To do that, you first access the Initial Codes option of the Setup command. Then, you access the Format command (from within the Setup command) to set the system defaults for this command.

In the top portion of figure 8-27, you can see the *WordPerfect* default settings for the Format command. These are the ones that are set when you install *WordPerfect* on your system. For most PC users, though, at least a few of the defaults aren't set the way they ought to be. So if you change these defaults to those recommended in the bottom portion of this figure, you'll take the first step toward improved formatting efficiency.

Use the Document screen of the Format command to set the Initial Base Font and Initial Codes for a document   Near the start of this chapter, I showed you how to use the Document screen of the Format command to set the Initial Base Font and Initial Codes for a document. Now that you know more about formatting, you should get in the habit of setting all of the options that apply to the entire document in this way. Often, that will include the Paper Size/Type and Tab Set option.

Discussion

When you master the skills presented in this section, you will have mastered the most practical formatting skills. These skills are all that you will need for preparing letters, memos, reports, and resumes in an attractive and convincing style. In fact, most people in business don't need all of the skills presented in this chapter. As a result, you only need to master those skills that apply to the types of documents that you prepare frequently. Later, when you need one of the other skills, you can use this chapter for reference.

You should realize, though, that *WordPerfect* provides many formatting features that aren't presented in this chapter. If, for example, you're going to prepare a screen play or a newsletter, *WordPerfect* provides for documents that have two or more columns. It also lets you import a graphic illustration or chart from another program into your document. And if your PC has a laser printer, you can use *WordPerfect* as a complete desktop publishing system. Most of these formatting features, though, go way beyond the original intent of a word processing program, way beyond the requirements of a typical word processing user in business, and way beyond the scope of this book.

The View Document screen at 100%

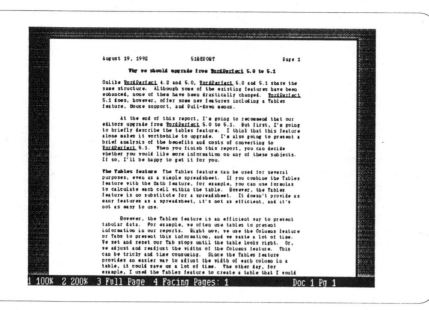

How to access the View Document screen

Print > View Document

Figure 8-26   How to view a document before printing it

Terms

font	initial base font
type family	scalable font
serif	non-scalable font
sans serif	justification
type size	justified text
cpi	ragged-right text
point	absolute tab stop
line height	relative tab stop
leading	single code
mono-spaced font	paired codes
proportionally-spaced font	indent
current printer	margin release
base font	outdent

hanging indent
dot leader
soft hyphen
normal hyphen
hard hyphen
competing codes
WYSIWYG

Objectives

1. Describe these terms as they apply to fonts:

    type family
    serif and sans serif type
    type size
    line height
    leading
    mono-spaced and proportionally-spaced fonts
    scalable and non-scalable fonts

2. Use the Print command to select the printer for a document.

3. Use the Format command to set the Initial Base Font and Initial Codes for a document without inserting codes into the document.

4. Use the Format command to set any one of the Line, Page, or Other options that are presented in this chapter.

5. Describe the function of each of the formatting codes of the Format command that are presented in this chapter.

6. Use the Font command to change the base font or the appearance of the base font within a document.

7. Use the commands and keystroke combinations for indenting, outdenting, centering, right aligning, boldfacing, and underlining.

8. Set and use tab stops for aligning tabular data with or without the use of the Tab Align command.

9. Use soft hyphens for hyphenating at the ends of lines.

10. Use the Reveal Codes screen to solve formatting problems.

11. View a document before printing it.

The *WordPerfect* default settings

Option	Default setting
Initial base font	Printer dependent
Justification	On for *WordPerfect* 5.0; Right for *WordPerfect* 5.1
Line spacing	1
Left margin	1"
Right margin	1"
Tab settings	Every 0.5"
Top margin	1"
Bottom margin	1"
Paper Size	8.5" x 11"
Widow/Orphan Protection	No (Off)

Recommended changes in the settings

Option	Recommended setting
Initial base font	The one you're going to use for most of your documents.
Justification	Off for *WordPerfect* 5.0; Left for *WordPerfect* 5.1.
Left margin Right margin	This depends on the base font. In general,the margins should be set so there are 66 or fewer characters in each printed line.
Tab set	*WordPerfect* 5.0 users should make sure that the defaults are consistent with the left margin setting.
Widow/Orphan Protection	Yes (On).

Figure 8-27   The *WordPerfect* default settings for formatting options and the recommended changes in the settings

Chapter 9

The most useful file-handling skills

When you use a hard disk, its directories and files can quickly get out of control. If you use *WordPerfect* for a year or two, for example, it's easy to create a couple hundred files. Then, if you don't organize these files logically and manage them efficiently, you're likely to have dozens of files on your hard disk that you no longer need and at least a few files that you need but can't find. That's why it's important that you learn how to do an effective job of managing your directories and files.

As I explained in chapter 2, DOS provides the commands that you need for managing files and directories. Many people, though, find that these commands are hard to use. If you're one of those people, you'll be glad to know that *WordPerfect* provides excellent file-handling functions. Since you can use these functions without exiting from *WordPerfect*, you'll probably want to use them even if you are an experienced DOS user. Often, it's more efficient to use the *WordPerfect* functions than it is to use either the DOS commands or a DOS shell.

To use the *WordPerfect* file-handling functions, though, you still need to know how to give valid DOS specifications for files and directories. In particular, you need to know how to specify a valid drive designation, a valid directory path, and a valid file name, and you should be able to combine those specifications in partial or complete file specifications. If you're not sure how to do those tasks, you should read chapter 2 again to make sure you have the concepts right.

Although this chapter presents all of the *WordPerfect* file-handling functions, you may not need them all. As a result, you should first read through this chapter to acquaint yourself with the functions. Then, you should try to master those skills that you expect to use frequently. Later, if you need to refresh your memory or if you need to learn a new file-handling skill, you can refer to this chapter for quick and effective reference.

How to set the default directory for your document files

When you start a *WordPerfect* session, the default directory may already be set to the directory that you're going to use for your document files. If it isn't, one of the first tasks that you should do is to set the default directory to the one that you're going to use. After I show you how to change the default directory, I'll show you two ways to set the default directory so it's the one you want when you start *WordPerfect*.

How to use the List command to set the default directory

Figure 9-1 presents two procedures for changing the default directory to the one you're going to use for your documents. In both procedures, you start by accessing the List command. Although this command is identified as the List Files command when you use *WordPerfect* 5.0, I'll refer to both the List and the List Files commands as the List command throughout this chapter and book.

In step 2 of the first procedure, you type an equals sign to tell *WordPerfect* that you want to change the directory that's displayed in the status line. Then, in step 3, you modify the directory specification so it's the way you want it, and you press the Enter key to complete the directory change. At that point, the new default directory is displayed in the status line. So in step 4, you can either press the Enter key to display the List screen for the new directory, or you can press the Esc or Cancel key to return to the Edit screen.

In the first two steps of the second procedure in figure 9-1, you access the List command and press the Enter key to display the List screen for the default directory. Then, in step 3, you select Other Directory from the bottom of the screen. This displays a prompt that asks you for the specification for the new default directory. In step 4, you modify the specification shown so it's the way you want it for the new directory, and you press the Enter key. Then, in step 5, you can either display the List screen for the new directory or return to the Edit screen.

How to use the Setup command to set the permanent default directory (*WordPerfect* 5.1 only)

If you only use one directory for your *WordPerfect* documents, it makes sense to set your system up so you don't have to change the default directory each time you start *WordPerfect*. If you have *WordPerfect* 5.1, you can use the Setup command to do that as summarized in the first procedure in figure 9-2. This command is explained in detail in chapter 6, but it's easy to use for setting the default directory. Just access the command, select Location of Files from the first menu, select Documents from the second menu, type the specification for the default directory, and press the Enter key.

How to use equals (=) to change the default directory

1. Access the List command (F5).

    `Dir C:\WP51\*.*   (Type = to change default Dir)`

2. Type equals (=).

    `New Directory = C:\WP51`

3. Type the drive and path that you want for the default directory and press the Enter key.

    `Dir c:\data\wprpts\*.*`

4. If you want to see the List screen for the new default directory, press the Enter key. If you want to return to the Edit screen, press the Esc or Cancel key.

How to use the Other Directory option to change the default directory

1. Access the List command (F5).

    `Dir C:\WP51\*.*   (Type = to change default Dir)`

2. Press the Enter key to display the List screen.

3. Select Other Directory.

    `New Directory = C:\WP51`

4. Type the drive and path that you want for the default directory and press the Enter key.

    `Dir c:\data\wprpts\*.*`

5. If you want to see the List screen for the new default directory, press the Enter key. If you want to return to the Edit screen, press the Esc or Cancel key twice.

Figure 9-1   How to use the List command to change the default directory

How to use DOS to set the default directory before you start *WordPerfect* (DOS 3.0 or later)

If you're using *WordPerfect* 5.0 or if you use more than one directory for your work, you can use DOS to set the default directory before you start *WordPerfect*. This is summarized in the second procedure in figure 9-2. In step 1, you use the Change-drive command at the command prompt to change the default drive to the one that your directory is stored on. In step 2, you use the Change-directory command to change the current directory to the one that you want to use as the default directory. In step 3, you start *WordPerfect*. In this step, though, you must include the drive and path for the *WordPerfect* directory as well as the command to start *WordPerfect*, and you can only do that if you're using DOS version 3.0 or a later version.

How to use the Setup command to set the starting default directory using *WordPerfect* 5.1

1. Access the Setup command (Shift+F2).
2. Select Location of Files.
3. Select Documents.
4. Type the drive and path that you want for the default directory and press the Enter key. This changes the default directory immediately. This directory also becomes the default directory each time you start *WordPerfect* release 5.1.

How to use DOS version 3.0 or later to set the default directory before you start *WordPerfect* 5.0

1. Change the drive to the one you want as the default drive as in this example:

   `C:\>d:`

2. Change the directory to the one you want as the default directory as in this example:

   `D:\>cd \wpdocs`

3. Start *WordPerfect* 5.0 by giving the path for the program along with its command name as in this example:

   `D:\WPDOCS>c:\wp51\wp`

Figure 9-2   Two ways to set the default directory so that it's in effect for all *WordPerfect* work sessions

If you're a competent DOS user, you shouldn't have any trouble using the procedure in figure 9-2. Also, you should be able to create a batch file that contains the three commands shown in this figure. Then, you can set the default directory and start *WordPerfect* just by entering the name of the batch file. If, for example, you create a batch file for this purpose that is named WP.BAT, you can set the default directory and start *WordPerfect* by typing *wp* at the command prompt and pressing the Enter key.

How to use the Save, Retrieve, and Exit commands

By the time you read this chapter, you should already know how to use the Save, Retrieve, and Exit commands. As a result, the summary in figure 9-3 should be all that you need for using these commands. If it isn't, please go back to chapters 3 and 4 to get a detailed description of how these commands work.

The Save command   When you use the Save command to save a new document, *WordPerfect* assumes that you want to save it in the default directory. If you don't, you must give a file specification that includes the path for the directory that you want the file saved in. This specification must also

Command	Access	Function	Prompts
Save	F10	Saves a document from internal memory to disk. For a new document, the default directory is assumed unless you override it by giving a complete file specification.	`Document to be saved:`
		For an old document, you are asked whether the current document should replace the old document.	`Replace D:\WPDOCS\SLSRPT? No (Yes)`
Retrieve	Shift+F10	Retrieves a document from disk into internal memory. The default directory is assumed unless you override it by giving a complete file specification. If a document is already in internal memory, the document is retrieved into the current document at the cursor location without any warning message.	`Document to be retrieved:`
Exit	F7	To start, this command asks whether you want to save the current document.	`Save document? Yes (No)`
		If the document hasn't been changed, a message is displayed on the right side of the status line that says that the document hasn't been changed.	`(Text was not modified)`
		If you decide to save the document, you get the same prompts that you get from the Save command.	`Replace D:\WPDOCS\SLSRPT? No (Yes)`
		After the document has been saved or you pass the opportunity to save it, this command either clears the screen or exits from *WordPerfect*.	`Exit WP? No (Yes)`

Figure 9-3   A summary of the Save, Retrieve, and Exit commands

include the drive if the drive is different from the one for the default directory. As a result, this command works best when you've got the default directory set up right.

When you use the Save command to save an old file (a file that you have already saved once), the complete file specification is displayed along with a message that asks whether you want to replace the old file. If you do, you select Yes. Otherwise, you can modify the file specification that's shown so it's the way you want it. Then, you can continue with the Save function.

The Retrieve command   When you use the Retrieve command to retrieve a file, *WordPerfect* assumes that you want to retrieve it from the default directory. If you don't, you must give a file specification that includes the path for the directory that you want the file retrieved from. This specification must also include the drive if the drive is different from the one for the default directory. As a result, this command works best when you've got the default directory set up right.

If you are working on a document when you use the Retrieve command, the second document is immediately retrieved into your current document at the cursor location. Unlike the Retrieve function of the List command that you'll learn about later in this chapter, the Retrieve command doesn't let you confirm the retrieve operation before it happens.

The Exit command   When you're through working on a document, you use the Exit command to either clear the screen or to exit from *WordPerfect*. When you access this command, you are first given the chance to save the document you've been working on. But if you haven't made any changes to the document since the last time you saved it, a message is displayed that tells you that the document hasn't been modified. Then, you can select No when you see this prompt:

Save document? Yes (No)

Otherwise, you can select Yes to save the document. If you do that, you get the same prompts that you do with the Save command, and *WordPerfect* assumes that you want to save the document in the default directory.

After you've saved the document or selected No to tell *WordPerfect* that you don't want to save the document, this prompt is displayed:

Exit WP? No (Yes)

If you select No, the Edit screen is cleared so you can start work on a new document. If you select Yes, you exit from *WordPerfect* and return to DOS or to the program that you started *WordPerfect* from.

To simplify the Exit procedure, I always use the Save command to save the document I've been working on before I access the Exit command. Then, I respond with *n* and *n* if I want to clear the screen and start work on a new document. And I respond with *n* and *y* if I want to exit from *WordPerfect*. This doesn't save any keystrokes, but it simplifies the Exit procedure because you don't save the document as part of it.

If you use the Switch command as described in chapter 8 to work on two documents at the same time, you use the Exit command to exit from one document at a time. I won't describe this procedure, though, because the Exit command works the same for each document.

How to use the List command to display and print directory listings

One of the most important uses of the List command is to display directory listings. You can use these displays to help you find and manage files. The directory that you display doesn't have to be the default directory, and it doesn't have to be a *WordPerfect* directory. You can use wildcards to display just those files in a directory that have certain types of names. And once you display a directory listing, you can print it.

How to display the List screen for a directory without changing the default directory
Figure 9-4 shows you how to display a directory without changing the default directory. The simplest way to do that is shown in the first procedure in this figure. In step 1, you access the List command. *WordPerfect* then displays the default directory. But if you want to display another directory, you modify the directory specification shown in the status line. Then, you press the Enter key. If, for example, you change the directory specification to

> C:\DATA\wprpts*.*

a List screen like the first one in figure 9-5 is displayed. This doesn't change the default directory because you didn't press the equals sign before you modified the directory.

How to interpret the List screen
Once a directory listing is displayed, you can use it to help you find the file you're looking for. If you're using *WordPerfect* 5.0, you may notice that your List screen is a little different than the ones shown in figure 9-5. In particular, a couple of the options at the bottom of the screen are different. However, the basic elements of the screens are the same.

On the top two lines of both the 5.0 and 5.1 screens, *WordPerfect* gives some information about the directory. As you can see in the screens in figure 9-5, the first line gives the current date and time as well as the drive and path of the directory. The second line tells you the number of bytes in the document you're working on (document size), the number of bytes left on the disk you're working on (free), the number of bytes in the directory that's displayed (used), and the number of files in the directory that's displayed (files). If you access the List screen from a blank Edit screen, the document size should be zero since you haven't started working on a document.

How to specify the directory that you want before the List screen is displayed

1. Access the List command (F5) to display the current directory:

   `Dir C:\DATA\WPMEMOS\*.*  (Type = to change the default directory)`

2. Modify the directory in the prompt so it specifies the directory that you want displayed. But don't press the equals sign (=) before you make the change. Then, press the Enter key to display the List screen for the directory that you specified.

How to move from one directory to another after the List screen is displayed

1. To display the parent directory, move the highlight to this item:

   `..  <PARENT>        <DIR>`   (for release 5.0)
   `..     Parent        <DIR>`   (for release 5.1)

   and press the Enter key. Then, the parent directory is shown at the prompt:

   `Dir C:\DATA\*.*`

   Press the Enter key again to display the List screen for the directory. If this isn't the directory you want, you can modify the directory specification before you press the Enter key.

2. To display a directory that's listed on the List screen, move the highlight to the directory and press the Enter key. Then, that directory is shown at the prompt:

   `Dir C:\DATA\WPRPTS\*.*`

   Press the Enter key again to display the List screen for the directory. If this isn't the directory you want, you can modify the directory specification before you press the Enter key.

3. If you want to respecify the directory while a List screen is displayed, access the List command to display a directory prompt that you can modify:

   `Dir C:\DATA\WPRPTS\*.*`

   Then, you can modify the directory specification

   `Dir C:\DATA\wpltrs`

   so it's the one you want displayed before you press the Enter key again.

Figure 9-4   How to display the List screen for a directory without changing the default directory

The middle part of the List screen presents an alphabetized listing of the subdirectories and files in the directory. The first screen in figure 9-5, for example, displays a list of ten files. For each file, *WordPerfect* lists the number of bytes in the file and the date and time that the file was last modified. If you're not sure which version of a file is the current version, you can often figure that out by checking the size of the file and the date and time it was last modified. If a directory contains more files than can be displayed on the List screen, you can use the Arrow keys and the Page-up and Page-down keys to expose the files that aren't initially shown.

The List screen for C:\DATA\WPRPTS*.*

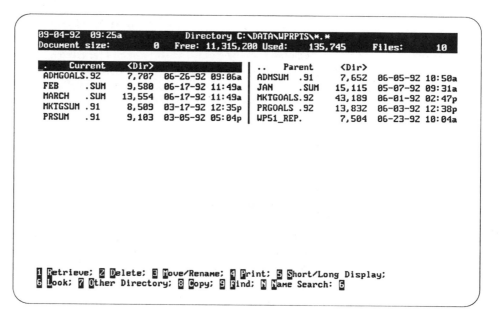

The List screen for C:\DATA*.*

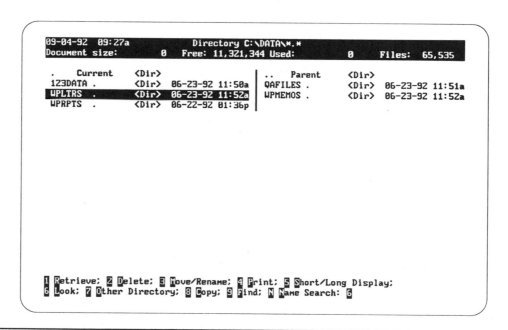

Figure 9-5   The List screens for C:\DATA and C:\DATA\WPRPTS

The top line in the listing portion of the List screen always gives entries for two directories. You can tell these entries are for directories instead of files because they both end with <Dir>. The *current directory* just refers to the directory that is being displayed, and the *parent directory* refers to the directory that the current directory is subordinate to. For the first screen in figure 9-5, the current directory is

    C:\DATA\WPRPTS

so the parent directory is

    C:\DATA

For the \DATA directory, the parent directory is the root directory. If a directory contains subdirectories, their entries are always listed before the entries for the files in the directory.

At the bottom of a List screen, you can see a selection line with ten options. After I finish showing you how to display and print directories, I'll show you how to use the eight options that perform file-handling functions.

How to move from one directory to another without changing the default directory   Once a directory is displayed, you can move from one directory display to another by using the techniques summarized in the second procedure in figure 9-4. If, for example, you want to move to the parent directory, you move the highlight to the directory on the top right of the List screen and press the Enter key. For the first screen in figure 9-5, this displays a prompt like this:

    Dir C:\DATA*.*

If that's the directory you want displayed, just press the Enter key. Then, a List screen like the second one in figure 9-5 is displayed.

If you want to display a directory that's displayed on the List screen, you move the highlight to that directory and press the Enter key. If, for example, you move the highlight to the WPLTRS entry of the second List screen in figure 9-5 and press the Enter key, a prompt like this is displayed:

    Dir C:\DATA\WPLTRS*.*

Then, if you press the Enter key again, this directory is displayed.

If you want to give a new directory specification while you're at a List screen, you can press the Enter key or access the List command again. This displays a prompt in the status line that you can modify to create the new directory specification. Then, when you press the Enter key, the new directory is displayed.

How to change the default directory to the highlighted directory
When a directory is highlighted on the List screen, you can make that directory the default directory by typing 7 for Other Directory. *WordPerfect* then asks whether you want that directory to be the new default directory. When you press Enter to indicate that you do, the displayed directory becomes the default directory.

Wildcard	Meaning
*	One or more characters of any kind
?	One character of any kind

Examples	Meaning
.	All files
*.wpm	All files with WPM as the extension
*.	All files that don't have an extension
m*.*	All files that start with M
c?.*	All one or two character files that start with C

A List screen for C:\DATA\WPRPTS*.92

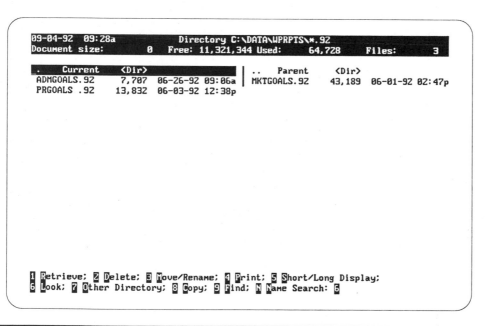

Figure 9-6   How to use wildcards to limit the number of files on the List screen

How to use wildcards to limit the display of files   If you've used DOS much, you probably know that it provides two *wildcards* you can use to limit directory listings. These wildcards are summarized in figure 9-6. In *WordPerfect*, you can use these wildcards when you use the List command to access a List screen.

A printed directory listing

```
09-10-92  02:51p              Directory D:\DATA\*.*
Free:  8,677,376

 .    Current        <Dir>                    | ..    Parent        <Dir>
BIOS    .            2,808  08-21-92 09:08a    | CATLET   .          1,411  07-06-92 01:37p
CATLET  .FM          1,346  07-06-92 02:17p    | CIPINFO .          2,828  02-19-92 11:32a
CNVNTNS .            5,812  07-06-92 04:50p    | DOSBCRTN.          1,914  11-12-91 04:36p
DWPSUM  .MMO         1,959  08-06-92 09:23a    | INVNTRY .TBL       6,829  04-01-92 10:56a
LSUN    .LTR         1,341  08-28-92 01:27p    | LWPPTS  .          1,783  07-07-92 11:15a
MOEND   .RPT         3,220  09-02-92 09:06a    | NETBAK   .         4,928  06-01-92 10:14a
NETWRK  .            4,047  05-27-92 11:05a    | PROOFING.MMO       3,059  03-03-92 04:22p
REPRINT .FRM         1,849  04-10-92 10:49a    | RESUME   .DP       1,896  08-06-92 12:11p
RESUME  .ST          1,775  08-03-92 08:31a    | RESUME   .ST2      2,328  08-06-92 12:05p
STEVEFIG.MEM         2,672  04-27-92 01:37a
```

How to print a List screen

Access the Print command (Shift+F7) while a List screen is displayed.

This prints a list of all the files that are in the specified directory, not just those that can be displayed on a single List screen.

Figure 9-7   How to print the files displayed on a List screen

The first wildcard represents one or more characters of any kind. It's referred to as the *asterisk wildcard* or the *star wildcard*. If you use wildcards, this is the one you'll use most. This wildcard makes it easy to list all the files in a directory that have a specific extension. For example, figure 9-6 shows a List screen for C:\DATA\WPRPTS*.92. If you look at the files on this screen, you can see that all of the files have this extension: 92.

The second wildcard represents one character of any kind. It's referred to as the *question mark wildcard*. Although you may never need it, it can be useful every once in a while. For example, a specification like this

C?FIGS

includes files with names C1FIGS, C2FIGS, and C9FIGS, but it excludes files with names like C19FIGS and C20FIGS.

How to print a directory listing   If you want to use a directory listing for reference, you can print it out by accessing the Print command. This is summarized in figure 9-7. As you can see, the printed directory listing has the same format as the one on the List screen. However, the printed listing includes all of the files in the directory, not just those that can be displayed on one screen.

When and how to use the long directory display (*WordPerfect* 5.1)

In this book, all of the List screens use the short directory display. If you're using *WordPerfect* 5.1, though, you can create long file names of up to 68 characters in addition to the short, 8-character names required by DOS. In theory, this lets you create names that are more descriptive so you'll be able to find your documents more easily. In practice, though, this also means that you have to take the extra time to create the long names; that the List screen is only able to display half as many names in the long form as in the short form; and that most file-handling functions work more slowly when you use long names than they do when you use only the short names. As a result, if your system asks for long names when you save a file, I recommend that you use the Setup command to turn this option off as described in chapter 6.

However, if you do use long names when you save your files, you can change the List screen display by using the Short/Long Display function that is listed at the bottom of the List screen. When you change the display to the long form, the listing portion of the screen provides for long names as well as short names. As a result, it takes *WordPerfect* longer to compose the long form of the screen. But otherwise, the List functions work the same whether you use the short or long display.

How to use the List command to manage files

Figure 9-8 summarizes the eight functions of the List screen that you can use for managing files. This summary includes seven functions that are the same for both *WordPerfect* 5.0 and 5.1, as well as one function that differs slightly. This function is called the Word Search function in *WordPerfect* 5.0 and the Find function in *WordPerfect* 5.1.

As you see in this summary, you can use the List command to retrieve, delete, rename, move, copy, and print files. You can also use it to find files with certain characteristics and to look at files without taking the time to retrieve them. To perform a function on one file, you just move the highlight to that file and select the function you want. Then, you respond to the prompts that are displayed. If you decide to cancel a function when you're at a prompt, you just press the Esc or Cancel key.

With that as background, you can probably use the functions that are summarized in figure 9-8 without any more help. If you want more information before you start experimenting with these functions, though, a description of each follows. After I describe how to use each of the functions on a single file, I'll show you how to use four of the functions on more than one file at a time.

The Retrieve function   This function retrieves the file that the highlight is on. Although you can often retrieve a file more quickly by using the

Option	Function	Prompt
Retrieve	Retrieves the highlighted file	Retrieve into current document? No (Yes)
Delete	Deletes the highlighted file or the marked files	Delete **D:\WPDOCS\SLSRPT?** No (Yes)
Move/Rename	Renames the highlighted file or moves the highlighted file or the marked files to another directory	New name: D:\WPDOCS\SLSRPT
Print	Prints the highlighted file or the marked files	Page(s): (All)
Look	Displays the contents of the highlighted file	(5.0) Press **Exit** when done (5.1) **Look: 1 N**ext Doc; **2 P**rev Doc: **0**
Copy	Copies the highlighted file or the marked files	Copy this file to:
Word Search (WP 5.0)	Finds and marks the files in the current directory that contain specific characters or words in the component of the file you select to search	See figure 9-11.
Find (WP 5.1)	Finds and lists the files in the current directory that contain specific characters or words in the component of the file you select to search	See figure 9-12.
Name Search	Moves the cursor to the first file name that starts with the characters you enter after you select this function	(Name Search; the Enter key or arrows to Exit.)

Figure 9-8   A summary of the file-handling functions that are available from the List screen

Retrieve command, the Retrieve function of the List command lets you retrieve a file when you're not quite sure how to spell its file name. It also warns you when you try to retrieve a file into the current document:

Retrieve into current document? No (Yes)

Then, if you didn't intend to do that, you can select No or press the Cancel key to cancel the command.

Keep in mind, though, that the Retrieve command has the potential to be more efficient than the Retrieve function of the List command. If you set the default directory right and use file names that are easy to remember, you can usually retrieve a file more quickly using the Retrieve command than you can using the Retrieve function of the List command.

The Delete function   This function can be used to delete the file that's highlighted. Before the file is deleted, though, *WordPerfect* gives you a warning message like this:

Delete C:\DATA\WPRPTS\ADMGOALS.92? No (Yes)

Then, to delete the file, you select Yes.

Although you can use the Cancel key to restore text that you delete from a file, you can't use it to restore a file that you delete. In fact, *WordPerfect* doesn't provide an "undelete" function to restore a file once it's deleted. That's why you should pay attention to the warning prompt and use the Delete function carefully.

The Move or Rename function   You can use this function to rename a file in the directory or to move a file to another directory. First, you highlight the file; then, you select this function. When you do, *WordPerfect* displays a prompt like this:

New Name C:\DATA\RPTS\ADMGOALS.92

Then, if you want to rename the file, you leave the path specification as it is and change the file name. But if you want to move the file to another directory, you change the path specification. If you want to change the name and move the file at the same time, you change both the path and the file name. To complete the function, press the Enter key.

The Print function   You can use this function to print the file that's highlighted. When you select this function, *WordPerfect* displays this prompt:

Page(s): (All)

Then, if you want all of the pages in the document printed, you just press Enter. Otherwise, you can specify the pages that you want printed using the symbols summarized in figure 9-9.

If you look at the summary in figure 9-9, you can see that *WordPerfect* 5.1 provides specifications for printing just the odd or even pages of a document. This can be useful when you want to print a document on both sides of the page, but your laser printer doesn't have this capability. To print on both sides, you first print the odd pages of a document. Then, you turn the pages over, put them in the form feeder of the printer, and print the even pages.

The Look function   The *WordPerfect* Look function lets you look at the contents of a document file without retrieving the document into memory.

Symbols	Function
,	Separates the entries in a list
-	Indicates that printing should include the page number to the left of the symbol, the page number to the right, and all pages in between
E	Indicates that only even-numbered pages should be printed (*WordPerfect 5.1*)
O	Indicates that only odd-numbered pages should be printed (*WordPerfect* 5.1)

Examples	Meaning
4	Print page 4
3,7	Print page 3 and page 7
2-10	Print from page 2 through page 10
5-	Print from page 5 to the end of the document
-6	Print from the first page of the document through page 6
3-5,7	Print from page 3 through page 5 and page 7
8-99	Print from page 8 to the end of the document
E	Print the even-numbered pages in the document
O	Print the odd-numbered pages in the document
E4-	Print the even-numbered pages from page 4 to the end of the document
O3-9	Print the odd-numbered pages from page 3 through page 9

Figure 9-9   How to specify the pages to be printed when you use the Print function

This can save you time when you're not sure which file contains the document that you want. To use this function, you first move the highlight to the file that you want to look at. Then, you can press the number *6* or the letter *l* to start the Look function. Usually, though, you just press the Enter key because the default value in the prompt is the number *6*, and that starts the Look function.

When you start the Look function for a *WordPerfect* document file, your screen will look like one in figure 9-10. Then, you can use the keystroke summary in this figure to move the cursor through the document. However, you can't edit the document when you're using this function. When you're sure that the document is the one you want, you can press the Enter key to end the Look function. Then, you can use the Retrieve function to retrieve the document, or you can perform one of the other functions on the file.

If you look at the keystroke summaries for *WordPerfect* 5.0 and 5.1 in figure 9-10, you can see that the Look function doesn't work quite the same for both of these releases. When you're using release 5.0, the Page-up and Page-down keys move one page back and one page forward in the document.

The Look screen for *WordPerfect* 5.1

```
File: C:\DATA\WPRPTS\ADMGOALS.92          WP5.1      Revised: 06-26-92 09:06a

Administrative goals for 1992

Customer service    Although our customer service is already
excellent, our goal is to continue to improve it.  For instance, I
would like us to ship all orders within one day from the time we
receive them.

Productivity standards    In 1991, salaries and wages for the
administrative group went up 38.3 percent, but sales only
increased 13 percent.  To some extent, that means that our people
weren't as productive in 1991 as they were in 1990.  That's why
our goal for 1992 is to not only provide the best (and most
personal) customer service in the industry, but also to do it with
maximum efficiency and productivity.

Training    In 1992, I'd like to continue to emphasize training.
Our goal should be to train all the people in the department so
that next year at this time they're more valuable to us...and to
themselves.  That means on-the-job training for everyone and in-
class training for some.

Look: 1 Next Doc; 2 Prev Doc: 0
```

Keystrokes for using the Look screen with *WordPerfect* 5.1

Down arrow	Scrolls down
Up arrow	Scrolls up
Home Home Up	Views the first page of the file
Home Home Down	Views the last page of the file
Page-down	Views the next file in the directory
Page-up	Views the previous file in the directory
Enter	Ends the Look function
Exit	Ends the Look function

Keystrokes for using the Look screen with *WordPerfect* 5.0

Down arrow	Scrolls down
Up arrow	Scrolls up
Home Home Up	Views the first page of the file
Home Home Down	Views the last page of the file
Page-down	Views the next page in the file
Page-up	Views the previous page in the file
Enter	Ends the Look function
Exit	Ends the Look function

Figure 9-10   How to use the Look screen

To look at another document, you have to end the function for the current document, move the highlight to the next document, and start the Look function again. When you're using release 5.1, though, the Page-up and Page-down keys move one document back and one document forward on the List screen. This makes it more efficient to look at one document after another as you try to find the one you want. If you look at the bottom of the Look screen in figure 9-10, you can see that you can also use the numbers *1* and *2* and the letters *n* and *p* to move the Look function from one document to the next.

If you try to use the Look function on a file that doesn't contain a *WordPerfect* document file, *WordPerfect* may not be able to read the contents of that file. If, for example, you use this function to look at a program file, the Look screen displays characters that are incomprehensible. On the other hand, if you use this function to look at an ASCII file or a document from another word processing program, some of the characters will be understandable, but others will be incomprehensible.

The Copy function   You can use this function to copy a file within a directory or from one directory to another. You can also use it to copy a file from a directory on the hard disk to a diskette. When you select this function, *WordPerfect* displays a prompt like this:

Copy this file to:

Here, you can type a file name, a path, or a complete file specification including drive, path, and file name. If you type just a file name, the highlighted file is copied to a file in the same directory but with a new file name. If you type a path without a file name, the highlighted file is copied to a file in the new directory but with the old file name. And if you type just a diskette drive specification like *a:*, the highlighted file is copied to a file in the root directory of the diskette in that drive.

The Word Search function (*WordPerfect* 5.0)   You can use this function to find files that contain a specific word pattern. You can search for this pattern in document summaries, first pages, or entire documents. If, for example, you want *WordPerfect* to find all the documents that contain a reference to "networking," you can search for this word pattern: network. This search works just like the search done by the Search command, but it will continue through all the documents that are displayed by the List command.

Figure 9-11 summarizes the use of this function. In step 1, you select this function while the List screen is displayed. In step 2, you select the option that you want *WordPerfect* to search through. If you use document summaries with your documents, you can select Doc Summary to search just the document summaries for the word pattern. (I haven't presented document summaries in this book because I don't recommend their use.) More likely, you will select First Pg or Entire Doc to tell *WordPerfect* that you want to

A List screen with the files marked by the Word Search function

```
09/04/92  09:53              Directory C:\DATA\WPRPTS\*.*
Document size:        0   Free: 11321344  Used:     67884       Marked: 3

. <CURRENT>      <DIR>                    .. <PARENT>     <DIR>
ADMGOALS.92      7707  06/26/92 09:06     ADMSUM  .91      7652  06/05/92 10:50
FEB     .SUM     9580x 06/17/92 11:49     JAN     .SUM    15115x 05/07/92 09:31
MARCH   .SUM    13554  06/17/92 11:49     MKTGOALS.92     43189* 06/01/92 14:47
MKTGSUM .91      8509  03/17/92 12:35     PRGOALS .92     13832  06/03/92 12:38
PRSUM   .91      9103  03/05/92 17:04     WP51_REP.        7504  06/23/92 10:04




1 Retrieve; 2 Delete; 3 Move/Rename; 4 Print; 5 Text In;
6 Look; 7 Other Directory; 8 Copy; 9 Word Search; N Name Search: 6
```

How to use the Word Search function to mark the files that contain the specified word pattern

1. Select the Word Search function when the List screen is displayed.

   Search: 1 Doc Summary; **2 F**irst Pg; **3 E**ntire Doc; **4 C**onditions: **0**

2. Select one of the first three options to search the document summaries, the first pages, or the entire documents for the files on the List screen. After you select an option, this prompt is displayed:

   Word pattern:

3. Type the word pattern that you want *WordPerfect* to look for. Then, press the Enter key. If the word pattern consists of more than one word, the pattern must be started and ended with a quotation mark ("). When *WordPerfect* finishes the search, it displays just the files that contain the specified word pattern in the component of the file that you specified in step 2.

Figure 9-11   How to use the Word Search function (*WordPerfect* 5.0)

search only the first pages of the documents or the entire documents. The fourth option in the prompt for this step lets you search for a few more conditions. Since you shouldn't ever need to do that, though, I won't present that option in this book.

In step 3, you type the word pattern that you want *WordPerfect* to search for. If this pattern contains only one word, you just type that word after the prompt. But if it contains more than one word, you must put quotation marks around the word pattern as in this example:

"networking options"

You can also use wildcards in the word pattern, although I doubt that you'll ever need to.

When *WordPerfect* finishes its search, it displays a screen like the one at the top of figure 9-11. Here, the files that are tagged with an asterisk are called *marked files*. These are the ones that contained the specified word pattern. You can then print the List screen so you'll have a record of the marked files. Or you can perform functions on the marked files like deleting, moving, or copying them. I'll show you how to do that in a moment.

The Find function (*WordPerfect* 5.1)   You can use this function to find the files that contain a specific word pattern. You can search for the pattern in file names, document summaries, first pages, or entire documents. If, for example, you want *WordPerfect* to find all the documents that contain a reference to "networking," you can have it search for this word pattern: network. This search works just like the search done by the Search command, but it will continue through all the documents that are displayed by the List command.

Figure 9-12 summarizes the use of this function. In step 1, you select this function while the List screen is displayed. In step 2, you select the option that you want *WordPerfect* to search through. If you want to search through just the file names, you select Name. If you use document summaries with your documents, you can select Doc Summary to search just the document summaries for the word pattern. (I haven't presented document summaries in this book because I don't recommend their use.) More likely, you will select First Pg or Entire Doc to tell *WordPerfect* that you want to search only the first pages or the entire documents. The fifth option in the prompt for this step lets you search for a few more conditions, but you shouldn't ever need to do that so I won't present this option in this book.

In step 3, you type the word pattern that you want *WordPerfect* to search for. If this pattern contains only one word, you just type that word after the prompt. But if it contains more than one word, you must put quotation marks around the word pattern as in this example:

"networking options"

You can also use wildcards in the word pattern, although I doubt that you'll ever need to.

When *WordPerfect* finishes its search, it displays a List screen with only the files that contained the specified word pattern. You can then print the List screen so you'll have a record of these files. Or you can perform functions on these files like deleting, moving, or copying them. I'll show you how to do that in a moment.

A List screen with the three files selected by the Find function

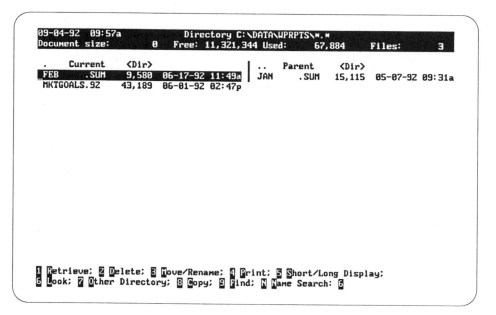

How to use the Find function to display just the files that contain the specified word pattern

1. Select the Find function while the List screen is displayed.

2. Select one of the first four options to search the file names, the document summaries, the first pages, or the entire documents for the files on the List screen. After you select an option, this prompt is displayed:

   Word pattern:

3. Type the word pattern that you want *WordPerfect* to look for. Then, press the Enter key. If the word pattern consists of more than one word, the pattern must be started and ended with a quotation mark ("). When *WordPerfect* finishes the search, it displays just the files that contain the specified word pattern in the component of the file that you specified in step 2.

4. To cancel all selections, you select Find again and select the Undo option from the prompt.

Figure 9-12   How to use the Find function (*WordPerfect* 5.1)

If you decide that you want to return the List screen to the way it was before you performed the Find function, you can select the Find function again. Then, when you select the Undo option, the screen is returned to the way it was before the last Find function.

The Name Search function   This function moves the cursor to the file or group of files that start with the characters you specify. After you select this function, you type the first character or two of the file name that you want to move the cursor to. When you do this, *WordPerfect* shows the characters you type on the bottom left corner of the List screen, and it moves the cursor to the first file name that starts with those characters. If, for example, you type the letter *t*, the cursor jumps to the first file name that starts with that letter. Then, if you type the letter *o*, the cursor jumps to the first file name that starts with the letters *to*. You can continue in this way until the cursor reaches the file name that you want. Often, though, you only need to type a character or two to reach the file or group of files that you want. As a result, this method of moving the cursor is frequently more efficient than using the Arrow keys. However, you have to at least know the first character of the file name. To end this function, you can press an Arrow key or the Enter key.

How to perform the List functions on more than one file at a time

To perform one of the List functions on more than one file at a time, you first mark the files that you want to perform the function on. Then, you select the appropriate function and respond to any prompts that appear.

How to mark files   To *mark a file*, you move the highlight to the file that you want to mark. Then, you type an asterisk (the uppercase symbol on the 8-key on the typewriter keyboard or the asterisk on the numeric key pad). This puts an asterisk next to the file as illustrated by the List screen in figure 9-11. If you're using *WordPerfect* 5.0, you can also use the Word Search function to mark files as I explained earlier. If you want to remove an asterisk that's next to a file name, type another asterisk in the same spot. In other words, the asterisk works as a toggle switch.

To mark all of the files in the directory of a List screen, you can access the Mark Text command (Alt+F5). You can also press the Home key followed by the asterisk. If you change your mind and want to remove all marks, you just perform those keystrokes again.

How to delete, move, copy, or print the marked files   Figure 9-13 gives a complete procedure for deleting, moving, copying, or printing more than one file at a time. After you mark the files in step 2, you select the function that you want to perform in step 3. To complete the function, you respond to the prompts listed in this figure. After you select Yes to tell *WordPerfect* that you want to perform the function on all the marked files, you continue like you do when you perform the function on a single file. If, for

How to delete, move, or copy more than one file at a time

1. Access the List screen for the directory that the files are in.
2. Type an asterisk next to the files that you want to mark. Or if you want to mark all of the files, access the Mark Text command or press Home followed by an asterisk. If you're using *WordPerfect* 5.0, you can also use the WordSearch function to mark files.
3. Select Delete, Move/Rename, Copy, or Print.
4. Respond to the prompts.

Delete prompts

```
Delete marked files?  No (Yes)
Marked files will be deleted. Continue?  No (Yes)
```

Move prompts

```
Move marked files?  No (Yes)
Move marked files to:
```

Copy prompts

```
Copy marked files?  No (Yes)
Copy marked files to:
```

Print prompts

```
Print marked files?  No (Yes)
Page(s): (All)
```

Figure 9-13   How to delete, move, copy, or print more than one file at a time

example, you want to print just the first page of the marked files, you select the Print function, select Yes at the first prompt, and enter *1* at the Page(s) prompt.

How to use the List command to manage directories

In general, you should use DOS or a DOS shell when you want to create or delete a directory. Then, before you create a directory, you can use the DOS Tree command or the Tree display of a DOS shell to display the directory structure. That way, you can review this structure to make sure that you're adding the new directory in a logical place. You can also review this structure after you've created or deleted a directory to make sure that the function worked the way you wanted it to.

How to create a directory

1. Access the List command (F5) to display a directory prompt.

   `Dir C:\WP51\*.*   (Type = to change default Dir)`

2. Type equals (=).

   `New Directory = C:\WP51`

3. Type the specification for the drive and directory that you want to create and press the Enter key.

   `Create C:\DATA? No (Yes)`

4. Select Yes.

How to delete a directory

1. Delete all files in the directory, or move all the files in the directory to a new directory.
2. Highlight the directory that you want to delete on a List screen.
3. Select the Delete function. To do this, you can use the Delete key or the Delete option at the bottom of the screen.

   `Delete C:\DATA\WPLTRS?  No (Yes)`

4. Select Yes. If the directory isn't empty, *WordPerfect* will give you an error message like this:

   `ERROR: Directory not empty`

   Otherwise, the directory is deleted.

Figure 9-14   How to create or delete a directory

But if you're uncomfortable with DOS, you can also use *WordPerfect* to create and delete directories. And since you can do this without exiting from *WordPerfect*, even experienced DOS users will occasionally want to use *WordPerfect* to create or delete directories.

How to create a directory   The first procedure in figure 9-14 shows you how to use the List command to create a new directory. In step 1, you access the List command and get the List prompt. In step 2, you type equals (=), type the specification of the directory that you want to create, and press the Enter key. Then, if the directory that you specified doesn't exist, *WordPerfect* displays a prompt like this:

Create C:\DATA\WPLTRS? No (Yes)

To create the directory, select Yes. Sometimes, though, you get this prompt by accident when you try to change the default directory and you give an incorrect directory specification. In that case, select No.

Before you can create a directory named C:\DATA\WPLTRS, you must first create the C:\DATA directory. If the \DATA directory doesn't exist when you try to create a subordinate directory, *WordPerfect* displays an error message that says you have specified an invalid path. If you understand DOS, you won't have any trouble with prompts like this. And if you don't understand DOS that well, you probably shouldn't be creating directories. Instead, you should either get help or learn more about DOS.

How to delete a directory   The second procedure in figure 9-14 shows you how to use the List screen to delete a directory. Before you can delete a directory, it must be empty. So in step 1, you delete or move any files in the directory that you want to delete.

In step 2, you highlight the directory that you want to delete on the List screen. To delete the C:\DATA\WPLTRS directory, for example, you access the List screen for the C:\DATA directory. Then, you move the highlight to the \WPLTRS directory.

In step 3, you select the Delete function. You can do this by selecting the Delete function at the bottom of the screen or by pressing the Delete key. When you do, *WordPerfect* displays a prompt like this:

Delete C:\DATA\WPLTRS? No (Yes)

To delete the directory, select Yes. Then, if the directory isn't empty, *WordPerfect* displays an error message to alert you to that fact. Otherwise, the directory is deleted.

Four file-handling skills for occasional use

You now know how to use all of the *WordPerfect* file-handling functions. With a little practice, you should be able to apply those functions to whatever file-handling requirements you encounter. Here, though, are four specific skills that you're likely to need occasionally.

How to combine two or more documents   Figure 9-15 shows you how to combine two documents. In step 1, you retrieve a document. In step 2, you move the cursor to the point in the first document where you want the second document to be retrieved. In step 3, you retrieve the second document into the first document to combine the two. Then, if you want to combine more than two documents, you can continue in this way.

When one document is retrieved into another document, it is given the formatting defaults of the first document. However, if formatting codes have been inserted into the second document, the inserted codes override the defaults. If that's not what you want, you have to search for the inserted codes and delete them.

To avoid this problem, you can use the Document options of the Format command to set the default options for the documents that you intend to combine. This use of the Format command is described in chapter 8. The

1. Retrieve the first document.
2. Position the cursor where you want the second document to be retrieved.
3. Retrieve the second document. If you use the Retrieve command, no warning message is displayed. If you use the Retrieve option of the List command, this message is displayed:

   `Retrieve into current document? No (Yes)`

   Select Yes to complete the retrieve.
4. To combine more documents, repeat steps 1-3.

Figure 9-15   How to combine two or more documents by using multiple retrieves

advantage of using the Document options for formatting is that no formatting codes are inserted into a document. Then, when you combine documents that are formatted in this way, inserted codes aren't a problem. Instead, all of the combined documents get the default formats of the first document.

When you save a combined document, *WordPerfect* gives it the same name as the first document that you retrieved. If that's not what you want, be sure to modify the name before you save the combined document. Also, if you don't want the individual documents to remain on your hard disk, you can delete them after you've combined them.

How to apply new system defaults to an old document by retrieving it into a document that contains one space   When you create a new document, it is given the formatting defaults of the system. Then, if you retrieve the document on a system that has different defaults, the document retains the defaults that it was created with. Often, though, that's not what you want.

Figure 9-16 shows you an easy way to apply new system defaults to an old document. In step 1, you clear the screen to start a new document. In step 2, you press the Spacebar once. This makes *WordPerfect* think that you've started a document. In step 3, you retrieve the old document into the document that consists of one space. In effect, this procedure is the same as the one for combining two documents. So when the old document is retrieved, it is given the defaults of the first document, and those are the new system defaults. Here again, though, inserted codes override the system defaults. So you may have to delete the inserted codes that conflict with the system defaults. In step 4, you delete the space at the top of the document.

When you save the document with the new codes, *WordPerfect* doesn't assume a name for it. Instead, it treats it like a new document. Normally, you use the name of the old document at the save prompt. Then, when you save the document, it replaces the previous version of the document.

1. Clear the Edit screen to start a new document.
2. Press the Spacebar to enter one space into the new document. That space is now the first document in internal memory so it is given the default settings for the system.
3. Retrieve the document that you want to apply the system defaults to. If you use the Retrieve command, no warning message is displayed. If you use the Retrieve option of the List command, this message is displayed:

   Retrieve into current document? **No** (**Yes**)

   Select Yes to complete the retrieve. The document defaults of this document are now replaced by the system defaults.
4. Use the Backspace key to remove the space at the top of the document.

Figure 9-16   How to apply the system defaults to a document by retrieving it into a document that contains one space

How to use a diskette to transfer *WordPerfect* files from one PC to another   If you want to move one or more *WordPerfect* files from one PC to another, you can use the List command as summarized in figure 9-17. In the first procedure, you mark the hard-disk files that you want to transfer, and you copy them to a diskette. In the second procedure, you mark the diskette files that you want to transfer, and you copy them to an appropriate directory on the hard disk.

When you're working with diskettes, make sure the diskettes are formatted. If they aren't, *WordPerfect* displays an error message something like this:

Diskette in drive A not formatted

You must also make sure that the diskettes that you're using are compatible with both PCs. If, for example, you're using a high capacity, 3-1/2 inch, diskette drive to transfer files to a PC with a standard capacity, 3-1/2 inch, diskette drive, you must use a standard capacity diskette for the transfer. Today, however, most PCs have both 5-1/4 and 3-1/2 inch disk drives that support high capacity diskettes. Consequently, diskette compatibility usually isn't a problem.

How to save a block within a document   If you use the Block command to block a portion of a document, you can use the Save command to save the block. Once you access the Save command, it works the same way it does when you save an entire document.

Four guidelines for managing directories and files

Now that you've learned how to use *WordPerfect* to manage your directories and files, here are four guidelines that will help you do a better job of

How to copy files from a hard drive to a diskette

1. Access the List screen for the directory that contains the files that you want to copy.
2. Highlight the file you want to copy or mark each of the files that you want to copy.
3. Select Copy.

    `Copy marked files? No (Yes)`

4. Select Yes.

    `Copy all marked files to:`

5. Insert the diskette in drive A, type *a:* after the prompt, and press the Enter key.

    `* Please Wait *`

    While this message is displayed, *WordPerfect* copies the file or files to the diskette.

6. Press the Cancel key to return to the Edit screen.

How to copy files from a diskette to a directory on a hard drive

1. Insert the diskette into drive A.
2. Access the List screen for drive A by entering a: at the prompt:

    `Dir a:`

3. Highlight the file you want to copy or mark each of the files that you want to copy.
4. Select Copy.

    `Copy marked files? No (Yes)`

5. Select Yes.

    `Copy all marked files to:`

6. Type the drive and directory that you want to copy the files to and press the Enter key.

    `* Please Wait *`

    While this message is displayed, *WordPerfect* copies the file or files to the hard drive.

7. Press the Cancel key to return to the Edit screen.

Figure 9-17   How to transfer files between PCs using a diskette

managing them. You should know these guidelines whether you use *WordPerfect* or DOS to manage your directories and files. Because these guidelines are all fairly obvious, I'll go through them quickly.

Store your files in logically organized directories   If you use a logical directory structure, you will be able to find your files more easily, manage them more effectively, and back them up more efficiently. To illustrate what I mean by a logical directory structure, figure 9-18 illustrates three types of logical directory structures.

In the first example, the PC has only a C drive, and all the program directories are subordinate to the root directory: DOS, UTIL, WP51 (for *WordPerfect* 5.1), 123 (for *Lotus 1-2-3*), and QA (for *Q&A*). Then, all of the data or document directories are subordinate to the related program directories. For instance, the WK1 directory that is subordinate to the 123 directory contains the spreadsheet files for *Lotus 1-2-3*. The MEMOS directory that is subordinate to WP51 directory contains the document files for memos prepared with *WordPerfect*. The DOCS directory that's subordinate to the QA directory contains the document files for *Q&A*. This is an acceptable directory structure because separate directories are used for programs and data; the directory names are short and easy to remember; and the directory structure is logical. If several people use the same PC, you can expand this type of structure so there is one set of directories for each PC user.

In the second example in figure 9-18, the PC has only a C drive, and all the program directories are subordinate to the root directory. However, all of the data directories are subordinate to the \DATA directory. This makes it easier to back up the data directories without backing up the program directories. As a result, I prefer this structure to the first structure.

In the third example in figure 9-18, the PC has both a C and a D drive. Then, all the program directories are stored on the C drive, and all the data directories are stored on the D drive. This makes it even easier to back up data directories without backing up program directories. This also makes it easier to give more structure to the organization of the data directories. If, for example, three people share one PC, the directory structure for drive D can be expanded so it's easy to tell which people use which directories.

Limit the number of files in each of your directories   When a directory reaches a certain size, it becomes more difficult to find the files you're looking for. For *WordPerfect*, you usually reach that point when a directory contains more files than can be displayed on one List screen. Then, it make sense to look for ways to reduce the number of files in the directory.

Often, all you have to do to reduce the number of files in a directory is to delete the files that you no longer need. With *WordPerfect*, you can easily find and delete those files by using the Look and Delete functions of the List screen. If that doesn't solve the problem, you can consider organizing the files of one directory into two or more directories. Here again, *WordPerfect* makes it easy for you to create new directories, to look at and mark old files, and to move the marked files.

Use consistent file names   A good file name is one that's descriptive enough to tell you what's in the file and distinct enough to distinguish it from

A typical directory structure for a PC that only has a C drive

C Drive

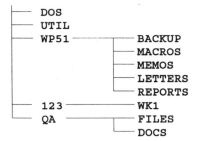

A better directory structure for a PC that only has a C drive

C Drive

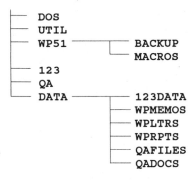

An efficient directory structure for a PC that has a C drive and a D drive

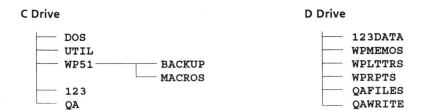

Figure 9-18   Three typical directory structures

other files with similar names. Unfortunately, you can't always create good file names with a limit of eight characters for the name and three for the extension. That's why it's so important that you organize your data files in logical directories and that you keep those directories small.

Within each data directory, you should try to create file names that are consistent. If you only use one directory for *WordPerfect* data, for example, you may want to use extensions to help distinguish your files. For instance, you can use .RPT for reports, .LTR for letters, and .MEM for memos.

Whenever practical, put each document's file name in its heading

Because you can't always create distinctive file names, you should try to include the file names in the headings of your documents whenever that's practical. Then, if you need to modify a document, you can tell what its file name is by reading the heading. Usually, you don't need to include the directory name along with the file name in the heading, but if there's any chance for confusion, include the directory path too.

Discussion

As thoroughly as this chapter covers file-handling skills, it doesn't present those functions that are related to the use of document summaries. These functions aren't presented for two reasons. First, if you use a logical directory structure, keep your document directories small, and use meaningful file names, you shouldn't need document summaries to help you keep track of your files. Second, your productivity usually goes down when you use document summaries. They slow you down because they require more entries, and they slow *WordPerfect* down too.

If you have any trouble using the file-handling functions like the Move or Copy functions of the List command, it's probably because your DOS background isn't as strong as it ought to be. If, for example, you have trouble specifying the path for the Copy function, that's probably because you don't have a clear idea of how your specification is going to be interpreted. The remedy for that problem, of course, is to learn more about DOS. Although the *WordPerfect* List command lets you perform most of the file-handling functions that you need without using DOS, you should at least know what the directory structure is for your PC and what the appropriate specifications are for using the directories in that structure.

Terms

current directory
parent directory
wildcard
asterisk wildcard
star wildcard
question mark wildcard
marked file

Objectives

1. Describe two ways for setting the default directory for your *WordPerfect* documents before you start *WordPerfect*.

2. Use the List command to set the default directory after you start *WordPerfect*.

3. Use the Save and Retrieve commands to save documents to and retrieve documents from the default directory. And use the Exit command to either clear the Edit screen or exit from *WordPerfect*.

4. Use the List command to display or print any directory on a disk drive without changing the default directory. If necessary, use wildcards to limit the number of files displayed.

5. Use the Name Search function of the List command to move the highlight to a file; use the Look function to display the contents of the file; and use the Retrieve function to retrieve the file.

6. Use the List command to perform any of the following functions on one or more files:
    Delete
    Move or Rename
    Copy
    Print

7. Use the Find function (5.1) or the Word Search function (5.0) of the List command to find all of the documents that contain a specific word pattern on the first page of the document or anywhere in the entire document.

8. Use the List command to create or delete a directory.

9. Combine two or more documents into a single file.

10. Apply new system defaults to an old document by retrieving it into a blank document.

11. Use a diskette to transfer *WordPerfect* files from one PC to another.

Chapter 10

The most useful printing skills

In chapters 3 through 5, you learned how to use the Print command for printing a full document or one page of a document. With that as background, you shouldn't have any trouble learning the printing skills presented in this chapter.

To start, you'll learn several different ways to print entire documents and specific pages from within multi-page documents. You'll also learn how to view a document before you print it. Next, you'll learn how to use the Control Printer screen to manage the printing operations. Then, you'll learn how to use the options of the Print command. To finish, you'll learn how the Paper Size/Type option of the Format command can affect printing operations and how the printer itself can affect printing operations.

How to use the primary functions of the Print command

When you access the Print command, *WordPerfect* displays one of the Print screens shown in figure 10-1; these are the screens for *WordPerfect* 5.0 and 5.1. As you can see, the top portion of each screen is a menu that provides seven printing functions. Of these, six are the same for both releases of *WordPerfect*. In contrast, the bottom portion of each screen is a menu of printing options. Here, the screen for *WordPerfect* 5.0 provides five options, and the screen for release 5.1 provides those five plus a sixth.

When you print in *WordPerfect*, you can print an entire document or one or more pages from a document that's on your Edit screen. This is known as *printing from the screen*, or *printing from memory*. You can also print an entire document or one or more pages from a document that's stored on disk without retrieving the document. This is known as *printing from disk*. In the Print functions listed in figure 10-1, the Full Document function and the Page functions print from the screen, and the Document on Disk function prints from disk. Later on in this chapter, you'll also learn how to use the Print function of the List command to print from the disk.

When you start a printing function, there is a short pause while *WordPerfect* creates a *print job* for the document and sends the print job to the printer. Then, *WordPerfect* lets you continue work while the job is printing. *WordPerfect* also lets you start other print jobs before the first one is finished, and it lets you manage the list of jobs by using the Control Printer function of the Print screen. This capability can be referred to as *print spooling*, and it is one of the features that makes *WordPerfect* a powerful word processing program.

While a job is being printed from the screen, you can continue working on it. Or you can exit from that document and begin working on another one. However, you can't exit from *WordPerfect* while a document is printing. If you try to do that, *WordPerfect* displays a warning prompt like this:

Cancel all print jobs? No (Yes)

If you select No at this prompt, *WordPerfect* returns you to the Edit screen. If you select Yes at this prompt, *WordPerfect* cancels all print jobs and completes the exit operation.

With that as background, you're ready to learn how the functions and options of the Print command work. In this chapter, you'll learn how to use all of the print functions and options of the Print screens in figure 10-1. I'll start by showing you how to use the five primary functions of the Print command.

The Full Document function   You should already know that you use the Full Document function of the Print command to print the entire document that's on the Edit screen. The procedure for this function is the first one in figure 10-2. You can start this function no matter what page the cursor is on.

The Page function   You use the Page function to print one page from the document on the screen. To do that, you use the second procedure in figure 10-2. In this case, you must make sure that the cursor is on the page you want to print before you start this function.

The Document on Disk function   You can use the Document on Disk function to print all of the pages or just specific pages from a document that's on disk. To do that, you use the third procedure in figure 10-2. In step 3, you type the name of the document file that you want to print and press the Enter key. If the document is in the default directory, you enter the file name only. Otherwise, you need to enter a specification that identifies the drive and directory as well as the file name.

In step 4, you press the Enter key to print all of the pages of the document. If you want to print a specific page or pages, you enter a page specification as summarized in figure 10-3. Since *WordPerfect* 5.0 doesn't provide a way to specify pages when you print from the screen, this function is particularly useful for users of release 5.0. To print selected pages of the

The Print screen for
WordPerfect **5.0**

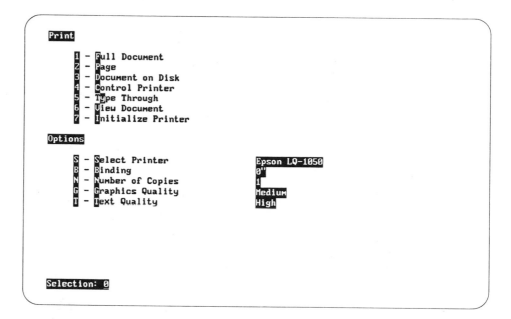

The Print screen for
WordPerfect **5.1**

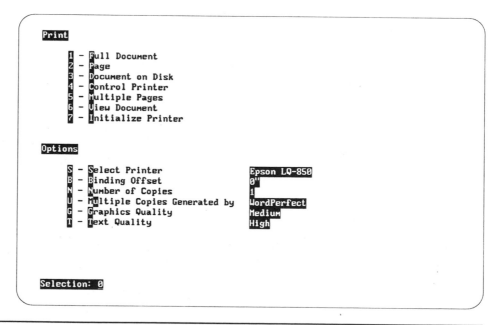

Figure 10-1   The Print screens for *WordPerfect* 5.0 and 5.1

document you're working on, first save it to disk. Then, use the Document on Disk function to print it.

When you print a document from disk using *WordPerfect* 5.0, you may get an error message like this:

ERROR: Document was Fast Saved — Must be retrieved to print

This means that the Fast Save option was on when the document was saved, so the document can't be printed from disk. Then, you must retrieve the document before you can print it. To turn the Fast Save option off so your documents aren't saved in this format, you use the Setup command as described in chapter 6.

If you look at the summary in figure 10-3, you can see that *WordPerfect* 5.1 provides specifications for printing just the odd or even pages of a document. This can be useful when you want to print a document on both sides of the page, but your laser printer doesn't have this capability. To print on both sides, you first print the odd pages of a document. Then, you turn the pages over, put them in the form feeder of the printer, and print the even pages.

The Multiple Pages function (*WordPerfect* 5.1 only)

If you're using *WordPerfect* 5.1, you can use the Multiple Pages function to print specific pages from the document that's on the Edit screen. To do that, you use the third procedure in figure 10-2. Here again, you use the specifications that are summarized in figure 10-3 to specify the pages that you want printed.

The View Document function

WordPerfect for DOS is not a *WYSIWYG* (what-you-see-is-what-you-get) program. As a result, the Edit screen doesn't show you how a document is going to look when it's printed. If, for example, a document has a header or a footer or if it's going to be printed with right justification, that's not shown on the Edit screen.

When you select the View Document option, however, a screen like the one in figure 10-4 is displayed. Although the text on this screen may be more difficult to read than the text on the Edit screen, the View Document screen shows you how the document is going to look when it is printed. Then, if something doesn't look right, you can correct the document on the Edit screen before you print it.

When you're at the View Document screen, you can use the normal keystroke combinations to move the cursor from one page to another and from one area of a page to another. You can also select any one of the four options shown in figure 10-4. If, for example, you want to see what an entire page is going to look like, select the full page option. You probably won't be able to read any of the text when you use this option, but you'll able to see the format of the entire page. Then, if you want to display the text in a larger size, you can select the 100% or 200% option. To return to the Print screen, press the Cancel key. To return to the Edit screen, press the Exit key.

If you discover a formatting problem when you use the View Document screen, you have to return to the Edit screen to make any formatting changes.

How to print a document from the Edit screen

1. Access the Print command (Shift+F7).
2. Select Full Document.

How to print a page from the Edit screen

1. Move the cursor to the page you want to print.
2. Access the Print command (Shift+F7).
3. Select Page.

How to print a document from disk

1. Access the Print command (Shift+F7).
2. Select Document on Disk.

   `Document name:`

3. At the prompt, type the name of the document and press the Enter key. If the document is in the default directory, you need to enter just the file name for the document. Otherwise, you need to enter a complete file specification that includes the drive and path.

   `Page(s): (All)`

4. At the prompt, press the Enter key to print all of the pages. Otherwise, enter a page specification as summarized in figure 10-3 to identify the pages that you want to print.

How to print multiple pages from the Edit screen (*WordPerfect* 5.1 only)

1. Access the Print command (Shift+F7).
2. Select Multiple Pages.

   `Page(s):`

3. Enter a page specification as summarized in figure 10-3 to identify the pages that you want to print and press the Enter key.

Figure 10-2   How to use the Print command to print documents

If you find several problems, you may have to go back and forth between the Edit screen and the View Document screen several times. Since this can be time consuming, it is often more efficient to print out the document to identify problems. This is particularly true if your document is short or if your PC takes a long time to prepare the View Document screen.

Symbols	Function
,	Separates the entries in a list
-	Indicates that printing should include the page number to the left of the symbol, the page number to the right, and all pages in between
E	Indicates that only even-numbered pages should be printed (*WordPerfect* 5.1)
O	Indicates that only odd-numbered pages should be printed (*WordPerfect* 5.1)

Examples	Meaning
4	Print page 4
3,7	Print page 3 and page 7
2-10	Print from page 2 through page 10
5-	Print from page 5 to the end of the document
-6	Print from the first page of the document through page 6
3-5,7	Print from page 3 through page 5 and page 7
8-99	Print from page 8 to the end of the document
E	Print the even-numbered pages in the document
O	Print the odd-numbered pages in the document
E4-	Print the even-numbered pages from page 4 to the end of the document
O3-9	Print the odd-numbered pages from page 3 through page 9

Figure 10-3   How to specify the pages to be printed when you use the Print function

Two other functions of the Print command

Now that I've presented the primary functions of the Print command, I'd like to introduce two functions that you may never need to use.

The Type Through function (*WordPerfect* 5.0 only)   If you select this function, *WordPerfect* sends all keystrokes directly to the printer without creating a document. In theory, this function is supposed to let you use your PC as if it were a typewriter. That way, you can use your PC to fill out forms. In practice, though, it's just too difficult to get the form correctly aligned in the printer. As a result, you shouldn't have any use for this function.

The Initialize Printer function   You can buy *soft fonts* for some printers that allow you to expand the number of fonts that the printer can print. Before you can use the soft fonts, though, you must use the Select Printer option of the Print screen to mark the fonts you want to use. In addition, you

The View Document screen at 100%

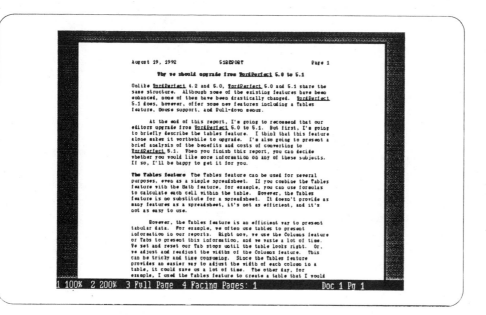

How to access the View Document screen

> Print > View Document

The four viewing options

Option	Meaning
100%	Display the current page at the size it's going to be when it's printed
200%	Display the current page at twice the size it's going to be when it's printed
Full page	Display the current page in its entirety
Facing pages	Display the current page and the facing page with odd numbered pages on the right and even numbered pages on the left

Figure 10-4   How to view a document before printing it

may be required to use the Initialize Printer function to load the fonts into your printer's memory. This, however, depends upon how your system is set up.

If you use soft fonts, you may also have to initialize the printer each time your printer's memory is erased. This memory is erased when you turn your printer off. But it's also erased when you use the Stop function of the Control Printer menu that you'll learn about in a moment. For the purposes of this book, I assume that you're not using soft fonts, so I won't say any more about the Initialize Printer function.

Two other ways to print a document or a portion of a document

Most of the time, you use the Print command to print a document or a portion of a document. But you should also know how to use the List command to print a document on disk. And you should know how to use the Print command to print a block from within a document on the Edit screen.

How to use the List command to print documents   Figure 10-5 shows you how to use the List command to print one or more documents on disk. In the first procedure, you access the List command and display the directory that contains the document that you want to print. Then, you highlight the document and select the Print function from the prompt at the bottom of the List screen. If you want to print selected pages from the document, you enter page specifications as summarized in figure 10-3. Then, when you press the Enter key, the document is printed.

The second procedure in figure 10-5 shows you how to print two or more documents from a List screen. In step 1, you access the List command and display the directory that contains the files you want to print. In step 2, you mark the files that you want to print. If you don't know how to do this, it's explained in detail in chapter 9. In step 3, you select Yes to tell *WordPerfect* that you want to print all of the marked files. In step 4, you usually press Enter to indicate that you want to print all of the pages of all of the marked files. However, if you only want to print selected pages of the files, you can enter page specifications in this step of the procedure. If, for example, you want to print just the first page of each marked file, you can enter a *1*.

Because the List command prints from disk, you may get an error message with *WordPerfect* 5.0 that says a document can't be printed because the Fast Save option was on when the document was saved. Then, you must retrieve the document before you can print it. To turn the Fast Save option off so your documents aren't saved in this format, you use the Setup command as described in chapter 6.

How to print a block from within a document   If you want to print a portion of a document, you can use the Block command to block that portion

---

How to use the List command to print a single document

1. Access the List command (F5) and display the directory that contains the file you want to print.
2. Move the highlight to the file name.
3. Select Print.

   `Page(s): (All)`

4. At the prompt, press Enter to print all pages, or enter a page specification as summarized in figure 10-3 to identify the pages that you want to print.

How to use the List command to print multiple documents

1. Access the List command (F5) and the List screen for the directory that contains the files you want to print.
2. Mark the files that you want to print.
3. Select Print.

   `Print marked files?  No (Yes  )`

4. Select Yes.

   `Page(s): (All)`

5. Press the Enter key to print all the pages of all the documents. However, you can also enter a page specification as summarized in figure 10-3 to identify the pages that you want to print from each of the documents. For example, you can print just the first page of each document.

Figure 10-5 How to use the List command to print documents

of the document. Then, you can use the Print command to print the block. When you access the Print command, *WordPerfect* displays a prompt like this:

Print block? No (Yes)

To print the block, select Yes.

How to use the Control Printer function of the Print command to control print jobs

When you print a document or a portion of a document, *WordPerfect* creates a print job for the document. Then, it sends the print job to a print file. If you start several print jobs, *WordPerfect* stores all of them while it waits for the printer to print them. While the jobs are printing, you can use the Control Printer function of the Print command to control the jobs. For instance, you can use the Cancel function to cancel a job or the Rush function to move a job up in the print sequence, or *print queue*.

When you select the Control Printer function from the Print screen in figure 10-1, a screen like the top one in figure 10-6 is displayed. As you can see in this figure, the top portion of the screen gives information about the job that is currently being printed (the *current job*). This information includes the job number, the paper size, the paper location (like the continuous form feed or the manual form feed), the page number that is currently being printed, and the copy number that is currently being printed.

If a job isn't printing properly, this portion of the screen may display a message that helps you solve the problem. If, for example, the printer is turned off when you start a print job, the Message line says, "Printer not accepting characters," and the Action line says "Check cable, make sure printer is turned ON." So whenever you start a print job and it doesn't start printing, one of the first steps you should take is to access the Control Printer screen to see if there's a message that will help you solve the problem.

The middle portion of the Control Printer screen displays up to three of the jobs that are waiting to be printed. This display can be referred to as the *job list*. In figure 10-6, for example, you can see that three jobs are listed and that two additional jobs aren't shown. This means that there are five jobs in the job list. If a job is printed from disk, the file specification for the document file is shown in the Document column of the job list. If a job is printed from the screen, the word *screen* is shown in the Document column. At the bottom of the Control Printer screen is a selection line that provides for five control functions. Of the five, you should know how to use the Display Jobs and the Cancel Jobs functions, and you have to know how to use the Go function. On the other hand, you may never need the Rush Jobs or the Stop Jobs functions.

The Display Jobs function   On the Control Printer screen, the number after "Additional jobs not shown" tells you how many print jobs aren't shown on the job list. To display the entire job list, you select the Display Jobs function from the selection line at the bottom of the screen. This displays a screen like the second one in figure 10-6. Then, you can get the job number for each print job. This number identifies the job, and you need it to perform some of the other control functions on the job.

The Cancel Jobs function   The first procedure in figure 10-7 shows you how to cancel the printing of one or more print jobs. After you access the Print command in step 1, you select the Cancel Jobs function from the Control Printer screen in step 2. In step 3, you enter the number of the job you want to cancel. Or you enter an asterisk (*) to cancel all of the jobs in the job list. When you cancel all print jobs, *WordPerfect* cancels all of the print jobs in the job list, not just those shown on the Control Printer screen.

When you cancel a print job, the printer doesn't stop printing immediately. Instead, it finishes printing the contents of its memory. This

The Control Printer screen

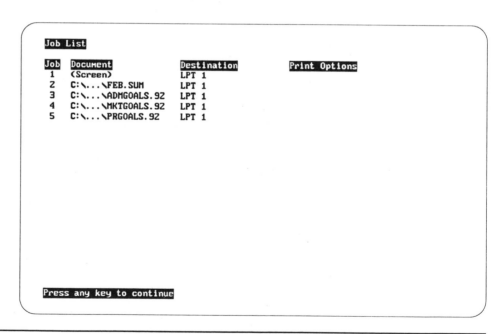

```
Print: Control Printer

Current Job

Job Number: 1                              Page Number:  1
Status:      Printing                      Current Copy: 1 of 1
Message:     None
Paper:       Standard 8.5" x 11"
Location:    Continuous feed
Action:      None


Job List

Job  Document              Destination      Print Options
 1   (Screen)              LPT 1
 2   C:\...\FEB.SUM        LPT 1
 3   C:\...\ADMGOALS.92    LPT 1

Additional Jobs Not Shown: 2



1 Cancel Job(s); 2 Rush Job; 3 Display Jobs; 4 Go (start printer); 5 Stop: 0
```

The Display Jobs screen

```
Job List

Job  Document              Destination      Print Options
 1   (Screen)              LPT 1
 2   C:\...\FEB.SUM        LPT 1
 3   C:\...\ADMGOALS.92    LPT 1
 4   C:\...\MKTGOALS.92    LPT 1
 5   C:\...\PRGOALS.92     LPT 1













Press any key to continue
```

Figure 10-6   The Control Printer screen and the Display Jobs screen

portion of the printer's memory is called the *print buffer*. The size of this buffer ranges from less than a page to several pages, depending on the printer.

The buffer size of the printer has a direct effect on the Control Printer screen. If a buffer is large, for example, the screen may indicate that page 10 is being printed when the printer is actually printing page 6. That's because the print buffer holds four or more pages. Similarly, if you send four one-page jobs to the printer, the Control Printer screen may indicate that no jobs are in the job list, even though the printer is printing just the first of the four jobs. That's because all four jobs are already stored in the print buffer.

The Rush Jobs function   The second procedure in figure 10-7 shows you how to rush a job by moving it to the top of the print queue. After you select the Rush function in step 2 of the procedure, you enter the number of the job you want rushed in step 3. Then, in step 4, you decide whether you want to interrupt the current job or move the rush job to the top of the queue so it will print after the current job. If you select Yes to interrupt the current job, *WordPerfect* will print the rushed job after it prints the current page. Then, when *WordPerfect* finishes printing the job you rushed, it finishes printing the job you interrupted.

When you complete step 4 of this procedure, the Action line on the Control Printer screen says, "Press R to rush the job immediately." You don't want to do this, though. If you do, *WordPerfect* is likely to start printing the rushed document right in the middle of the page for the current document. As a result, neither document prints the way you want it to.

The Stop function   The third procedure in figure 10-7 shows you how to stop printing a job. You can use this function if your printer has a malfunction (like a paper jam) while you're printing a long document. Then, after you fix the problem and reload the paper, you can tell *WordPerfect* what page to resume printing on. If, for example, your printer jams on the seventh page of a ten-page document, you can restart the print job on page seven.

Because the Stop function keeps track of what page the job was stopped on, it makes it easy for you to restart the print job. Otherwise, this procedure has the same effect as turning the printer off and on. This means that your printer's memory is erased. So if you're using soft fonts, you may have to initialize your printer before you continue with other print functions.

As you can see, the Stop function is of minimal value because you can stop a print job almost as easily by turning the printer off. This stops the print job immediately and clears the print buffer. Then, you can use the Control Printer screen to cancel the job if part of it hasn't been sent to the printer. To restart, you turn the printer back on, adjust the form in the printer so printing will resume at the top of a new form, and put the printer back on line. Next, if you're using soft fonts, you may have to initialize the printer.

How to cancel one or more print jobs

1. Access the Print command (Shift+F7) and select the Control Printer function from the Print screen.
2. Select Cancel.

   `Cancel which job? (* = All) 1`

3. To cancel one job, type the number of the job and press the Enter key. To cancel all jobs, type an asterisk and press the Enter key.

How to rush a print job

1. Access the Print command (Shift+F7) and select the Control Printer function from the Print screen.
2. Select Rush.

   `Rush which job? 3`

3. Type the number of the job you want to rush and press the Enter key.

   `Interrupt current job? No (Yes)`

4. If you select Yes, *WordPerfect* prints the job you're trying to rush after it finishes printing the current page. If you select No, *WordPerfect* prints the job you're trying to rush after it finishes printing the current job.

How to stop a print job

1. Access the Print command (Shift+F7) and select the Control Printer function from the Print screen.
2. Select Stop.

   `WARNING: If you use this option, you will need to initialize your printer before you can continue printing. You will also need to make sure all forms are in their original positions. Are you sure? No (Yes)`

3. Select Yes.
4. Adjust the paper in the printer and select the Go function.
5. Select the Go function again to restart the printer.

   `Restart on page:`

6. Type the page number you want to resume printing on and press the Enter key. The default number *WordPerfect* gives is the page that was printing when you accessed the Stop function.

Figure 10-7   How to use the Cancel, Rush, and Stop functions of the Control Printer screen

Then, you can use the Print command to print the document again. If you print the document from disk or use the Multiple Pages function, you can also specify the right starting page for the document.

The Go function   When you use the Printer Control screen, you sometimes need to use the Go function to start or restart the print job. The Action line at the top of the Control Printer screen tells you when to use this function with a message like this:

>   **Press "G" to continue**

If, for example, you use the Stop function, you need to use the Go function to restart the job. And if you use manual forms in your printer, you may have to access the Go function after you load each page into your printer.

How to set the options at the bottom of the Print screen

Figure 10-8 summarizes the options that are displayed at the bottom of each Print screen in figure 10-1. If you only use one printer on your PC and it's set up the way you want it, you may never need to access any of these options. However, you should at least know what they can do for you.

On most PCs, the system defaults for the print options in figure 10-8 are set the way you want them to be. As a result, you only have to change one of these options when you want to affect the printing for the current document. You should realize, though, that the defaults for all of these options except the Select Printer option are changed by using the Setup command. To do that, you access the Setup command, select Initial settings, and select Print Options. Then, you change the default option just as you would change one of the print options on the Print screen. To change the default printer and its related settings, however, you use the Select Printer option of the Print screen.

The Select Printer option   On the Print screen in figure 10-1, you can see that the name of the current printer is displayed to the right of the Select Printer option. Then, if you have more than one printer installed on your system, you can use this option to change the current printer.

When you select the Select Printer option, *WordPerfect* displays a screen like the first one shown in figure 10-9. In this example, two printers are available for selection. To select one of them, you move the highlight to it and press the number *1*, the letter *s*, or the Enter key. When you select a printer, it stays in effect until you change it. In other words, it becomes the default printer.

If you select a printer after you've inserted the base font codes for another printer into a document, *WordPerfect* tries to convert the codes for the old printer to equivalent codes for the new printer. As it converts each code, *WordPerfect* puts an asterisk in front of the code that you can see when you reveal codes. If both the new printer and the old printer support a font

Option	Function	Choices	Applies to	In force until
Select Printer	Select the printer that you want to use from a list of the printers that have been installed on your version of *WordPerfect*, whether or not the printer is actually attached to your PC	Any installed printer	Current document and new documents	You change this option
Binding Offset	Specify how far from the paper edge you want your formatted documents printed; this offset distance is added to the left margin on odd pages and to the right margin on even pages		Current document	You exit from the document, or you change this option
Number of Copies	Specify the number of copies that you want printed		Current document	You exit from the document, or you change this option
Multiple Copies Generated by	Specify how the copies should be generated	WordPerfect Printer	Current document	You exit from the document, or you change this option
Text Quality	Select a text quality	Do not print Draft Medium High	Current document	You exit from the document, or you change this option
Graphics Quality	Select a graphics quality	Do not print Draft Medium High	Current document	You exit from the document, or you change this option

Figure 10-8   A summary of the options that are available from the Print screen

that's used within a document, *WordPerfect* will probably convert that code correctly. However, if the new printer doesn't support a font that's been inserted into a document, *WordPerfect* will convert that code to the default font for the new printer. If the conversion doesn't work the way you want it to, you have to change the initial base font for the document and the base font codes within the document so they're appropriate for the new printer. The use of the Format and Font commands for these purposes is described in detail in chapter 8.

If you want to add a printer to the Select Printer list, you can use the Additional Printers option that's in the selection line at the bottom of the

Select Printer screen. This option lets you choose from a list of printers that are supported by *WordPerfect*. You can add one of these printers to the Select Printer list even if the printer isn't attached to your PC. That way, you can create a document that is formatted properly for a printer that's attached to another PC. Then, you can use a diskette to transfer the document from your PC to the other PC, and you can print the document on the other PC without making any changes to it.

If you want to change the initial base font for a printer, you can use the Edit option that's in the selection line at the bottom of the Select Printer screen. When you select this option, *WordPerfect* displays a screen like the second one in figure 10-9. When you select the Initial Base Font option, a list of the available fonts is displayed so you can select the one that you want. This font then becomes the default base font for all new documents. This process is described in detail in chapter 6, and you can learn how to change fonts within a document in chapter 8.

You can also use an Edit Printer screen like the one in figure 10-9 to identify the port that your printer is attached to. You can use this screen to tell *WordPerfect* that your printer has a special sheet feeder attached to it. You can use this screen to tell *WordPerfect* which *font cartridges* you are going to plug into your printer or which soft fonts are available to your printer. And you can use this screen to give a path for the directory that contains the soft fonts. Once your printer has been installed properly on your system, though, you shouldn't have to use the Edit function for these purposes. As a result, I'm not going to show you how to use the Edit Printer screen for these purposes in this book.

The Binding Offset option   If you're going bind a document after you print it, you can use this option to increase the margins on the left side of odd numbered pages and on the right side of even numbered pages. If, for example, you enter a value of .5 inches as the binding offset and the left and right margins are both 1 inch, the left margins on odd numbered pages and the right margins on even numbered pages become 1.5 inches. Then, if you use a laser printer to print the documents with odd numbered pages on one side of the paper and even numbered pages on the other, the pages will be ready for binding. Or if you print the pages on just one side but use a copier to copy them on two sides, they will be ready for binding.

The Number of Copies option   If you want to print more than one copy of a document, you can use this option. If, for example, you want to print three copies of a memo, you can select this option, type *3*, and press the Enter key. Then, you print the document.

The Multiple Copies Generated by option (*WordPerfect* 5.1)   If you're using *WordPerfect* 5.1, you can use this option to specify whether

The Select Printer screen

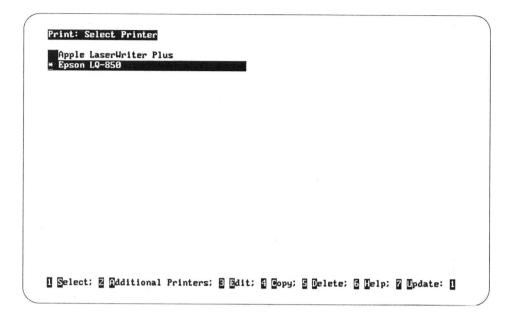

The Edit Printer screen

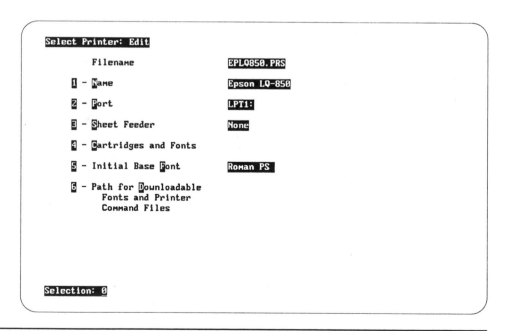

Figure 10-9   The Select Printer screen and the Edit Printer screen

WordPerfect or the printer should generate the copies. When *WordPerfect* generates the copies, it generates each set of copies individually. In other words, the sets are collated. In contrast, when the printer generates the copies, it generates all the copies for the first page, all the copies for the second page, and so on. Because the way the printer generates the copies is more efficient, this option is particularly useful when you're printing complex pages on a laser printer. However, this option doesn't work on dot-matrix printers, and it doesn't work on all laser printers either.

The Text Quality option   You can use this option to print text in draft, medium, or high quality. Since you can continue working on documents while *WordPerfect* is printing and since high quality text is the easiest to read, you usually want this option set to high. But if you want to print a long document quickly, you can use this option to print in draft quality mode. My printer, for example, takes about 40 seconds to print a full page of text in either medium or high quality mode, but it takes only 15 seconds to print the same page of text in draft quality mode. On the other hand, draft quality printing is much harder to read than either the medium or high quality printing.

The Graphics Quality option   You can use this option to print graphics in draft, medium, or high quality. You can also use this option to not print the graphics at all. This makes sense when you want to review the text for a page, but you don't want to take the time to print the graphics. Although this book doesn't teach you how to use graphics, you should realize that this option works the same way that the Text Quality option does.

How the Paper Size/Type option of the Format command can affect printing operations

In chapter 8, I showed you how to use the Paper Size/Type option of the Format command to specify the size and type of the paper that you're going to use for a document. If you always print on the same sized paper on standard forms and the default settings are correct, you won't ever have to use this option. But if you change from one paper size to another, from continuous to manual forms, or from paper in one form feed to paper in another, you should know how this option can affect printing operations.

The Paper Size setting just tells *WordPerfect* what size paper you're going to use so the proper commands are sent to the printer. If, for example, you're using continuous forms on a dot-matrix printer, *WordPerfect* needs to know what the paper size is so it can tell the printer how far to skip to get to the top of the next form. Once you get the size set right, the printing procedures for one size form should be the same as for another size form, regardless of form type.

In contrast, the Paper Type setting for *WordPerfect* 5.0 can be used to tell *WordPerfect* whether the paper is a standard continuous form or some other type of form. If the type isn't a standard continuous form, *WordPerfect* won't start printing a document until you respond to one of its messages. To do that, you have to select the Control Printer function of the Print screen. Then, you usually have to select the Go function to start a job printing. For some paper types, you may have to select the Go function to start the printing for each page of the document.

If you're using *WordPerfect* 5.1, you can use the Paper Size/Type option to tell *WordPerfect* more specifically how you want the printing operations handled. To start, when you select this option of the Format command, a Paper Size/Type screen like the one in figure 10-10 is displayed. If you're going to use one of the forms listed, you move the highlight to that form and press the Enter key. If, for example, you select the third form in the first screen in figure 10-10, the form will be 9.5 x 4 inches (envelope size), it will be a manual form, and *WordPerfect* will prompt you to load the form.

If you want to add a form to the listing or change the specifications for one of the listed forms, you can use the Add or Edit functions that are listed at the bottom of the first screen in figure 10-10. Either way, that leads you to an Edit Paper Definition screen like the second screen in figure 10-10. Here, you can set several other options that can affect printing operations. For instance, can use the Font Type option to tell *WordPerfect* whether you want to print the document the normal vertical way (portrait) or sideways (landscape). You can use the Prompt to Load option to tell *WordPerfect* whether you want it to require a response before it starts printing. You can use the Location option to tell *WordPerfect* whether the form that you're going to use is a manually fed form or a continuous form. If it's a manual form and your printer has more than one form feed (bin), you can also use this option to tell *WordPerfect* which bin the form is going to come from. And you can use the Double Sided Printing option to tell *WordPerfect* to print on both sides of the form.

Of course, most of these options are closely related to the printer that you're using. If, for example, your printer can't print in landscape mode, it makes no sense to set it for landscape printing. Similarly, if your printer has only one form feed, it makes no sense to set the Location option to Bin 2. Although *WordPerfect* may accept settings that don't make sense, the settings will be ignored when the documents are printed.

When you set the Paper Size/Type option for a document, you should realize that your settings may not work quite the way you want them to. As a result, you should be prepared to experiment with the settings until you get them right. This is one of the frustrations of working with printers. But once you establish the right settings for each form that you use on each printer, you can reuse those settings whenever appropriate.

The Paper Size/Type screen for *WordPerfect* **5.1**

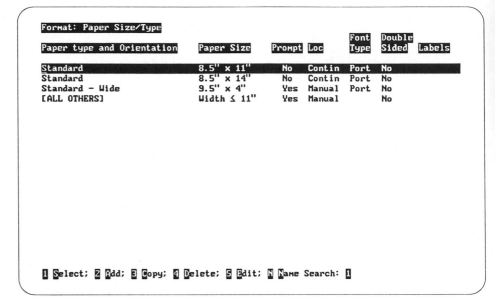

The Edit Paper Definition screen for *WordPerfect* **5.1**

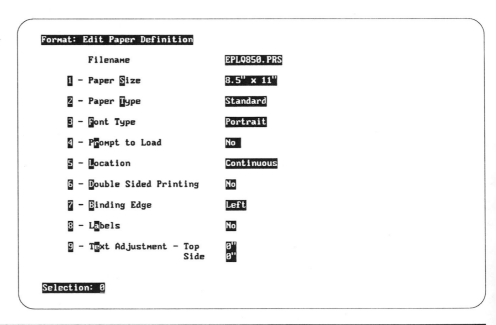

Figure 10-10   The Paper/Size Type screen and the Edit Paper Definition screen for *WordPerfect* 5.1

How the printer can affect printing operations

Today, most printers are either dot-matrix printers or laser printers, but there are many variations from one printer to another. Most dot-matrix printers, for instance, provide for the use of both continuous and manual forms, but some have two different form feeders. Then, one feeder can be used for one form (like letterhead paper) and the other feeder can be used for another form (like envelopes). Similarly, most laser printers have only a single form feeder, but some have two or more. And most can print on only one side of the paper, but some can print on both.

As you would expect, the operating procedures also vary widely from one printer to another. And often, these procedures determine how efficiently you can use a printer for printing certain types of forms. That's why it's worth taking the time to learn how to use your printer the way it was designed to be used. Perhaps the best way to do that is to ask an experienced colleague to show you the tricks for efficient operation. Otherwise, you should take the time to read the manual for your printer.

Discussion

This chapter probably presents more printing skills than you need to use on a regular basis. So now that you've been introduced to the most useful printing functions, you can decide which ones you should take the time to master. Later, if you decide that you want to use one of the other functions, you can use this chapter for quick and easy reference.

Terms

printing from the screen	soft font
printing from memory	print queue
printing from disk	current job
print job	job list
print spooling	print buffer
WYSIWYG	font cartridge

Objectives

1. Use the Print command to print one or more pages from a document on the screen or a document on disk.

2. Use the Print command to view a document before printing it.

3. Use the List command to print one or more pages from a document on disk.

4. Use the Block and Print commands to print a block from within a document.

5. Use the Control Printer function of the Print command to cancel, rush, stop, or start a print job.

6. Use the Select Printer option of the Print command to select a printer for a document.

7. Use the Binding Offset, Number of Copies, Multiple Copies Generated By, and Text Quality options of the Print command to set the printing specifications for a document.

8. If you're using *WordPerfect* 5.0, use the Paper Size/Type option of the Format command to specify the size and type of paper to be used for a document. If appropriate, these specifications should provide for manual and continuous forms and for efficient operational procedures.

9. If you're using *WordPerfect* 5.1, use the Paper Size/Type option of the Format command to specify the Paper Definition for the form to be used for a document. If appropriate, this definition should provide for manual and continuous forms, for the correct form bin, and for efficient operational procedures.

Chapter 11

How to use the spelling checker and thesaurus

WordPerfect's spelling checker is so quick and easy to use that you'll probably want to use it on every document you create. *WordPerfect*'s thesaurus is also quick and easy to use so it comes in handy whenever you're trying to think of a synonym or an antonym for a word. In this chapter, you'll learn how to use both of these *WordPerfect* features with maximum efficiency.

How to use the spelling checker

You can use *WordPerfect*'s Spell command to check a document for spelling and for certain types of typographical errors. To check for spelling, *WordPerfect* looks up each word its dictionary that contains about 115,000 words. If the word is in the dictionary, *WordPerfect* assumes it's correct. If it isn't, *WordPerfect* displays a screen that lets you correct the word. This feature of *WordPerfect* is often referred to as the *spell check feature* or as the *spelling checker*. *WordPerfect*'s spelling checker runs so fast on most PCs that you'll be able to check most documents in less than 30 seconds.

Although the spelling checker usually finds most of the errors in a document, it won't catch all spelling and typographical errors. If, for example, you spell *there* as *their*, the checker won't catch the error because both words are in its dictionary. Similarly, if you type *though* when you mean to type *through*, the checker won't catch the error. Nevertheless, the spelling checker is a useful feature that you should use on most of the documents that you create.

Figure 11-1 shows you a general procedure for using the spelling checker. In step 1, you access the Spell command by pressing the Ctrl+F2 key combination. This displays a prompt with six options. The first three options:

Check: 1 Word; 2 Page; 3 Document

are the ones you'll use most often. I'll explain how to use the other three options later in this chapter. In step 2, you select one of these options to check the spelling of a single word, a single page, or the entire document.

Once the spelling checker starts checking the spelling, you simply respond to the screens that are displayed as indicated in step 3 of figure 11-1. For the most part, your responses are obvious, but I'll explain the options in detail in a moment. Then, when all the words have been checked, *WordPerfect* displays a message line like the one after step 3 in figure 11-1. This shows you how many words were checked. In step 4, you press any key to return to the Edit screen.

If you want to cancel the spelling checker at any time during its operation, you can press the Cancel key (F1). When you do, *WordPerfect* displays a message that gives you a count of the number of words that were checked before the cancellation. Then, you press any key to return to the Edit screen.

How to respond to the three screens of the spelling checker   Once you start the spelling checker using the Word, Page, or Document option, *WordPerfect* starts checking for errors. Whenever it finds one, it displays a screen with options that you can select to correct the error. When you correct an error, the spelling checker continues to search for the next error.

Both release 5.0 and 5.1 display two types of error screens: the Not Found and the Double Word screens. The Not Found screen indicates a spelling error. The Double Word screen indicates the use of the same word two times in a row (a common typing error). If you're using release 5.1, the spelling checker also displays a third screen: the Irregular Case screen. This screen indicates that a word is spelled in a way that usually isn't correct, like *firSt* instead of *first*.

You can see a typical Not Found screen in figure 11-2. Here, the highlighted word *analysis* is the one that *WordPerfect* couldn't find in its dictionary. Then, right below the horizontal line that divides the screen, *WordPerfect* lists some possible corrections for the word. At the bottom of the screen, *WordPerfect* displays a selection line.

If one of the listed words is correct, type its letter. Then, *WordPerfect* replaces the incorrect word with the word you selected, and it continues the spelling check. If, for example, you press *a* for *analysis*, *WordPerfect* replaces the word *analisis* in the document with the word *analysis*. Since you use letters to select from the list of possible corrections, you must use numbers to select the options from the selection line at the bottom of the screen.

Figure 11-2 summarizes the options for the Not Found screen. If the word that's highlighted is correct, you can press *1* to skip it for this time only or *2* to skip it for the rest of the spelling check. If you want to add the word to the supplemental spelling dictionary, you press *3*. You'll learn more about this dictionary in a moment. Once you add a word to this dictionary, the word won't show up on subsequent Not Found screens because it will be found by the spelling checker.

If you want to edit the word that's highlighted by the Not Found screen, press *4*. You use this when *WordPerfect* doesn't display any words as possible

1. Access the Spell command (Ctrl+F2).

   `Check: 1 Word; 2 Page; 3 Document; 4 New Sup. Dictionary; 5 Look up; 6 Count: 0`

2. Select the Word, Page, or Document option.

3. Respond to the Not Found, Double Word, and Irregular Case screens that *WordPerfect* displays until all the words have been checked. If you want to cancel the spell check before completion, press the Cancel (F1) key.

   `Word Count: 1204                              Press any key to continue`

4. Press any key to return to the Edit screen.

Figure 11-1   How to use the spelling checker

corrections or it doesn't display the right word. When you press *4*, *WordPerfect* moves the cursor to the highlighted word so you can correct it. Then, you can use the Left and Right arrow keys to move to the part of the word that you want to correct. After you correct it, you press the Enter or Exit key to continue with the spelling check.

If you want to look up a word in the dictionary when the Not Found screen is displayed, press *5* to select the Look Up option. You can also select this option from the opening prompt of the Spell command that is shown in step 1 of figure 11-1. This option lets you look up the spelling of a word in *WordPerfect*'s dictionary when you know only a few letters of the word's proper spelling. When *WordPerfect* stops at the word *occrance*, for example, it doesn't recognize it as an attempt to spell *occurrence*. As a result, the Not Found screen doesn't include any possible corrections. Then, if you select the Look Up option, *WordPerfect* displays this prompt:

Word or word pattern:

Here, you can type how you think the word should be spelled. You can even type a phonetic spelling (how the word sounds) to look up the word. If you type *okurance*, for example, *WordPerfect* will list *occurrence* as a possible correction. Then, you can select it to replace the misspelled word.

If you know how to use wildcards, you can use the * wildcard and the ? wildcard when you enter a word pattern for *WordPerfect* to look up as in this example:

Word or word pattern: occ*r*ce

For this pattern, *WordPerfect* finds only the word *occurrence*. When you use wildcards, the * (asterisk) represents one or more characters and the ? (question mark) represents just one character. If you refer to chapter 9, you can learn how to use wildcards, and you can see examples of the use of wildcards within file names in figure 9-6.

If the highlighted word on the Not Found screen consists of a combination of letters and numbers like F6, you can press *6* if you want to ignore words with embedded numbers for the rest of the spelling check. This is useful when you're doing some types of technical writing, like writing this book.

Figure 11-3 illustrates the Double Word screen and summarizes its options. As you can see, this screen and its options work much like those for the Not Found screen. For a double word, you can press *2* to skip it, *3* to delete the second word, *4* to edit it, or *5* to stop checking for this type of error for the rest of the spelling check.

Figure 11-4 illustrates the Irregular Case screen and its options. This type of checking, however, is only done by *WordPerfect* 5.1, not by *WordPerfect* 5.0. Once the Irregular Case screen is displayed, you can press *2* to skip the irregular case, *3* to replace it, *4* to edit it, or *5* to stop this type of checking. You should realize, though, that the Replace option doesn't always work the way you would expect. That's why I suggest that you use the Edit option instead of the Replace option to correct an irregular case. That way, you can make sure that the word is corrected properly.

How to use the default supplemental dictionary

When *WordPerfect* checks the spelling of the words in a document, it uses both a *main dictionary* and a *supplemental dictionary*. If it doesn't find a word in either the main or the supplemental dictionary, *WordPerfect* displays the Not Found screen in figure 11-2. Then, if you select the Add option, *WordPerfect* adds the word to the supplemental dictionary and continues with the spelling check. From that time on, *WordPerfect* will find the word that has been added to the supplemental dictionary so it won't be displayed as an error.

Figure 11-5 gives the file names that are used for the main dictionary and the *default supplementary dictionary*. These dictionaries are stored in the directory that's identified by the Location of Files option of the Setup command. You can learn how to use this command in chapter 6, and figure 6-8 shows you the Location of Files screens for *WordPerfect* 5.0 and 5.1. On many PCs, both the main dictionary and the default supplemental dictionary are stored in a directory named \WP50 for *WordPerfect* 5.0 and \WP51 for *WordPerfect* 5.1.

If you use the default supplemental dictionary for all of your work, you probably won't ever have to know what the name of this dictionary is or what directory it's located in. Occasionally, though, you may want to edit the supplemental dictionary. If, for example, you accidently add a misspelled word to your supplemental dictionary, you can just retrieve the file, delete the word, and save the corrected file. When you retrieve the file, you'll notice that the words are arranged in alphabetical order. After you edit the dictionary file, you can save it just as you would save any other *WordPerfect* document.

How to use a named supplemental dictionary

If you work on several different types of projects, you may want to use a different

The Not Found screen

```
        At the end of this report, I'm going to recommend that our
editors upgrade from WordPerfect 5.0 to 5.1.  But first, I'm going
to briefly describe the tables feature.  I think that this feature
alone makes it worthwhile to upgrade.  I'm also going to present a
brief analisis of the benefits and costs of converting to
WordPerfect 5.1.  When you finish this report, you can decide
whether you would like more information on any of these subjects.
If so, I'll be happy to get it for you.

The Tables feature  The Tables feature can be used for several
                                            Doc 1 Pg 1 Ln 15 Pos 24
{                                                          }

        A. analysis          B. analyses          C. analysts
        D. analyzes          E. annalists         F. annuluses



Not Found: 1 Skip Once; 2 Skip; 3 Add; 4 Edit; 5 Look Up; 6 Ignore Numbers: 0
```

Option	Function
Letter	Replaces the highlighted word with the one you select
1 Skip Once	Skips the word this time only
2 Skip	Skips the word for the rest of the spell check
3 Add	Adds the word to the supplemental dictionary
4 Edit	Changes to edit mode so you can edit the word
5 Look Up	Looks up the spelling of the word that you enter at the prompt that follows
6 Ignore Numbers	Stops checking for words with embedded numbers for the rest of the spell check

Figure 11-2   The options of the Not Found screen

supplemental directory for each type of project. The easiest way to do that is to use the New Sup Dictionary option of the starting screen for the Spell command as summarized in figure 11-6. When you use this option, you specify a *named supplemental dictionary*. Then, *WordPerfect* uses the named dictionary as the supplemental dictionary instead of the default supplementary dictionary. The named supplemental dictionary is stored in

The Double Word screen

```
        At the end of this report, I'm going to recommend that our
editors upgrade from WordPerfect 5.0 to 5.1.  But first, I'm going
to briefly describe the Tables feature.  I think that this feature
alone makes it worthwhile to upgrade.  I'm also going to present a
brief analysis of the benefits and costs of converting to
WordPerfect 5.1.  When you finish this report, you can can decide
whether you would like more information on any of these subjects.
If so, I'll be happy to get it for you.

The Tables feature  The Tables feature can be used for several
purposes, even as a simple spreadsheet.  If you combine the Tables
                                        Doc 1 Pg 1 Ln 3.51" Pos 5.75"
```

Double Word: 1 2 Skip; 3 Delete 2nd; 4 Edit; 5 Disable Double Word Checking

Option	Function
2 Skip	Skips the double word this time only
3 Delete 2nd	Deletes the second word
4 Edit	Changes to edit mode so the words can be edited
5 Disable Double Word	Stops checking for double words for the rest of the spell check

Figure 11-3   The options of the Double Word screen

the directory that is specified by the Location of Files screen along with the default supplemental dictionary.

To tell *WordPerfect* that you want to use a named supplemental dictionary, you use the procedure in figure 11-6. In steps 1 and 2 of this procedure, you access the Spell command and select the New Sup Dictionary option. Then, in step 3, you type the name of the named supplemental dictionary that you want to use. If, for example, you're working on a group of projects with the code DDBS, you can use that name for the supplemental dictionary that's associated with these projects. When you press the Enter key, this dictionary becomes the default supplementary dictionary, and it stays in force until you

The Irregular Case screen

```
brief analysis of the benefits and costs of converting to
WordPerfect 5.1.  When you finish this report, you can decide
whether you would like more information on any of these subjects.
If so, I'll be happy to get it for you.

The Tables feature  The Tables feature can be used for several
purposes, even as a simple spreadsheet.  If you combine the Tables
feature with the Math feature, for example, you can use formulas
to calculate each cell within the table.  However, the Tables
feature is no substitute for a spreadsheet.  It doesn't provide as
many features as a spreadsheet, it's not as efficient, and it's
                                       Doc 1 Pg 1 Ln 4.18" Pos 3.5"
[                                                   }

Irregular Case: 1 2 Skip; 3 Replace; 4 Edit; 5 Disable Case Checking
```

Option	Function
2 Skip	Skips irregular case this time only
3 Replace	Converts the irregular case to the standard case
4 Edit	Changes to edit mode so word can be edited
5 Disable Case Checking	Stops checking for irregular case for the rest of the spell check

Figure 11-4   The options of the Irregular Case screen (*WordPerfect* 5.1 only)

exit from *WordPerfect* or you use the New Sup Dictionary option to change to another named supplemental dictionary.

If you create several dictionaries for several different projects, you should store all of the your supplemental dictionary files in a subdirectory of the \WP50 or \WP51 directory. If you're using release 5.0, for example, you can store your supplemental dictionaries in a directory named C:\WP50\SPELL. Then, you need to use the Location of Files screen of the Setup command to tell *WordPerfect* what directory contains your supplemental dictionaries. Storing all your supplemental dictionaries in one directory like this makes them easier to find and manage.

The file names for the main and default supplemental dictionaries

Main dictionary name: WP{WP}US.LEX (5.1)
                         WP{WP}EN.LEX (5.0)

Default supplemental dictionary name: WP{WP}US.SUP (5.1)
                                         WP{WP}EN.SUP (5.0)

Figure 11-5   The file names for the main dictionary and the default supplemental dictionary

How to count the number of words in a document   When *WordPerfect* finishes checking the spelling of the words in a document, it displays the number of words that it has checked in the lower left corner of the screen. However, you can also get this count by using the Count option of the starting screen for the Spell command. Then, *WordPerfect* counts the words without checking their spelling. As a result, the count goes much faster. So if you want just a word count for your document, use this option.

How to check the spelling in a block   If you add some text to a document after you check its spelling, you may want to check the spelling for the new text only. If the new text doesn't fit conveniently on a single page, you can block it and run the spell checker on the block. To do that, you use the Block command to block that portion of the document. Then, you access the Spell command.

How to use the thesaurus

When you use *WordPerfect*'s thesaurus, you can look up one, two, or three words at a time. In the first screen in figure 11-7, for example, you can see how *WordPerfect*'s thesaurus displays the synonyms and antonyms for one word, *efficient*. In the second screen, you can see how *WordPerfect*'s thesaurus feature displays synonyms and antonyms for three words: *efficient*, *productive*, and *useful*.

At the top of the screens in figure 11-7, you can see a small window that shows four lines of the Edit screen. Below the four lines, you can see three columns. In one of the columns, letters are used to identify the words in the column. The bottom line of the screen is a selection line that offers four options: Replace word, View Doc, Look Up Word, and Clear Column.

Figure 11-8 summarizes the keystrokes that you need for using the thesaurus. To look up a word that's on your Edit screen, move the cursor to the word and access the Thesaurus command by pressing Alt+F1. If, for example, you move the cursor to the word *efficient* and access the thesaurus feature, *WordPerfect* displays a screen like the first one in figure 11-7. Then, if none of these choices are what you're looking for, you can look up any of the

1. Access the Spell command (Ctrl+F2).

    `Check: 1 Word; 2 Page; 3 Document; 4 New Sup. Dictionary; 5 Look up; 6 Count: 0`

2. Select New Sup. Dictionary.

    `Supplemental dictionary name:`

3. Type the name of the supplemental dictionary to be used and press the Enter key. This dictionary file must be in the directory specified for the Supplemental Dictionary on the Location of Files screen of the Setup command. The new supplemental dictionary stays in force until you change it or exit from *WordPerfect*.

Figure 11-6   How to use a named supplemental dictionary

words on the thesaurus screen that have dots to the left of them. A dot means that *WordPerfect* has synonyms and antonyms for that word.

To look up a word with a dot next to it, you press the letter next to the word. When you do that, *WordPerfect* fills up one of the columns with the synonyms and antonyms for that word. If you select a word without a dot, *WordPerfect* displays a message that says:

Word Not Found

After you look up a couple of words, two or more columns of the screen are used as illustrated by the second screen in figure 11-7. Then, you can use the Left and Right arrow keys to move the letters from one column to the next. And if there isn't enough room on the screen for all of the choices in one or more of the columns, you can use the Up and Down arrow keys to scroll to the synonyms and antonyms that don't fit on the screen.

To replace the word *efficient* on the Edit screen with the word *effective* on the thesaurus screen, select the Replace Word option by pressing the number *1*. Since you use letters to look up words, you have to use numbers to select the options at the bottom of the screen. Then, press the letter next to the word you want to use as the replacement. In figure 11-7, for example, you press the letter *a*. *WordPerfect* then replaces the word *efficient* with the word *effective*. To end the Thesaurus command and return to the Edit screen, you press the Enter key.

Besides the Replace option, the Thesaurus command provides three other options as summarized in figure 11-8. The View Document option moves the cursor to the portion of the Edit screen that's at the top of the Thesaurus screen. Then, you can scroll through that document to review other parts of it. If you find another word that you want to look up, you can access the Thesaurus command with the cursor on that word. Or if you press the Enter or Exit key, you return to the original Thesaurus screen, and the cursor moves back to its original location in the Edit screen.

The Look Up Word option lets you look up a word that you enter instead of a word on the screen. And the Clear Column option lets you clear the column that the letters are on so there's more room on the Thesaurus screen for other words.

When and how to use an electronic dictionary

Neither the thesaurus nor the spelling checker lets you look up the precise meaning of a word. To write well, though, it's far more important to use the right word than it is to use a variety of words. That's why an electronic dictionary is likely to be more valuable than an electronic thesaurus.

Although *WordPerfect* doesn't include an electronic dictionary, several of them are available as *third-party products*. This means that the dictionaries are supplied by other companies, not WordPerfect Corporation. These dictionaries are designed to work with *WordPerfect* as well as with most other word processing programs.

After you install an electronic dictionary on your PC, you can access it by pressing a special keystroke combination called a *hot key*. On my PC, for example, the hot key combination is the Ctrl key plus the letter *a*. When you press the hot key, the electronic dictionary looks up the word that the cursor is on and displays the definition as shown in figure 11-9. In this case, the definition is displayed in a box on the *WordPerfect* Edit screen. You can then use the dictionary to look up other words in the box, or you can press the Esc key to return to *WordPerfect*.

If you frequently use a dictionary as you write, an electronic dictionary can pay for itself by helping you look up words more quickly. Although the definitions aren't as complete as they are in the larger, printed dictionaries, the definitions are acceptable for many purposes. The dictionary illustrated in figure 11-9 is an excellent product called *Definitions Plus!* that retails for about $100. It's one of several good electronic dictionary programs on the market today.

Discussion

WordPerfect's spelling checker and thesaurus are two of its outstanding features. Both are quick and easy to use so you should be able to master them with a minimum of experimentation. Later, if you find that you frequently use a dictionary while you work with *WordPerfect*, you should consider buying an electronic dictionary.

Terms

spell check feature
spelling checker
main dictionary
supplemental dictionary

default supplemental dictionary
named supplemental dictionary
third-party product
hot key

The Thesaurus screen after it has looked up the word *efficient*

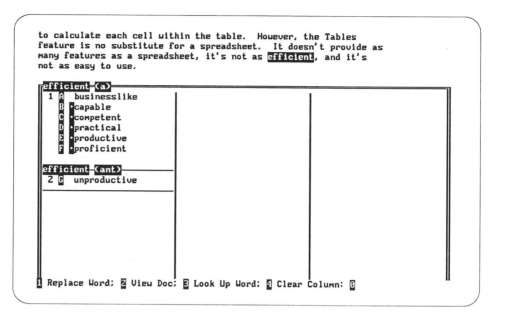

The Thesaurus screen after it has looked up *efficient, productive, and useful*

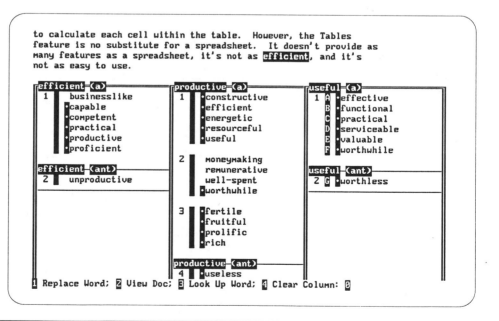

Figure 11-7   Two Thesaurus screens

How to access the Thesaurus command

Alt+F1

The keystrokes for using the thesaurus

Keystrokes	Function
Letters	Looks up the synonyms and antonyms for the word next to the letter
Left or Right arrow	Moves the selection letters one column in the direction of the arrow.
Up or Down arrow	Scrolls up or down the column to display words that don't fit on the screen

The four options of the thesaurus

Option	Function
1 Replace Word	Replaces the highlighted word on the Edit screen with the word that you select by letter at the prompt that follows.
2 View Document	Moves the cursor to the document at the top of the thesaurus screen so you can scroll through it. Press the Enter or Exit key (F7) to stop viewing the document and return to the thesaurus screen.
3 Look Up Word	Looks up the word that you enter at the prompt that follows.
4 Clear Column	Clears the column that the selection letters are in.

Figure 11-8 How to use the Thesaurus command

Objectives

1. Use the Spell command to check the spelling of a word, page, or document.

2. If necessary, use more than one supplemental dictionary with the spelling checker.

3. Use the Spell command to count the words in a document or to check the spelling in a block within a document.

4. Use the Thesaurus command to look up the synonyms or antonyms for a word.

whether you would like more information on any of these subjects.
If so, I'll be happy to get it for you.

The Tables feature   The Tables feature can be used for several
purposes, even as a simple spreadsheet. If you combine the Tables
feature with the Math feature, for example, you can use formulas
to calculate each cell within the table. However, the Tables
feature is no substitute for a spreadsheet. It doesn't provide as
many features as a spreadsheet, it's not as efficient, and it's
not as easy to use.

```
                                                     icient way to present
t ┌─────────────────────────────────────┐           les to present
i │ efficient                        1   │           se the Columns feature
o │                                      │           waste a lot of time.
W │   ef·fi·cient                        │           le looks right.  Or,
w │     adjective.                       │           umns feature.  This
c │       1. Acting or producing         │            Tables feature
p │          effectively with a minimum of │          f each column in a
t │          waste or effort.            │           other day, for
e │       2. Exhibiting a high ratio of  │            a table that I would
h │          output to input.            │           .0.  Although I'm
s │     efficiently adverb.              │           , I finished this
  └─────────────────────────────────────┘
ta
D:\LWPDOCS\51REPORT                              Doc 1 Pg 1 Ln 5.51" Pos 5.42"
```

Figure 11-9   The definition of the word *efficient* that's supplied by an electronic dictionary called
Definitions Plus!

Chapter 12

How to develop and use a practical set of macros

The macro feature of *WordPerfect* lets you "play back" many keystrokes and commands by entering just a few keystrokes. For example, you can create a macro that lets you insert "International Association for Environmental Research" into a document just by pressing the letter *e* while you hold down the Alt key. Or you can create a macro that lets you change the default directory to the one you usually use by pressing the letter *d* while you hold down the Alt key. Obviously, then, a practical set of macros can help you work more productively.

In this chapter, you'll learn how to create and use three different types of macros. You'll also learn how to replace, edit, and manage your macros. When you finish this chapter, you should be able to develop a practical set of macros that will help you improve your productivity right away.

How to define and execute three types of macros

Many programs, including word processing and spreadsheet programs, provide for the use of *macros*. In general terms, a *macro* is a collection of keystrokes or commands that can be accessed and performed by using just a few keystrokes. As a result, macros can help you work more efficiently.

Before you can use a macro, you need to create or "record" the macro. In *WordPerfect* terminology, this is known as *defining a macro*. Then, you can use or "play back" the keystrokes or commands that the macro represents. In *WordPerfect* terminology, this is known as *executing a macro*. To define a macro using *WordPerfect*, you use the Macro Define command. Then, to execute certain types of macros, you use the Macro command. These commands are summarized in figure 12-1.

To complicate matters, though, *WordPerfect* provides for three different types of macros. These can be referred to as *Alt+letter macros*, *named macros*, and *temporary macros*. Since all three have their special uses, I'll start by showing you how to define and execute each type of macro.

Command name	Access	Function
Macro Define	Ctrl+F10	Defines or "records" a new macro. Replaces or edits an existing macro. Ends the define, replace, or edit procedure.
Macro	Alt+F10	Executes or "plays back" a named macro.

Figure 12-1 The Macro Define command and the Macro command

How to define and execute an Alt+letter macro   The first procedure in figure 12-2 shows you how to define an Alt+letter macro. In step 1, you access the Macro Define command. Then, in step 2, you provide a name for the macro. For an *Alt+letter macro*, you provide the name by pressing any one of the 26 letter-keys while you hold down the Alt key. If, for example, you're going to create a macro that changes the default directory to the one that you usually use, Alt+D is a suitable name for the macro.

If you use an Alt+letter combination that has already been used for a macro, *WordPerfect* displays a warning message. Then, you can use the Cancel key to cancel the macro definition, or you can replace or edit the existing macro. If you cancel the definition, you have to start the Macro Define command again and use another name.

In step 3, you type a description for the macro; then, you press the Enter key. You can use up to 39 characters in the description. A good description is one that is descriptive enough to tell you what the macro does and distinct enough to distinguish the macro from your other macros. If you decide that you don't want to take the time to provide a description for the macro, you press the Enter key. However, I recommend that you take the time to enter a description because it will save you time later on. As you'll soon see, using descriptions makes it easier for you to manage your macros.

After you finish entering the description for the macro, *WordPerfect* returns you to the Edit screen so you can enter the actual keystrokes for the macro in step 4. A "Macro Def" prompt flashes in the bottom left corner of the screen to remind you that your keystrokes are being recorded for a macro. At this point, you type the keystrokes or perform the task that you want *WordPerfect* to record. As you do this, *WordPerfect* shows you the keystrokes or performs the tasks. As a result, you can tell what the macro is going to do when you finish it. When you're done, you access the Macro Define command again in step 5 to end the macro. When you do, the "Macro Def" prompt stops flashing and you are at the Edit screen.

How to define an Alt+letter macro

1. Access the Macro Define command (Ctrl+F10).

   Define macro:

2. Hold down the Alt key and press the letter of the Alt+letter macro.

   Description:

3. Type up to 39 characters that describe the macro and press the Enter key.

   Macro Def

4. As the prompt flashes, type the keystrokes that you want to record. If, for example, you want the macro to insert "International Association for Environmental Research" into a document, type those letters.

5. Access the Macro Define command (Ctrl+F10) to stop recording the macro.

How to execute an Alt+letter macro

Hold down the Alt key and press the letter of the macro. If, for example, you want to execute the Alt+E macro, use that keystroke combination.

Result of executing the Alt+E macro described above

These words are inserted into the document at the cursor location:

International Association for Environmental Research

Figure 12-2   How to define and execute an Alt+letter macro

In step 4, if you decide that you want to cancel the macro definition and start over, you can't use the Cancel command. If you access this command, it gets recorded in the macro instead. As a result, the only way to stop the macro definition is to access the Macro Define command. This, however, finishes the macro definition and creates a macro, even though the macro isn't going to work the way you want it to. Then, you can replace the macro. I'll show you how to do that later on in this chapter.

You can create simple or complicated macros, short or long macros. Within a macro, you can record keystrokes, commands, and even the Alt+letter combination for another macro. Often, though, the simplest macros save you the most time. In figure 12-2, for example, the macro consists of 52 keystrokes and no commands: "International Association for Environmental Research." But after you define this macro, you can insert all 52 keystrokes into a document just by executing the macro.

As you can see in the second procedure in figure 12-2, you execute an Alt+letter macro by using one keystroke combination. To execute the Alt+E macro, for example, you press the letter *e* while you hold down the Alt key. As you will see, this is the easiest way to execute macros. That's why you'll probably want to use Alt+letter macros for the macros that you use most frequently.

If you try to execute a macro and it doesn't exist or *WordPerfect* can't find it, *WordPerfect* displays a warning message like this for a few seconds:

ERROR: File not found — ALTE.WPM

Here, the message means that *WordPerfect* can't find the Alt+E macro. When you get a prompt like this, you should check to make sure that you used the right Alt+letter combination for executing the macro. If that's not the problem, the macro either doesn't exist or *WordPerfect* is looking in the wrong directory for it. Later on in this chapter, you'll learn how to list the macros in the macro directory so you can tell what the problem is.

When you execute a complicated macro for the first time, it may not work the way you want it to. If a macro runs for an unexpectedly long time, for example, it isn't working properly. Then, you can cancel the macro execution while it is running by pressing the Cancel key. For simple macros, though, you shouldn't have this problem.

How to define and execute a named macro   The first procedure in figure 12-3 shows you how to define a *named macro*. With the exception of step 2, this is the same procedure that you use for defining an Alt+letter macro. The difference in step 2 is that you type the name that you want to use for the named macro instead of pressing an Alt+letter key combination. You can use up to eight characters for the name. If, for example, you're going to create a macro that changes the default directory to one named DDBSDOCS, DDBS is a suitable name for the macro. If you use a name that has already been used for a macro, *WordPerfect* displays a warning message.

As you can see in the second procedure in figure 12-3, you execute a named macro in two steps. In step 1, you access the Macro command. In step 2, you type the name of the macro and press the Enter key. Because this takes longer than executing an Alt+letter macro, you usually use named macros for those macros that you use less frequently than Alt+letter macros. You also use named macros when you don't want them executed by accidentally pressing an Alt+letter key combination. If, for example, you define a macro that completely reformats a document, you should probably use a named macro.

How to define and execute a temporary macro   *WordPerfect* provides for two types of *temporary macros* as summarized in figure 12-4. The first type is comparable to a named macro, but the name is blank. To define this type of macro, you access the Macro Define command in step 1. Then, in step 2, you press the Enter key to tell *WordPerfect* that you're defining a temporary macro. In step 3, you enter the commands and keystrokes for the macro, and you access the Macro Define command again in step 4 to end the macro. To execute this first type of macro, you access the Macro command and press the Enter key.

How to define a named macro

1. Access the Macro Define command (Ctrl+F10).

   `Define macro:`

2. Type from one to eight characters for the name of the macro and press the Enter key. Suppose, for example, that you decide to name the macro *ddbs*.

   `Description:`

3. Type up to 39 characters that describe the macro and press the Enter key.

   `Macro Def`

4. As the prompt flashes, type the keystrokes that you want to record. If, for example, you want to create a macro that changes the default directory to d:\ddbsdocs, you do these steps: (1) Access the List command; (2) Press the equals sign; (3) Type *d:\ddbsdocs* and press the Enter key; and (4) press the Cancel key to return to the Edit screen.

5. Access the Macro Define command (Ctrl+F10) to stop recording the macro.

How to execute a named macro

1. Access the Macro command (Alt+F10).

   `Macro:`

2. Type the name of the macro that you want to execute and press the Enter key. If, for example, you want to execute a macro named DDBS, type those letters and press the Enter key.

The result of executing the DDBS macro described above

The default directory is changed to: D:\DDBSDOCS

Figure 12-3   How to define and execute a named macro

The second type of temporary macro is comparable to an Alt+letter macro. It can be called an *Alt+number macro*. To define this type of macro, you use the second method in figure 12-4. In step 1, you start by pressing the Ctrl+Page-up key combination. In step 2, you name the temporary macro by pressing one of the number keys from 0 through 9 while you hold down the Alt key. Then, in step 3, you record the macro. In this case, though, you are limited to a total of 79 keystrokes, and you are not allowed to use commands in the macro. To execute this type of macro, you press the number for the macro while you hold down the Alt key.

A temporary macro is erased as soon as you exit from *WordPerfect*. As a result, you use these macros when they can save you time for one *WordPerfect* session, but they're not so valuable that you want to save them. If, for example, you're typing a document that requires the use of several lengthy terms, you can use a different Alt+number macro for each of the terms. Then, when you finish the document and have no more use for the macros, you know that the macros will be erased at the end of the session.

Because you can easily get by without them, temporary macros are the least useful of the three types of macros. If, for example, you want to create three temporary macros for use on one document or project, you can name them Alt+X, Alt+Y, and Alt+Z. This has the same benefit as creating Alt+number macros, but the Alt+letter macros are still available if you aren't able to finish the document or project in a single *WordPerfect* session.

Seven typical macros

To give you a better idea of what macros can do, figure 12-5 presents seven typical macros. For each, you can see the macro name, the file name, the macro description, and the keystrokes and commands that have been recorded for the macro. These macros illustrate the types of jobs that a practical set of macros can do. After you read about these macros, you can try them on your own PC to see how easy it is to create and use macros.

An Alt+letter macro that types text   Using a macro to type text is the simplest use of a macro. This type of macro can be called a *keystroke macro*. If you use the same technical terms in many of the documents that you create, the use of keystroke macros for these terms can quickly improve your productivity.

In figure 12-5, the first macro is a keystroke macro that types the signature block for a letter. To record this macro when you reach step 3 in figure 12-2, you type the keystrokes for the Sincerely line, press the Enter key three times, type the keystrokes for the Name line, press the Enter key, and type the keystrokes for the Title line. To end the macro definition, you access the Macro Define command again.

An Alt+letter macro that accesses italics   Besides typing text, you can use macros to access *WordPerfect* commands. In chapter 8, for example, you can learn that it takes several keystrokes to insert the paired code that italicizes text. So if you use italics much, you'll want to create an Alt+letter macro that inserts the italics code.

In figure 12-5, the second macro inserts the paired italics codes into a document. To record this macro in step 3 of the procedure in figure 12-2, you first access the Font command. Then, you select Appearance and Italics by pressing the letters *a* and *i*. In the last column of figure 12-5, you can see how this gets recorded in the macro. Then, to end the macro definition, you access the Macro Define command.

An Alt+letter macro that contains a nested macro   The third macro in figure 12-5 types the book title *War and Peace* in italics whenever you use

Method 1: How to define a temporary macro that lets you use commands

1. Access the Macro Define command (Ctrl+F10).
   Define macro:
2. Press the Enter key.
   Macro Def
3. Type the keystrokes that you want to record.
4. Access the Macro Define command (Ctrl+F10) to stop recording the macro.

How to execute this type of temporary macro

1. Access the Macro command (Alt+F10).
   Macro:
2. Press the Enter key.

Method 2: How to define a temporary macro that limits you to 79 characters and no commands

1. Press Ctrl+Page-up.
   Variable
2. Type a number from 0 through 9 and press the Enter key if you're using *WordPerfect* 5.1. If you're using *WordPerfect* 5.0, you just type the number.
   Value:
3. Type up to 79 characters or spaces and press the Enter key.

How to execute this type of temporary macro

Hold down the Alt key and press the number that you entered in step 2.

Figure 12-4   How to define and execute a temporary macro

the Alt+W key combination. To record this macro, you start by using the Alt+I macro for accessing the paired italics codes (assuming that you have already created this macro). Then, you type the book title and press the Right arrow key to move the cursor past the second italics code in the pair.

When one macro contains another macro, the macros can be referred to as *nested macros*. Although you can nest a named macro within another macro, this is more complicated than nesting an Alt+letter macro. So if you know that you're going to nest a macro within one or more other macros, you should make the macro an Alt+letter macro.

An Alt+letter macro that boldfaces the line that the cursor is on
The fourth macro in figure 12-5 boldfaces the line that the cursor is on, and

the cursor doesn't have to be at the start of the line. If you look at the keystrokes for this macro, you can see that the macro starts by using Home Home Home Left to move the cursor to the start of the line before any codes. Then, the next three keystrokes start the Block command, move the cursor to the end of the line, and access the Bold command. This boldfaces the block and completes the macro. If you write reports that have boldfaced headings within them, this macro can make it easier for you to boldface the headings.

A named macro that types the heading for a memo   The fifth macro in figure 12-5 is a named macro that types the heading for a memo. In the first line of the memo, this macro accesses the Date command and selects the date code. Then, this macro types the To, From, and RE lines of the memo. This macro ends with six Up arrows and the End key to move the cursor to the proper location for entering the rest of the To line of the memo. If you write many memos, a macro like this can save a minute or two each time you use it.

A named macro that changes the default directory   The sixth macro in figure 12-5 changes the default directory to D:\DDBSDOCS. This macro starts by accessing the List command and pressing the equals key to change the default directory. Then, it types a complete specification for the new default directory. It finishes by pressing the Enter key to complete the directory change and the Cancel key to return to the Edit screen.

A named macro that executes a series of global replacements
The last macro in figure 12-5 is a named macro that executes three global replacements. You can use a macro like this to "clean up" documents that have been imported from another program. You can also use a macro like this to prepare documents that are going to be used with other programs. If, for example, you are going to transfer a *WordPerfect* document to a desktop publishing program, you should get rid of the tabs, hard returns, and spaces that aren't needed by the desktop publishing program.

Although the last macro in figure 12-5 is simplified for instructional purposes, it illustrates what a macro like this can do. It starts the first global replacement by using the Home Home Up keystrokes to move the cursor to the top of the document. Then, it uses the Replace command to replace all Tab characters with no characters. For the second global replacement, the macro moves the cursor to the top of the document and uses the Replace command to replace all occurrences of two Enter keystrokes in a row with one. This takes away the blank line between paragraphs. The macro then moves the cursor back to the top of the document.

If you want to experiment with a macro like this, retrieve any document that has a few paragraphs in it. Then, start the definition for a macro named *dtprep* and give it an appropriate description like *prepare wp document for dtp*. When you do this, *WordPerfect* returns you to the Edit screen. At this point, you can record the replacements shown in figure 12-5, or you can record your

Macro Name	File name	Description	Keystrokes
Alt+S	ALTS.WPM	Types the signature block for a letter	Sincerely,{Enter} {Enter}{Enter} Ed Williams{Enter} Marketing Manager
Alt+I	ALTI.WPM	Inserts paired italics codes	{Font}ai
Alt+W	ALTW.WPM	Types *War and Peace* in italics	{ALT I}War and Peace{Right}
Alt+B	ALTB.WPM	Boldfaces the line that the cursor is on	{Home}{Home}{Home}{Left} {Block}{End}{Bold}
MEMO	MEMO.WPM	Types the heading for a memo	Date:{Tab}{Tab}{Date/Outline}c {Enter}{Enter} To:{Tab}{Tab}{Enter}{Enter} From:{Tab}{Tab} Joe Murach{Enter}{Enter} RE:{Tab}{Indent}{Enter}{Enter} {Up}{Up}{Up}{Up} {Up}{Up}{End}
DDBS	DDBS.WPM	Changes the default directory to D:\DDBSDOCS	{List}= d:\ddbsdocs{Enter}{Cancel}
DTPREP	DTPREP.WPM	Prepares a document for desktop publishing	{Home}{Home}{Up} {Replace}n{Tab}{Search}{Search} {Home}{Home}{Up} {Replace}n{Enter}{Enter} {Search}{Enter}{Search} {Home}{Home}{Up}

Figure 12-5   Seven typical macros

own replacements. When you're done, access the Macro Define command to stop recording your keystrokes.

To test the macro, clear the screen but don't save the document that you modified while you defined the macro. Then, retrieve the original document and execute the DTPREP macro. It should work the same way it did when you recorded the keystrokes. It's that easy to create a macro like this.

How to repeat the execution of a macro a specific number of times

Occasionally, you may want to execute a macro several times in a row. If, for example, you define a macro that types an underline across a page, you can execute it 20 times in a row to put 20 lines on a page.

To repeat a macro, you use the Esc key as described in chapter 7. When you press the Esc key, *WordPerfect* displays a prompt like this:

Repeat Value = 8

Then, you can change the number on this prompt to the number of times you want to execute the macro. When the number is correct on the screen, just execute the macro. However, this technique doesn't work with Alt+-number macros.

How to replace a macro

Figure 12-6 presents the procedure for replacing an existing macro. This procedure varies slightly depending on which release of *WordPerfect* you use. First, you access the Macro Define command, and you enter the Alt+letter combination or the name of the macro that you want to replace. Then, *WordPerfect* displays a message that says that the macro already exists. When you select Replace, *WordPerfect* 5.1 displays a message that gives the file name of the macro that you're about to replace. *WordPerfect* 5.0 doesn't display this message. After you make the selection to replace the macro, *WordPerfect* displays a prompt for the new description. Even if the description is the same, you must enter it at this prompt. Otherwise, the macro won't have a description. After you enter the description, *WordPerfect* returns you to the Edit screen so you can record a new macro.

You use this procedure when you want to replace an old macro that you no longer use with a new macro. However, you can also use this procedure when you want to change a short macro by re-entering it. If, for example, a short macro has a minor error, you can correct the error by re-entering the entire macro the right way. Most of the time, though, it's more efficient to correct a macro by editing it than by replacing it.

How to edit a macro

Figure 12-7 gives the procedure for editing a macro when you use *WordPerfect* 5.0, and figure 12-8 gives the procedure for editing a macro when you use *WordPerfect* 5.1. In the first two steps of both procedures, you access the Macro Define command and enter the name of the macro that you want to edit.

For *WordPerfect* 5.0, you select Edit in step 3 of the procedure in figure 12-7. This displays the Macro Edit screen shown in this figure. In step 4, you select Description if you want to edit the description of the macro. After you edit the description that's shown, you press the Enter key. In step 5, you select Action to edit the keystrokes and commands of the macro. When you finish editing the macro, you press the Exit key to return to the Edit screen.

For *WordPerfect* 5.1, you can select Edit or Description in step 3 of the procedure in figure 12-8. If you don't want to edit the description, you select

How to replace a macro using *WordPerfect* 5.1

1. Access the Macro Define command (Ctrl+F10).

    `Define macro:`

2. Enter the Alt+letter combination for an Alt+letter macro or the name of a named macro.

    `Already exits: 1 Replace; 2 Edit; 3 Description: 0`

3. Select Replace.

    `Replace C:\WP51\MEMO.WPM? No (Yes)`

4. Select Yes.

    `Description`

5. Enter a new description, and press the Enter key. This returns you to the Edit screen with this prompt flashing:

    `Macro def`

6. Enter the keystrokes that you want to record. These replace all of the keystrokes of the old macro.

7. Access the Macro Define command (Ctrl+F10) to stop recording the macro.

How to replace a macro using *WordPerfect* 5.0

1. Access the Macro Define command (Ctrl+F10).

    `Define macro:`

2. Enter the Alt+letter combination or the name of the named macro.

    `Already exits: 1 Replace; 2 Edit: 0`

3. Select Replace.

4. Enter a new description, and press the Enter key. This returns you to the Edit screen with this prompt flashing:

    `Macro def`

5. Enter the keystrokes that you want to record. These replace all of the keystrokes of the old macro.

6. Access the Macro Define command (Ctrl+F10) to stop recording the macro.

Figure 12-6   How to replace a macro

Edit to display the Macro Edit screen shown in this figure. If you do want to edit the description, you select Description. A prompt is then displayed for this purpose. Then, after you edit the description and press the Enter key, the Macro Edit screen is displayed. Once the Macro Edit screen is displayed, you can edit the macro. When you finish editing the macro, you press the Exit key to return to the Edit screen.

How to interpret the Macro Editor screen   Figures 12-7 and 12-8 display the Macro Editor screen for releases 5.0 and 5.1. As you can see, the file name and macro description are displayed at the top of each screen. Here, the file name is DTPREP.WPM and the description is "Prepare wp document for dtp." The macro definition is displayed in a box in the middle of each screen.

Within the macro definition, commands and control keystrokes are represented by words within braces {}. For instance, {Replace} refers to the Replace command, {Tab} refers to the Tab key, and {Up} refers to the Up arrow key. In contrast, the characters that aren't in braces represent typewriter keystrokes. For instance, the *n* and the period after the first Replace command are keystrokes from the typewriter keyboard. If you enter a space in a macro definition, it is represented by a light dot on the Macro Editor screen as illustrated by the two spaces following the *n* and the period in the third line of the macro definition.

How to use edit mode and insert mode   Figure 12-9 summarizes the keystrokes you need for using the Macro Editor. As you can see, the Ctrl+F10 keystroke combination lets you toggle between the *edit mode* and the *insert mode*. Although it's difficult to tell which mode you're in, you always start in edit mode. After that, you can tell which mode you're in by the way the keystrokes work when you press them.

When you're in edit mode, you can use the Arrow keys to move the cursor anywhere in the macro definition. Then, you can use the Delete and Backspace keys to delete any of the codes or characters. If, for example, you want to delete the Replace command, you move the cursor to it and press the Delete key. While you're in edit mode, you can also insert commands and typewriter characters into a document. As a result, you are likely to use edit mode most of the time when you're editing a macro definition.

When you're in edit mode, however, you can't insert the codes for the Tab and Enter keystrokes into a macro definition. Instead, these keystrokes change the alignment of a macro definition without changing its function. In the definitions in figures 12-7 and 12-8, for example, I've pressed the Enter key at the end of each line to make the macro easier to read. Otherwise, the breaks at the end of the line are often in illogical places.

If you want to insert the codes for keys like the Tab, Enter, Delete, and Backspace keys, you must switch from edit mode to insert mode. In this mode, every keystroke inserts a code into the Macro Edit screen. As a result, you can't move the cursor or delete a code. That's why you usually have to switch back and forth between the two modes as you edit a macro definition.

Why you probably won't want to use *WordPerfect*'s macro commands   When you're in edit mode at the Macro Editor screen, you can access a set of *macro commands* by pressing the Ctrl+Page-up key combination. If you have any programming experience, you can quickly see that these

The Macro Edit screen for *WordPerfect* **5.0**

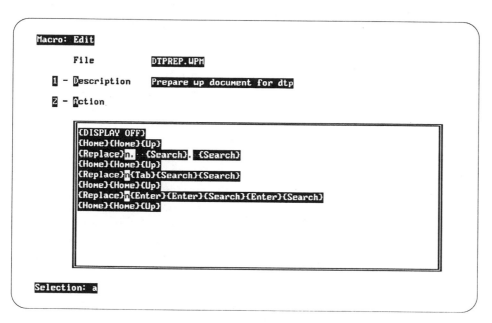

How to edit a macro

1. Access the Macro Define command (Ctrl+F10).

   Define macro:

2. Enter the Alt+letter combination for an Alt+letter macro or the name of a named macro.

   Already exits: 1 Replace; **2** Edit: **0**

3. Select Edit to edit the macro. This displays the Macro Edit screen shown above.

4. If you want to edit the description of the macro, select Description. This moves the cursor to the description portion of the screen. When you finish editing the description, press the Enter key.

5. If you want to edit the macro, select Action. This moves the cursor to the portion of the screen that displays the keystrokes and commands of the macro. You can then edit the macro using the keystrokes summarized in figure 12-9. If you decide later that you don't want to save the changes that you've made to the macro, press the Cancel key.

6. Press the Exit key to return to the Edit screen.

Figure 12-7   How to edit a macro using *WordPerfect* 5.0

commands let you add programming logic to a macro definition. For instance, these commands let you use If-Then logic within a macro. They also let you repeat the execution of portions of a macro. As a result, you can use the macro commands to create extremely complex macros.

If you're like most *WordPerfect* users, though, you won't need to use these macro commands. Instead, you'll create relatively simple macros that provide obvious improvements in your efficiency. For that reason, the macro commands aren't presented in this chapter or this book.

How to manage your macro files

When you define a macro, *WordPerfect* stores it in a file. If you look back to figure 12-5, you can see how *WordPerfect* names these files. For an Alt+letter macro, the file name is ALT followed by the letter for the macro. For a named macro, the file name is the macro name. For both types of macros, the extension for the file name is .WPM. As a result, the file name for the Alt+I macro is ALTI.WPM, and the file name for the DDBS named macro is DDBS.WPM.

If you create macros for all of the repetitive tasks that you do, you'll soon have a few dozen macros on your PC. Before long, you're likely to have several macro files that you no longer use. And you're likely to have at least a few macro files that you ought to use but have forgotten about. That's why it's important that you learn how to do an effective job of managing your macro files.

Since macros are stored in files, you can use the file-handling skills of chapter 9 to manage macro files. For instance, you can use the List command to look at, delete, and rename files. Before you can do that, however, you need to know which directory your macro files are stored in.

How to find the directory that contains your macro files   To find the directory that contains your macro files, you use the Setup command to display the Location of Files screen. This command is explained in detail in chapter 6, but all you have to do is access the Setup command and select Location of files option. In figure 6-8, you can see the Location of Files screens for both *WordPerfect* 5.0 and 5.1. On both of these screens, the directory for the macro files is displayed after the Keyboard/Macro Files option.

Often, the directory that's used for macro files is the same as the directory for the other *WordPerfect* files. In *WordPerfect* 5.0, this directory is usually C:\WP50; in *WordPerfect* 5.1, this directory is usually C:\WP51. To manage your macro files more effectively, though, I recommend that you store them in a separate directory. I'll show you how to do this in a moment.

If no directory is displayed for the Keyboard/Macro Files option on the Location of Files screen, *WordPerfect* stores any macros you create in the default directory. In that case, however, the macros can only be used when

The Macro Edit screen for *WordPerfect* 5.1 in edit mode

```
Macro: Action

    File            DTPREP.WPM

    Description     Prepare wp document for dtp

    {DISPLAY OFF}
    {Home}{Home}{Up}
    {Replace}n.  {Search}.  {Search}
    {Home}{Home}{Up}
    {Replace}n{Tab}{Search}{Search}
    {Home}{Home}{Up}
    {Replace}n{Enter}{Enter}{Search}{Enter}{Search}
    {Home}{Home}{Up}




Ctrl-PgUp for macro commands;  Press Exit when done
```

How to edit a macro

1. Access the Macro Define command (Ctrl+F10).

   Define macro:

2. Enter the Alt+letter combination for an Alt+letter macro or the name of a named macro.

   Already exits: 1 Replace; 2 Edit; 3 Description: 0

3. If you don't want to edit the description of the macro, select Edit. This displays a Macro Edit screen like the one shown above.

   If you want to edit the description of the macro, select Description. Then, this prompt is displayed:

   Description:

   After you edit the description and press the Enter key, a Macro Edit screen like the one shown above is displayed.

4. Edit the macro using the keystrokes summarized in figure 12-9. If you decide that you don't want to save the changes that you've made, press the Cancel key.

5. Press the Exit key to return to the Edit screen.

Figure 12-8   How to edit a macro using *WordPerfect* 5.1

Keystrokes	Function
Ctrl+F10	Toggles between Edit mode and Insert mode
Edit mode	
Arrow key	Moves the cursor in the direction of the arrow
Delete key	Deletes the code or keystroke at the cursor
Backspace key	Deletes the code or keystroke to the left of the cursor
Tab key	Moves the codes and keystrokes that follow to the right one tab stop without altering their function
Enter key	Moves the codes and keystrokes that follow one line down without altering their function
WordPerfect command	Inserts the code for the command
Insert mode	
WordPerfect command	Inserts the macro code for the command
Control keys like the Arrow, Delete, and Backspace keys	Inserts the macro code for the key

Figure 12-9   The keystrokes for using the Macro Editor

the directory that the macros are in is the default directory. If that's not what you want, you need to specify a Macro File directory on the Location of Files screen.

How to use the List command to display a listing of just the macro files in a directory   If you know how to use the List command as described in chapter 9, you should know how to use it to display a listing of just the macro files in a directory. After you access the List command, you can type a specification like this to do that:

    c:\wp51*.wpm

This means that the files in the \WP51 directory on the C drive should be listed, but only those files with the extension .WPM. In other words, only the macro files should be listed.

How to use the List command to look at, delete, rename, or move macro files   Once the macro files are displayed on the List screen, you can perform any of the List functions on the highlighted or marked file. If, for example, you want to look at the highlighted file, you press the Enter key. In

1. Create a directory for macros and keyboard files (see chapter 9).
2. Move all existing macro and keyboard files to the new directory (see chapter 9).
3. Use the Setup command to change the directory for the macro and keyboard files on the Location of Files screen (see chapter 6)

Figure 12-10 How to set up a separate directory for macro and keyboard files

this case, you can see the macro description at the top of the screen, but the rest of the macro is unintelligible. As a result, you can't tell what the macro file does unless you've given it a description.

If you want to Delete or Rename a file, you just move the highlight to the file and select the appropriate function. If, for example, you want to delete a macro that you no longer use, you select the Delete function. If you want to rename a macro so it's easier to remember the name, you select the Move/Rename function. When you use this function, you can convert named macros to Alt+letter macros and vice versa. Remember, though, that you can't change the extension of the file name. If you do, *WordPerfect* won't know that the file is a macro.

If you want to delete two or more files, you can mark the files before accessing the Delete function. Similarly, if you want to move all the macro files to a new macro directory, you can mark all of the files before accessing the Move/Rename function. If you don't already know how to mark files, that's covered in detail in chapter 9.

How to set up a separate directory for your macro files If your macro files are stored in the same directory as the other *WordPerfect* files, it's worth taking the time to set up a separate directory for them. Then, you'll be able to manage your macro files more efficiently. To set up a separate directory for your macro files, you can use the procedure in figure 12-10.

In step 1, you create the directory that you're going to use for your macro files. You can use *WordPerfect* to create this directory as described in chapter 9. Or you can use DOS to create this directory. For simplicity, you can create a directory named MACROS that is subordinate to the directory that contains the other *WordPerfect* files. In *WordPerfect* 5.0, this directory is usually C:\WP50\MACROS; in *WordPerfect* 5.1, it's C:\WP51\MACROS.

In step 2, you need to move all of the macro files from the old directory to the new directory. You also need to move all keyboard files to the new directory. Since all macro files have .WPM as the extension and all keyboard files have .WPK as the extension, it's easy to identify the files that have to be moved. Then, you can use DOS commands to move the files. Or you can use *WordPerfect* to move the files. In *WordPerfect*, you can mark the files that need to be moved on the List screen and then access the Move function.

In step 3, you use the Setup command to change the directory that's specified on the Location of Files screen. Otherwise, *WordPerfect* won't be able to find your macros when you try to execute one of them. Once you change the directory specification, *WordPerfect* will store all new macros in the new directory.

How to develop a practical set of macros

Once you master the skills and concepts presented in this chapter, it's up to you to develop and use a practical set of macros. In general, you should consider defining a macro whenever you find yourself doing the same sequence of commands and keystrokes repetitively. But you have to keep your perspective. If it's going to take longer to create a macro than the time that you're likely to save by using it, you should think twice before you define the macro.

Figure 12-11 lists some of the macros that we use in our shop to help us work more productively. For instance, the Alt+E macro takes the inside address from a letter and prints an envelope from it; the Alt+H macro starts the preparation of a standard heading for reports; and the MEMO, LETTER, and REPORT macros do all the formatting for these types of documents. This list, however, is only meant to give you ideas. Only you can decide which macros are going to help you work more efficiently.

The first step, though, is to take an hour or two to develop a beginning set of macros. As you use these macros, you'll see how valuable they can be. You'll also get ideas for other macros that can save you time. Then, you'll add these macros to your set. Before long, you'll have a practical set of macros that improve your productivity and make *WordPerfect* easier to use.

Terms

macro   Alt+number macro
defining a macro   keystroke macro
executing a macro   nested macros
Alt+letter macro   edit mode
named macro   insert mode
temporary macro   macro command

Objectives

1. Define and execute either an Alt+letter macro or a named macro.

2. Define and execute an Alt+number macro.

3. Use the Macro Define command to replace a macro.

4. Use the Macro Define command to edit a macro.

5. Use the List command to list and manage your macro files.

Name	Function
Alt+letter macros	
Alt+B	Boldfaces the line that the cursor is on
Alt+D	Changes the default directory to the one you use most frequently
Alt+E	Blocks the inside address in a letter, moves it to document 2, formats that document for envelope printing, prints the envelope, and exits from document 2 to return to the letter
Alt+H	Starts the preparation of a standard heading for a document
Alt+I	Inserts the paired code for italics
Alt+S	Types the signature block for a letter
Named macros	
memo	Sets the codes on the Document Initial Codes screen to the ones that you use for memos, types the heading for a memo, and moves the cursor to the To line
letter	Sets the codes on the Document Initial Codes screen to the ones that you use for letters, types the form of a letter including the signature block, and moves the cursor to the start of the inside address
report	Sets the codes on the Document Initial Codes screen to the ones that you use for reports
dtprep	Uses a series of global replacements to convert a *WordPerfect* document to the form that's required for desktop publishing

Figure 12-11   Some ideas for a practical set macros

Chapter 13

How to troubleshoot the most common *WordPerfect* problems

Sooner or later, you'll run into a perplexing problem when you're using *WordPerfect*. Your formatting codes won't work the way you intended them to; your screen will freeze; your printer won't print; or *WordPerfect* will display a message that you don't understand. In most cases, though, problems like these are easy to solve.

In this chapter, you'll learn how to solve some of the most common *WordPerfect* problems. As you read about the solutions, you'll realize that the material in chapters 6 through 12 prepares you for solving most problems without any help. This chapter just relates the skills presented in those chapters to specific *WordPerfect* problems. Once you learn how to solve these problems, you'll be a more independent *WordPerfect* user.

When and how to use the Help feature

By the time you read this chapter, you should already know how to use the Help feature as summarized in figure 13-1. To access this feature, you use the F3 key. If you're using *WordPerfect* 5.1, this key displays *context-sensitive information* that's related to the function you're using. If you're not using a function or if you're using *WordPerfect* 5.0, you can use the other keys summarized in figure 13-1 to display help information. For the most part, the Help feature is self-explanatory, but you can refer to chapter 5 (figures 5-10 through 5-13) if you want more information about it.

The Help feature is useful when you already know how to use a *WordPerfect* function or feature, but you can't remember some of the details for using it. However, the Help feature usually doesn't give you the perspective that you need for learning how to use a function or feature. And it usually doesn't give you enough information to help you solve a problem.

How to access and exit from the Help feature

Keystrokes	Function
F3	Accesses the Help feature
Enter or Spacebar	Exits from the Help feature

How to access the Help information that you want

Keystrokes	Function
F3	Displays the *WordPerfect* command template so you can find the keystroke combination for the command that you want to get information about. You shouldn't need to do this unless you don't have a template of your own.
Function or control key	Accesses the screen that explains the related command or function. Often, these screens lead to other screens that present more detailed information.
Any letter	Displays the Help Index, an alphabetic list of the Help topics, for the letter entered. If the list doesn't fit on one screen, you go to the next screen by pressing the letter again (5.1) or the number *1* (5.0).

Figure 13-1   How to access and use the Help feature

How to solve problems with codes

When you use commands like the Format, Font, Boldface, and Underline commands, codes are inserted into your document. If the right codes are inserted in the right places, the codes work correctly. But if two codes compete or if certain codes aren't inserted at the top of a page, they don't work correctly. Here, then, is a brief description of these common coding problems.

Competing codes   When you insert a single code into a document, it remains in effect until you override it with the same single code later in the document. Sometimes, though, you insert a code in the wrong place so it overrides a preceding code when you don't want it to. This problem can be referred to as *competing codes*.

Figure 13-2 illustrates the problem of competing codes. In the Edit screen at the top of the figure, you can see that the second margin code of 1.5 inches overrides the first margin code:

[L/R Mar:1",1"][Center Pg][L/R Mar:1.5",1.5"]

Then, if you want the first margin code to take effect, you must delete the second margin code.

All of the codes that apply to your document may not appear when you reveal codes. In the bottom screen in figure 13-2, you can see the Initial

Codes that are set for the document through the Document option of the Format command. This screen shows the codes that are applied to a document, even though they aren't inserted into the document. Although you can override these codes by inserting codes at the top of a document, you're better off changing the codes that apply to the entire document on this Initial Codes screen. If, for example, you want left and right margins of 1.5 inches, you don't have to insert a margin code into the document because the Initial Codes screen provides for those margins. And if you want margins of 1 inch, you don't have to insert a margin code into the document; you just delete the margin code on the Initial Codes screen because the *WordPerfect* default is for 1 inch margins.

If you use the Document option to set the Initial Codes that apply to the entire document, you're less likely to have a problem with competing codes. You're also less likely to delete those codes accidentally. If you want to know when and how to use the Document option of the Format command to set Initial Codes, you should read chapter 8.

Codes not placed at the top of a page   Figure 13-3 lists codes that must be placed at the top of a page or document to work properly. This figure also tells you what happens if the code isn't placed at the top of the page. All of the codes in this summary are assigned with the Page option of the Format command.

When a code isn't at the top of a page, you can use the Search command to search for it. Then, you can block the code and move it to the top of the page. Or you can delete the code and insert it at the top of the page. Since it takes several keystrokes to access the Format Page screen, and it takes several more keystrokes to set these options, it's often more efficient to move the code.

What to do when your screen freezes

If you work with *WordPerfect* long enough, the screen will eventually "freeze" or "lock up." Usually, the cause is an error within *WordPerfect* (a programming bug) that happens when you use a certain sequence of commands and keystrokes. However, a screen can also freeze due to static electricity or a hardware failure.

When the screen freezes, none of the keys on your keyboard affect the screen. Then, you have to *reboot* your PC to unfreeze your screen. To reboot, you can use the On/Off switch to turn your PC off and then back on. Or you can reboot your PC using the Ctrl+Alt+Delete key combination. This has the same effect as turning the PC on and off, but it's faster.

After you reboot and restart *WordPerfect*, you'll get the messages shown in figure 13-4. The first message asks whether other copies of *WordPerfect* are

The Edit screen for the document with the codes revealed

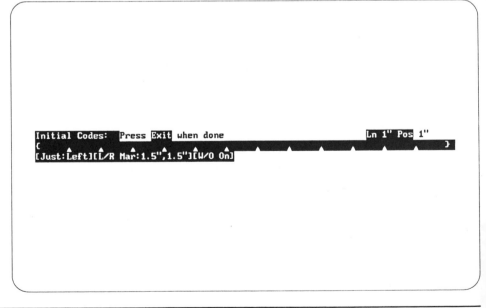

The Initial Codes screen of the Format command

Figure 13-2   Competing margin codes for a document

Name of code	Code	Result if not at top of page
Paper Size/Type	[Paper Sz/Typ:]	Takes effect on the next page
Center Page	[Center Pg]	Doesn't center the page
Top/Bottom Margins	[T/B Mar:]	Takes effect on the next page
Header	[Header A:]	Prints on the next page
Footer	[Footer A:]	Prints on the next page
Page Numbering	[Pg Numbering:]	Prints on the next page

Figure 13-3   Codes that must be inserted at the top of a page before any text to work properly

running on your PC. If you exit from *WordPerfect* without using the Exit command, *WordPerfect* doesn't know that you exited from the copy of the program that you were using. Assuming that you're using *WordPerfect* on a stand-alone PC, not on a network, you select No. *WordPerfect* then displays the Edit screen so you can start working.

If you're using the Timed Document Backup option of *WordPerfect* that's described in chapter 6, the second message in figure 13-4 is displayed when it's time for backing up. This message means that the backup files from your previous *WordPerfect* session are still on the disk because you didn't exit from *WordPerfect* using the Exit command. If you want to recover the document or documents that you were working on when the screen froze, you can rename the old files as I'll explain in a moment. Otherwise, you can tell *WordPerfect* to delete the files so it can complete its timed backup.

How to recover a document that has been backed up by *WordPerfect*

If your *WordPerfect* session ends before you can use the Save and Exit commands, the document or documents that you were working on aren't saved to named files. This happens when the screen freezes and you have to reboot the PC. This also happens when you shut off the PC before you exit from *WordPerfect* or when the electric power fails while you're working on your PC.

If you're using the Timed Document Backup option of *WordPerfect*, though, you can recover the document or documents that you were working on. You turn this option on by using the Setup command as described in chapter 6. Then, the documents that you're working on are saved at timed intervals in backup files (one backup file for document 1, another backup file for document 2). When you exit from *WordPerfect* normally, these backup files are deleted because you don't need them. But if you exit abnormally due to a power failure or user error, the backup files aren't deleted. As a result, you can use them to recover the documents that you were working on.

How to exit from *WordPerfect* and reboot your PC when the screen is frozen

Press the Ctrl+Alt+Delete key combination

How to respond to the messages that you get when you restart *WordPerfect*

`Are other copies of WordPerfect running? Yes (No)`

If you're using a stand-alone PC, select No.

`Old backup file exists. 1 Rename; 2 Delete: 1`

WordPerfect displays this message when it's time to perform a timed backup of the current document or documents. However, this message is only displayed if the old backup files still exist. Then, if you've already recovered your document or documents from the old backup files or if you don't want to recover them, you select Delete to tell *WordPerfect* that the old backup files are no longer needed. Otherwise, you use the recovery procedure presented in figure 13-5.

Figure 13-4   How to exit from *WordPerfect* and re-start it when your screen freezes

Figure 13-5 gives a procedure for recovering your documents from the backup files. In step 2, assuming that you're working on a stand-alone PC, not a networked PC, you select No. In step 3, you find out where the backup files are stored by displaying the Location of Files screen. If you need more information about how to do this, it's explained in detail in chapter 6.

Then, in step 4, you recover the backup files. You can do this by retrieving a backup file, looking at it on the Edit screen to make sure it's the one you want, and saving it to the file that you were working on. You can also do this by using the Look function and the Move/Rename function of the List command.

After you recover the backup files or perhaps while you're recovering them, *WordPerfect* may display this message:

Old backup file exists. 1 Rename; 2 Delete: 1

This message is displayed the first time *WordPerfect* does a timed backup after an abnormal exit, but only if the old backup files still exist. Then, if you've already recovered your documents from the backup files, you select Delete so *WordPerfect* can complete the timed backup. Otherwise, you should rename the backup files so you can recover their contents later on.

What to do when your printer doesn't print or doesn't print correctly

Printers are a major source of problems for most PC users. Because printers are mechanical, form feeding is frequently a problem. And because there are

1. Restart *WordPerfect*.

   Are other copies of *WordPerfect* running? Yes (No)

2. If you're using a stand-alone PC, select No.

3. If you don't know where the backup files are stored on your system, access the Setup command and select Location of Files. Then, note the drive and path that's given for the Backup Files.

4. Access the List screen for the directory that's used for Backup Files on the Location of Files screen in step 3. The backup files for documents 1 and 2 are named as follows:

   Document 1 = WP{WP}.BK1
   Document 2 = WP{WP}.BK2

   To recover one of these files, you move the highlight to it. Then, you can use the Look function to make sure it's the document that you want to recover. If it is, you can use the Move/Rename function to change the name of the document to the one you were working on before you exited from *WordPerfect*. Or you can use the Retrieve function to retrieve the file and you can save it with the name of the document you were working on.

5. When it's time for *WordPerfect* to perform a timed backup of the current document or documents, it displays this message if the old backup files still exist:

   Old backup file exists. 1 Rename; 2 Delete: 1

   Then, if you've already recovered your document or documents, you select Delete to tell *WordPerfect* that the old backup files are no longer needed. But if you haven't yet recovered your document or documents, you select Rename so you can rename the backup files. After you've renamed them, *WordPerfect* completes the timed backup.

Figure 13-5   How to recover a document from a timed backup file after an abnormal exit from *WordPerfect*

so many different kinds of printers, the coordination between a printer and an application program like *WordPerfect* is often a problem. Once you install an application program for a specific printer, most of the problems disappear, but some don't. Figure 13-6 summarizes some of the most common printing problems and error messages that you get when you use *WordPerfect*.

The printer doesn't print   After you tell *WordPerfect* to print a document or a portion of a document, the most common problem is that nothing prints. This is the first problem listed in figure 13-6, and five probable causes for this problem are listed. The first two are: (1) that your printer isn't turned on, and (2) that you haven't pressed the On-line button or its equivalent to make the printer ready for printing.

The third probable cause is that *WordPerfect* is waiting for a response. To see whether it is, you access the Print command and select the Control Printer option. This displays a screen like the one in figure 13-7. Here, the message in the Action line indicates that you should insert paper into the printer and press the letter *g*. If you're not familiar with this screen, it's explained in detail in chapter 10. Often, the messages in the Message and Action lines are self-explanatory. For instance, the third set of messages in figure 13-7 indicates that the format of the document that you're trying to print is incompatible with the current printer. Then, you can press the letter *c* to cancel the print job so you can correct the problem.

Often, the printer waits for a Go response because the Paper Size/Type code for the document indicates a change in the size or type of paper. You can learn more about this option in chapters 8 and 10. However, the printer also waits for a Go response after you use the Control Printer screen to stop the printing of a job.

The fourth probable cause in figure 13-6 is that the wrong port has been specified for a printer. This shouldn't happen if you've installed a printer correctly. If it does happen, however, it's an easy problem to detect. In the screen in figure 13-7, for example, you can see that the second document in the job list is going to be printed on port 2 (LPT2) instead of port 1 (LPT1). But if the printer isn't attached to LPT2, the document can't be printed. Then, you have to use the Select Printer option of the Print screen to edit the printer definition and change the port specification.

The fifth probable cause in figure 13-6 is that the cable between the systems unit of your PC and the printer isn't connected properly. This often occurs after you move a PC from one location to another. The solution is to check the cable connections and make sure that they're secure.

The document doesn't print the way you expected it to   If your printer prints the document, but the document isn't printed the way you expected, there are two probable causes. These are listed in figure 13-6. First, if the document doesn't look anything like what you had on your Edit screen, the document was probably formatted for a different printer than the one you're using. To correct this, you can use the Select Printer option to change the current printer to the one that's appropriate for your document. If you need help selecting a printer, please refer to chapter 10.

The second probable cause is that you didn't use the right font or formatting codes in your documents. If you've read chapters 6 and 8, you should be able to figure out what has gone wrong without much trouble. Chapter 6 shows you how to set the default font and the default formats for new documents. Chapter 8 shows you how to override the default font and formats for a document and how to insert font and formatting codes into a document.

A document on disk isn't formatted for the default printer   The first error message in figure 13-6 is displayed when you try to print a

Problem	Probable causes	Action
The printer isn't printing.	The printer isn't on.	Turn the printer on.
	The printer isn't on-line.	Press the On-line button or its equivalent.
	The printer is waiting for you to access the Go function from the Control Printer screen.	Access the Print command and select Control Printer. Then, press the letter *g*.
	The wrong printer port is specified for the current printer.	Access the Print command and select the Select Printer option. From the screen that follows, select Edit. Then, change the port specification to the one that's correct.
	The cable between the systems unit and the printer isn't connected properly.	Make sure that the printer cable is connected properly.
The document isn't printed in the font or with the formatting that you expected.	The document has been formatted for a printer that is different from the current printer.	Use the Select Printer option of the Print command to change the current printer to the one that the document has been formatted for.
	The Initial Codes and Initial Font for the document or the codes in the document itself aren't correct.	Edit the codes so they're correct and print the document again.

Error message	Meaning	Action
Document Not Formatted for Current Printer. Continue?	The document on disk has been formatted for a printer that isn't the current printer. If you continue, the document may not print correctly.	If the document doesn't print the way you expect, retrieve it, change the current printer, and print it again.
File was Fast Saved — Must be retrieved to print (*WordPerfect* 5.0)	The document on disk has been fast saved so it can't be printed from disk. Instead, it must be retrieved before printing.	Retrieve the document and print it. If you want to turn the Fast Save option off, use the Setup command as described in chapter 6.

Figure 13-6   Common printer problems and error messages

document from disk that was formatted for another printer. Then, if you select No, *WordPerfect* cancels the print function. But if you select Yes, *WordPerfect* formats the document for the current default printer as best it can, and it prints the document.

When *WordPerfect* formats a document for the default printer, it tries to convert all the printer specific codes (like font codes) to codes that the new printer can understand. If the old printer and the new printer are similar, this often works the way you want it to. If the printers aren't similar, though, this usually leads to the second problem listed in figure 13-6. In this case, the document is printed, but it doesn't look the way you want it to. If, for example, *WordPerfect* tries to convert the codes in a document that was formatted for a dot-matrix printer to codes for a laser printer, the printed document may not be recognizable.

A document on disk was fast saved (*WordPerfect* 5.0)   If you use *WordPerfect* 5.0, you get this message when you try to print a document from disk that has been fast-saved. Before you can print the fast-saved document, you must retrieve it and press the Home Home Down keys. After that, you can print the document from the screen. To turn the Fast Save option off, you use the Setup command that's presented in chapter 6.

How to handle the most common error messages for file-handling problems

Figure 13-8 lists the most common error messages that *WordPerfect* displays for file-handling problems. These messages are divided into three types: file handle messages, file specification messages, and disk space messages.

File handle messages   When *WordPerfect* is in operation it uses many files besides the document file or files that you're working on. As a result, your PC has to be set up with enough *file handles* to accommodate *WordPerfect*. When you install *WordPerfect*, it sets the number of file handles specified in the CONFIG.SYS file to an appropriate number. But if someone changes the CONFIG.SYS file, either one of the file handle messages in figure 13-8 may be displayed when you start *WordPerfect*. Then, you can't use *WordPerfect* until you correct this problem.

To increase the number of file handles, you need to edit the CONFIG.SYS file. This file should be stored in the root directory of the C drive. Specifically, the CONFIG.SYS file must include a FILES= command that specifies a number of 20 or more. However, the CONFIG.SYS file is a DOS file, not a *WordPerfect* file, so you can't use *WordPerfect* to edit it.

If you know how to use DOS and how to edit DOS files, you can make the required change to the CONFIG.SYS file in just a minute or two. Then, when you're done editing the CONFIG.SYS file, you must reboot your PC so the new CONFIG.SYS file takes effect. Once the CONFIG.SYS file has been set up correctly, you shouldn't get any more file handle messages.

The Control Printer screen

```
Print: Control Printer

Current Job

Job Number: 4                          Page Number:  1
Status:     Printing                   Current Copy: 1 of 1
Message:    None
Paper:      Standard 9.5" x 4"
Location:   Manual feed
Action:     Insert paper
            Press "G" to continue

Job List

Job  Document              Destination        Print Options
 4   (Screen)              LPT 1
 5   (Screen)              LPT 2


Additional Jobs Not Shown: 0



1 Cancel Job(s); 2 Rush Job; 3 Display Jobs; 4 Go (start printer); 5 Stop: 0
```

Common Message and Action lines

Message:	Printer not accepting characters
Action:	Check cable, make sure printer is turned ON
Message:	None
Action:	Insert Paper
	Press "G" to continue
Message:	ERROR: Incompatible file format
Action:	Press "G" to restart, "C" to cancel

Figure 13-7   The Control Printer screen and three of the most common Message and Action lines

File specification messages   If you know how to create and use DOS file specifications as described in chapter 2, you shouldn't have any trouble responding to the file specification messages in figure 13-8. When you use the Retrieve command to retrieve a file, for example, *WordPerfect* displays the File Not Found message when it can't find the file. If you gave a complete specification for the file, this message means that the file isn't in the directory you specified. If you gave only the file name, this means that the file isn't in the default directory.

The File Not Found message is also displayed when *WordPerfect* can't find one of the files it needs for a function such as a macro file, a dictionary file, or a print file. *WordPerfect* looks for these files in the directories that are specified on the Location of Files screen of the Setup command. If, for example, the Location of Files screen says that macro files are stored in a directory named \WP51\MACROS, that's where *WordPerfect* looks for them. Then, if *WordPerfect* can't find a macro in this directory, it displays the File Not Found message. Once you get *WordPerfect* set up right, it shouldn't have any trouble finding its own files. But you need to know how the Setup command can affect the directories that contain files that you create. As a result, you should read chapter 6 if you haven't already because it explains the use of the Location of Files screen in detail.

The Can't Rename File message is displayed when you try to rename a file in a way that is invalid. If, for example, you try to rename a file using a file name or specification that doesn't follow the rules listed in chapter 2 of this book, the Can't Rename File message is displayed. Usually, though, the problem is obvious so it's easy to correct.

The Invalid Drive/Path Specification message is displayed when you try to save or retrieve a file with an invalid specification. Here again, if you know DOS, the problem is usually obvious. If necessary, you can use the List command to check the directories on your drives as described in chapter 9. That way, you can be sure to get the specification right the next time you try it.

The Directory Not Empty message is displayed when you try to delete a directory that isn't empty. This function is explained in detail in chapter 9. In general, though, this message means either that the directory still contains some files or that you're trying to delete the current directory. Then, you must either delete the remaining files in the directory or change the current directory before trying the delete function again.

Disk space messages   You get a disk space message when you try to save a file on a diskette or hard disk drive that doesn't have room for the file. Then, you can delete one or more files from the diskette or hard drive to make room for the file, or you can save the file on a different diskette or hard drive.

Discussion

If you haven't read them already, you should take the time to read all of the other chapters in this section (chapters 6 through 12). These chapters will enhance your problem solving skills because they present the concepts and details that underlie the solutions presented in this chapter.

Also, if you're not already comfortable with DOS, you should take the time to learn more about it. For that purpose, I recommend a companion

Message	Meaning	Action
File handle messages		
No Available File Handles	The CONFIG.SYS file isn't set up correctly.	Add a FILES=30 command to the CONFIG.SYS file.
Insufficient File Handles to Run WordPerfect. Increase FILES= in CONFIG.SYS and Reboot Your Computer	The CONFIG.SYS file isn't set up correctly.	Increase the number of files in the FILES= command in the CONFIG.SYS file to FILES=30.
File specification messages		
File Not Found	The file that *WordPerfect* is trying to find can't be found in the directory that's specified or in the default directory (if no directory is specified).	Make sure that the file name and directory specification are correct. Or if you're not using a directory specification, make sure that the default directory is correct.
Can't Rename File	You're trying to rename a file in a way that is invalid, or you're trying to rename a protected file.	Correct your renaming specification, or get the access rights to the protected file.
Invalid Drive/Path Specification	The drive/path specification doesn't identify an existing directory.	Correct the drive/path specification.
Directory Not Empty	You're trying to delete a directory that isn't empty, or you're trying to delete the current directory.	Delete the files in the directory before trying to delete the directory. Or, if you have already deleted all the files, change the current (default) directory so it isn't the one that you're trying to delete.
Disk space messages		
Insufficient Disk Space—Insert New Diskette and Press Any Key	The diskette doesn't have any more room for files.	Delete one or more files from the current diskette or insert a new diskette into the diskette drive.
Disk Full—Press Any Key to Continue	The hard disk drive doesn't have any more room for files.	Delete one or more files from the current hard drive or change the current drive to another hard drive.

Figure 13-8   Common error messages for file-handling problems

book to this one called *The Least You Need to Know About DOS*. Once you master the skills that it teaches, you'll never again have problems with messages like the ones in figure 13-8.

Terms

context-sensitive information
single code
paired code
competing code
reboot
file handle

Objectives

1. Identify and solve any problems caused by the codes that have been inserted into a document.

2. Restart *WordPerfect* after your screen freezes and respond appropriately to the messages that you receive after you restart it.

3. Use the backup files from the Timed Document Backup feature to recover the document or documents you were working on at the time of an abnormal exit from *WordPerfect*.

4. Identify and solve any of the common printing problems.

5. Respond appropriately to any of the common error messages for file handling.

Section 4

Some additional perspective

Many *WordPerfect* users will never need the *WordPerfect* functions and features that aren't presented in section 3 of this book. But some users will. Accordingly, the one chapter in this section introduces you to the *WordPerfect* functions and features that aren't part of "the least you need to know about *WordPerfect*." If you do need one or more of the functions and features introduced in this section, you can probably learn them from your *WordPerfect* manual now that you know the essential *WordPerfect* skills.

Chapter 14

Other *WordPerfect* features that you ought to be aware of

When you master the commands and functions that are presented in section 3 of this book, you'll be able to use *WordPerfect* to prepare most types of business documents. But as you work with *WordPerfect*, you'll realize that some of the commands on the template haven't been presented in this book. As a result, you'll probably have questions like: What do these commands do? Do I need to know how to use them? Should I take the time to learn them?

To answer those questions, this chapter introduces you to the commands and features that aren't presented in the other sections of this book. As you read about these commands and features, you may realize that you don't need any of them. In that case, the "least you need to know about *WordPerfect*" will also be "everything you need to know about *WordPerfect*." However, you may discover that some of the features introduced in this chapter are just what you need. Then, you can figure out how to use them by using the *WordPerfect* manual, the *WordPerfect* Help feature, or an advanced *WordPerfect* book.

Figure 14-1 summarizes the commands that are introduced in this chapter. As you can see, these commands are accessed by 11 of the 40 keystroke combinations of the command template. If you have read the chapters in section 3 of this book, you know how to use the commands that are accessed by 29 of the 40 keystroke combinations. In addition, you should know how to use Screen command to divide the screen into two windows; the Date/Outline command to insert a date into a document; and the Mark Text command to mark all the files on the List screen. As a result, you're already familiar with 32 of the 40 keystroke combinations on the command template.

This chapter introduces you to the commands and features that are designed for special purposes. For instance, you can use the Merge feature to prepare repeat letters. You can use the desktop publishing features to improve a document's appearance. And you can use the tables feature to prepare tables. If you need one of these features, *WordPerfect* becomes more

Key name	Access	Options	Function
Shell	Ctrl+F1	Go to DOS	Exits temporarily from *WordPerfect* to DOS
		DOS Command (5.1)	Executes a DOS command without exiting from *WordPerfect*
Screen	Ctrl+F3	Line Draw	Draws lines
		Rewrite	Reformats the screen without moving the cursor down it
Date/Outline		Outline	Turns the Outline feature on and off
		Paragraph Numbering	Inserts a paragraph number code
		Define	Defines the numbering scheme for the paragraph number codes
Mark Text	Alt+F5		Marks the blocks of text that you want to use in a table of contents, a list, an index, or a Table of Authorities
		Subdoc	Identifies the documents that are subordinate to a master document
		Define	Defines the tables, lists, or indexes that are going to be generated
		Generate	(1) Generates the tables, lists, or indexes from the marked text; (2) Removes the redlining and the strikeout text from a document; (3) Compares two documents to generate redline and strikeout codes
Text In/Out	Ctrl+F5	DOS Text	Saves or retrieves a text file
		Password	Assigns a password to a file
		Save As	Saves a file in a generic word processing or a *WordPerfect* format
		Comment	Inserts a comment into a document that isn't printed with the rest of the document
		Spreadsheet (5.1)	Imports a spreadsheet into a document
Math/Columns (5.0) Columns/Table (5.1)	Alt+F7	Columns	Formats a portion of a document into two or more columns
		Tables (5.1)	Creates or edits a table
		Math	Performs mathematical operations on data that's in a table

Figure 14-1 A summary of the functions that are introduced in this chapter (part 1 of 2)

Key name	Access	Options	Function
Style	Alt+F8		Creates or edits a style sheet; or applies the styles in a style sheet to blocks in a document
Merge R (5.0) End Field (5.1)	F9		Marks the end of a field within a record within a secondary merge file
Merge Codes	Shift+F9		Marks the end of a record within a secondary merge file or marks the locations of the fields to be merged in the primary merge file
Graphics	Alt+F9	Figure Table Box Text Box User Box	Defines one of four different types of graphic boxes
		Line	Defines a horizontal or vertical line
		Equation (5.1)	Defines a box for a mathematical equation
Merge/Sort	Ctrl+F9	Merge	Merges a primary merge file with a secondary merge file
		Sort	Sorts the records in a secondary merge file or sorts the lines or paragraphs in a document

Figure 14-1   A summary of the functions that are introduced in this chapter (part 2 of 2)

valuable to you. That's why you should be aware of all of the features that *WordPerfect* offers.

The Merge feature and the Sort feature

You can use the Merge feature to merge data from one file into a document that's in another file. If, for example, you create a file that contains the names and addresses of the people on a mailing list, you can merge those names and addresses into a letter that you want to send to all of the people on the list. The result is one letter for each person on the list.

Figure 14-2 shows the codes that you use with the Merge feature of *WordPerfect* 5.1 (the codes for *WordPerfect* 5.0 are slightly different). Here, you can see that the *secondary merge file* is the file that contains the names and addresses, and the *primary merge file* is the file that contains the letter. In the secondary file, the data for each person is called a *record*, and each unit of information in a record is called a *field*. As you create the secondary file, you use the End Field command (*WordPerfect* 5.1) or the Merge R command (*WordPerfect* 5.0) to mark the end of a field. And you use the Merge Codes command to mark the end of a record. In figure 14-2, two complete records are shown in the secondary file, and each record has nine fields.

In the primary file, you use the Merge Codes command to tell *WordPerfect* where you want fields from the secondary file inserted when the two files are merged. In figure 14-2, you can see that you don't have to use all of the fields from the secondary file in the primary file, and you don't have to use the fields in the same sequence in both files. Also, you can insert a field into the primary file more than once.

To merge a primary and a secondary file, you use the Merge/Sort command. If, for example, you merge the two files in figure 14-2, the result is letters like those shown on the screen in figure 14-3. Here, there is one letter for each record in the secondary file. After the files have been merged on the screen, you can check the documents to make sure that the merge function has worked the way you wanted it to. Then, you can print the documents.

Before you perform a merge function, you can use the Sort function to sort the records in the secondary file. For example, you can use the Sort function to alphabetize all the records in the secondary file in figure 14-2 by last name. You can also use the Sort function to select certain types of records from a secondary file before sorting them. For example, you can use this function to select just the records in which the last-name field begins with an *m*.

The Sort feature can also be used independent of the Merge function to sort the lines or paragraphs within a document in alphanumeric order. If, for example, you want to sort the lines in an index that you've created for a document, this feature lets you sort them quickly and efficiently.

The Merge feature can be useful if you use it for a small file of records with a limited number of fields. But if you try to use this feature for a file that consists of dozens of records with many fields in each record, you'll soon discover that entering and maintaining the records is an inefficient and error prone process. As a result, you're better off using a database program like *Q&A* for creating and maintaining files of records because the program is designed for that purpose. *Q&A* is also designed for merging a document with the records in a file, and it can use a *WordPerfect* document for the merge function without any conversion difficulties.

Desktop publishing features

Figure 14-4 lists eight desktop publishing features that are introduced in this chapter. Once you learn how to use these features, you can create documents that look as though they have been prepared by traditional publishing

A secondary merge file with nine fields in each record

```
Mr.{END FIELD}
Bill{END FIELD}
Curtis-Ostrow{END FIELD}
Foothill Hardwoods{END FIELD}
P.O. Box 576{END FIELD}
Coarsegold{END FIELD}
CA{END FIELD}
93658{END FIELD}
(209) 689-6729{END RECORD}
======================================================================
Ms.{END FIELD}
Katherine{END FIELD}
Halls{END FIELD}
Wood Pro. Distributing{END FIELD}
1600 Cummings Street, Building 5{END FIELD}
Manteca{END FIELD}
CA{END FIELD}
94809{END FIELD}
(415) 527-8745{END RECORD}
======================================================================
Ms.{END FIELD}
Michelle{END FIELD}
Dowling{END FIELD}
RKR, Inc.{END FIELD}
```
Field: 1   Doc 1 Pg 1 Ln 1" Pos 1.25"

A primary merge file

```
                                   September 4, 1992

     {FIELD}1~ {FIELD}2~ {FIELD}3~
     {FIELD}4~
     {FIELD}5~
     {FIELD}6~, {FIELD}7~ {FIELD}8~

     Dear {FIELD}1~ {FIELD}3~:

     Last month we moved our production division.  The new address
     is on our purchase orders.  Please tell your shipping department
     about the change and have them ship our orders to the new
     address.

                                   Sincerely,


                                   John Lockwood
                                   Vice President, Production
```
C:\DATA\WPLTRS\ADDRESS   Doc 1 Pg 1 Ln 1" Pos 1.5"

Figure 14-2   The two types of files required by the Merge feature

```
                                      September 4, 1992


       Mr. Bill Curtis-Ostrow
       Foothill Hardwoods
       P.O. Box 576
       Coarsegold, CA 93658

       Dear Mr. Curtis-Ostrow:

       Last month we moved our production division.  The new address
       is on our purchase orders.  Please tell your shipping department
       about the change and have them ship our orders to the new
       address.

                                      Sincerely,



                                      John Lockwood
                                      Uice President, Production
       =============================================================================
                                      September 4, 1992

       Ms. Katherine Halls

                                             Doc 1 Pg 1 Ln 1" Pos 1.5"
```

Figure 14-3   The merge letters derived from the files in figure 14-2

methods. To take full advantage of the desktop publishing features of
WordPerfect, though, you need a laser printer.

As you read about its desktop publishing features, you should realize that
WordPerfect isn't the right program for desktop publishing if your
requirements are extensive. After all, *WordPerfect* is a word processing
program that has some desktop publishing capabilities; it is not a desktop
publishing program. Perhaps its major weakness is that you can't see how the
document will look while you work on it. This makes the program far more
difficult to use for desktop publishing than it ought to be. That's why many
people prefer to use desktop publishing programs like *Aldus Pagemaker* or
Ventura Publisher when it's time to prepare a document for printing. After
they prepare a document using *WordPerfect*, they transfer the document to the
desktop publishing program for final formatting and printing.

Because *WordPerfect for Windows* has improved desktop publishing
capabilities and because you can see how a document will look when it's
printed, you should consider converting to this program if desktop publishing
is one of your major applications. Then, you can use the same program for
word processing and desktop publishing. However, this program runs
considerably slower than *WordPerfect* for DOS on most PCs. As a result, some

Desktop publishing features

Feature	Function
Newspaper columns	You can use the Columns option from the Math/Columns command (5.0) or the Columns/Tables command (5.1) to define and use newspaper style columns.
Graphic lines	You can use the Line option from the Graphics command to create vertical and horizontal graphic lines in your documents.
Graphic boxes	You can use any of the first four options from the Graphics command to create four different types of graphic boxes in a *WordPerfect* document. Then, you can import graphic images, text, or spreadsheets into these boxes.
Styles	You can use the Style command to create style sheets and attach styles from the style sheets to blocks within a document. The use of style sheets can improve the consistency and quality of your document's presentation.
Automatic hyphenation	You can use the Hyphenation option from the Line screen of the Format command to turn on *WordPerfect*'s Automatic Hyphenation feature. Then, *WordPerfect* uses the Spell dictionary to automatically hyphenate words for you.
Force Odd/Even	You can use the Force/Odd Even Page option from the Page screen of the Format command to force a page to be an odd or an even page.
Line Height	You can use the Line Height option from the Format Line screen to manually adjust the height of the lines in a portion of a document. If you don't use this feature, *WordPerfect* automatically adjusts the Line Height based on the size of the font that you're using.
Line Draw	You can use the Line Draw option from the Screen command to draw graphic lines in a *WordPerfect* document.

Figure 14-4   Desktop publishing features

people use *WordPerfect* for DOS for preparing their documents. Then, they use *WordPerfect for Windows* for desktop publishing the documents.

If your desktop publishing requirements are limited, though, *WordPerfect* for DOS may offer all of the features that you need. If, for example, you just need the features for producing a newsletter like the one in figure 14-5 with the same format each month, you can do that efficiently with *WordPerfect* for DOS. Similarly, if you just need desktop publishing for preparing proposals that always have the same format, you can do that efficiently with *WordPerfect* for DOS. Here, then, is a brief introduction to the desktop publishing features of *WordPerfect* for DOS.

Newspaper columns   In figure 14-5, you can see that the newsletter is divided into two columns. In *WordPerfect* terminology, these columns are known as newspaper columns. When you use this type of column, you can divide text into as many as 24 columns. Most of the time, though, two or three columns are all that you need. Because this feature is relatively easy to use, it is one of the more practical desktop publishing features of *WordPerfect*. To access this feature, you use the Math/Columns command in *WordPerfect* 5.0 or the Columns/Table command in *WordPerfect* 5.1.

Graphic lines   If you look again at the newsletter in figure 14-5, you can see that horizontal lines are used to separate portions of the page. To create these lines, you can use the Line option of the Graphics command. When you create graphic lines, though, they don't appear on your Edit screen. As a result, you can't easily control the length, width, and placement of these lines.

Graphic boxes   The Graphics command lets you create and edit four different types of graphic boxes. Then, you can import text, graphics, or spreadsheets into these boxes. This feature is illustrated by the box on the newsletter in figure 14-5. In this example, the box contains text. Like graphic lines, though, graphic boxes don't appear on your Edit screen. As a result, you can't control the length, width, appearance, and placement of the boxes easily. And it's even harder to control the text, graphics, or spreadsheets that you import into these boxes.

Styles   The Styles command lets you create and edit *style sheets* that consist of *styles* that can be applied to blocks of text. Within each style are codes that specify the font to be used for the blocks of text that the styles are applied to. For instance, you can use a style that specifies a 12 point, boldface font for one type of heading in a newsletter. And you can use a style that specifies a 10 point, boldface, italic font for another type of heading.

When you use style sheets and styles, you can quickly and consistently format a document. Then, if you want to change the font that you used for one of the styles, you just change the style in the style sheet. When you do that, all of the text in the document that the style has been applied to is reformatted. You don't have to edit the document at all.

Although the Styles feature is often associated with desktop publishing, it can be useful whether or not you use any of the desktop publishing features. However, this feature is relatively difficult to use so it takes time to master it. And once you've mastered it, it can take a considerable amount of time to set up the style sheets that you're going to use. Once you get your style sheets set up the way you want them, though, you can work more efficiently with styles than without them. Also, as you will see in a moment, it's much easier to use *WordPerfect*'s automatic generation features when you use styles.

The Writer's Bulletin

September 1992

How to get the most from your word processor... and from your PC

Just a few years ago, most business writing was tedious work. To start, you usually wrote the first draft of a document in longhand. Then, if you were lucky, someone else would type it for you or enter it into a word processing system. If your document required visual aids, you drew rough drafts by hand, and you frequently drew the final drafts too.

As you moved up the organization chart, of course, you got more clerical help for your typing and drawing. But you still did a lot of proofing as you reviewed the several drafts of a typical business document.

Today, thanks to Personal Computers (PCs), you don't have to work that way. When you switch from typing to a word processing program like *WordPerfect*, you should easily be able to double your productivity. You should also be able to make dramatic improvements in the quality of your writing.

Between the idea and the reality, though, the shadow often falls. So today, after the installation

of over 50 million PCs in business, white-collar productivity has gone up less than ten percent. And the quality of the writing in most businesses hasn't improved at all.

In this issue of the Writer's Bulletin, we're going to give you some ideas that will help you get the most from your word processor...and from your PC. Specifically, we'll introduce you to four types of software and three writing methods that can help you improve your writing.

Why PCs and word processing haven't helped most managers

Even today, the business managers who use PCs are in the minority. To all too many of them, dictating letters, holding meetings, and reviewing the work of others is managerial, while using a keyboard is menial. These managers just don't realize how

much they could improve their productivity if they learned to do their own PC work. But until this attitude changes, the productivity potential of PCs and word processing will never be realized.

Fortunately, the next generation of managers won't have this problem. Most of them are learning to use PCs in college, and they expect to use PCs in business. In fact, they're likely to be sorely disappointed if they don't have access to a PC whenever they want to use one.

In this bulletin
- How a proven writing procedure can help you improve your writing
- What's new in CD ROM databases for writers
- The least you should know about on-line information services
- How the CEO of Wilkins, Inc. led the way to PC productivity
- Two writing analyzers that can help you improve the quality of your writing

Figure 14-5 A newsletter that uses newspaper columns, graphic lines, and a graphic box

Automatic hyphenation   When you use narrow columns of text, like those in the newsletter in figure 14-5, hyphenation at the ends of lines becomes more important. By hyphenating, you can remove large gaps at the ends of lines when you're using ragged right text. And you can eliminate large gaps between words when you're using justified text.

To turn on *WordPerfect*'s automatic hyphenation feature, you use the Line screen of the Format command. Then, *WordPerfect* uses the dictionary of the spelling checker to hyphenate all words in the document. If a word that isn't in the dictionary needs to be hyphenated, *WordPerfect* prompts you for the location of the hyphen. If this prompt is distracting as you create a document, you can turn off this feature until just before you print the document.

Force Odd/Even Page   You can use one of the Page options of the Format command to specify that a page should begin on an odd numbered (right) page or an even numbered (left) page. This can be useful when you work on a document that consists of several sections. If, for example, you want each section to start on a right page, you use this option to insert the proper code at the start of the first page of each section. Then, *WordPerfect* inserts blank pages whenever they are necessary.

Line Height   You can use the Line Height option of the Line screen of the Format command to manually adjust the heights of the lines used in a document. Otherwise, *WordPerfect* automatically selects the line height for each font. Usually, though, the automatic line height is satisfactory. So the average *WordPerfect* user never needs to use this feature.

Line Draw   *WordPerfect*'s Line Draw feature lets you draw graphic lines on your Edit screen. Theoretically, then, you could use this feature to draw a simple illustration for a document. In practice, though, this feature is difficult to use. That's why you're usually better off using a drawing program for this purpose. Then, if necessary, you can import the drawing into a graphic box within your document.

Features for presenting tabular data

Chapter 8 shows you how to use tab stops for presenting tabular data. However, both *WordPerfect* 5.0 and 5.1 offer a Parallel Columns feature that is useful for some types of columnar data. And *WordPerfect* 5.1 offers a powerful feature for preparing tables.

Parallel Columns   To access this feature, you use the Math/Columns command of *WordPerfect* 5.0 or the Columns/Table command of *WordPerfect* 5.1. Then, instead of specifying newspaper columns, you specify parallel columns.

Perhaps the best use of this feature is for preparing scripts. Otherwise, if you prepare simple tables, you can probably prepare them more efficiently by using tab stops. And if you prepare complex tables, the Tables feature of *WordPerfect* 5.1 is far more efficient than the Parallel Columns feature. In fact, if you frequently need to prepare complex tables and you're still using *WordPerfect* 5.0, you should consider upgrading to release 5.1.

Tables (*WordPerfect* 5.1)   If you need to prepare tables like those in figure 14-6, the Tables feature is surprisingly powerful and easy to use. You access this feature from the Columns/Table key. In the first table in this figure, graphic lines separate the columns and rows of the table. But you can remove these lines if you want to, as illustrated by the second table. When you remove the lines, *WordPerfect* prepares a table for printing much faster than when the lines are present. This is particularly obvious if you're using an older, slower PC.

Features for managing long documents

WordPerfect's features for managing long documents aren't easy to learn. In addition, they are often hard to set up so they work the way you want them to. However, if you frequently work on long documents, these features can help you improve your productivity.

Automatic generation features   You can use the Mark Text command to automatically generate a table of contents, a list of terms, or an index for a document. For instance, once you've used this command to mark the headings in a report, you can automatically generate a table of contents like the one shown in figure 14-7. As you can see in this example, *WordPerfect* can automatically generate the page numbers along with the headings or terms that you've marked in a document.

Styles   As I mentioned earlier, you can use the Styles feature to help you consistently format a document. This feature is even more useful when you're working with long documents. In addition, you can use the styles to mark the text that you want to include in a table of contents, a list, or an index. If, for example, you use styles to format the headings in a document, all you have to do is include the codes for marking the text in the style definition. Then, when you format your headings, you also mark them for use in the table of contents for the document.

Master document   Sometimes a writing project is so large that it makes sense to divide it into a number of documents. If, for example, you're working on a book, you can store each chapter in a separate file. Then, if you want to generate a table of contents, list, or index for the entire project, you can use the Master Document feature to link the separate documents together. You access this feature from the Mark Text key.

Features for working with legal or government documents

If you work with government or legal documents, *WordPerfect* provides several features that can help you work more efficiently.

Line numbering   This feature lets you number the lines in a document with numbers in the left margin. You access this feature from the Line screen of the Format command, and it gives you several numbering options. For example, you can set up this feature so it doesn't number blank lines and so it only places the number on every fifth line.

Redline and strikeout   You can use the Font command to insert redline and strikeout codes around text. When you're working with legal or government documents, for example, you may have to mark suggested additions to a document as redline and suggested deletions as strikeout. Then, when the document is printed, the redlined portions can be shaded and the strikeout portions can be crossed out by hyphens. Later, when the changes are agreed upon, you can use the Remove feature to automatically remove the redline markings from the additions and to delete the text that was marked for strikeout. The Remove feature is accessed from the Mark Text key.

If you make just a few additions and deletions to a document, you can sometimes use the Compare feature to automatically insert redline and strikeout markings. This feature is accessed from the Mark Text key. To insert these markings, *WordPerfect* compares the edited document on your screen with the unedited document that's on disk. However, if you make a lot of changes to a document, this feature doesn't work well. In fact, this feature sometimes doesn't work well even when you only make a minor change to a document.

Table of Authorities   If you need to prepare a Table of Authorities for a document, you can use the Mark Text command to generate one in either the short or the long form. To prepare a Table of Authorities, you usually mark all the cases, statutes, regulations, and so on as you create the document. Next, you insert the code that defines the Table of Authorities into your document, and you generate the table. As it generates the Table of Authorities, *WordPerfect* separates the authorities into the sections that you marked them for. Then, *WordPerfect* sorts the authorities within each section alphanumerically.

A table with lines

Five types of programs you can use for a mailing list		
Program type	**Typical strengths**	**Typical weaknesses**
Word Processing	Preparing form letters	Preparing directories Maintenance functions Sorting functions Selection functions
Database	Preparing labels Preparing directories Maintenance functions Sorting functions Selection functions	
Integrated	Preparing form letters Relatively easy to use	
Mailing list	Low cost Easy to use Preparing labels Preparing directories	Preparing form letters General inflexibility
Spreadsheet		Preparing form letters Preparing labels Preparing directories Maintenance functions Selection functions

A table without lines

Five types of programs you can use for a mailing list		
Program type	**Typical strengths**	**Typical weaknesses**
Word Processing	Preparing form letters	Preparing directories Maintenance functions Sorting functions Selection functions
Database	Preparing labels Preparing directories Maintenance functions Sorting functions Selection functions	
Integrated	Preparing form letters Relatively easy to use	
Mailing list	Low cost Easy to use Preparing labels Preparing directories	Preparing form letters General inflexibility
Spreadsheet		Preparing form letters Preparing labels Preparing directories Maintenance functions Selection functions

Figure 14-6   Two tables created with the Table feature of *WordPerfect* 5.1

Outline   You access the Outline feature from the Date/Outline key. This feature makes it easier for you to create an outline. However, it is limited when compared to an outline processing program like *ThinkTank* or *GrandView*. As a result, you should only use this feature when your outlining requirements are limited. If you frequently use outlines to help organize your thoughts, you should consider buying an outline processor.

Features for working with academic documents

If you're a student, a professor, or work in an academic environment, here are two features that can help you work more efficiently.

Footnote   *WordPerfect* provides an excellent feature for preparing documents that require footnotes or endnotes. You access this feature from the Footnote key. It is relatively easy to master, and it takes much of the drudgery out of working with footnotes.

Outline   You access the Outline feature from the Date/Outline key. This feature makes it easier for you to create outlines in the traditional academic style. So if you have to develop an occasional outline, this feature may be useful to you.

Math-related features

If you need to perform calculations on rows or columns of numbers, you should probably use a spreadsheet program like *Lotus 1-2-3* or *Quattro Pro*, not a word processing program like *WordPerfect*. However, *WordPerfect* does provide a feature for performing calculations on the data in a document. And it does provide a feature for entering and editing mathematical equations into a document. For some *WordPerfect* users, these features have practical applications.

Math   *WordPerfect*'s Math feature can be used to perform calculations on numbers that are aligned in tabular columns. This feature is accessed from the Math/Columns key of *WordPerfect* 5.0 or the Columns/Table key of *WordPerfect* 5.1. If, for example, you set up a document in the form of an invoice, you can use this feature to calculate the extensions of the line items and the total amount billed. For occasional math requirements, though, it's usually easier to use a calculator to get the results that you need and then to enter the results into your document.

If you're using *WordPerfect* 5.1, you can use the Math feature in combination with the Tables feature. In this case, the table approximates a spreadsheet. Then, you can enter formulas into the cells of the table just as

Chapter 1
When and how to back up your hard disk

How backups work	1
The types of hardware you can use to back up a hard disk	2
Diskette drives	2
Backup tape drives	3
Other hardware	3
Two types of programs you can use to back up a hard disk	3
The DOS commands	4
Commercial backup utilities	4
Two types of backups	5
Full backups	5
Incremental backups	5
How the drives, directories and files on your hard disk affect backups	6
Disk and diskette drives	6
Directories and subdirectories	7
File names	7
How to do separate program and data backups	7
How to use drives to do separate program and data backups	7
How to use directories to do separate program and data backups	8

Figure 14-7 A table of contents generated from the headings within a document

you can enter formulas into the cells of a spreadsheet. This brings the math capabilities of *WordPerfect* closer to those of a spreadsheet program. However, the math capabilities still don't compare with those of a complete spreadsheet program like *Lotus 1-2-3* or *Quattro Pro*.

Equation (*WordPerfect* 5.1) You access this feature from the Graphics key, and it lets you create and edit complex mathematical equations within a document. However, it only prints these equations; it doesn't calculate them. Although this feature is difficult to use, it can be valuable if you need to use mathematical equations in your documents.

Miscellaneous commands and options

Figure 14-8 summarizes some miscellaneous commands and options that aren't presented in this book. These are accessed from the Shell, Screen, and Text In/Out keys.

Shell The Shell command lets you temporarily exit to DOS so you can execute a DOS command. The *WordPerfect* 5.1 version of this command also lets you execute a DOS command without exiting from *WordPerfect* at all. Both versions of this command can cause problems, though, because *WordPerfect* remains in internal memory. As a result, DOS may not have enough memory to execute the command that you issue. In the worst case, this causes your screen to freeze. Then, you have to reboot your PC and recover your document from the *WordPerfect* backup file as described in chapter 13. For this reason, I recommend that you avoid using this command.

Screen You can use the Rewrite option on the Screen command to "rewrite" the text on your edit screen. This reformats the screen based on any changes that you've made to the formatting codes. If you move the cursor down the screen, *WordPerfect* rewrites the screen automatically so you don't ever need the Rewrite function. But sometimes, the Rewrite function works more quickly than moving the cursor.

Text In/Out If you look at the options available from the Text In/Out command in figure 14-8, you can see that the first option lets you save and retrieve *text files*. These files are also known as *ASCII files*. They have a general format that is often useful for transferring files from one program to another. You can also use this option to retrieve a DOS file like the AUTOEXEC.BAT or CONFIG.SYS file. Then, after you edit it, you can use this option to save the file in the ASCII format.

The second set of options for this command in figure 14-8 lets you save a document in the format of an earlier version of *WordPerfect*. It also lets you save a document in a generic word processing format. These options are useful when you have to transfer a document to another release of *WordPerfect* or to another word processing program.

The third option for this command in figure 14-8 lets you protect a document by attaching a password to it. The fourth option lets you put comments in a document that are displayed on the Edit screen but aren't printed. The fifth option lets you import a spreadsheet from another program into a document. These options can be useful occasionally, but it's likely that you'll never need any of them.

The Convert program

The Convert program that comes with *WordPerfect* provides the conversion capabilities that are summarized in figure 14-9. As you can see, these capabilities go beyond the conversion capabilities provided by the Text In/Out command. The Convert program lets you convert a document to the format of another release of *WordPerfect*. It also lets you convert a document

Option	Function
Shell command	
Go to DOS	Lets you temporarily exit to DOS without clearing your document or the *WordPerfect* program from memory
DOS command (5.1)	Lets you execute a DOS command without exiting from *WordPerfect*
Screen command	
Rewrite	Lets you rewrite the Edit screen without running the cursor through the document to show the current format of the document
Text In/Out command	
DOS text	Lets you save a document as a DOS text file and lets you retrieve a DOS text file into *WordPerfect* format
Save As (5.1) Save Generic (5.0) Save As WP 4.2 (5.0)	Lets you save a document in generic word processing format or in the format of an older version of *WordPerfect*
Password	Lets you protect a document with a password
Comment	Lets you create a comment within a document that won't get printed with the rest of the document
Spreadsheet (5.1)	Lets you import spreadsheets from other programs into a document

Figure 14-8   Some miscellaneous commands and options

to three general formats and to two specific word processing formats. For instance, the Convert program lets you convert a secondary merge file into *DIF format*, a general format for use with spreadsheet programs.

If you're converting to *WordPerfect* from another word processing program or if you frequently convert documents from other word processing programs to *WordPerfect*, the conversion capabilities of the Convert program can be invaluable. If, for example, you're converting from *Word 4.0* or *DisplayWrite* to *WordPerfect* 5.1, the Convert program makes it easy for you. In all, the Convert program for *WordPerfect* 5.1 provides for the conversion of four general formats and five specific word processing formats to the *WordPerfect* 5.1 format.

Discussion

If you want to use any of the commands or features that I introduced in this chapter, you can probably figure out how to use them by using the

From *WordPerfect* format to	To *WordPerfect* format from
Other *WordPerfect* releases	Other *WordPerfect* releases
IBM DCA format	IBM DCA format
Navy DIF standard	Navy DIF standard
Secondary Merge format to Spreadsheet DIF	Spreadsheet DIF to Secondary Merge format
Seven-Bit transfer format	Seven-Bit transfer format
Wordstar 3.3	*Wordstar* 3.3
MultiMate Advantage II	*Multimate Advantage II*
	Word 4.0
	DisplayWrite
	Mail Merge

Figure 14-9   The file conversion capabilities provided the Convert program of *WordPerfect* 5.1

WordPerfect Help feature or the *WordPerfect* manual. Some of the commands and features, in fact, are quite easy to use so you don't really need to learn more about them before you experiment with them. Others, however, are quite complicated. As a result, learning how to use them on your own can be both a frustrating and an inefficient experience. Once you master the *WordPerfect* skills presented in section 3 of this book, though, you have a foundation of knowledge that makes it easier for you to learn new commands and features, no matter what instructional or reference materials you use.

Terms

secondary merge file
primary merge file
record
field
style sheet

style
text file
ASCII file
DIF format

Objective

Decide whether you need any of the commands or features that are introduced in this chapter.

Appendix A

How to install *WordPerfect*

This appendix describes how to install the *WordPerfect* 5.1 program, and it describes two ways to install the *WordPerfect* 5.0 program. In addition, this appendix describes how to use either *WordPerfect* 5.0 or 5.1 to install a printer. However, since these procedures differ from *WordPerfect* 5.0 to 5.1, you only need to read the instructions that apply to your release of *WordPerfect*. But before you install either version of *WordPerfect*, you should know some preliminary concepts that apply to both versions of *WordPerfect*.

Preliminary concepts

When you install *WordPerfect* on a hard disk, you copy the *WordPerfect* program files to a directory on your hard disk. Then, you may need to edit your CONFIG.SYS file, and you may want to edit your AUTOEXEC.BAT file. And finally, you need to install a printer. While both *WordPerfect* 5.1 and 5.0 come with Install programs that can help you accomplish these tasks, only the Install program that comes with *WordPerfect* 5.1 helps you install a printer. A little later in this chapter, you'll learn how to use the Print command to install a printer in *WordPerfect* 5.0.

The CONFIG.SYS and AUTOEXEC.BAT files   The CONFIG.SYS and AUTOEXEC.BAT files are DOS files that are found in the root directory of the C drive. When you turn on or "boot" your PC, your PC reads these files to set itself up. If you use the Install program to install *WordPerfect*, the program modifies these files so that *WordPerfect* runs properly. If you need to modify these files yourself, you have to use DOS to edit them.

Within the CONFIG.SYS file, there is a FILES= command that determines the number of file handles that are available to application programs. In order for *WordPerfect* to run properly, it needs at least 20 file handles. Then, if necessary, the Install program sets the number of file handles to 20. However, if you plan to run any TSRs (terminate-and-stay-resident programs) with *WordPerfect*, you may need to use DOS to edit the CONFIG.SYS file and set the number of file handles to 25 or 30.

Within the AUTOEXEC.BAT file, there is a PATH command that establishes a list of directories that DOS searches whenever it receives a command. The Install program for *WordPerfect* 5.1 inserts the *WordPerfect* program directory (usually \WP51) into the PATH command in the AUTOEXEC.BAT file. Then, you can start *WordPerfect* at the DOS prompt from any directory. Although it isn't necessary to have the program directory in the PATH command in order to use *WordPerfect*, sometimes it's helpful to be able to start the program this way.

Print drivers and printer files   When you install a printer, *WordPerfect* creates a file that translates *WordPerfect* codes to codes that your printer can understand. This file is referred to as a *print driver*. In *WordPerfect*, all print driver files have this extension: PRS. In order to create a print driver, *WordPerfect* must be able to access a file that contains general information about your printer and related printers. These *printer files* have this extension: ALL. And they are sometimes referred to as *ALL files*.

How to install *WordPerfect* 5.1 on a hard disk

Since the files on the *WordPerfect* 5.1 diskettes are compressed, you must use the Install program to expand and copy the files to your hard disk. If you use DOS to copy these files, they won't be expanded and they won't run properly.

Figure A-1 shows how to use the Install program to install *WordPerfect* 5.1 for the first time. Here, the right column shows the DOS commands you must enter at the DOS command prompt. After you start the Install program in step 2, it displays a screen like the one shown in figure A-2. At this Installation screen, you select the Basic option as indicated in step 3.

In step 4, you respond to the Install program's prompts that are shown in figure A-3. In step 5, you insert each program disk as *WordPerfect* prompts you for it, and you press Enter. If you have plenty of disk space, the easiest way to respond to the prompts is to select Yes for all of them. Although this copies some files that you won't need onto your hard disk, you can delete these files later once you're comfortable with *WordPerfect*.

If you want to conserve disk space, you can use figure A-4 to decide which files you want to copy to your hard disk. If you use just the skills presented in this book, you won't need the Utility Files, the Learning Files, the Style Library, the PTR Program Files, or the Graphic Images. In addition, you won't need the Keyboard Files unless you want to use the ALTRNAT keyboard that's described in chapter 6.

In step 6, you respond to the Install program's prompts to edit your CONFIG.SYS and AUTOEXEC.BAT files. Again, the easiest way to respond to these prompts is to select Yes. If either of these files needs to be modified, *WordPerfect* prompts you to reboot your PC and start the Install program

Step	DOS Command
1. Insert the *WordPerfect* diskette labeled *Install/Learn/Utilities 1* into the diskette drive and log onto that drive.	`C:\>a:`
2. Start the Install program.	`A:\>install`
3. Select the Basic installation option from the screen shown in figure A-2.	
4. Answer the prompts shown in figure A-3 to specify the files that you want *WordPerfect* to install on your hard disk.	
5. Insert the appropriate program diskettes as prompted by the Install program and press Enter.	
Repeat steps 4 and 5 until you're through all of the prompts.	
6. Respond to the Install program's prompts to change your CONFIG.SYS and AUTOEXEC.BAT files.	
7. Respond to the Install program's prompts to install a printer or printers.	

Figure A-1   A 7-step procedure for installing *WordPerfect* 5.1 on a hard disk

```
Installation

   1 - Basic        Perform a standard installation to C:\WP51.

   2 - Custom       Perform a customized installation.  (User selected
                    directories.)

   3 - Network      Perform a customized installation onto a network.
                    (To be performed by the network supervisor.)

   4 - Printer      Install updated Printer (.ALL) File.

   5 - Update       Install WordPerfect 5.1 Interim Release program file(s).
                    (Used for updating existing WordPerfect 5.1 software.)

   6 - Copy Disks   Install every file from an installation diskette to a
                    specified location.  (Useful for installing all the
                    Printer (.ALL) Files.)




   Selection: 1
```

Figure A-2   The main installation screen for *WordPerfect* 5.1

again. That's because the modifications to these files won't take effect until you reboot your PC. After you reboot, you repeat steps 1 and 2 to restart the Install program.

In step 7, you insert the Printer 1 diskette and press Enter. When you do, the Install program displays a master list of printers like the one shown in figure A-5. As you can see on this screen, you can use the Name search option at the bottom of the screen or the Page-up and Page-down keys to search for your printer. When you find your printer, type the number that identifies it and press Enter to select it. Then, respond to any prompts or screens that the Install program displays. For example, the Install program might show you a Printer Helps and Hints screen that gives you some information that's specific to your printer. When you install a printer in *WordPerfect* 5.1, the Install program copies the ALL file for the printer to the hard disk, and it creates a PRS file for the printer you selected.

Installing a printer completes the installation process. When the Install program returns you to the DOS prompt, *WordPerfect* has been installed on your PC. Later, if you want to add another printer, you can use one of the two methods that follow.

How to install a printer in *WordPerfect* 5.1

After you install the printer or printers you need with the Install program, you may never need to install a printer again. If you do need to, however, you have two options. First, if the printer (ALL) file for the printer you want to install has been expanded and copied to your hard disk, you can use the Print command to install a new printer. Second, you can always use the Install program to install a printer.

To use the Print command to install a new printer, you use the first three steps of figure A-9. First, you start *WordPerfect*, access the Print command, and select the Select Printer option. Then, *WordPerfect* displays the printers that are currently installed. If you want to add a printer to the Select Printer list, you can use the Additional Printers option that's in the selection line at the bottom of the screen. This option lets you choose from a list of printers that are supported by *WordPerfect*. However, if the printer you want isn't on this screen, or if *WordPerfect* tells you that it can't find the printer files, you have to use the Install program to install the printer.

To use *WordPerfect* 5.1's Install program to install a printer, start the program as directed in figure A-1. If the Install program finds that all of the *WordPerfect* 5.1 files are already installed on your system, it prompts you to insert the Printer 1 diskette and press Enter. Then, *WordPerfect* displays a list of printers like the one shown in figure A-5. At this screen, you find the printer, type the number that identifies it, and press Enter. To complete the selection, you respond to any prompts and screens that *WordPerfect* displays.

Do you want to install Utility Files? Yes (No)

Do you want to install the Learning Files? Yes (No)

Do you want to install the Help File? Yes (No)

Do you want to install Keyboard Files? Yes (No)

Do you want to install the Style Library? Yes (No)

Do you want to install the WordPerfect program? Yes (No)

Do you want to install the Speller? Yes (No)

Do you want to install the PTR Program? Yes (No)

Do you want to install the Graphic Drivers? Yes (No)

Do you want to install Graphic Images? Yes (No)

Figure A-3　　The *WordPerfect* 5.1 installation prompts

Type of files	Function
Utility	These are various utilities like Convert and Capture for advanced features of *WordPerfect* that go beyond simple word processing. You don't need these files to run *WordPerfect*, but some of them are useful.
Learning	These files contain the *WordPerfect* tutorial material. You don't need them unless you want to use *WordPerfect*'s tutorial or the *WordPerfect Workbook*.
Help	These files are necessary to run the Help feature.
Keyboard	These files are for various keyboard layouts. You don't need these files unless you want to use a pre-defined *WordPerfect* keyboard. If, for example, you want to use the ALTERNAT keyboard, you'll need the ALTERNAT.WPK file.
Style Library	These files contain *WordPerfect*'s pre-formatted styles for formatting text. You probably don't need these files.
WordPerfect Program	These files are necessary to run *WordPerfect*.
Speller	These files are necessary to run *WordPerfect*'s Spell checker.
PTR Program	These files let you modify and install printer files. You probably don't need them.
Graphic Drivers	These files let *WordPerfect* operate on graphics files. If your monitor supports graphics, you probably want to install these files.
Graphic Images	These files contain graphic images that you can directly import into *WordPerfect* documents. You probably don't need these files.

Figure A-4　　The *WordPerfect* 5.1 files and their function

If the Install program finds that some, but not all, of the *WordPerfect* 5.1 files are already installed on your system, the Install program displays the main Install screen shown in figure A-2. At this screen, you select the Custom option. Then, you select the Install Printer option. Next, if you follow the prompts, the Install program displays a list of printers like the one shown in figure A-5. At this screen, use the techniques I described earlier to select a printer.

How to install *WordPerfect* 5.0 on a hard disk

There are two ways you can install *WordPerfect* 5.0 on your hard disk. You can use the *WordPerfect* 5.0 Install program, or you can use DOS. When you use the Install program, it creates a directory on your hard disk, copies all the *WordPerfect* files to that directory, and it automatically checks and alters your CONFIG.SYS file. In addition, the Install program creates a LEARN subdirectory and copies some tutorial files into this directory. If you have plenty of disk space and aren't comfortable with DOS, this is the method you should use. If you are comfortable with DOS, however, you can save disk space by using it to manually install *WordPerfect*. This method gives you more flexibility over what files you want to install. In addition, this method doesn't automatically alter your CONFIG.SYS.

How to use the Install program to install *WordPerfect* 5.0 on a hard disk   Figure A-6 shows you how to use Install program to install *WordPerfect* 5.0 for the first time. Here, the right column shows the DOS commands you enter at the DOS command prompt. After you insert the Learning diskette and start the Install program in steps 1 and 2, the program displays a screen like the one shown in figure A-7. As you can see, the Install program creates a C:\WP50 directory, copies all *WordPerfect* files to that directory, creates a C:\WP50\LEARN directory, copies tutorial files to that directory, and modifies your CONFIG.SYS file. At this screen, you select Yes as indicated in step 3.

In step 4, the Install program prompts you to insert the *WordPerfect* diskettes. After you insert all of the diskettes, the program checks your CONFIG.SYS file. If the number of file handles is less than 20, *WordPerfect* tells you that it's altering your CONFIG.SYS file. Next, the Install program returns you to DOS. If your CONFIG.SYS file has been altered, you have to reboot your PC before the new CONFIG.SYS file takes effect.

At this point, *WordPerfect* is installed on your PC. However, the Install program doesn't install your printer for you. To do that, you have to start *WordPerfect* and use the Print command. I'll show you how to use the Print command to install a printer in just a moment.

```
 1   Epson FX-80                          Printers marked with '*' are
 2   Epson FX-85                          not included with shipping
 3   Epson FX-850                         disks.  Select printer for
 4   Epson FX-86e                         more information.
 5   Epson LQ-1000
 6  *Epson LQ-1000 (Additional)
 7   Epson LQ-1050
 8  *Epson LQ-1050 (Additional)
 9  *Epson LQ-1050 (M8 ROM Additional)
10   Epson LQ-1050 (M8 ROM)
11   Epson LQ-1500
12   Epson LQ-2500
13  *Epson LQ-2500 (Additional)
14   Epson LQ-2550
15  *Epson LQ-2550 (Additional)
16   Epson LQ-500
17  *Epson LQ-500 (Additional)
18   Epson LQ-510
19  *Epson LQ-510 (Additional)
20   Epson LQ-800
21  *Epson LQ-800 (Additional)
22   Epson LQ-850

N Name Search; PgDn More Printers; PgUp Previous Screen; F3 Help; F7 Exit;
Selection: 22
```

Figure A-5   *WordPerfect* 5.1's master list of printers

Step	DOS Command
1. Insert the *WordPerfect* diskette labeled *Learning* into the diskette drive and log onto that drive.	`C:\>a:`
2. Start the Install program.	`A:\>install`
3. At the main Install screen shown in figure A-7, select Yes to continue.	
4. Insert the appropriate program diskettes as prompted by the install program and press Enter.	
5. If necessary, reboot your PC so that the new CONFIG.SYS file is in force.	
6. Start *WordPerfect* and use the Print command to select a printer (see figure A-9).	

Figure A-6   A 6-step procedure for using the Install program to install *WordPerfect* 5.0 on a hard disk

How to use DOS to install *WordPerfect* 5.0 on a hard disk   Figure A-8 shows you how to use DOS to install *WordPerfect* 5.0. First, you create a directory. Then, you copy the *WordPerfect* 5.0 program files to your hard disk. Here, you can decide what diskettes you want to copy to your hard disk. For example, you don't need to copy the diskettes labelled Conversion, PTR, or Learning to your hard disk for *WordPerfect* to run correctly. And you don't need to copy any of the Printer diskettes to your hard disk. Next, if necessary, you use DOS to edit your CONFIG.SYS and AUTOEXEC.BAT files. If you alter either of these files, remember that you must reboot your PC before the edited file takes effect.

At this point, *WordPerfect* is installed on your system. However, you still need to start *WordPerfect* and use the Print command to install the printer. I'll explain how to that next.

How to install a printer in *WordPerfect* 5.0

Figure A-9 shows you how to use the Print command to install a printer in *WordPerfect* 5.0. In step 1, you start *WordPerfect* and press Shift+F7 to access the Print command. In step 2, you select the Select Printer option. Then, *WordPerfect* displays the Select Printer screen. This screen lists the printers that are already installed. If it's blank, no printers are currently installed.

In step 3, you select the Additional Printers option. If *WordPerfect* finds printer (ALL) files on your hard disk, it displays a list of printers that are available. If one of these printers is the printer you want, select it, and *WordPerfect* creates a print driver for that printer. In this case, your printer installation is complete.

However, if *WordPerfect* doesn't find any printer files on your hard disk, or if the printer you want to install isn't displayed, you select the Other Disk option. When you do, *WordPerfect* displays a prompt like this:

Directory for printer files:

At this prompt, you type the directory that the print files are in. Usually, that means inserting a *WordPerfect* Printer diskette into the disk drive of your PC and entering the letter of that drive. However, it sometimes means specifying a directory on your hard disk.

Once you tell *WordPerfect* where the printer files are, it displays a list of printers. If you're inserting the Printer diskettes into your PC, you may have to search through them all before you find your printer. When you find your printer, type the number that identifies it and press Enter.Then, *WordPerfect* creates a print driver for the printer, and the printer is added to the list on the Select Printer screen.

```
This installation program will perform the following:

   1) Copy all files necessary to execute WordPerfect 5.0
      into the subdirectory C:\WP50. If the subdirectory
      C:\WP50 does not exist it will be created. You will
      be prompted to insert the various system disks into
      drive A: at the appropriate times.

   2) Copy all files necessary to execute the WordPerfect
      Tutor into the subdirectory C:\WP50\LEARN. If the
      subdirectory C:\WP50\LEARN does not exist it will be created.

   3) Insert the string FILES=20 into your CONFIG.SYS file. A
      copy of your original CONFIG.SYS file will be retained in
      a new CONFIG.OLD file.

   Do You Want to Continue? (Y/N) Y
```

Figure A-7   The main installation screen for *WordPerfect* 5.0

Step	DOS Command
1. Create a directory for the *WordPerfect* program files.	`C:\>md\wp50`
2. Change to the WP50 directory.	`C:\>cd wp50`
3. Insert the *WordPerfect* diskettes into the diskette drive and copy the *WordPerfect* program files into the WP50 directory.	`C::\WP50>copy a:*.*`

Repeat step 3 for each *WordPerfect* diskette.

4. Use DOS to edit your CONFIG.SYS and AUTOEXEC.BAT files.

5. If necessary, reboot your PC so that the new CONFIG.SYS and AUTOEXEC.BAT files are in force.

6. Start *WordPerfect* and use the Print command to select a printer (see figure A-9).

Figure A-8   A 6-step procedure for using DOS to install *WordPerfect* 5.0 on a hard disk

1. Start *WordPerfect* and press Shift+F7 to access the Print command.

2. Select the Select Printer option from the Print screen. When you do, *WordPerfect* will give you the Select Printer screen. (This screen is explained in chapter 10.) This screen lists the printers that are already installed. If it's blank, no printers are currently installed.

3. Select the Additional Printers option. If *WordPerfect* finds printer files, it will display a list of printers that it can install. If one of these printers is the printer you want, you can select it, and *WordPerfect* will create a print driver for that printer. However, if *WordPerfect* doesn't find any printer files, or if the printer you want to install isn't displayed, go to step 4.

4. Select the Other Disk option.

   Directory for printer files:

5. Insert one of the *WordPerfect* diskettes labelled *Printer* into the A drive, type a:, and press Enter. When you do, *WordPerfect* will show the list of printers that's on that diskette. Since the print files on the *WordPerfect* 5.1 diskettes are compressed, this doesn't work in 5.1.

   Repeat step 5 until you find your printer.

6. When you find your printer, type the number to the left of your printer and press Enter.

Figure A-9   A 6-step procedure for using the Print command to install a Printer for *WordPerfect* 5.0

Some perspective on installing printers

You may be surprised that *WordPerfect* allows you to install more than one printer. If you read chapter 10, however, you'll learn how to use the Select Printer screen to switch between two or more printers. Also, you'll learn that you can install printers that aren't attached to your PC and when this can be useful.

When you try to select a printer, the exact make and model of your printer might not be listed. If so, select what you think is the closest option. If your printer doesn't work correctly, you can delete the PRS file for that printer and install another printer. With a little experimentation, you should be able to find a print driver that runs your printer properly.

Some perspective on setting defaults

After you install *WordPerfect*, you should set it up so that it works the way you want it to. For example, you should use the Print command to set the default font for each printer. And you should use the Setup command to set the margins, justification, and tabs stops so that they work for most of your documents. To learn more about these default settings and how to set them up, you can read chapter 6.

Appendix B

When and how to use the
WordPerfect 5.1 menus

If you read chapter 3, you know that I recommend using the function keys to access *WordPerfect* screens and commands. As a result, this book is designed to be used with the function key interface. However, in *WordPerfect* 5.1, you have the option to use a system of menus, like the menus shown in figure B-1, to access *WordPerfect* screens and commands. In addition, *WordPerfect* 5.1 supports the use of a mouse.

If you want to use the menus, this appendix will show you how. First, you'll learn how to use the menus with or without a mouse. Then, you'll learn how to set up the menus so you can use them efficiently. Next, you'll learn how to use a mouse with *WordPerfect* screens, selection lines, and prompts. And finally, I'll show you how to use the menus to access the *WordPerfect* screens and commands that are presented in this book. But first, you need to learn some terms that apply to the menu interface.

An introduction to pull-down menus

If you look at figure B-1, you will see several different elements that make up the *WordPerfect* 5.1 menu system. There is a *menu bar* across the top of the screen that has the names of the nine different *WordPerfect* menus on it. These menus are called *pull-down menus* because you pull them down in order to select items from them. In figure B-1, for example, the Font menu is pulled down.

If you look closely at the items on the Font menu, you will see that there is a triangle to the right of the Appearance item. When you select an item with a triangle, *WordPerfect* gives you another menu with more items. Since this menu cascades off to the right side of the pull-down menu, it's called a *cascading menu*. In figure B-1, for example, the Appearance menu cascades off to the right side of the Appearance item on the Font menu. When you select an item that doesn't have a triangle, *WordPerfect* executes that item immediately.

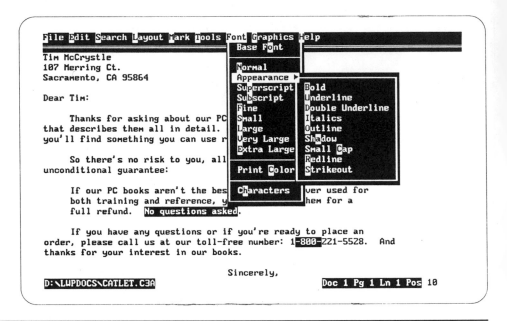

Figure B-1   The pull-down menu for the Font command

As you work with the pull-down menus, you'll realize that they are just another way of doing the same things you can do with the function keys. In other words, there are no additional features that you can use with the menus. And in most cases, the menus lead to the same *WordPerfect* screens, selection lines, and prompts that the function keys lead to.

How to use the pull-down menus

There are three steps to using the menus. First, if the menu bar is not visible, you must display it. Then, you pull down a menu and select an item from it. Figure B-2 shows how to use the menus with a mouse or with the keyboard.

With a mouse   If you are using a mouse, you can display the menu bar by clicking the right button. Then, to pull down the menu you want, move the mouse cursor to that menu and click the left button. To select an item, move the mouse cursor to it and click the left button. If you make a mistake or change your mind, you can back out of the menus by clicking the right button.

With the keyboard   If you're using the keyboard, you can display the menu bar by holding down the Alt key while you press the Equals (=) key. Then, to pull down the menu you want or to select an item from a menu, you press the highlighted letter of the menu or item. Or you can move the cursor

How to access the menus and items with a mouse

Right button	If you are at the Edit screen, click the right button to display the menu bar.
	If you are in a menu, click the right button to back out of all the menus and return to the Edit screen.
Left button	Move the mouse cursor to an item and click the left button to select it.

How to access the menus and items with the keyboard

Alt key+Equals	Displays the menu bar.
Alt key	Displays the menu bar if you've set this default for your system. (Figure B-5)
Cursor control keys	Moves the cursor through the menus and items to highlight your selection.
Highlighted letter	Selects the menu or item.
Enter key	Selects a menu item that has been highlighted by the cursor.
Esc key	Backs out of menus one by one. If you are at the menu bar, it returns you to the Edit screen.
Cancel key (F1)	Backs out of menus one by one. If you are at the menu bar, it returns you to the Edit screen.
Exit key (F7)	Backs out of all menus and returns you to the Edit screen.

Figure B-2   How to access the pull-down menus and select items

to the menu or item to highlight it, and then press the Enter key. But this method requires more keystrokes, so I don't recommend it. If you make a mistake or change your mind, you can cancel your selection by using the Esc, Cancel, or Exit keys as shown in figure B-2.

How to use a mouse with *WordPerfect* 5.1

If you're used to using a mouse to select items in a WYSIWYG (what-you-see-is-what-you-get) environment, you may find that using a mouse with *WordPerfect* 5.1 is frustrating. That's because *WordPerfect* for DOS wasn't developed with mouse support in mind. Still, if you're used to using a mouse, you may be delighted that you can now use one to block text on the Edit screen and to make selections from *WordPerfect* screens, selection lines, and prompts.

1. Position mouse cursor and hold down the left button.
2. Drag the mouse cursor to the end of the text that you want blocked.
3. Release the left mouse button.

Figure B-3   How to use the mouse to block text

How to block text on the Edit screen   Figure B-3 shows you how to block text on the Edit screen. First, you position the mouse cursor where you want to begin the block. Then, you press and hold down the left mouse button as you drag the mouse cursor to the end of the text that you want to block. This is referred to as the *click-and-drag* technique. To complete marking the block, you release the left mouse button.

How to make selections at the *WordPerfect* 5.1 screens, selection lines, and prompts   Figure B-4 shows you how to use the mouse to make selections at the *WordPerfect* 5.1 screens, selection lines, and prompts. To select an item from a screen or selection line, you move the mouse cursor to the highlighted letter or number of the item. Then, you click the left mouse button.

You can also use the mouse to confirm operations at the prompt line. If, for example, you use the Save command to save an existing document named CATLET in the D:\WPLTRS directory, *WordPerfect* displays this prompt:

Document to be saved: D:\WPLTRS\CATLET

To confirm the save operation, you position the mouse cursor on the prompt and press the right mouse button.

How to set up the pull-down menus so they work the way you want them to

WordPerfect 5.1 gives you several options for setting up the pull-down menus. Then, you set the options so that the menus are displayed and pulled down the way you want them. You set the options for the pull-down menus at the Menu Option screen shown in figure B-5. To access the Menu Option screen, you pull down the File menu and select the Setup item. Then, you select the Display option from the Setup menu. And finally, you select the Menu Options from the Display screen. The two most important options on this screen are the Alt-Key-Selects-Pull-Down-Menu option and the Menu-Bar-Remains-Visible option.

The Alt-Key-Selects-Pull-Down-Menu option   If you use the keyboard to select menus, you'll probably want to set this option to Yes. Then, you can

Left button	To select an item, move the mouse cursor to a highlighted number or letter and click the left button.
Right button	To confirm a prompt, position the mouse cursor on the prompt and click the right button.
	To back out of menus, selection lines, or prompts and return to the Edit screen, click the right button.

Figure B-4   How to use the mouse to select, confirm, and exit from screens, selection lines, and prompts

display the menu bar by pressing the Alt key. Otherwise, you have to press the Alt+Equals key combination to display the menu bar.

The-Menu-Bar-Remains-Visible option   Whether or not you keep the menu bar visible is up to you. If it's visible, you save a keystroke or mouse click every time you want to select a menu. And you might feel more comfortable with the menu bar shown at the top of the screen. On the other hand, when the menu bar is visible, you can't see as many lines of text on the Edit screen.

How to use pull-down menus to access the Setup and Format screens

Figure B-6 shows you how to access the Setup and Format screens with the pull-down menu system. If you've read this book, you know that to use *WordPerfect* effectively and efficiently you must know how to use the Setup and Format screens. To set up *WordPerfect* so it works the way you want it, you use the Setup and Format commands as described in chapter 6. You also need to know how to use the Format command as described in chapter 8 to set defaults that affect an entire document.

How to use pull-down menus to access the *WordPerfect* commands presented in this book

Figure B-7 is an alphabetical list of the *WordPerfect* commands that are presented in this book. So, if you can't figure out how to access a command with the menus, you can use this figure for reference.

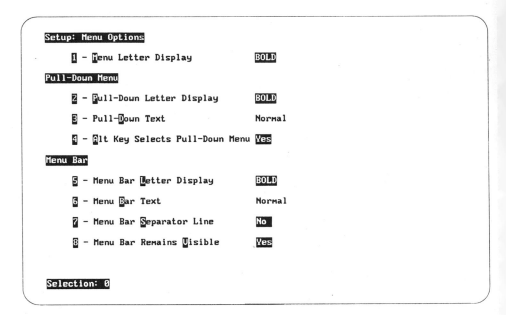

Figure B-5   The Menu Options screen

Setup screens	Menu access
Setup screens	**Menu access**
Mouse	File > Setup > Mouse
Display	File > Setup > Display
Environment	File > Setup > Environment
Initial Settings	File > Setup > Initial Settings
Keyboard Layout	File > Setup > Keyboard Layout
Location of Files	File > Setup > Location of Files
Format screens	**Menu access**
Line	Layout > Line
Page	Layout > Page
Document	Layout > Document
Other	Layout > Other

Figure B-6   How to use the menus to access the Setup and Format screens

Command name	Menu access
Block	Click-and-drag mouse
	Edit > Block
Bold	Font > Appearance > Bold
Cancel	Esc
	Edit > Undelete
Center	Layout > Align > Center
Date	Tools > Date Text
	Tools > Date Code
	Tools > Date Format
Exit	File > Exit
Flush Right	Layout > Align > Flush Right
Font	Font
Help	Help > Help
	Help > Index
	Help > Template
Indent, single	Layout > Align > Indent ->
Indent, double	Layout > Align > Indent -><-
List Files	File > List Files
Macro Define	Tools > Macro > Define
Macro	Tools > Macro > Execute
Move	Edit > Select
	Edit > Move
	Edit > Copy
	Edit > Delete
	Edit > Paste
Print	Edit > Print
Replace	Search > Replace
Retrieve	File > Retrieve
Reveal Codes	Edit > Reveal Codes
Save	File > Save
Screen, window	Edit > Window
Search, backward	Search > Backward
Search, forward	Search > Forward
Spell	Tools > Spell
Switch	Edit > Switch Document
	Edit > Convert Case
Tab Align	Layout > Align > Tab Align
Thesaurus	Tools > Thesaurus
Underline	Font > Appearance > Underline

Figure B-7   An alphabetical listing of the commands presented in this book

Appendix C

A summary of the *WordPerfect* keystrokes and commands presented in this book

This appendix summarizes the keystrokes and commands that are presented in this book. Within each summary, the keystrokes and commands are grouped by function. If a command can logically be placed in two or more of these groups, it's placed in all of them. For each command, you are referred to the primary figures in the text that present the command. Since some commands and keystrokes function differently if text is blocked on the screen, I've presented a summary of commands that you can use on blocked text. Because this appendix presents the keystrokes and commands in a new order, it can help you review the *WordPerfect* skills presented in this book.

Keystroke summary

Keystrokes	Function

How to move the cursor

The Ctrl key and the Arrow keys

Ctrl+Right	Moves the cursor right one word at a time.
Ctrl+Left	Moves the cursor left one word at a time.
Ctrl+Up (5.1)	Moves the cursor up one paragraph at a time.
Ctrl+Down (5.1)	Moves the cursor down one paragraph at a time.

The Home key and the Arrow keys

Home Left	Moves the cursor to the left of the line after all codes.
Home Right	Moves the cursor to the right of the line after all codes.
Home Up	Moves the cursor to the top of the Edit screen.
Home Down	Moves the cursor to the bottom of the Edit screen.
Home Home Up	Moves the cursor to the top of the document after all codes.
Home Home Down	Moves the cursor to the bottom of the document after all codes.
Home Home Home Up	Moves the cursor to the top of the document before all codes.
Home Home Home Left	Moves the cursor to the left of the line before all codes.

The End key

End	Moves the cursor to the right of the line after all codes.

The Page keys

Page-up	Moves the cursor to the top of the previous page.
Page-down	Moves the cursor to the top of the next page.

The Plus (+) and Minus (-) keys on the numeric pad with Num-lock off

+	Moves the cursor to the bottom of the Edit screen.
-	Moves the cursor to the top of the Edit screen.

The Go to command

Ctrl+Home	Moves the cursor to the top of the page you specify at the Go to prompt by entering the page number.

How to delete text

Keystrokes	Function
Ctrl+Delete	Deletes the word at the cursor.
Ctrl+Backspace	Deletes the word to the left of the cursor.
Ctrl+End	Deletes from the cursor to the end of the line.
Ctrl+Page-down	Deletes from the cursor to the end of the page.

How to work with pages

Ctrl+Enter	Inserts a hard page break [HPg] into the document.
Ctrl+B	Inserts an automatic page number into the document.

How to indent and outdent text on the tab stops

Tab	Indents the current line one tab stop.
Shift+Tab	Outdents the current line one tab stop; often used to release the left margin.

How to work with hyphens

Ctrl+Hyphen	Inserts an invisible hyphen that *WordPerfect* uses only if the word needs to be hyphenated at the end of a line.
Hyphen	Inserts a visible hyphen that *WordPerfect* uses only if the words needs to be hyphenated at the end of a line.
Home Hyphen	Inserts a visible hyphen that tells *WordPerfect* not to break the word at the hyphen.

How to move between *WordPerfect* screens

Highlighted letter or number	Selects an option.
Esc	Returns to the previous screen.
Cancel (F1)	Returns to the previous screen.
Zero (0)	Returns to the previous screen.
Exit (F7)	Returns to the Edit screen.

Editing commands

Key name	Function	Refer to figure
Block	Turns block on to block if no text is blocked; turns block off if text is already blocked.	7-2
Cancel	Undeletes the blocked text shown on your Edit screen.	7-6
Date/Outline	Automatically types the current date into your document, or inserts a code for the current date.	7-13
Esc	Repeats a function n times	7-18
Format	Accesses the commands for Headers, Footers, and Page Numbers.	7-14, 7-15, 7-17
Move	Moves, copies, or deletes a sentence, paragraph, page, or block.	7-3, 7-5
Replace	Searches for a string of text and replaces that string of text with another string of text.	7-9
Reveal Codes	Toggles between the Edit screen and the Reveal Codes screen.	8-25
<Search	Searches for a string of text from the cursor to the beginning of the document.	7-7, 7-8
>Search	Searches for a string of text from the cursor to the end of the document.	7-7, 7-8
Screen	Divides the screen into two parts. The top half shows Document 1 and the bottom half shows Document 2.	7-11
Switch	If no text is blocked, it switches between Document 1 and Document 2. If text is blocked, you can use it to convert blocked text to uppercase or lowercase.	7-10, 7-12

Formatting commands

Key name	Function	Refer to figure
Bold	Boldfaces text.	8-21
Center	Centers text.	8-20
Flush Right	Aligns text with right margin.	8-20
Font	Changes size and appearance of text relative to the base font; changes the base font.	8-16, 8-17
Format	Accesses the Line, Page, Document, and Other options for setting tabs, margins, line spacing, and so on.	8-4 through 8-14, 8-22
>Indent	Indents a paragraph one tab stop from the left margin.	8-19
>Indent<	Indents a paragraph one tab stop from the left margin and an equal amount from the right margin.	8-19
Print	Selects the current printer.	8-3
Reveal Codes	Toggles between the Edit screen and the Reveal Codes screen.	8-25
Setup	Accesses the Document option for setting the initial codes for a document.	6-6
Underline	Underlines text.	8-21

File handling commands

Exit	Clears the document, *WordPerfect*, or both from internal memory.	9-3
List	Sets the default directory and accesses the List screen.	9-1, 9-4 through 9-8, 9-10 through 9-14
Retrieve	Retrieves a document from disk into internal memory.	9-3, 9-15, 9-16
Save	Saves a document from internal memory to disk.	9-3
Setup (5.1)	Sets the default directory so that it's in effect for all work sessions.	9-2

Printing commands

Key name	Function	Refer to
Print	Accesses the Print screen (see Print screen functions and Print screen options).	8-3, 9-9, 10-1 through 10-3, 10-6 through 10-10
List	Accesses the List screen (see the Print option on the List screen options).	9-7, 9-8, 10-5

Spelling checker, Thesaurus and Help commands

Spell	Accesses the spelling checker.	11-1 through 11-6
Thesaurus	Accesses the Thesaurus.	11-7, 11-8
Help	Accesses the Help feature.	5-14 through 5-17

Macro commands

Macro Define	Defines or "records" a new macro. It also replaces or edits an existing macro.	12-1 through 12-8
Macro	Executes or "plays back" a named macro.	12-1 through 12-8

Commands that you can use on a block of text

Key Name	Function
Move	Moves or copies a block of text.
Delete	Deletes a block of text.
Print	Prints a block of text.
Save	Saves a block of text to a named file (the default directory is assumed unless you override it by giving a complete file specification).
Spell	Checks the spelling of the words in the block and counts the number of words in the block.
Switch	Changes the case of the letters in the block from upper- to lowercase or from lower- to uppercase.
Bold	Boldfaces the blocked text.
Underline	Underlines the blocked text.
Font	Changes the size or appearance of the blocked text when it's printed.

Index

1073741824

Comment Form

Your opinions count

If you have any comments, criticisms, or suggestions for us, I'm eager to get them. Your opinions today will affect our products of tomorrow. And if you find any errors in this book, typographical or otherwise, please point them out so we can correct them in the next printing.

Thanks for your help.

Mike Murach

Book title: The Least You Need to Know about *WordPerfect*

Dear Mike: _____

_____

_____

_____

_____

_____

_____

_____

_____

_____

_____

_____

_____

_____

_____

_____

_____

_____

Name_____

Company (if company address) _____

Address _____

City, State, Zip _____

Fold where indicated and tape closed.
No postage necessary if mailed in the U.S.

fold

BUSINESS REPLY MAIL

FIRST-CLASS MAIL   PERMIT NO. 3063   FRESNO, CA

POSTAGE WILL BE PAID BY ADDRESSEE

Mike Murach & Associates, Inc.

4697 W JACQUELYN AVE
FRESNO CA 93722-9888

fold

fold

fold

Order Form

Our Ironclad Guarantee

To our customers who order directly from us: You must be satisfied. Our books must work for you, or you can send them back for a full refund...no questions asked.

Name & Title _____

Company (if company address) _____

Street address _____

City, State, Zip _____

Phone number (including area code) _____

Fax number (if you fax your order to us)_____

Qty	Product code and title	*Price
WordPerfect		
____ LWP	The Least You Need to Know about *WordPerfect*	$20.00
____ LWIG	Least/*WordPerfect* Instructor's Guide --Please call for information	
Lotus 1-2-3		
____ LLOT	The Least You Need to Know about *Lotus 1-2-3*	$20.00
____ GLOT**	The Practical Guide to *Lotus 1-2-3*	25.00
Multiple Programs		
____ DWPL	DOS, *WordPerfect*, and *Lotus* Essentials	$25.00

Qty	Product code and title	*Price
DOS		
____ LDOS	The Least You Need to Know about DOS	$17.95
____ DOSB	The Only DOS Book You'll Ever Need	24.95
____ DOS2**	The Only DOS Book You'll Ever Need (2nd Ed.)	27.50
____ BACK	How to Back Up Your PC	15.00
Business Writing		
____ WBPC	Write Better with a PC	$19.95

☐ Bill the appropriate book prices plus UPS shipping and handling (and sales tax in California) to my ____VISA ____MasterCard:

    Card number_____

    Valid thru (month/year) _____

    Cardowner's signature _____

☐ Bill me.

☐ Bill my company. P.O. #_____

☐ I want to **save** UPS shipping and handling charges. Here's my check or money order for $_____. California residents, please add sales tax to your total. (Offer valid in the U.S.)

* Prices are subject to change. **Please call for current prices.**

** Available February 1993

To order more quickly,

Call **toll-free** 1-800-221-5528

(Weekdays, 8 to 5 Pacific Standard Time)

Fax: 1-209-275-9035

Mike Murach & Associates, Inc.

4697 West Jacquelyn Avenue
Fresno, California 93722-6427
(209) 275-3335

fold

BUSINESS REPLY MAIL

FIRST-CLASS MAIL   PERMIT NO. 3063   FRESNO, CA

POSTAGE WILL BE PAID BY ADDRESSEE

Mike Murach & Associates, Inc.

4697 W JACQUELYN AVE
FRESNO CA 93722-9888

fold   fold

A 3-in-1 guide to the most popular PC programs

DOS, *WordPerfect*, and *Lotus* Essentials

Patrick Bultema and Joel Murach

The books in our *Least* series are designed for people who use a PC at least a couple of hours each day for fairly lengthy applications. In that case, they'll teach you the minimum set of skills you need to use your software efficiently.

But if you have only limited PC requirements—you don't use a PC that often, for example, or you use it only for fairly simple, one- or two-page documents—you may not need to know as much about the software as the *Least* books teach. You may be satisfied with an abridged approach—a least-of-the-*Least*, if you will.

That's exactly what this book is. The first 3 chapters give you some background on PC hardware and software. Then, the rest of the book is divided into 3 sections—one each on DOS, *WordPerfect*, and *Lotus 1-2-3*.

Each section begins with a tutorial that teaches you to use the software from scratch in just a couple of hours—the same tutorial that's in each of the *Least* books. Then, each section teaches you addi-

tional skills that will save you time and frustration every time you use the software. These skills are all taught in the *Least* books, too, but here they've been cut down to their bare essentials. So the sections in this book present about half of what you'd learn in the corresponding *Least* book.

In short, this book will quickly train you in the essentials of DOS, *WordPerfect*, and *Lotus 1-2-3*, and yet give you the overall perspective that's missing in other "quick-start" books. And because our books are designed in conjunction with each other, you can easily move up to one or more of the *Least* books if you start using the software more extensively and need to expand your skills.

3 books in one plus an introduction, 520 pages, $25.00
ISBN 0-911625-69-0

 To order by phone, call toll-free 1-800-221-5528 (Weekdays, 8 to 5, Pacific Standard Time)

Covers all releases through 2.4 and 3.1

The Least You Need to Know about *Lotus 1-2-3*

Patrick Bultema

Lotus 1-2-3 isn't a difficult subject. Like all software products, though, it's evolved far beyond its original design. So its menu structure isn't particularly logical. And it offers far more functions than any one PC user is ever likely to use. And some of its functions are hidden behind function keys. And the notation used in its formulas is probably confusing to people without a strong algebraic background. And ...

Well, maybe it *is* difficult to learn how to use *Lotus 1-2-3*! That's where this book comes in. It zeroes in on the essential skills you need, so you'll be creating and using your own spreadsheets in less time than you thought possible...even if you're not a math major.

But this book is also for you if you already know the *Lotus* basics, but you're frustrated because you know you're not working as efficiently as you should be. It will teach you all the features and shortcuts you need to know to get the most out of *Lotus*.

- Section 1 presents the hardware and software background you need to understand if you're new to *Lotus* or to PCs

- Section 2 presents a *Lotus* tutorial that will have you creating and using your own spreadsheets in just a couple of hours

- Section 3 gives you the additional skills that will let you use *Lotus* proficiently and professionally every day (the chapters in this section are designed for quick reference, and can be read at any time, in any order)

- Section 4 gives you some perspective by telling you about other *Lotus* features you might want to use, depending on the type of work you do

Each section is filled with spreadsheet and screen examples that help you learn faster...even if you're not in front of a PC. And later on, these examples make quick and easy references for functions that you don't use often enough to have memorized.

So whether you need to learn *Lotus 1-2-3* from scratch or you want to hone your *Lotus* skills so you can work more productively, this book is for YOU.

12 chapters, 261 pages, $20.00
ISBN 0-911625-65-8

For spreadsheet users in business who want to get more done in less time

The Practical Guide to *Lotus 1-2-3*

Patrick Bultema

This book is a complete reference to all the *Lotus 1-2-3* features that are most useful for business applications. So if you decide you can benefit from some of the features presented in section 4 of *The Least You Need to Know about Lotus 1-2-3*, this book will teach you how to use them in a minimum of time. You'll learn:

- the most useful @functions for business applications
- how to use range names to organize a spreadsheet
- how to protect areas of a spreadsheet
- how to share data between spreadsheets
- how to convert data to or from *Lotus 1-2-3*
- how to manage *Lotus 1-2-3* files
- how to use add-in programs
- how to use *Lotus* presentation features, like graphing and the WYSIWYG add-in program

- the basics of using the macro and database features
- when and how to upgrade to a later release of *Lotus*
- when and how to upgrade your PC hardware

In order for this book to be a *complete* reference, it also covers the essential *Lotus* skills that are taught in section 3 of *The Least You Need to Know about Lotus 1-2-3*. So keep this book close at hand, ready to use whenever you want to learn a new *Lotus* feature or whenever you need to refresh your memory about a feature you don't use very often.

22 chapters, approx. 500 pages, $25.00
ISBN 0-911625-70-4

Available February 1993

 To order by phone, call toll-free 1-800-221-5528 (Weekdays, 8 to 5, Pacific Standard Time)

Covers DOS 2.0 through 5.0 for hard disk users

The Least You Need to Know about DOS

Patrick Bultema

It seems like every time you get to working on your PC, some "little" problem brings you to a screeching halt. Like you can't start one of your programs because someone else has been using your PC. Or it takes you half an hour to transfer data from one PC to another because the diskette you're using won't work right in both machines. Or you can't find a file that you know is there somewhere. And often, you can't get going again until someone else helps you out.

But you can handle problems like these easily on your own...or avoid them altogether...if you have just a minimum set of DOS skills. That's where this book comes in. Its tightly focused approach will quickly teach you the essential DOS skills you need to become a more competent, more independent PC user:

- how to start your application programs from DOS or a shell, no matter who was using the PC last or what application was being run

- how to manage your directories and files, so you can always find what you're looking for

- how to refer to DOS directories and files from your application programs

- how to transfer data from one PC to another using diskettes

- how to back up the hard disk data on your PC

- how to change the CONFIG.SYS and AUTOEXEC.BAT files, in case you don't like the way your system starts up or operates

- how to use the DOS 5.0 shell to work more efficiently, in case you have DOS 5.0 installed on your PC

- and nothing more!

So if you're tired of asking for PC help from the PC support group, the "help" line, your colleagues, your friends, or your spouse, this book is for YOU.

14 chapters, 276 pages, $17.95
ISBN 0-911625-61-5

 To order by phone, call toll-free 1-**800**-221-5528 (Weekdays, 8 to 5, Pacific Standard Time)

Covers DOS 2.0 through 5.0 for hard disk users

The Only DOS Book You'll Ever Need

Doug Lowe and Patrick Bultema

This book is for anyone who wants...or needs...to know more about DOS than what's covered in *The Least You Need to Know about DOS*. So if you don't have anyone to set your PC up for you or to help you solve more technical problems, this book is for you. It's also the ideal book for people who provide support to less technical PC users. As a result, we recommend it for every corporate "help desk," for every PC support person, and for the lead technical person in every user department.

Everything in the *Least* book is also in this book, though much of it is in expanded form. So there are chapters on managing files and directories, backing up your hard disk, working with diskettes, using the DOS 5.0 shell, and making changes to the CONFIG.SYS and AUTOEXEC.BAT files. In addition, though, this book covers:

- how to prevent, detect, and recover from disk problems and user errors
- how to improve the performance of your PC without buying new hardware

- the commercial utility programs that actually improve upon DOS (why, for example, should you use DOS to do a function like backup when you can use an inexpensive utility to do it far more efficiently?)
- when and how to install a new version of DOS
- how to partition and format a hard disk
- how to use the DOS 4.0 shell (it isn't nearly as helpful as the DOS 5.0 shell)
- more commands for CONFIG.SYS and AUTOEXEC.BAT
- how to use some of the advanced capabilities of DOS that you'll seldom (if ever) need

So if you want to expand your DOS knowledge...or if you're looking for a resource for PC support...get a copy of *The Only DOS Book You'll Ever Need* TODAY!

27 chapters, 550 pages, $24.95
ISBN 0-911625-58-5

 To order by phone, call toll-free 1-800-221-5528 (Weekdays, 8 to 5, Pacific Standard Time)

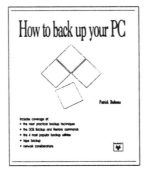

How to Back Up Your PC

Patrick Bultema

You know that you should back up the hard disk on your PC. If you don't, you will eventually lose one or more of your valuable files due to a software problem or operational error. Or you'll lose all of your files due to a hard disk failure. And without a current backup, you probably won't be able to recover any of the files.

But right away, you get mired in questions and problems. What software should you use to do backups? In fact, what are the software options? Should you back up to diskette or tape? How often do you have to do backups? Is this going to be more trouble than it's worth? How do you even get started?

How to Back Up Your PC provides the answers. In chapter 1, you'll learn how to analyze your backup requirements. This chapter will also tell you about your hardware and software options and guide you to the ones that are best for you. At that point, you can go directly to those chapters that apply to your situation. These chapters cover subjects like:

- how to use the DOS commands to back up and restore your hard disk (this is only recommended if your backup requirements are minimal)

- how to use the 4 most popular backup utilities (all are far more efficient and reliable than the DOS commands):

  ✓ Central Point Backup
  ✓ Norton Backup
  ✓ PC Fullbak+
  ✓ Fastback Plus

- when to consider backing up to tape...and what software and hardware you'll need if you decide that's the right option for you

- how to handle backups if you're on a network

- how to design your backups so they're quick and reliable no matter what hardware or software you decide to use

So don't wait for a hard disk disaster to strike. Let this book show you how to do fast and effective backups starting TODAY. Someday soon, you'll be glad you did.

6 chapters, 202 pages, $15.00
ISBN 0-911625-63-1